Report on the War in Vietnam

Report on the War in Vietnam

Section I

Report on Air and Naval Campaigns against
North Vietnam and Pacific Command-Wide support of the War
June 1964–July 1968

By

Admiral U. S. G. Sharp, USN
Commander in Chief Pacific

Section II

Report on Operations in South Vietnam
January 1964–June 1968

By

General W. C. Westmoreland, USA
Commander, U. S. Military Assistance Command, Vietnam

GOVERNMENT REPRINTS PRESS
Washington, D.C.

© Ross & Perry, Inc. 2001 All rights reserved.

No claim to U.S. government work contained throughout this book.

Protected under the Berne Convention. Published 2001

Printed in The United States of America

Ross & Perry, Inc. Publishers
717 Second St., N.E., Suite 200
Washington, D.C. 20002
Telephone (202) 675-8300
Facsimile (801) 459-7535
info@RossPerry.com

SAN 253-8555

Government Reprints Press Edition 2001

Government Reprints Press is an Imprint of Ross & Perry, Inc.

http://www.GPOreprints.com

Library of Congress Control Number: 2001093149

ISBN 1-931641-47-1

Cover *Mig Sweep* © 1975 Keith Ferris - keithferrisart.com

☉ The paper used in this publication meets the requirements for permanence established by the American National Standard for Information Sciences "Permanence of Paper for Printed Library Materials" (ANSI Z39.48-1984).

All rights reserved. No copyrighted part of this publication may be reproduced, stored in a retrieval system, or transmitted, in any form or by any means, electronic, photocopying, recording, or otherwise, without the prior written permission of the publisher.

PREFACE

This is a report on the Vietnam War by Admiral U. S. Grant Sharp, Commander in Chief Pacific (CINCPAC), and General William C. Westmoreland, Commander, United States Military Assistance Command, Vietnam (COMUSMACV). It covers events up to 30 June 1968.

Because of security considerations for military operations still underway in Vietnam, classified information on the war has not been included. This does not detract significantly from the report's usefulness as a record of the struggle against Communist aggression in South Vietnam.

The report is in four parts: CINCPAC's account of the air and naval campaign against North Vietnam, Pacific Command-wide efforts in support of the war, COMUSMACV's command account of the war in South Vietnam, and a prologue that welds the other three parts together.

More comprehensive but classified reports are prepared annually by CINCPAC and COMUSMACV for official use. These reports are available only on a "need to know" basis, and will remain so for the foreseeable future. The present report will serve in the interim as an additional current reference on the Vietnam War.

My viewpoint of the war in Vietnam is conditioned first of all by the comprehensive nature of CINCPAC's responsibilities in the entire Pacific and Asian area. As CINCPAC, I was responsible for all United States military operations—naval, ground, and air—in this entire region. Therefore, while Vietnam has been the focal point of our military effort in the Pacific Command, I have, by command necessity, viewed that conflict against the broader perspective of United States national interests throughout the area.

Our operations in Vietnam have been conducted to block Communist aggression in Southeast Asia, but this aggression is only the most visible portion of the Communist threat to United States security interests in the Pacific. Less obvious components of the total Communist threat are manifested by the provocative actions of North Korea, the mounting pressures of the North Vietnamese presence in Laos and Cambodia, and the rising level of Communist inspired insurgency in Thailand and Burma. These situations have required careful and continuing evaluation to insure the most efficient allocation of available resources in the Pacific Command to conduct the war in Vietnam and, at the same time, the protection of vital United States interests in an area stretching from the Bering Sea in the north to the eastern Indian Ocean in the south.

To meet the pervasive Communist threat, CINCPAC and his Pacific Command Service component commanders and subordinate unified commanders have developed a vast and complex support structure to provide the basis for Southeast Asia operations and continued United States operations in other areas. This support structure is necessary for the deployment of Free World forces to South Vietnam and provides a readiness posture to assure an adequate and flexible response to any threat to United States vital interests.

During the period covered by this report, the war in Vietnam has been the major part of the total CINCPAC effort to protect vital United States interests in the Pacific, and of the total national effort to protect American interests throughout the world.

The success of our efforts in Vietnam and throughout the Pacific has been dependent to a large degree upon the outstanding support and cooperation of an array of commands and agencies external to the Pacific Command. This report does not detail the extent of their participation but due recognition must be given their significant contribution to the total effort involved.

U. S. G. SHARP

COMMAND STRUCTURE

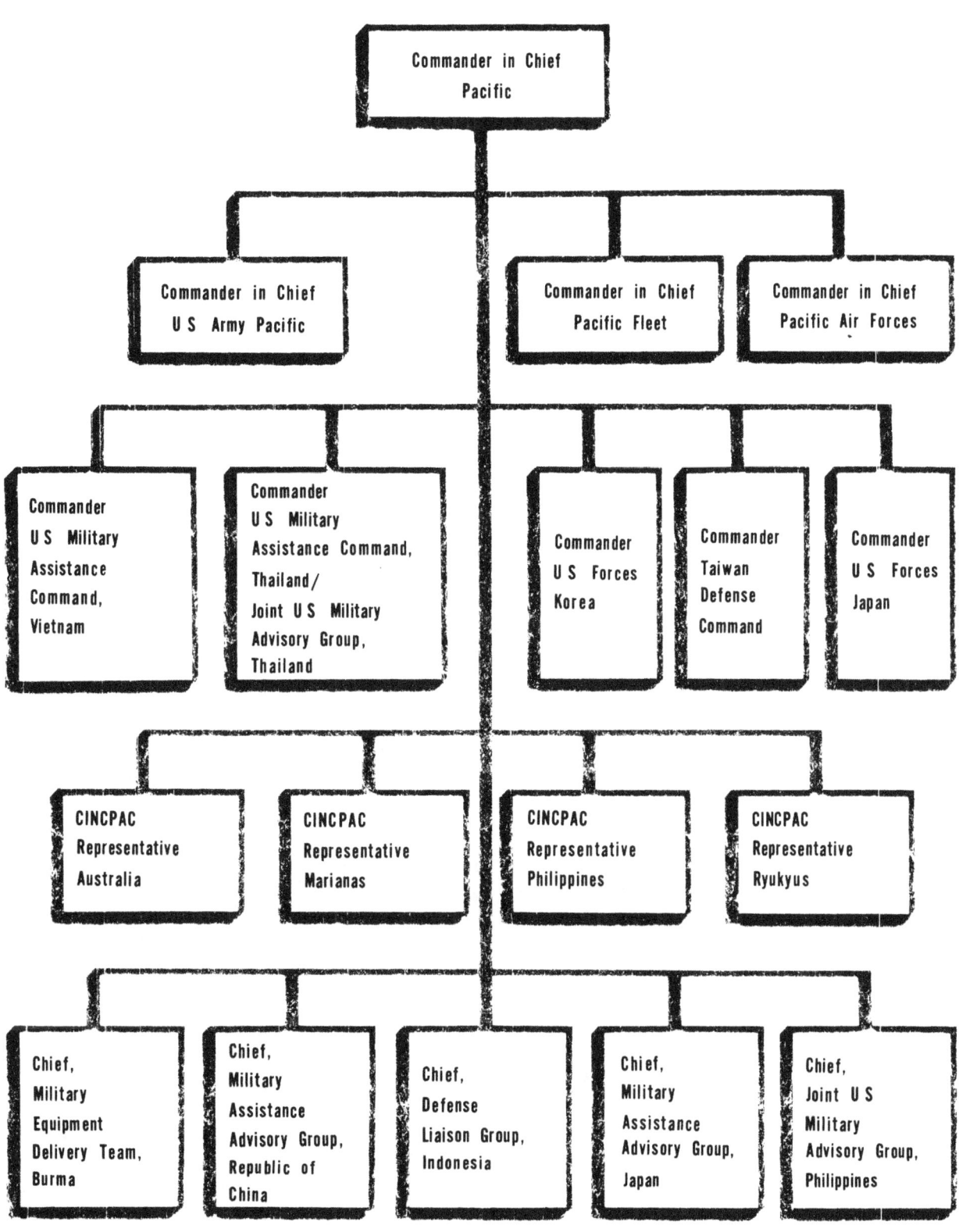

CONTENTS

SECTION I
	Page
Preface	i
Command Structure	iii
Prologue	1
Air and Naval Campaigns Against North Vietnam	11
Air and Naval Actions Against North Vietnam—1965	14
Inception of ROLLING THUNDER Operations	16
ROLLING THUNDER Operations—1966	23
ROLLING THUNDER Operations—1967	31
ROLLING THUNDER Operations—January through March 1968	44
Curtailment of ROLLING THUNDER Operations	47
Naval Surface Operations	49
Effects of ROLLING THUNDER	53
Pacific Command-Wide Efforts in Support of the War	55

SECTION II
COMUSMACV Report on Operations in South Vietnam	69

PROLOGUE

Every war has its own distinctive features. The Vietnam War has been characterized by an invading army that denied its own existence, by guerrilla fighters who lived among the people they threatened, by the employment of highly sophisticated modern Communist weapons systems, and by carefully controlled limitations on the activities of American field commanders imposed less by the capabilities of their own forces and weapons than by considerations of international politics.

For over 20 years South Vietnam has fought to preserve its freedom against unremitting, ruthless aggression. The aggression has been no less real for the fact that it has been by Vietnamese against Vietnamese and by techniques of subversion, infiltration, terror, and attack rather than overt invasion on the classic pattern. The military effort which we and our allies have mounted in assistance to our Vietnamese ally has been one of constant innovation in resistance to a form of attack new in our experience.

In one way this war has not differed from others. The tests of battle have been met by our fighting men with unsurpassed dedication and courage, upholding the finest traditions of our military services.

The Vietnam War has had the most intense press coverage and has been the most thoroughly documented, most centrally controlled, most computerized, and most statistically analyzed in history. This was due in part to the necessity to measure the progress of a war in which there were no clearly drawn battle lines—no front, no safe rear. Because so much has been publicized about the war, this report contains no accounts that have not been reported before, nor revelations not previously expressed. Our goals, our efforts to meet them, our achievements, and our reversals are all part of the public record.

The weapons in this war have ranged from sharpened bamboo sticks through the entire spectrum of modern conventional weapons. Through an evolutionary growth reaching astounding proportions, the war has had one underlying theme—North Vietnam, supported by world Communist interests, has maintained a fierce determination to take over the government and people of South Vietnam, at whatever cost in lives or material. The Communists initially attempted to gain control by subversive methods—simple terrorism and assassination. When those techniques met strong resistance, Hanoi applied all of its resources and all of the aid it could accommodate from its allies, resorting to overt aggression. This report will sketch the profile of this Communist aggression and outline what we have done to counter it.

The United States had no desire to become involved in a war in Asia. One reason we did not send troops to Indochina at the end of World War II to support the French effort to regain control was that we did not want to help reinstate a colonial authority. The indigenous anti-French resistance, which began in late 1946, was not just a nationalist movement, although it sometimes took that guise. The Viet Minh had been organized in 1941 as a coalition of various groups—Democrats, Socialists, Communists, and other less well-defined sections of the independence movement. Its organization was dominated by the Communists, led by Ho Chi Minh who had been trained in Moscow.

The war in Korea later proved to the world the seriousness of the threat of Asian Communism and in the early 1950's, after the Viet Minh had revealed itself as an instrument of communism, the United States, therefore, started sending more military aid to France for use against the Communist Viet Minh.

GENEVA—1954

Despite this aid, France's attempt to reinstate colonial rule in Indochina was already failing when the United States, Great Britain, the USSR, and France met in Geneva in 1954. They sought a political settlement in Korea and a truce in Indochina. In May while the conference was in progress, General Vo Nguyen Giap and his Viet Minh forces defeated the besieged French forces at Dien Bien Phu and with this defeat the French decided to leave Indochina.

At Geneva, agreement was reached to partition Vietnam near the 17th Parallel with a provisional demarcation line cushioned by a demilitarized zone. Neither North nor South Vietnam was to interfere with the internal affairs of the other. Elections to reunify the two parts were to be held within two years of the signing.

Of great importance was the agreement banning the introduction of new troops and weapons or the establishment of new military bases. The manpower and materiel already in Vietnam could be replaced but not augmented, according to the treaty. Neighboring Laos and Cambodia were barred from military alliances, and foreign bases in either country were prohibited. All Viet Minh and French troops were to be withdrawn from both countries. To enforce the terms of the armistice, a three-country International Control Commission was created.

The United States and Vietnam did not sign the Geneva Accords, but endorsed them in principle and adhered to them in action until Communist violations had emptied them of meaning and rendered the International Control Commission powerless.

President Eisenhower, speaking for the United States, on 10 October 1954 offered "to assist the Government of Vietnam in developing and maintaining a strong, viable state, capable of resisting attempted subversion or aggression through military means" in the hope "that such aid, combined with . . . continuing efforts, will contribute effectively toward an independent Vietnam endowed with a strong government." Our involvement stems from this commitment.

DETERIORATION OF THE SITUATION IN SOUTH VIETNAM

North Vietnam hoped that the newly formed South Vietnamese Government would, if given enough time, fall of its own accord. The Hanoi leaders were ready to step into the resulting political void and reap a cheap victory. Such was not to be the case, however, for in the years immediately following the cessation of hostilities the Republic of Vietnam, beset though it was with problems, made steady if unspectacular progress.

The Geneva Accords called for national elections in both parts of Vietnam. But in 1956 the Saigon government refused to hold elections in South Vietnam on the grounds that elections in North Vietnam under the Communists would not guarantee the voters a free choice.

Hanoi had not anticipated this and now set about to gain control of the South by other means. The Viet Minh had left many cadres in the South in 1954. Under Hanoi's orders, they were organized into a political-paramilitary organization.

In 1960 the Central Committee of the Lao Dong Party, the Communist Party of North Vietnam, passed a resolution that South Vietnam was to be "liberated" and that North and South Vietnam were to be unified under a "progressive socialist" administration.

The Hanoi radio then announced the formation in South Vietnam of the National Front for the Liberation of South Vietnam, a front which Hanoi claimed was made up of several political parties of South Vietnamese. Subsequent Hanoi broadcasts identified a "People's Revolutionary Party" as the leading party in this so-called front. It is significant that no announcement of this came out of South Vietnam, and no nationally-known South Vietnamese figure was ever identified with any of the political parties, which were on paper only, mentioned by the Hanoi radio.

Now the insurgent effort was infused with new cadres from the North—South Vietnamese who went, or were taken, North after the 1954 armistice.

The new organization, referred to as the Viet Cong, talked of land reform, a benevolent socialism, freedom from taxes, and the evils of American capitalistic influence. In some areas the Viet Cong were accepted by the people and the organization established local councils. Where the people rejected the Viet Cong, terrorism and armed attack were applied.

All the while, the Viet Cong were strengthening their organization, acquiring arms and experience. A cold-blooded campaign of elimination of local and national government officials, doctors, school teachers, and public health workers was instituted. This campaign, and the turbulent situation within the Saigon government, left the country weakened.

The overthrow and assassination of the country's first President, Ngo Dinh Diem, in late 1963 was the prelude to a series of rapidly changing governments. Internal ethnic and religious differences were exacerbated—often by the Communists—and plagued the country during these years. One consistent factor, however, was that all leaders of the various governments asked for increasing military assistance from the United States, for they knew that without it their country could not survive against the determined efforts of North Vietnam to take over South Vietnam.

The Communists exploited the confusion in South Vietnam whenever they could. Still, the insurgents in the South, despite their support from the North, were not able to gain full control of the country. In 1964 Hanoi decided that the introduction of battle-ready North Vietnamese Army Regulars was needed to bring about the defeat of the South.

The troops left their North Vietnamese training bases for what was often a clandestine journey of many months along the trails through Laos and Cambodia (a trail system named for their President, Ho Chi Minh) or infiltrated the zone which had been "demilitarized" at Geneva. They often remained in areas across the South Vietnamese border, where they were safe from South Vietnamese forces, until they were ready to invade. Although the Geneva Accords prohibited the presence of foreign troops in Laos or Cambodia, this did not inhibit the Communists.

Arrivals of United States advisors requested by the government of South Vietnam were announced on the front pages of the world's newspapers. Movement of the Communist forces was made secretly under cover of night and the jungle. The arrival of the Communists and their increasingly advanced weapons often could not be detected until they were met in battle.

For this reason, facts regarding troop escalation lagged behind the estimates. We were able to estimate rates of infiltration, however, and found continuing increases. Until mid-1964 the majority of the infiltrees were ethnic South Vietnamese members of the Viet Minh who had regrouped to the North after the 1954 cease-fire. In late 1964 the number of infiltrators began to increase greatly as regular North Vietnamese soldiers began to be introduced. By the end of 1964 a minimum of 12,000 North Vietnamese had been infiltrated, including the first North Vietnamese Army regiment to come as a unit. In the ensuing years large unit infiltrations have been the rule. As of June 1968 we estimate that more than 300,000 North Vietnamese troops have entered South Vietnam.

THE COMMUNIST AID PROGRAM

North Vietnam could not have supported such a military effort alone. During the period 1954 through 1967, assistance to North Vietnam from other Communist countries totaled some $2.9 billion, most of which came from the USSR. Annual aid agreements with the USSR, Communist China, North Korea, Mongolia, Rumania, Bulgaria, and Cuba have underscored Hanoi's heavy dependence on this outside aid, both to maintain essential production and services and to support the war in South Vietnam.

Russia has equipped North Vietnam with about 35 surface-to-air missile battalions and has supplied a sophisticated communications and radar network, numerous aircraft (including IL-28 jet light bombers and MIG-15, MIG-17, and MIG-21 fighter planes), and large quantities of antiaircraft weapons. All of these weapons contributed to establishing the most sophisticated air defense system ever faced by any force in combat. In addition, the USSR has supplied North Vietnam with modern ground force equipment such as 122- and 140-mm rockets, 120-mm mortars, and 130-mm field guns.

Priority attention has been given to North Vietnam's transportation system. The USSR has supplied not only a large portion of the vehicles needed to move supplies south, but also the road construction equipment needed to keep existing roads serviceable and to build new military roads in North Vietnam, Laos, and Viet Cong controlled areas of South Vietnam. In addition, the USSR has supplied railroad equipment, barges, bridge equipment, and petroleum for North Vietnam's transportation system.

Communist China's percentage of total aid has declined steadily since 1965. Such aid was significant, however, and has included the rehabilitation and development of North Vietnam's railways, highways, and communications facilities, reconstruction and improvement of irrigation systems, and construction of heavy and light industrial facilities. In 1966 it was reported that 40,000 Chinese were being used in North Vietnam for road and rail maintenance and other repair work. By early 1968 this figure had grown to 50,000. Some personnel were also believed to be in antiaircraft units. Military equipment from China continues to be mostly small arms, ammunition, and light antiaircraft artillery; but some MIG-17 jet fighters have been provided.

In the early stages of the war the enemy was handicapped by weapons and ammunition shortages and he relied often on homemade and captured items. Today there is an abundance of the latest models from the Communist conventional weapons arsenals.

SOUTH VIETNAM REQUESTS OUTSIDE ASSISTANCE

South Vietnam has also relied on massive external aid, from the United States and many other countries. In December 1961 South Vietnam sent an urgent appeal to President Kennedy for immediate further help. The President agreed to increase our military assistance. The political and military situation, however, continued to deteriorate. North Vietnam became emboldened by the eroding situation and misjudged American determination. American naval ships on patrol in the Gulf of Tonkin were involved in clashes with North Vietnamese torpedo boats on 2 and 4 August 1964, which led to approval of the Joint Congressional Resolution of 7 August 1964—the Tonkin Resolution—which not only approved retaliatory attacks but also stated that:

". . . the Congress approves and supports the determination of the President, as Commander-in-Chief, to take all necessary measures to repel any armed attack against the forces of the United States and to prevent further aggression. . . . The United States regards as vital to its national interest and to world peace the maintenance of international peace and security of Southeast Asia. Consonant with the Constitution and the Charter of the United Nations, and in accordance with its obligations under the Southeast Asia Collective Defense Treaty, the United States is, therefore, prepared, as the President determines, to take all necessary steps, including the use of armed force, to assist any member or protocol state of the Southeast Asia Collective Defense Treaty requesting assistance in defense of its freedom."

UNITED STATES COMMITMENT OF FORCES

During January and February 1965 the general situation in South Vietnam continued to worsen, the military threat increased, political tensions in Saigon deepened, and morale plummeted. It became increasingly apparent that the existing levels of United States aid could not prevent the collapse of South Vietnam. Even as deliberations on how best to deal with the situation were in progress within our government, the Viet Cong launched a series of attacks on American installations in South Vietnam. These attacks indicated that North Vietnam was moving in for the kill. It appeared that they would succeed, perhaps in a matter of months, as things were developing. Acting on the request of the South Vietnamese government, the decision was made to commit as soon as possible 125,000 United States troops to prevent the Communist takeover. At the same time President Johnson indicated that additional forces would be sent as requested by the Republic of Vietnam and the Commander of the United States Military Assistance Command, Vietnam.

As the need increased and as North Vietnam moved in more of its own troops, requests for additional United States troops followed. By December 1965 we had about 184,000 troops in Vietnam. The year of greatest buildup was 1966, when our strength more than doubled. Increases have since been at a slower rate but have continued.

SOUTHEAST ASIA TREATY ORGANIZATION REACTION

The SEATO Council and the Military Advisers, at each of their regular meetings since April 1964, condemned the Communist aggression and Hanoi-directed subversion of South Vietnam. The communiqués following these meetings have become progressively stronger in this regard. Each of the meetings was an occasion for the council to express its appreciation for the contributions from Free World nations assisting the South Vietnamese. The council further evinced its interest and growing concern, as well as support, for South Vietnam, a SEATO Protocol State, by encouraging increasing participation in its meetings by the South Vietnamese observer.

Each of the troop-contributing member nations of SEATO declared publicly that its support of South Vietnam was as a result of, and in accordance with, its obligations under the SEATO Treaty. The United Kingdom and France, though not contributing troops, contributed money, medical aid, technical assistance, and other forms of help.

The government of South Vietnam did not make a formal request for assistance from the Organization per se. Rather, such requests were made directly to each member nation individually. Significantly, all SEATO member nations, in one way or another and in varying degrees, assisted the South Vietnamese in their defense against Communist terrorism and aggression.

FREE WORLD ASSISTANCE TO SOUTH VIETNAM

In April 1964 President Johnson urged all the nations of the Free World to come to the assistance of South Vietnam. South Vietnam itself made formal requests to certain nations for assistance.

In response, nonmilitary assistance from 39 countries other than the United States totaled $55 million from April 1964 to June 1968. Most of those nations preferred to provide civic action and medical assistance rather than active military participation.

Prior to April 1964 Australia was the only nation other than the United States to supply military assistance. In 1962 Australia furnished a 30-man Army training team and in August 1964 augmented this team with an aviation detachment. In May 1965 Australia agreed to send a task force to South Vietnam and Australian forces there now total about 7,500 men.

In July 1964 New Zealand furnished a military engineer team and in May 1965 decided to replace this detachment with a combat force. New Zealand forces in 1968 totaled over 500.

Other than the United States the nation supplying the greatest assistance to the Republic of Vietnam is the Republic of Korea. By the end of

1965, 20,620 Korean troops were in South Vietnam and those forces now total approximately 50,000.

By the end of 1965 Thailand and the Republics of the Philippines and China also had given aid in the form of noncombatant personnel to act in either advisory or civic action roles. In addition, Canada, Japan, the Netherlands, the Federal Republic of Germany, and many other nations were contributing economic and technical assistance to South Vietnam, including many nonmilitary advisors and technicians.

In December 1966 a Royal Thai Government decision to assist in the ground war in Vietnam received enthusiastic support from the Thai people. The first element of the Royal Thai Army Volunteer Regiment arrived in Vietnam in July 1967 and the main body of approximately 2,500 men followed in September. Later in the year Thailand decided to send a division, with a total strength of over 11,000 men, to replace the Royal Thai Regiment. This division is scheduled to arrive in Vietnam in two increments, the first by August 1968. The second will follow upon completion of outfitting and training.

THE REPUBLIC OF VIETNAM'S ARMED FORCES

The Armed Forces of the Republic of Vietnam have been fighting without respite for many years. They have carried the heaviest load of casualties and the greatest personal hardships. Most Vietnamese soldiers have served their country gallantly, faithfully, and responsibly throughout the years. With the help and training of their allies they have acquired knowledge of modern military tactics and techniques, which they have applied effectively.

STRATEGY FOR THE CONDUCT OF THE WAR

Our basic objective in South Vietnam has been to establish a safe environment within which the people of South Vietnam could form a government that was independent, stable, and freely elected—one that would deserve and receive popular support. Such a government could not be created in an environment dominated by Communist terrorism. The Viet Cong and the North Vietnamese Army occupied large parts of the country and subjected large areas to armed attacks and acts of terrorism and assassination. These acts were most often directed at the representatives of government in provinces, villages, and hamlets throughout the countryside, the government officials most closely associated with the people.

The United States' military goal was to provide a secure environment in which the citizens could live and in which all levels of legal government could function without enemy exploitation, pressure, or violence. Our strategy to achieve this goal consisted of three interdependent elements—the ground and air campaign in South Vietnam, the nation building effort in South Vietnam, and our air and naval offensive against North Vietnam. Through these integrated efforts we have sought to convince the Hanoi regime that its aggression could not succeed and that such aggression would be too costly to sustain.

To this end United States, South Vietnamese, and other Free World forces went into battle to defeat the Communists and their organizations in South Vietnam. When the enemy was driven out of an area, United States and other Free World forces assisted the Vietnamese people in that area with projects such as building construction, sanitation, and medical care. Skills in these and other specialties were supplied by our soldiers, sailors, airmen, and Marines in their changing roles as both fighting men and workers in civic action.

But before major civic action programs could proceed, the enemy had to be blocked in his aggression. Efforts to defeat enemy aggression in South Vietnam will be detailed in another portion of this report.

As almost all of his war-making material came from or through North Vietnam, we took the war to the enemy by a vigorous and unremitting—but highly selective—application of our air and naval power. Aircraft from land bases in South Vietnam and Thailand and from our aircraft carriers at sea applied this power. We attacked the enemy's military installations and power plants, petroleum products storage areas and industrial facilities which supported the war effort, and the vehicles and roads by which war material moved south—his means of provisioning the aggression. The bombing has been the most precise in history with less damage to nontargets and noncombatants than was ever experienced in previous wars. Communist support of the war was made extremely costly in terms of goods and facilities destroyed.

Our naval forces curbed the movement of men and their food and war-making material as they attempted to infiltrate by sea or by the great river systems of Southeast Asia. Naval gunfire assisted in coastal operations with marked effectiveness.

From a military standpoint, both air and naval programs were inhibited by restrictions growing out of the limited nature of our conduct of the war. The key port of Haiphong in North Vietnam, for example, through which 85 percent of North Vietnam's imports flowed, and at which ships of many nations called, has been a prohibited target. Our planes could not bomb it. Nor was mining of that harbor permitted. Materials shipped from Haiphong were sought out later and bombed on their journey south, when they could be found. The primitive road and trail networks of Southeast Asia and the frequently heavy tree cover made such moving targets and sheltered small storage areas very difficult to find, even with our sophisticated weapons and equipment.

Despite these difficulties, strikes on railroad lines, roads, and waterways greatly impeded the flow of war material. These attacks created additional management, distribution, and manpower problems for North Vietnam.

The bombing of North Vietnam was unilaterally stopped by the United States a number of times, for varying periods of time, in the hope that the enemy would respond by stopping his aggressive activities and reducing the scope and level of conflict. In every case the Communists used the bombing pause to rush troops and supplies to reinforce their army in South Vietnam. Such unilateral truce efforts, while judged politically desirable, accrued some temporary military disadvantages to successful prosecution of the war.

SUMMARY OF PROGRESS—1965 TO 1968

By mid-March 1965 United States forces were exerting pressure on Communist forces in South Vietnam and the United States logistic capability was expanding. In 1966 we commenced deployment of a balanced and effective combat force. Successful spoiling operations during that year prevented a Communist military takeover and forced the enemy to revert to defensive employment of his main force units. A capable and resourceful enemy continued overt warfare, however. He had developed a strong logistic base, much of it in neighboring Laos and Cambodia. The enemy maintained the capability to deploy substantial additional North Vietnamese Army Regulars.

While our air operations over North Vietnam attrited but did not prevent the introduction of external assistance into North Vietnam, substantial progress was made in destroying war supporting industries and resources. Emphasis was directed toward harassing, disrupting, and impeding the movement of men and material to South Vietnam. Such movement was made costly and the enemy was forced to exert a prodigious effort to continue it. He adjusted to our attacks by ingeniously hiding and dispersing his logistics activity, however, and his recuperative capability along the routes of movement was remarkable.

In 1966 we were able to take the initiative against Communist main force units in South Vietnam. However, the enemy was able to disengage many units and to seek refuge in sanctuaries in Laos, Cambodia, and North Vietnam, where our ground forces were not permitted to strike him. This permitted him to establish the pace of the ground war to his advantage. Although it would be erroneous to suggest that the enemy at this stage had reverted purely to guerrilla actions as his primary mode of operations, he realized that he could not defeat and eject United States and Free World military forces by large unit operations. He was sufficiently flexible to hit at times and places of his choosing and under circumstances that offered a good probability of success. In 1966 the enemy's unit integrity had not been destroyed, nor had his logistic capabilities fallen below those needed to continue the war.

The Communists avoided major contact, using their sanctuaries, fighting defensively when forced to do so, and attempting to rebuild and reinforce for operations at an opportune time. Tactical guerrilla warfare was intensified without fragmenting main force units or discarding plans for their buildup and use. Hanoi continued the high rate of infiltration of Regular troops to replace losses and to augment units in the field. Enemy strategy hinged on continuing the war in the hope of outlasting our determination.

Another element of the Communists' basic strategy was a propaganda campaign directed at increasing both domestic and international pressure on the United States Government to stop the bombing of North Vietnam and to settle on terms favorable to the enemy.

By mid-1967 the combination of military operations against the enemy in all areas forced him to reassess his situation in light of his deteriorating military position. He was no longer capable of military victory. There were significant increases in the strength and capabilities of Allied forces in South Vietnam and combat operations were expanded accordingly. Our operations, supported by close air support and B–52 bomber strikes, increasingly neutralized enemy base areas, located and destroyed the supplies on which the enemy depended, and drove him into sparsely populated regions where food was scarce. The overall military trend in 1967 in enemy losses—those killed, wounded, and captured—was favorable to the allies, as was the overall trend in enemy defections. The number of persons and areas under Communist control declined slowly and the number of South Vietnamese impressed into Viet Cong service declined significantly. Consequently, the troop replacement burden fell increasingly on the North Vietnamese. There was evidence of manpower problems in North Vietnam, resulting in wider use of women in the labor force to free men badly needed for military replacements. Shortages of food, material, and medical supplies were taking their toll. Morale and combat effectiveness deteriorated in some of their units, especially those in isolated areas.

In 1967 the enemy did not win a major battle in South Vietnam. Many of his main force units had been driven to positions across the Laos and Cambodia borders where they took advantage of sanctuaries for protection and supply, in much the same way they had operated in 1965 and 1966 when hard pressed by our combat forces.

The Communist strategy continued to reflect an effort to draw Allied forces into remote areas, especially those areas adjacent to border sanctuaries, leaving populated areas unprotected. This enabled enemy local and guerrilla forces to harass, attack, and generally impede government efforts. Through these means the Viet Cong continued to exert a significant influence over large portions of the population. Although enemy capabilities were at times formidable in local areas, they were never overpowering. Through careful exploitation of the enemy's vulnerabilities and the application of our superior firepower and mobility, we were able to prevent him from making any spectacular gain in South Vietnam in 1967.

During 1967 the air and naval campaign against North Vietnam continued to be an element of our strategy in which we had the initiative. We continued to press this advantage. There was no doubt that our past efforts had hurt North Vietnam and that continued support of the war in South Vietnam was causing severe hardships. From a purely military view, additional operational latitude for air and naval forces would have enabled the execution of campaigns against North Vietnam which would have brought about a more rapid deterioration of the enemy's total war-supporting structure. If more effective curtailment of the Communist war effort had been achieved by drains on their resources, the result would have been a steady reduction of insurgency and aggression in South Vietnam.

In coordination with our military operations, the task of nation building in South Vietnam, the ultimate goal of our struggle, received its full share of attention. True, progress often was interrupted by enemy attacks or harassment, but the demonstration of government concern and aid for every village and hamlet in South Vietnam remained the aim. Efforts in this regard were not new. The French attempted *agrovilles* in the 1950's and the Diem regime tried a program of "strategic hamlets." These all failed for many reasons, not the least of which were failure to base goals on capabilities, to plan realistically, and to take into account the interests and aspirations of the people.

Subsequent efforts at nation building were more attuned to the needs of the people, but in 1966 growth was still slow and painstaking. Although the Vietnamese Armed Forces had the primary mission of supporting pacification, United States forces reinforced their efforts by direct support. Vietnamese Army units were redeployed and retrained to support these programs, but providing the motivation was difficult and progress in orienting those forces was slow.

In 1967 a new constitution was promulgated and the citizens of South Vietnam went to the polls and elected a new national government. Similarly, for the first time since the early days of the Diem regime, representative government was initiated at the village and hamlet level. There were fragmentary but nevertheless encouraging signs that the National Assembly was becoming constituent oriented.

Additionally, during 1967 there was a reorganization and consolidation of United States support of the pacification program. As a result the program was buttressed with added resources, increased military support, and unified civil-military staffing, thus creating a single, forcefully directed, United States pacification support effort.

Progress in the war from 1 January to 30 June 1968 can best be viewed in the context of the enemy's goals for his 1967–68 winter-spring campaign. Sometime in mid-1967 he revised his strategy in order to generate widespread internal uprisings, cause wholesale desertions from the ranks of South Vietnam's Army, and lay the groundwork for a political effort, including negotiations, along with his military effort to attain victory. The United States, the Communists hoped, faced with a collapsing ally, would lose the determination to pursue the war.

To carry out this new strategy, even larger numbers of North Vietnamese Regular Army troops and a heavier volume of supplies and equipment were infiltrated into South Vietnam. With the approach of *Tet,* the Vietnamese New Year season, the Communists felt that the time was ripe to go all out. They chose the first day of the *Tet* holidays for opening the offensive. Contrary to their expectations, the people of South Vietnam did not swing over to their side and there were few defections from the Vietnamese Army. Despite the surprise attack in violation of the Communists' own truce, the Vietnamese Army fought extremely well in throwing back the enemy while bearing the brunt of the assault. By coming out in the open, enemy troops were more vulnerable to our superior firepower, mobility, and flexibility. The result for the enemy was extremely high personnel losses. However, the tempo of the war was intensified. The enemy used new Soviet supplied rockets to initiate assaults on urban centers, notably Hue and Saigon, which were heretofore relatively free from attack.

During the first three months of 1968, the air campaign against North Vietnam was hampered by the rainy monsoon weather. As a result, most attack sorties were conducted against supply routes and military installations in southern North Vietnam.

On 1 April in a further attempt to get Hanoi to the peace conference table, the President of the

United States stopped bombing attacks over the principal populated and food-producing areas of North Vietnam, except in the area north of the Demilitarized Zone where enemy actions directly threatened United States and other Free World forces in South Vietnam. Militarily, this action resulted in further concentration of attack sorties in southernmost North Vietnam, primarily directed at traffic on roads and trails, to try to keep reinforcements and supplies from reaching South Vietnam where they would be brought into battle against our forces. Politically, the President's action brought the response from the North Vietnamese that they would come to the conference table.

The enemy continued his countrywide attacks in an attempt to give the South Vietnamese and the world public an impression of North Vietnamese strength while exaggerating the human and material costs of the war to the Allied side. Our tactical aircraft and B–52 bombers continued their support of ground operations in South Vietnam with B–52 effort concentrating primarily on truck parks, storage areas, and troop concentrations. The air effort further compounded the enemy's difficulties in getting supplies and equipment down the infiltration routes.

In early May the Communists mounted further harassing attacks throughout South Vietnam with primary emphasis on the Saigon area and in the northern part of the country. Because of their earlier *Tet* losses, these attacks were not nearly as fierce or well coordinated as the *Tet* offensive. The results, however, were essentially the same—heavy losses for the enemy, a broadening of the war into urban areas, and a quantum jump in civilian casualties. Still, the enemy continued to reconstitute and reposition his forces for further attacks.

Then in late May and early June 1968 the enemy launched new assaults, particularly on the city of Saigon. American military installations and Vietnamese government headquarters seemed to be the initial objectives, although again the enemy showed complete disregard for the lives of innocent South Vietnamese civilians. When these attacks were blunted, the enemy commenced a series of indiscriminate rocket attacks against the civilian populace of Saigon, creating widespread destruction, heavy civilian casualties, and increasing numbers of refugees. These assaults on Saigon obviously were designed to influence the talks that had begun on 13 May in Paris, where Hanoi showed no disposition to modify its hardline stand.

As of 30 June our estimate is that the enemy does not possess the means of achieving military victory in South Vietnam but he does retain a dangerous capability to mount serious attacks. There is no indication that he has abandoned his goal of a unified Communist Vietnam. Against the backdrop of the Paris talks, a major victory would loom large. The enemy no doubt remembers how well a combined military and political strategy worked for him in Geneva 14 years ago.

AIR AND NAVAL CAMPAIGNS AGAINST NORTH VIETNAM

By August 1964 the Viet Cong, strongly supported by regular units of the North Vietnamese Army, held the military initiative in South Vietnam, controlled much of the rural area, had seriously reduced the effectiveness of the South Vietnamese government's pacification program, and appeared to be building up to a final push against the largely demoralized armed forces and unstable government.

The Viet Cong were accomplishing these successes despite our ever increasing economic aid, training programs by our military advisors, and our combat support personnel serving with the Armed Forces of the Republic of Vietnam.

In keeping with normal military intelligence collection requirements, routine naval patrols had been periodically operating in international waters off the coast of North Vietnam observing junk traffic and naval activity, and collecting hydrographic data and intelligence concerning North Vietnamese electronic installations which might become necessary to United States forces in the event of hostilities. One such patrol was proposed in early 1964 for reconnaissance off the North Vietnamese coastline. The recommendation was approved with the patrol to start not later than 31 July 1964.

In the late afternoon of 2 August, about 28 miles off the coast of North Vietnam and on a course away from the coast, the radar of the destroyer *Maddox* detected three boats closing on the ship at high speed. Despite evasive action, the boats by their maneuvers demonstrated hostile intent. The *Maddox* fired three warning shots and, when that did not deter the attackers, opened destructive fire with its five-inch guns. One boat was disabled but managed to launch what appeared to be two torpedoes, which missed by approximately 200 yards. Another boat retired to the north and lost all power. The third boat, hit at least once, passed approximately 1,700 yards astern of the *Maddox* firing a machine gun. One of the 12.7-mm projectiles ricocheted into a ready service magazine. Aircraft from the carrier *Ticonderoga,* then in the Gulf of Tonkin, joined the action, and the *Maddox* broke off pursuit of its attackers. No further contact was made and the carrier aircraft and the *Maddox* retired from the area. This was an unprovoked attack on a ship of the United States on the high seas.

The next day the President warned North Vietnam that "United States ships have traditionally operated freely on the high seas in accordance with the rights guaranteed by international law . . . . "They will," he said, "continue to do so and will take whatever measures are appropriate for their defense." He further warned that "The United States Government expects that . . . North Vietnam will be under no misapprehension as to the grave consequences which would inevitably result from any further unprovoked military action against United States forces."

In accordance with a Presidential directive, the Tonkin Gulf patrol was reinforced by a second destroyer, the *C. Turner Joy,* and during daylight hours by a combat air patrol from the *Ticonderoga* operating off northern South Vietnam. To reduce the risk of night torpedo boat attacks, the two ships were ordered to retire each afternoon to a "night steaming area" 24 miles square, centered about 100 miles offshore.

On 3 August the *Maddox* and the *C. Turner Joy* entered the Gulf of Tonkin. On the evening of 4 August 1964 the two destroyers were proceeding on an easterly course at a speed of about 20 knots. Shortly after dark, the task group commander, aboard the *Maddox,* observed on the surface search radar at least five contacts at about 36 miles distance, which he evaluated as probable torpedo boats. The *Maddox* and the *C. Turner Joy* changed course and increased speed to avoid what appeared to be an attack.

About an hour later, both ships' radars held contacts approximately 14 miles to the east. At that time the two United States ships were approximately 60 miles from the North Vietnamese coast. When it became evident from the maneuvers of the approaching enemy craft that they were pressing in for an attack position, both *Maddox* and *C. Turner Joy* opened fire. At this time, the enemy boats were at a range of 6,000 yards from the *Maddox* when the radar tracking indicated that the contact had turned away and began to open range. Torpedo noises were then heard by the *Maddox*'s sonar and this information was immediately passed to the *C. Turner Joy,* at which time both ships took evasive action to avoid the torpedo. A torpedo wake was then sighted passing abeam of the *C. Turner Joy,* approximately 300 feet to port and on the same bearing as the *Maddox.*

One target was taken under fire by the *C. Turner Joy,* numerous hits were observed, and it then disappeared from all radars. The commanding officer and other *C. Turner Joy* personnel observed a thick column of black smoke from this target.

Later, but during the attack, a searchlight was observed and was seen to swing in an arc toward the *C. Turner Joy*. The searchlight was immediately extinguished when aircraft from the combat air patrol orbiting above the ships approached the vicinity of the boat.

The silhouette of an attacking boat was also seen when the boat came between the ship and the flares dropped by an aircraft.

In addition, two aircraft at altitudes of between 700 and 1,500 feet, in the vicinity of the two destroyers at the time of the torpedo attack, sighted gun flashes on the surface of the water as well as light antiaircraft bursts near their altitude. On one pass over the two destroyers both pilots positively sighted a "snakey" high speed wake one and one-half miles ahead of the lead destroyer, the *Maddox*.

At approximately midnight the action ended when radar contact was lost on the last enemy boat. Best estimates were that at least two of the enemy craft were sunk, possibly two more damaged. There was no damage to the United States destroyers.

Less than half an hour after the termination of the second attack on the patrol, CINCPAC recommended that authority be granted for immediate punitive air strikes against North Vietnam. Two hours later, a message from the Joint Chiefs of Staff alerted us to plan strikes for first light the following day.

At the same time that the strike order was issued by the Joint Chiefs of Staff, a series of comprehensive air and sea movements was undertaken to discourage enemy reaction to the attack.

At the time of launch of the strike aircraft on 5 August the President announced to the public that the United States was making a measured response to the North Vietnamese aggression but did not intend to start a war.

Sixty-four strike aircraft were launched from the aircraft carriers *Ticonderoga* and *Constellation*. They inflicted severe damage to the North Vietnamese gunboat and torpedo boat fleet, destroying eight and damaging 21 others. Smoke from the Vinh petroleum storage areas rose to 14,000 feet and those stores were estimated to be 90 percent destroyed. The strikes were not without cost to our forces. Two of the aircraft from the *Constellation* were lost to antiaircraft defense at Hon Gai and two other aircraft were hit but recovered safely.

Immediately after the strikes on 5 August, Secretary of State Dean Rusk stated that the United States made its retaliatory air strikes in order to prevent a Communist "miscalculation" that we would not reply in kind. President Johnson also warned North Vietnam and Communist China against being "tempted . . . to widen the present aggression," and stated that there was "no immunity from reply."

The remainder of 1964 was characterized by increased readiness throughout the Pacific Command to meet any new North Vietnamese aggression. Extensive plans were made for future punitive or retaliatory strikes to be made in response to any renewed overt acts of aggression.

On Christmas Eve 1964 the Communists exploded a large demolition charge in the Brink Bachelor Officers Quarters in downtown Saigon. A second aircraft carrier was ordered to the Gulf of Tonkin and retaliatory strikes were readied but not executed.

NORTH VIETNAM'S AIR DEFENSE SYSTEM—1964

Events subsequent to our air strikes on 5 August 1964 in retaliation for the Gulf of Tonkin incidents revealed how prior training and prompt military and technical aid from other Communist countries served to turn a rudimentary air defense system into one of imposing capabilities. On 7 August two days after our strikes, aerial photography of Phuc Yen Airfield near Hanoi revealed the presence of MIG-15's and 17's. It was obvious from this rapid response that the aircraft came from Communist China. Hanoi evidently decided it was prudent to prepare for a long war. North Vietnamese aggression in South Vietnam was moving ahead rapidly and there was no telling when the United States might retaliate against the North again.

In early November 1964 North Vietnamese Premier Pham Van Dong visited Moscow, ostensibly to celebrate the 47th anniversary of the Bolshevik Revolution. His primary mission, however, was to request major material and technical support in building a modern air defense system.

The North Vietnamese air defense system on the eve of the Gulf of Tonkin incidents was of low effectiveness. The aircraft inventory consisted of some 30 trainers, 50 transports, and four light helicopters, none of which had effective air defense capabilities. The airfields were primarily oriented towards handling light and medium transport activity. Gia Lam Airfield at Hanoi and Cat Bi Airfield at Haiphong were the only two modern airfields capable of sustained jet operations, although Phuc Yen, also near Hanoi, was nearly completed. Two other airfields, Kien An at Haiphong and Dong Hoi, just north of the Demilitarized Zone, had hard-surfaced runways capable of supporting jet aircraft. There were no missiles for defense. Conventional antiaircraft weapons (some 700 of all types) provided the air defense capability and there was little radar tracking capability. The radar complex consisted of about 20 early warning sets with very little capability for definitive tracking. Overall air defense was limited to key population areas and military installations, and mainly restricted to altitudes below 20,000 feet.

AIR AND NAVAL ACTIONS AGAINST NORTH VIETNAM—1965

At the outset of 1965 our air forces were engaged only in limited combat operations in Southeast Asia, but by late January of that year, there was widespread conviction among senior United States and Vietnamese military commanders and civilian authorities in Vietnam that the absence of a United States response to Viet Cong and North Vietnamese attacks against our personnel and forces in South Vietnam would encourage further anti-United States incidents. With this in mind and with the approval of the Joint Chiefs of Staff, an operation order—nicknamed FLAMING DART—was developed to detail the military actions for retaliatory air strikes to be executed on order of higher authority.

One destroyer patrol, ordered into the Tonkin Gulf, was scheduled to begin on 7 February. However, it developed that this was the date of a state visit by Soviet Premier Alexei N. Kosygin to Hanoi and the patrol was cancelled in order to avoid any incident that might worsen United States-Soviet relations. In addition to cancelling the naval patrol in the Gulf, the attack carriers *Coral Sea* and *Hancock* were ordered to stand down from a fully ready condition and on the morning of the seventh the two ships turned eastward for Subic Bay, leaving only the aircraft carrier *Ranger* in the Gulf of Tonkin.

Within hours of the release of the two carriers, the North Vietnamese-controlled Viet Cong launched a heavy mortar attack on United States forces and billets in the vicinity of the Pleiku Airbase. Eight Americans were killed, 109 wounded. This was the first of a series of Viet Cong attacks which coincided with Premier Kosygin's visit.

After this attack, our forces resumed promptly the operational readiness posture so recently relaxed. The aircraft carriers *Coral Sea* and *Hancock* were ordered to reverse course and steam toward the Tonkin Gulf. After alerting Pacific Command air and naval component commanders, CINCPAC informed the Joint Chiefs of Staff that our forces were ready to execute the FLAMING DART plan as appropriate retaliation. The Joint Chiefs of Staff responded promptly with "Execute" and the *Coral Sea* and the *Hancock* launched a total of 45 planes against North Vietnamese army barracks and port facilities at Dong Hoi, just north of the Demilitarized Zone.

Simultaneously the aircraft carrier *Ranger* launched a 34-plane strike against the Vit Thu Lu Barracks, 15 miles inland and five miles north of the Demilitarized Zone, but poor weather prevented these attacks from being carried out.

At Dong Hoi, ten buildings were destroyed, two others heavily damaged, and an undetermined number left burning. One A-4 Skyhawk and its pilot were lost.

Concurrent with these retaliatory actions, force augmentations of the Pacific Command were undertaken to deter or counter North Vietnamese or Chinese Communist reaction. At the same time, proposals were submitted to the Joint Chiefs of Staff to increase the military pressure against North Vietnam. CINCPAC proposed that our aircraft be authorized to participate on a continuing basis with the Vietnamese Air Force against the Viet Cong within South Vietnam, that frequent destroyer patrols be conducted in the Tonkin Gulf to place the Communists on the defensive in their home grounds, and that fighter escort be authorized for photographic reconnaissance missions in the southern portion of North Vietnam.

With Ambassador to South Vietnam Maxwell Taylor and General Westmoreland supporting the retaliatory action and emphasizing the importance of South Vietnamese Air Force participation, the Joint Chiefs of Staff authorized an additional strike on 8 February with South Vietnamese Air Force resources against the Vu Con Barracks, with the Chap Le Barracks (about 15 miles north of the Demilitarized Zone) as an alternate target in case of bad weather. The South Vietnamese Air Force, in association with our pathfinder and flak suppression forces, executed a successful strike against the Chap Le Barracks with 24 A-1H aircraft.

On 10 February the enemy blew up a United States enlisted men's billet at Qui Nhon, killing 23 Americans and wounding 21 others. Immediately after this action, CINCPAC recommended to the Joint Chiefs of Staff that we retaliate promptly and emphatically, and included a proposal that the South Vietnamese Air Force be used to strike the Vu Con Barracks. Ambassador Taylor and General Westmoreland again were in agreement with our views.

In response to CINCPAC's recommendation, the Joint Chiefs of Staff issued a warning order to be prepared to conduct coordinated attacks during daylight hours on 11 February. The execution order from the Joint Chiefs of Staff assigned United States strike forces to the Chanh Hoa Barracks, 35 miles north of the Demilitarized Zone. The Vu Con Barracks was to be handled by the South Vietnamese Air Force.

On 11 February FLAMING DART TWO was launched. Weather conditions forced the South Vietnamese Air Force to attack its alternate target, the Vit Thu Lu Barracks, with resulting destruction of five buildings. The United States naval aircraft strike at Chanh Hoa Barracks was successful but our forces suffered the loss of three aircraft.

INCEPTION OF ROLLING THUNDER OPERATIONS

Until mid-February 1965 all United States and South Vietnamese Air Force air strikes against North Vietnam had been in response to specific Communist violence directed against our forces. However, at CINCPAC's direction, plans had been prepared to undertake a program of air strikes against North Vietnam, not necessarily related to retaliatory action, should such operations be ordered. The objective of the air strikes was to cause the government of North Vietnam to cease its support and direction of the insurgencies in South Vietnam and Laos.

Before such strikes could be launched, it was essential for the United States and its allies to make preparations for possible reaction by North Vietnam and Communist China. Some preparatory moves were accomplished in connection with the FLAMING DART air strikes to include the evacuation of American dependents from South Vietnam and augmentation of air power in Southeast Asia.

Although there were no further FLAMING DART actions, there was continued planning for additional air strikes. Higher authority, in response to continued and increasing aggression by North Vietnam, soon authorized the use of United States forces for an air strike against the Quang Khe Naval Base and recommended employment of South Vietnamese Air Force aircraft to strike the Dong Hoi Airfield (just north of the Demilitarized Zone). These strikes, with a planning readiness date of 20 February, were given the nickname ROLLING THUNDER. That name came to be applied to our air campaign against North Vietnam with different strike series numbered in sequence.

ROLLING THUNDER STRIKES BEGIN

On 2 March 1965 the first ROLLING THUNDER strikes were launched when United States aircraft hit a supply area and the Vietnamese Air Force struck a port complex. Strategic Air Command B–52 night air strikes were included in the warning order for ROLLING THUNDER 5, but SAC participation was not included in the execute message. SAC B–52 operations were not to become a part of ROLLING THUNDER but became a separate operation, ARC LIGHT.

ROLLING THUNDER operations were initiated under strict controls and specific guidance. The strike day was specified, as well as the number of sorties by task and by target; strikes were dependent on Vietnamese Air Force participation prior to or concurrent with United States strikes; attacks were limited to primary targets or one of two alternates with unexpended ordnance to be dumped into the South China Sea; prestrike reconnaissance was not permitted; bomb damage assessment aircraft were to accompany strike aircraft or immediately follow the strike aircraft; subsequent bomb damage assessment was to be conducted at medium altitude only and unescorted; and no aircraft were to be recycled.

As the ROLLING THUNDER campaign progressed, restrictions were gradually reduced and greater latitude in air operations was authorized. Within the approved boundaries, armed reconnaissance aircraft (originally prohibited from doing so) were permitted to hit enemy vehicles on roads and rail lines, aircraft or vehicles on certain airfields, North Vietnamese naval craft, water craft firing on aircraft, radar and communications facilities, surface-to-air missile sites and equipment, and barges, ferries, and lighters.

North Vietnam was divided into seven geographic regions, identified as Route Packages, for ROLLING THUNDER operations. They were designed for the purpose of assigning responsibility for target development, collection of intelligence data, and target analysis. To insure economical and effective use of resources, operational procedures were developed between our Seventh Air Force and Seventh Fleet that provided for full coordination of air operations in the ROLLING THUNDER program and yet allowed both Services to operate in all areas.

As ROLLING THUNDER progressed and the operational commanders were granted increased flexibility in conducting operations, the subordinate commanders were reminded of the unique character of the campaign. For example, in an April message to subordinate commanders, CINCPAC noted that in the day-to-day pressure of an operational environment it was not easy to remember that the air campaign in North Vietnam was not just another war with the objective of inflicting maximum damage to the enemy. ROLLING THUNDER was described as a precise application of military pressure for the specific purpose of halting aggression in South Vietnam, and that there was no doubt as to the damage the strikes had accomplished. CINCPAC's message emphasized that the commanders could continue to expect various types of restrictions on their operations, some explicitly stated, others implied, and that the fundamental importance of the air campaign, conducted as ordered, required careful compliance with the spirit and intent of each instruction.

ROLLING THUNDER STRIKES SUSPENDED

On 12 May 1965 air strike and armed reconnaissance operations within North Vietnam were suspended. Strike aircraft released by this move were made available for use against the Viet Cong within South Vietnam. A special reconnaissance program was launched to observe the reaction of the North Vietnamese rail and road transportation systems.

RECOMMENDED FUTURE COURSE FOR ROLLING THUNDER

During the bombing pause, a comprehensive recommendation on the future course of the air campaign was submitted to the Joint Chiefs of Staff. CINCPAC stated that in developing the future course of the campaign it was necessary to weigh carefully the capabilities and limitations of United States air power when required to operate within specific political parameters, and to weigh the vulnerability of North Vietnam within that framework. A concept was then proposed for a demonstration of the ubiquity of our air power, characterized by an around-the-clock program of immobilization, attrition, and harassment of North Vietnamese military targets. The specific types of missions proposed for this purpose were extensive daytime armed reconnaissance on land and inland waterway routes south of 20° North coupled with night blockage tactics; increased route interdiction south of 20° North; repeated attacks against known military facilities south of 20° North that could be effectively attacked by a small strike force; attacks that sought out and destroyed dispersed supplies, equipment, and military personnel; and attacks on port facilities and recognized North Vietnamese shipping.

As a desirable alternative CINCPAC recommended that incremental attacks be authorized on the larger targets over a period of days, to be supported by bomb damage assessment. This type of attack was to be conducted against major targets south of 20° North and later extended northwest to Dien Bien Phu.

Intensified psychological operations were also suggested as an important adjunct to ROLLING THUNDER. CINCPAC proposed specific measures to transmit the message that the United States had no quarrel with the people of North Vietnam and that they should avoid all military installations. The targets and "strike zones" proposed were initially limited to the area from the Demilitarized Zone to 20° North, but these were to be extended to the northwest against specific targets. CINCPAC also recommended that, as the zone for strikes against major targets expanded to the north and west, the armed reconnaissance and small strike zone be expanded accordingly. In this plan, it was proposed to lift the numerical limit on armed reconnaissance sorties so that only our capability be considered in establishing the number of small, controlled air operations.

One purpose of this campaign was to drive home to the North Vietnamese leaders that our staying power was superior to their own.

ROLLING THUNDER STRIKES RESUMED

During the bombing suspension initiated in May 1965, information was collected to permit an evaluation of the results of ROLLING THUNDER. On 16 May CINCPAC suggested to the Joint Chiefs of Staff that further respite for North Vietnam would serve to make future problems more difficult in South Vietnam and Laos. On this basis CINCPAC recommended resumption of ROLLING THUNDER and received authorization from higher authority to resume operations on 18 May 1965.

Within ROLLING THUNDER 15, specified geographical areas were for the first time assigned for armed reconnaissance and one strike was authorized north of 20° North against Quang Suoi Barracks.

Continuing through the end of 1965, North Vietnamese military targets were subjected to air attack by ROLLING THUNDER operations. North Vietnamese freedom of troop and war supply movement was progressively impaired as the number and importance of ROLLING THUNDER fixed targets grew. The area and intensity of armed reconnaissance were expanded but at a carefully measured and moderate pace. By year's end, we had progressed from ROLLING THUNDER 16 on 25 May through ROLLING THUNDER 47, which was authorized on 24 December 1965.

EVALUATION OF ARMED RECONNAISSANCE

It was clear by September 1965 that despite the damage caused by air attacks in North Vietnam there was no indication of North Vietnamese willingness to negotiate or terminate support of the Viet Cong.

It must be noted that the principle of continual and steadily increasing pressure was basic to the concept of ROLLING THUNDER and thus to the achievement of our purposes through the use of air power. This principle had not been held to in the ROLLING THUNDER campaign, either in armed reconnaissance or in fixed target strikes. Armed reconnaissance sorties had leveled off for the two months previous to September 1965 and strikes on fixed targets had actually decreased.

The overall decrease in pressure was caused in part because the authorized armed reconnaissance area had fewer significant targets than before. Further, the reduced number of fixed targets for each succeeding ROLLING THUNDER period had lessened the pressure on North Vietnam. Finally, the most important targets were in the northeast and in the large sanctuaries around Hanoi and Haiphong, where air operations were not authorized.

On 26 November CINCPAC recommended destruction of major war supporting targets in the northeast, including those in the Hanoi and Haiphong areas, disruption of major port facilities, and subsequent increased armed reconnaissance directed at the road, rail, and coastal lines of communication from China and on inland waterways.

EXPANSION OF NORTH VIETNAM'S AIR DEFENSE SYSTEM—1965

In April 1965 photography revealed the first North Vietnamese surface-to-air missile (SAM) site under construction some 15 miles southeast of Hanoi. A second SAM site appeared about a month later and by mid-July 1965 several more sites had been discovered in various stages of construction, forming an incomplete irregular ring around Hanoi. Neither missiles nor missile-associated equipment was detected in any of the sites. On 24 July 1965 the first known successful SAM firing from a North Vietnamese site occurred, resulting in the loss of an F-4C aircraft. Subsequently the number of SAM sites increased rapidly in the area north of Thanh Hoa. By the end of 1965, more than 60 sites had been discovered protecting the vital military-industrial complex around Hanoi and Haiphong and the LOC south to Thanh Hoa. The SAM threat forced our aircraft to operate below the minimum effective altitudes of the missile system. This required more fuel and placed the aircraft within the kill envelope of small arms, automatic weapons, and light antiaircraft artillery. Evaluation of the effectiveness of the SAM system for 1965 indicated it took about 13 missiles launched for each aircraft shot down.

As SAM defenses were increased and improved, so also was North Vietnam's aircraft inventory. In late May 1965 eight IL-28 jet light bombers were identified at Phuc Yen Airfield and by mid-June the number of MIG-15 and MIG-17 fighter aircraft had climbed to almost 70. At Phuc Yen, the presence of unpacked crates indicated that there were more aircraft awaiting assembly. In late December 1965 an improved supersonic fighter, the delta-winged MIG-21, arrived to bolster North Vietnam's air defenses. Combat aircraft activity during 1965 was mainly devoted to training and only ten fighter engagements were reported, resulting in a total of two United States and six North Vietnamese fighter aircraft downed. The IL-28's were not involved in combat missions. North Vietnam's aircraft inventory at the end of 1965 numbered about 75 MIG jet fighters and eight IL-28 jet light bombers.

The most effective elements of North Vietnam's air defense system proved to be the automatic weapons and antiaircraft artillery (AAA). Antiaircraft weapons were credited with destroying about 80 percent of our aircraft shot down in North Vietnam during 1965, with the most damaging fire from light AAA and automatic weapons. This rate was to be expected, considering low-level attacks by fighter-bombers and flak suppression tactics.

During 1965 North Vietnam accomplished a rapid buildup of early warning and height-finding radar sites. An initial ground controlled intercept (GCI) capability was established in both the northern and southern portions of the country and into the Gulf of Tonkin.

On 4 April MIG aircraft possibly under GCI control surprised and shot down two F-105's over Thanh Hoa. The number of AAA fire control radars increased during the year but not as fast as the number of AAA weapons. At the end of 1965 the ratio of radars to occupied AAA installations was no more than 1 to 25.

THAILAND BASED AIRCRAFT OPERATIONS

Thai bases were used for strike aircraft from the outset of the ROLLING THUNDER program and for reconnaissance missions in Laos. This arrangement existed with the full consent of the Thai Government. The use of Thailand-based aircraft for operations in North Vietnam and Laos helped relieve pressure on the already congested air bases in South Vietnam, introduced an added increment of flexibility into our air operations, and permitted sortie levels which otherwise would have taxed the capability of our resources.

THE VIETNAMESE AIR FORCE'S ROLE IN ROLLING THUNDER

South Vietnamese Air Force (VNAF) participation was a significant element in ROLLING THUNDER. However, heavy Viet Cong pressure tended to drain VNAF resources to meet requirements in South Vietnam at the expense of the campaign in North Vietnam. Diverting carrier aircraft and increasing United States Air Force attacks within South Vietnam relieved pressure on the VNAF, thereby permitting increased VNAF participation in ROLLING THUNDER. Subsequently, the VNAF provided a minimum of three strike/

reconnaissance missions for each of the ROLLING THUNDER periods.

COMMAND AND CONTROL FOR ROLLING THUNDER OPERATIONS

The command and control arrangement for ROLLING THUNDER strike and armed reconnaissance operations basically consisted of CINCPAC's operational control of the strike forces through the Commanders in Chief of the Pacific Fleet (CINCPACFLT) and Pacific Air Forces (CINCPACAF) and the Commander, United States Military Assistance Command, Vietnam (COMUSMACV). Coordination authority was assigned to CINCPACAF with the tacit understanding that it would be further delegated to the Commander of the 2d Air Division, located in South Vietnam. This authority was granted to the extent it was required to preclude mutual interference of friendly forces during strike and armed reconnaissance missions. A Seventh Fleet liaison officer to the 2d Air Division accomplished liaison with the Commander of Task Force 77, who exercised operational command and control over the aircraft carriers on station off the Vietnam coast. The Commander of the 2d Air Division exercised operational control for CINCPACAF over the Air Force forces in Southeast Asia engaged in combat air operations.

This system conformed to accepted doctrine for unified control of our forces and it functioned smoothly for this purpose. It provided an effective means of exercising coordination of air operations over North Vietnam without a combined command structure. Although there were refinements within this system, there was no fundamental change.

ORDNANCE EXPENDITURE

The general purpose bomb was the weapon against the majority of ROLLING THUNDER targets. The Navy used principally the 500-pound bomb; our Air Force relied mainly on the 750-pound bomb supplemented by the 500-pound bomb. Special targeting required limited numbers of 250-, 1,000-, 2,000-, and 3,000-pound bombs.

Throughout ROLLING THUNDER operations there was no case in which sorties were cancelled because weapons were unavailable. In some cases, however, the optimum weapons necessary for achievement of maximum damage per sortie were not used when local shortages required substitution of alternate weapons for those preferred.

Use of napalm against North Vietnam targets was prohibited until ROLLING THUNDER 6; thereafter it was employed only against specific military targets not adjacent to a population center.

LEAFLET OPERATIONS

The initial leaflet program aimed at the North Vietnamese was approved on 9 April 1965. The concept was that prior to an airstrike we would warn the populace, by leaflets or by radio, that certain categories of targets were considered military objectives and that the people should evacuate all targets of the type described. The first leaflet mission was conducted on 14 April.

In June Washington authorities granted to CINCPAC and to the American Ambassador in Saigon the authority to conduct leaflet drops as part of the total air effort. It was intended that the targets for ROLLING THUNDER and the leaflet missions would be complementary. Further, it was directed that the leaflet operations would be expanded to two drops of about two million leaflets each per week.

Intensified psychological operations were directed and on 16 July CINCPAC recommended that leaflet operations be conducted on the major North Vietnamese population centers, to include Hanoi and Haiphong. This was approved by higher authority with the proviso that leaflet aircraft could not penetrate a 40-nautical mile circle around either Hanoi or Haiphong. Leaflets for Hanoi and Haiphong were targeted utilizing the wind-drift technique.

Until the early part of September 1965 all leaflet missions were executed by F–105 aircraft. On 10

September a C–130 was used for the first time in the leaflet program. On this, the first night mission of the program, 9,000 packets containing toys were dropped over North Vietnam in connection with Children's Day.

Responding to an October query from the Joint Chiefs of Staff, CINCPAC again proposed a relaxation of restrictions on leaflet aircraft in the interest of more effective operations. CINCPAC's proposal provided that the less stringent constraints applicable to some of the other air operations be applied to leaflet missions. After approval by the Joint Chiefs of Staff, the basic operation order of 17 December broadened the area of operations but still restricted aircraft from entering a 25-nautical mile radius from Hanoi, a 10-nautical mile radius from Haiphong, and a distance varying from 25 to 30 nautical miles from the Chinese border.

A total of 77 million leaflets and 15,000 gift kits were distributed under the leaflet program during 1965. There were indications that the material was reaching the populace, that in some instances the morale of the people was being lowered, and that the North Vietnamese authorities were forced to take counterpropaganda actions. On this basis the leaflet operation was termed worthwhile.

Leaflet operations were suspended during the latter part of December as part of the Christmas stand-down.

HOLIDAY CEASE-FIRE—1965

The Viet Cong announced a Christmas "truce" in South Vietnam in 1965. On our side, Secretary of State Dean Rusk proposed that the United States suspend bombing operations against North Vietnam for 24 hours and that air operations in South Vietnam be limited to support of forces in contact with the Viet Cong. Should this result in a real and similar restraint on the part of the enemy, we would continue to suspend bombing in the hope that negotiations could begin. CINCPAC concurred in Secretary Rusk's proposal, feeling that such operations could be suspended without significant military advantage to the Viet Cong.

We announced that air operations would be suspended over North Vietnam for a 24-hour period over Christmas and, as circumstances would have it, they were not resumed until the end of January 1966. Air and ground operations in South Vietnam were limited to defensive actions during the 24-hour Christmas period. Subsequently, the ground cease-fire period was extended by six hours, and ended on 26 December.

The enemy did not observe his own announced truce. Casualties reported for the period 24 through 26 December as a result of enemy violations were 3 United States personnel killed and 23 wounded, 54 members of the South Vietnamese Armed Forces killed and 55 wounded, and 15 South Vietnamese civilians killed and 19 wounded.

On 26 December CINCPAC commented to the Joint Chiefs of Staff on the difficulties faced by a commander in the presence of the enemy when a cease-fire was extended on short notice. It was pointed out that the advantage of a cease-fire accrued to the enemy, suggested that any future cease-fire should be planned in detail well in advance, and proposed that aerial observation of key enemy installations in North Vietnam should continue even during a cease-fire.

EFFECTS DURING 1965

Initial ROLLING THUNDER air operations during 1965 were relatively light and resulted in an ordnance expenditure of only about 200 tons of ordnance per week. As the campaign got under way and more targets were made available, up to 1,600 tons of ordnance were dropped each week with the major portion against industrial targets. Damage within the industrial sector was quite evenly distributed among all target systems. For example, an estimated 27 percent of North Vietnam's electrical capacity was destroyed by the end of 1965.

Damage to military targets was concentrated primarily against military barracks. However, attacks against other military facilities such as ammunition dumps and storage depots would have had more immediate impact since loss of military equipment required replacement from either the USSR or Communist China. By the end of 1965, approximately 1,500 waterborne logistic craft, 800 trucks, and 650 pieces of railroad rolling stock had been either damaged or destroyed as a result of offensive air action.

Indications were that enemy morale and tenacity were supported by a strong conviction that the patience of the American public would expire before we could attain a just peace. Hanoi officials stated publicly that enormous costs and casualties would persuade the United States to negotiate on North Vietnamese terms. In the eyes of a military commander, the objectives of the ROLLING THUNDER campaign had not been achieved—and to achieve them required adherence to the basic concept and principle of applying a continual and steadily increasing level of pressure.

ROLLING THUNDER OPERATIONS—1966

As 1966 opened, North Vietnam's airspace was free of United States combat air operations. The suspension which began on Christmas of 1965 in connection with our peace overtures was continued until 31 January 1966 when, all peace efforts having been spurned by the enemy, limited ROLLING THUNDER strikes and armed reconnaissance operations were resumed.

During the pause, enemy forces were deeply involved in actions preparing for the resumption of our operations. Our side, aware of this, made photographic reconnaissance and analyzed the information obtained. The enemy preparatory activity involved reconstructing and improving his lines of communication (LOC), improving and increasing the air defense of important areas, dispersing the military support base, and pushing a large number of trucks and supplies towards the infiltration corridors leading into Laos. Some 40 additional air defense positions were added in the vicinity of the northwest rail line between Hanoi and Communist China. Similarly, an increase of 26 guns protecting the LOC's below Vinh was noted.

The reconnaissance photography accomplished during the pause in our air attacks was of great value in determining enemy activity and was of material aid in planning future strikes. Analysis of the enemy effort expended to rehabilitate certain LOC's indicated the value he assigned to the various routes.

RESUMPTION OF ROLLING THUNDER OPERATIONS

Resumption of ROLLING THUNDER operations, which took place on 31 January, apparently came as no surprise to the North Vietnamese because the LOC associated activity resumed "normal" night time and dispersal procedures several days prior to this date. News media speculation and political and other developments presaged that the period of relative quiet was about to end.

On 12 January during the stand-down of offensive air operations against North Vietnam, a detailed discussion of the relationship of military operations in North Vietnam to the overall strategy of the war in South Vietnam was submitted to the Joint Chiefs of Staff. In this submission, CINCPAC noted that plans should be made to resume effective operations against North Vietnam if negotiations did not bring an early cease-fire. The relationship of military operations against North Vietnam to the overall strategy was discussed in terms of the following undertakings: (1) to deny to the Communists in South Vietnam the effective North Vietnamese direction and assistance vital to their war-making capability; (2) to assist the government of South Vietnam in protecting the South Vietnamese people from Communist subversion and oppression, to liberate areas dominated by the Viet Cong, and to assist in the establishment of a stable economy and the continuation of an independent non-Communist government; (3) to defeat the Viet Cong and North Vietnamese forces and destroy their base areas in South Vietnam.

We stated that it was necessary to achieve success in each of these three elements of strategy through simultaneous application of appropriate military force.

The first undertaking—to deny the Communists in South Vietnam effective North Vietnamese direction and assistance—was advocated as the basis for the renewed air campaign. The air campaign was to be conducted so as to accomplish this undertaking most effectively. Access to external assistance that permitted North Vietnam to sustain military operations must be denied and the resources already in North Vietnam and most needed to support aggression would be destroyed. All known military material and facilities would be destroyed and military activities and movements would be continuously harassed and disrupted. The foregoing would require operations quite different from those before the cease-fire.

While recognizing limited achievements in the air campaign, CINCPAC's view was that the nature of the war had changed since the air campaign began. ROLLING THUNDER had not forced Hanoi to the decision sought, and indications were that Ho Chi Minh intended to continue to support the Viet Cong until he was denied the capability to do so.

In summary, we felt that these three tasks, effectively accomplished, would either bring the enemy to the conference table or cause the insurgency to wither from lack of support. The alternative appeared to be a long and costly war—costly in lives and material resources.

EXPANSION OF ROLLING THUNDER OPERATIONS

ROLLING THUNDER 48 extended from 31 January to the end of February 1966. Weather was a limiting factor throughout the period. It caused a high percentage of cancellations or diversions and greatly limited the information obtained from bomb damage assessment.

Most ROLLING THUNDER operations during this period were limited to the southern area of North Vietnam and by the end of the month there was little to report in the way of results.

By the end of February the results obtained through ROLLING THUNDER, while showing that considerable enemy military material and facilities were destroyed or damaged, gave very little evidence of progress toward the objective of the program.

March weather was slightly better than February's, with an occasional day of good visibility throughout the ROLLING THUNDER area. More often, however, pilots found 100 percent cloud cover or haze to 12,000 or 14,000 feet. This caused a high rate of cancellations. Even so, the rate of damage to fleeting targets in the ROLLING THUNDER area improved significantly.

In March General Westmoreland urgently requested authority to bring military power to bear on the enemy approaches to the battlefield for which he was responsible. On 1 April the Basic Operation Order for ROLLING THUNDER assigned General Westmoreland the primary responsibility for armed reconnaissance and intelligence analysis in the southernmost portion of North Vietnam. To remove any doubt about where the emphasis might lie, Secretary of Defense McNamara stated on 16 April that operations north of this southernmost portion of North Vietnam would be conducted only when they could be performed without penalty to required operations in the "extended battlefield."

ROLLING THUNDER 50, effective 1 April, directed planning and preparation for attacks against the most significant targets yet considered, including the Viet Tri Railroad-Highway Bridge; the Haiphong Thermal Power Plant; the Haiphong Cement Plant; and petroleum, oil, and lubricants (POL) storage at Haiphong, Hanoi, Nguyen Ke, Bac Giang, Do Son, and Duong Nham. Another important target was the early warning-ground control intercept radar at Kep, a facility that supported the area's air defense. Authority to strike these targets was to be granted separately by the Joint Chiefs of Staff. In late April, however, ROLLING THUNDER 50 was indefinitely extended and at that time the strikes on the ten significant targets had not been authorized.

The ten fixed targets specified by ROLLING THUNDER 50 remained on the restricted list through early June, when an 11th target—Phuc Yen POL Storage—was added. Soon thereafter, an intensive search began for techniques that would minimize civilian casualties during strikes on POL storage at Haiphong and Hanoi and at the Haiphong Thermal Power and Cement Plants.

Then on 23 June CINCPAC received the authority to conduct air strikes, after first light on 24 June, on seven POL storage facilities and the Kep radar. It was specifically directed that same-day strikes against the POL facilities at Hanoi and Haiphong would initiate ROLLING THUNDER 50 ALPHA. Special care was to be taken to avoid damaging merchant shipping when attacking the Haiphong target. Steps were taken to minimize casualties among enemy civilians and the friendly operating forces. Special measures were devised to assure a rapid flow of detailed information to Washington.

Despite special precautions to insure the security of information pertaining to these operations, news media carried essential strike details at almost the same time the POL strikes were authorized. This prompted a postponement of the strikes, deferring damage to one of North Vietnam's basic resources for maintaining the military effort.

Shortly after noon on 30 June the program against POL facilities was launched with strikes on stores at Hanoi and Haiphong. About 95 percent damage was achieved by the Hanoi strike and an almost equal level was obtained after a second strike at Haiphong.

The POL system of North Vietnam was to be the primary target of ROLLING THUNDER 51. CINCPAC therefore promulgated a plan of action in late July to accomplish the maximum feasible POL system destruction while yet assuring a balanced effort against other North Vietnamese elements and their military capability to support the Viet Cong. However, the only fixed targets authorized by the Joint Chiefs of Staff for ROLLING THUNDER 51 were bridges.

On 12 November ROLLING THUNDER 52 was authorized, but armed reconnaissance objectives and operating areas remained the same as authorized in ROLLING THUNDER 51. The level of attack sorties per month was raised from 10,100 to 13,200. Strikes were authorized against one bridge, one railroad classification yard, two POL facilities, three surface-to-air missile storage areas, one vehicle depot, one cement plant, two power plants, and selected elements of the only steel plant in North Vietnam. However, the steel and cement plants and the two power plants were deferred from attack. On 15 December restrikes against the railroad classification yard and the vehicle depot were prohibited and by 23 December the delivery of ordnance within ten nautical miles of Hanoi had been prohibited.

In a message to the Joint Chiefs of Staff on 24 December CINCPAC recommended that authority to strike all ROLLING THUNDER targets be reinstituted. However, it was not until ROLLING THUNDER 55 and 56 in April and May of 1967 that some of these targets were reauthorized.

EFFECTS OF THE POL CAMPAIGN

By early 1965 North Vietnam, largely due to external assistance, possessed a good regional system of petroleum distribution facilities to meet the needs of industrial, transport, and military POL consumers. Nearly all of North Vietnam's POL storage capacity clustered around these centers of activity.

By June 1966 the air campaign had eliminated Nam Dinh and Phu Qui as centers of POL tank storage and had reduced Vinh to at most one-third of its original capacity. At the end of the month POL targets in Hanoi and Haiphong first came under attack. By early August these attacks had destroyed the largest storage facility in the Hanoi area and had lowered the capability of the Haiphong receiving terminal to marginal levels. Originally capable of storage of the equivalent of about four Soviet tanker loads, the Haiphong terminal could no longer hold more than one-third of a normal tanker's capacity.

As early as mid-1965 North Vietnam had begun taking remedial or precautionary measures against the air campaign. New farms of buried or bunkered tanks started dotting the country, the majority of them in or near the major military and industrial centers. Extremely large numbers of petroleum drums appeared. None of the POL farms approached pre-strike capacities. Characteristically, they consisted of varying numbers of tanks in the 2,200 to 3,300 gallon class, suggesting a possible modular relationship with Soviet-built tank trucks.

At Haiphong, tankers continued to arrive and discharge their cargo into lighters and barges that made deliveries to inland transhipment points and south along the coast. North Vietnam's 1968 POL receipt and distribution system continues to follow this pattern.

NORTH VIETNAM'S AIR DEFENSE SYSTEM—1966

Throughout 1966 the proliferation of SAM sites continued, and continuous SAM coverage extended from Yen Bai to Haiphong in the north to about Ha Tinh in the south. Additional SAM sites were discovered during the year, raising the total to about 150. As our strike operations expanded in North Vietnam the missile expenditure rate increased. Observed expenditures in 1966 totaled almost nine times the number of SAM's expended in 1965 and the effectiveness statistically of the SAM defenses dropped to an average of about 33 missiles

Nam Dinh Petroleum Storage

required per aircraft shot down. Our evasion tactics and electronics countermeasures degraded North Vietnam's efforts to maintain or improve SAM effectiveness.

During 1966 MIG aggressiveness against our strike forces increased from an average of only one engagement per month in the first half of the year to an average of about 12 per month during the last half. Interference by MIG's on numerous occasions served to force strike aircraft to jettison their ordnance in order to engage the attacking MIG's, or to evacuate the area. An increasingly effective air defense effort was evident as coordination between fighters, SAM's, antiaircraft artillery, and radar elements improved. In air encounters, we had a decided advantage with a total of 11 of our aircraft downed by MIG's compared to 29 MIG's lost to our fighters. By the end of 1966 some 70 fighter aircraft were in North Vietnam, including about 15 MIG-21's.

During 1966 the improvement of existing airfields and construction of new airfields maintained pace with other defense efforts. Phuc Yen and Kep remained the primary military airfields where the majority of the aircraft were deployed. Gia Lam at Hanoi and Cat Bi and Kien An at Haiphong were utilized as prime dispersal areas to provide for flexibility in the deployment of fighters to protect key areas. In January a new potential jet airfield at Yen Bai, about 60 miles northwest of Hanoi, was observed under construction which continued throughout the year. Harassing attacks against this field commenced in July and retarded construction efforts. In March Bai Thuong, 60 miles south of Hanoi, became almost operational, but our bombing attacks prevented it from becoming serviceable. Another new, potential jet airfield at Hoa Lac, 20 miles west of Hanoi, was observed under construction in June but was not operational during the remainder of the year.

The total number of radar sites at the end of 1966 numbered over 100, consisting of a well-balanced inventory of early warning, GCI, AAA fire control, and SAM-associated equipment.

HOLIDAY CEASE-FIRES

In anticipation of probable proposals for Christmas 1966 and the New Year and *Tet* (the Vietnamese New Year) cease-fires, CINCPAC presented his views well in advance so they might be considered in arriving at any decision made concerning a stand-down. In so doing, CINCPAC cited the conclusive disadvantages and risks that had accrued to friendly forces as a result of the extended 1965–1966 Christmas and *Tet* stand-downs.

At that time the enemy had achieved an increase of about 400 weapons in his antiaircraft artillery inventory in North Vietnam, the addition of more than 15 early warning and fire control radars, and construction of nearly 30 additional surface-to-air missile sites. The flow of men and material through Laos toward South Vietnam had also continued unabated and in fact had accelerated during the first three months of 1966. Large scale reconstruction of LOC's had been launched, key rail lines were repaired and traffic was resumed, and other measures taken to overcome the shortcomings and deficiencies caused by air attacks had increased the southward flow of men and material. In South Vietnam, the Viet Cong had initiated countrywide activity to position forces for the subsequent January–February 1966 campaign. And finally, the Viet Cong initiated 84 significant incidents during the 30-hour *Tet* stand-down.

Another Christmas-*Tet* stand-down would almost certainly result in a repeat performance by the enemy. While a stand-down of not more than 48 hours was militarily acceptable, CINCPAC felt there must be an unqualified understanding that it would not be unilaterally prolonged unless, of course, there was some indication that Hanoi was serious about negotiations. Commanders would need to be instructed and permitted to take all measures necessary, including increasing air reconnaissance (other than armed reconnaissance) and continuing activity away from their bases, to detect threatening enemy movements and concentrations. Friendly commanders would need to be allowed to retain contact until attacking North Vietnamese or Viet Cong forces withdrew and to resume offensive operations if necessary to provide for the safety of friendly forces. The risk of a stand-down of more than one or two days would serve only to the enemy's advantage and generate risks that we could not accept for our forces.

When the cease-fire for Christmas was directed, it provided for a stand-down in Vietnam from 24 to 26 December.

During the cease-fire period the enemy committed 101 violations. Total casualties for United States forces were three killed and 27 wounded; for South Vietnamese forces, 27 killed and 27 wounded; three civilians were killed and five wounded; and the Viet Cong-North Vietnamese had 26 killed and an unknown number wounded.

Along the coastal areas of North Vietnam, waterborne traffic increased substantially during the cease-fire period. Over 1,000 watercraft were sighted along the coast moving between the mouths of the Song Giang and Kien Giang (rivers) between 8 and 12 February 1967 (*Tet*). Of these, more than 15 were large steel-hulled cargo carriers, trawlers, or gunboats up to 140 feet long.

SEVENTH AIR FORCE ESTABLISHED

The bulk of our Air Force support in Southeast Asia had been provided by the 2d Air Division with headquarters in Saigon. With the continued expansion of 2d Air Division forces and activities, the Air Force Chief of Staff, General J. P. McConnell, determined that it would be appropriate to change the unit's title to Seventh Air Force. The change was made effective 1 April 1966 with 2d Air Division Commander Lieutenant General Joseph H. Moore, USAF, assuming command of the Seventh Air Force, with no alteration in existing command relationships.

EFFECTS DURING 1966

The existence of restricted areas around Hanoi and Haiphong and along the border of Communist China effectively insulated a large portion of industrial, military supply, and LOC targets from air attack. As a result, strikes were conducted against less significant targets generally consisting of transportation equipment, general military targets, and installations of the transportation system. This emphasis against transportation, combined with United States restraint, permitted the enemy to develop alternates and to overcome many

La Khe Thon railroad bridge.

NORTH VIETNAM TARGET ELEMENT SUMMARY 1966

TARGET CATEGORY	DESTROYED	DAMAGED	TOTAL DESTROYED & DAMAGED
AAA/AW SITES	493	479	972
SAM SITES	18	83	101
COMMUNICATIONS SITES	38	57	95
MILITARY AREAS	118	434	552
POL AREAS	3,903	578	4,481
STAGING/SUPPLY AREAS	76	1,065	1,141
BUILDINGS	4,941	3,363	8,304
LOC's	1,359	6,390	7,749
PORTS	24	98	122
POWER PLANTS	0	6	6
RAILROAD YARDS	10	119	129
MOTOR VEHICLES	2,067	2,017	4,084
RAILROAD VEHICLES	1,095	1,219	2,314
WATER VEHICLES	3,690	5,810	9,500
TOTAL	17,832	21,718	39,550

NOTE: SOME FIXED TARGETS WERE RESTRUCK NUMEROUS TIMES AND DAMAGE TO THEM MAY BE REPORTED ABOVE MORE THAN ONCE.

of his difficulties as they arose. The construction of alternate routes for infiltration; the use of shuttle services, ferries, floating bridges, and bypasses; and the employment of large numbers of road and bridge repair and construction labor crews permitted continued operation of most LOC's to support insurgency in the South. Equipment losses, especially truck losses, were generally compensated for by increased imports from Communist countries.

Authorization to strike POL facilities and distribution systems was obtained in mid-1966. Initial efforts at destroying storage sites were fairly successful but dispersal of these facilities, which was accomplished shortly after the December 1965 bombing pause, made finding the sites much more difficult. By the end of September and despite the heavy emphasis on this campaign, it was estimated that at the normal rate of consumption, North Vietnam retained sufficient reserves of POL to maintain its military and economic activity for up to four months.

By the end of 1966 approximately 9,500 waterborne logistic craft, nearly 4,100 trucks, and over 2,000 pieces of railroad rolling stock had been either damaged or destroyed as a result of air attacks.

Despite the fact that the enemy was able to compensate for a large portion of the damage suffered by his transportation system and industrial capability, the air offensive accomplished several tasks which, if left undone, would have resulted in an increased ground threat to South Vietnam. The combination of the air offensive against POL facilities and the transportation system increased the pressure to maintain adequate stocks, required increased imports, and added to port congestion in Haiphong. Constant harassment of the LOC's prevented uninhibited movement of military units to the south and caused them to move primarily at night, appreciably extending their transit time. Added to the disruption of the North Vietnamese timetable for operations in South Vietnam, these efforts brought about economic deterioration, disrupted normal transportation and logistic networks, and aggravated management problems and manpower shortages.

After a comprehensive review of ROLLING THUNDER operations, which included its objectives, results, and future courses of action, CINCPAC concluded that the basic objectives and tasks that had been set forth for ROLLING THUNDER were still valid and that an effective ROLLING THUNDER air campaign, together with continued successful operations in South Vietnam, offered the greatest prospects for bringing the war to a successful conclusion on terms advantageous to the United States and its allies.

ROLLING THUNDER OPERATIONS—1967

On 12 January 1967 General Earle G. Wheeler, Chairman of the Joint Chiefs of Staff, was briefed on the CINCPAC concept for conducting ROLLING THUNDER operations in 1967. The objective was to bring increasing pressure so as to cause North Vietnam to cease supporting, controlling, and directing insurgencies in Southeast Asia. Tasks to accomplish this objective were three: to deny North Vietnam access to the flow of external assistance, to curtail the flow of men and supplies from North Vietnam into Laos and South Vietnam, and to destroy in depth those resources in North Vietnam that contributed to support of the aggression.

These tasks were considered interdependent and, in a broad sense, represented a three-pronged approach that required an integrated targeting concept.

CINCPAC felt that accomplishment of these tasks was dependent on the application of continuous and steadily increasing pressures. The application of steadily increasing pressure was denied us in 1966 through operational restrictions and as a result the tasks were not accomplished. CINCPAC also felt that the best way to increase the pressure was to apply continuing steady power, on a long term targeting basis, against key target systems.

The CINCPAC concept for a long term targeting program emphasized target systems, rather than individual sites, and stressed weight of effort on a continuing basis. Since a majority of the targets was in the northern area of North Vietnam, the concept focused primarily on that area. There were six basic target systems: electric power, war supporting industry, transportation support facilities, military complexes, petroleum storage, and air defense.

On 18 January CINCPAC outlined the targeting and operational concept to the Joint Chiefs of Staff. CINCPAC recommended the following parameter in implementing the program against the six basic target systems—all targets in each of the target systems that required approval by higher authority should be approved as a package. This would allow maximum flexibility in the timing of strikes, taking into consideration intelligence and weather factors. Continuing pressure should be assured by striking about 15 new targets each month. The objective would be to avoid peaks and depressions. If we were to increase the pressure on Hanoi, a steady program of disruption against the basic target systems was necessary. The six target systems should be considered as a single package, with each system interrelated to the other, and elements of each system should be attacked, rather than one system at a time.

A breakdown by system of those targets proposed for strike under the concept was furnished to the Joint Chiefs of Staff with the comment that the concept had "finite limits" and "finite goals" and therefore could not be considered as "open ended." Of necessity the program was dynamic. Some targets would probably require periodic restrike, others would not. New targets would probably be generated as the enemy adjusted. When major targets were destroyed or disrupted, minor targets which had not originally been considered worth hitting would become of primary significance.

The ROLLING THUNDER campaign during the first quarter of 1967 was hampered by adverse weather typical of the northeast monsoon season, conditions which precluded full-scale attacks on fixed targets and greatly reduced armed reconnaissance. However, ground controlled radar delivery of ordnance in the southern Route Packages, small force attacks by Seventh Fleet A–6 aircraft, and attacks by Seventh Air Force F–105's and F–4's combined to keep pressure around-the-clock.

Of special importance was the implementation of ROLLING THUNDER 53 on 24 January and ROLLING THUNDER 54 on 23 February. Combined, they authorized strikes against 16 fixed targets in the vital industrial area in the northeast quadrant of North Vietnam.

The middle of April generally marked the end of the bad weather over North Vietnam, air activity was accelerated, and by 21 April all ROLLING THUNDER 54 targets had been struck.

On 23 April the execute order for ROLLING THUNDER 55 was received. Armed reconnaissance operating areas remained constant while fixed targets included one power transformer station, a cement plant, three bridges, a rail repair shop, an ammunition depot, a POL storage area, and the Kep and Hoa Lac MIG-capable airfields in the vicinity of Hanoi. Selected targets were authorized for strike within the ten mile circle around Hanoi. By 28 April all but one of the ROLLING THUNDER 55 targets had been struck.

The continued strikes in the Hanoi-Haiphong area caused intensified defensive reactions to our strikes. The enemy rapidly shifted concentrations of antiaircraft artillery and surface-to-air missiles to those areas.

ROLLING THUNDER 55 was replaced by ROLLING THUNDER 56 on 2 May. This added ten new fixed targets, all of which were struck by the end of May. The good weather period over North Vietnam permitted maximum effort against all authorized targets and LOC's. Of signal interest was the concentrated program against North Vietnam's land transportation system along the major supply lines from Communist China. The main effort was concentrated primarily on classification yards, repair facilities, railroad and highway bridges, and support areas. Results were excellent, particularly in the entrapment of rolling stock and its subsequent destruction. Simultaneous armed reconnaissance of the road and canal LOC's contributed to intensifying overall logistical problems throughout North Vietnam. This pattern of air attacks continued throughout 1967 with the over-

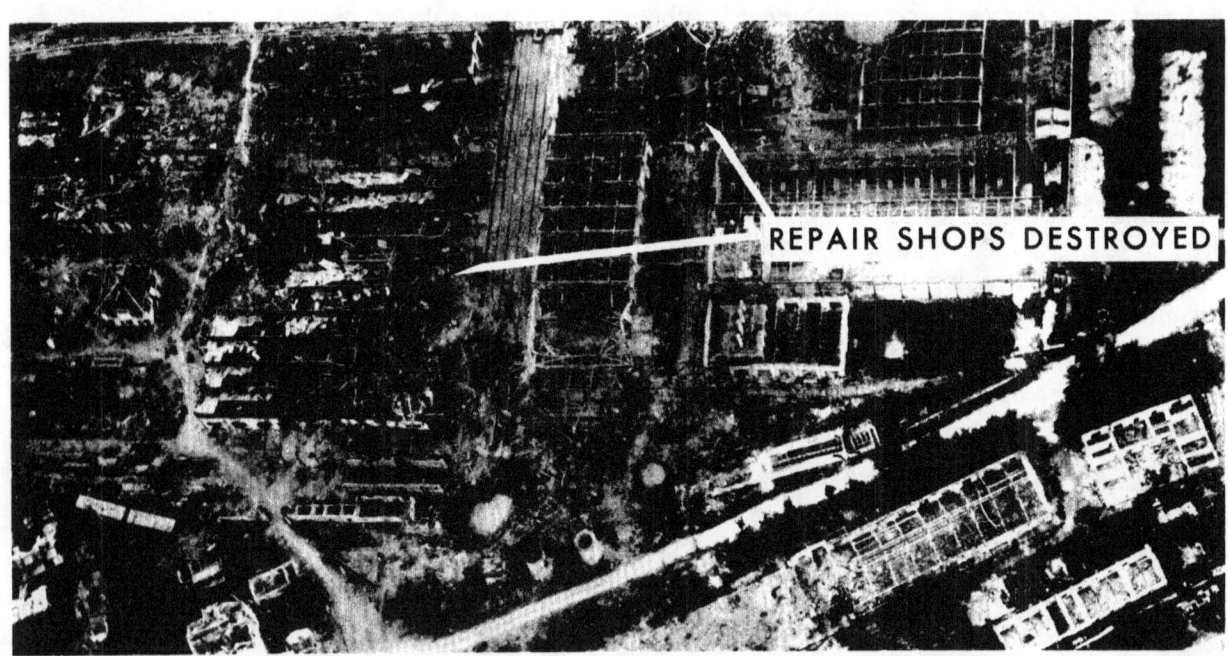

Hanoi railroad car repair shops.

all purpose of isolating Haiphong from Hanoi, and Hanoi and Haiphong from the rest of the country, especially those LOC's radiating southward to Laos and the Demilitarized Zone.

During July favorable weather existed in the northern areas of North Vietnam approximately 66 percent of the month. This allowed maximum effort to be applied throughout North Vietnam and resulted in a record number of attack sorties flown in the Hanoi and Haiphong areas and against the vital northern rail and road transportation system. On 20 July ROLLING THUNDER 57, with 16 new targets, was authorized.

The period of favorable flying weather during August was about 20 percent less than in July. The campaign in the north was stimulated by the follow-on authorization to ROLLING THUNDER 57 for attacks against selected LOC in the northeast. The new authorization increased the number of fixed targets from 16 to 46. These strikes resulted in marked attrition of railroad rolling stock and interdiction of the railroad lines. In the Hanoi and Haiphong area, 30 fixed targets were attacked. The targets exposed in these previously restricted areas consisted primarily of railroad and highway bridges and bypasses, and supply storage areas. Penetration of these sanctuaries, coupled with the high level of damage attained, further compounded the problem of transhipment of vital supplies to the South. On 24 August all targets in the Hanoi area were again placed in a restricted status.

Weather in the northern sections of North Vietnam during September was much worse than forecast and severely hampered air operations. Seventeen new targets were added to the ROLLING THUNDER 57 target list during September; eight were in the Hanoi restricted area and adverse weather limited our effort against the remainder. Despite the degraded effort in the northern Route Packages, constant pressure was maintained through the employment of the all-weather bombing systems of Air Force and Navy aircraft.

Improved weather during October, the lifting of the restriction on authorized targets within the Hanoi area on 23 October, and the addition of eight new targets to the ROLLING THUNDER

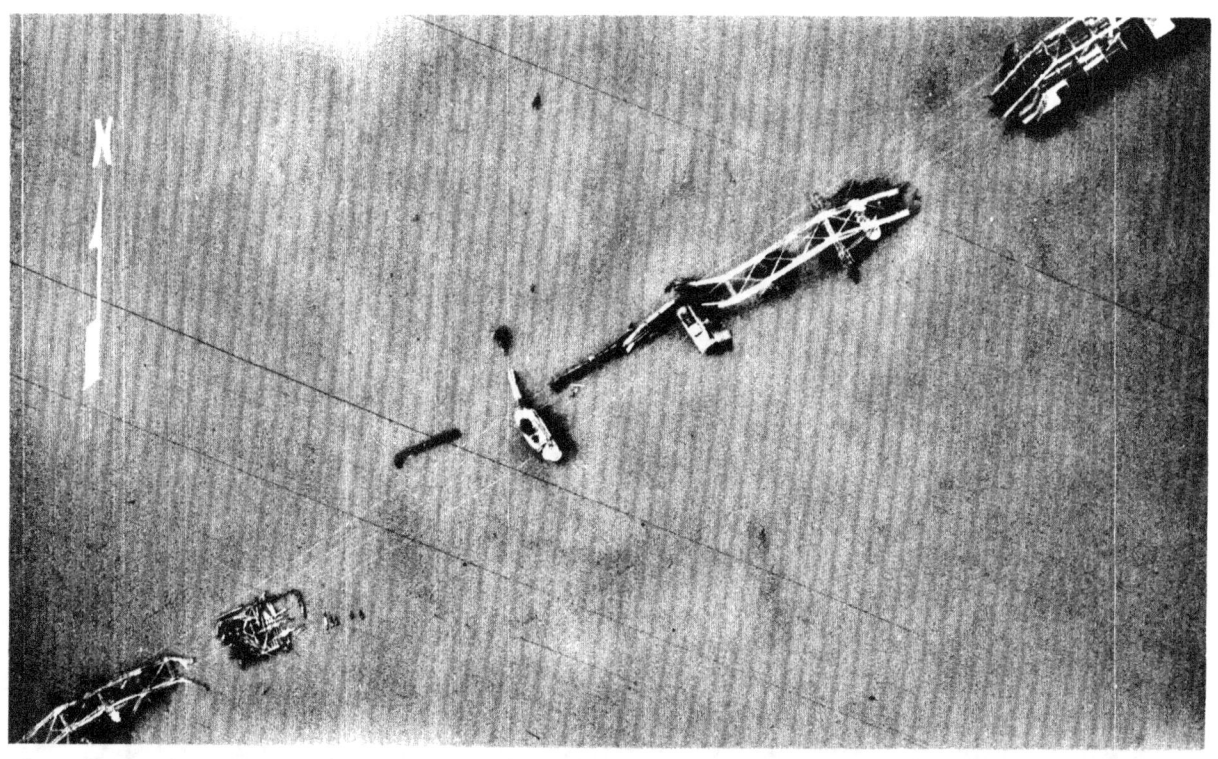

Hanoi railroad and highway bridge over the Red River.

Above, U.S. aircraft experiences near miss by enemy surface-to-air missile. *Below*, a missile detonating harmlessly.

57 target list permitted a 60 percent increase in attack sorties against these targets as compared to the September effort. The eight additional targets included seven new targets in the immediate Haiphong area plus a ship repair facility near Haiphong. The transportation, power, and air defense systems were dealt severe blows as a result of the 23 October authority to re-enter the Hanoi area and to strike the new targets in and near Haiphong.

During November 14 new targets were added to the ROLLING THUNDER 57 target list bringing it to a total of 85. Adverse weather throughout November precluded execution of the planned air effort in the northern areas. However, of the 85 targets, 25 were struck one or more times during the month.

Although no new targets were authorized during December and the damage level to the ROLLING THUNDER 57 targets remained relatively unchanged, strikes were conducted against previously authorized targets. Both the Doumer and Canal Des Rapides Railway and Highway Bridges at Hanoi were extensively damaged during the period 14 through 18 December. Other key targets struck included the Hai Duong, Haiphong, and Kien An Highway and Railroad Bridges and the Kien An, Yen Bai, Hoa Loc, Kep, and Phuc Yen Airfields. All were unserviceable for varying lengths of time. Weather continued to be the dominant factor influencing ROLLING THUNDER operations throughout North Vietnam during December. The poor weather conditions signified the true beginning of the northeast monsoon which would curtail air operations over North Vietnam for the next three or four months.

NORTH VIETNAM'S AIR DEFENSE SYSTEM—1967

Although MIG pilot aggressiveness, proficiency, and air tactics continued to improve in 1967, we maintained the lead in air engagements. Averaging some 20 encounters per month for the year, the North Vietnamese Air Force lost aircraft at a ratio of three to one (over 75 MIG's downed in air-to-air combat vs 25 of our aircraft). In addition to the air losses, strikes against three airfields resulted in the destruction of 15 MIG's on the ground. MIG losses, however, were soon replaced by shipments from the USSR and Communist China. At year's end, some 20 aircraft were operating in North Vietnam; the remainder were believed to be in southern China, probably for retraining and regrouping.

At the beginning of 1967 North Vietnam's fighter aircraft were utilizing four airfields: Gia Lam, Phuc Yen, Kep, and Cat Bi. In February newly constructed Hoa Lac Airfield became serviceable and in April our photography indicated that MIG aircraft had landed there. Harassing strikes against Hoa Lac and Kep began in April and Kien An at Haiphong was added to the list in May. By the end of the year, all of the jet-capable or jet-potential airfields had been attacked except for Gia Lam, the international airport at Hanoi, which had not been authorized for strike. Although vital ground equipment was destroyed, most of the major fields were returned to serviceability within a short time after each strike.

By 1967 approximately 25 SAM battalions were estimated to be operational in North Vietnam and by the end of the year more than 100 new SAM sites had been discovered. SAM coverage expanded to the northwest and to the area just north of the Demilitarized Zone. In October 1967 and again in December, the first known SAM's were fired at B-52 aircraft, but they failed to damage the aircraft. Although some 3,500 SAM visual firings were noted throughout 1967, compared to about 990 in 1966, SAM effectiveness again declined. An average of 55 SAM's was required to down one of our aircraft compared to 33 in 1966 and 13 in 1965. It was evident that our countermeasures and techniques were becoming more effective.

MINING OF NORTH VIETNAM WATERS

During 1966 the North Vietnamese made increased use of waterborne logistic craft to transport men and supplies southward. On 23 February 1967 the mining of selected areas of North Vietnam was authorized by higher authority. The use of air-delivered bottom-laid mines in selected river areas was determined to be an effective method of assisting in reduction of North Vietnamese coastal traffic.

Operations began in March, with all mines sown in the mouths of rivers. Haiphong, Hon Gai, and Cam Pha deepwater ports were not authorized for mining.

While the extent of the effectiveness of the mining operations has been impossible to document because of a lack of concrete intelligence and our inability to maintain near-constant surveillance, the slowdown in logistic traffic in these areas indicates that the operations had a significant impact on enemy activity.

TAKING THE WAR TO THE ENEMY IN NORTH VIETNAM—1967

In reporting the achievement of our objective in 1967, the three basic tasks we had set for ourselves provide the best means for discussing results.

Denying Access to External Assistance

The amount of external assistance to North Vietnam had increased every year since the war began and with it the tonnage of goods imported into the country. In 1967 sea import tonnages were almost 40 percent greater than the 930,000 metric tons delivered in 1966. Mining and air strikes against port facilities had not been authorized where third country shipping could be endangered. However, systematic strikes on LOC's greatly impeded the flow of imported goods once they were within the country. These sorties included attacks against war-supporting fixed targets as well as key LOC targets to reduce the flow of imported material.

The advent of good weather in late May 1967 permitted a concentrated strike effort against all of the northern rail lines and within the Hanoi and Haiphong complexes. Strikes in June, July, and August accounted for over 56 percent of the total trucks and rail rolling stock reported as damaged and destroyed for the entire year. A mid-year estimate indicated that approximately 30 percent of imported material was being destroyed by air strikes while in transit. Strikes against large military storage depots in the Hanoi and the Thai Nguyen areas destroyed additional supplies which had arrived in North Vietnam by rail and sea.

Beginning in August, a major campaign was launched to isolate Hanoi and Haiphong from each other and from the northern and southern logistic routes. The campaign rendered the main bridges in these areas unserviceable for varying lengths of time, thus making it more difficult for North Vietnam to move imports through these major distribution centers. Numerous bypasses were put into operation and both truck and watercraft activity increased, denoting North Vietnam's attempts to overcome the bombing effects. Transportation clearance capacity was considerably reduced. Watercraft were noted mooring near foreign ships in order to lessen the chance of their being attacked. Large open storage areas multiplied near the Haiphong docks and throughout the city as the full weight of the campaign became evident. By October some 200,000 tons of goods imported by sea had been accumulated and stacked in these areas. In early November intelligence indicated that the many air alerts slowed up work on the Haiphong docks as workers took shelter. In addition, absenteeism among stevedores had increased because of the dangers of coming to work. Hunger and weariness among dock workers were reported. Shortages of trucks and specific types of lighters slowed down the off-loading of ships and the clearing of cargo from the port. Effective dredging of the approaches to Haiphong was reduced by the mere presence of United States aircraft in the area and foreign merchant ships were unable to take advantage of their full load capacity.

The overall effect of our effort to impede the flow of external assistance resulted not only in destruction and damage to the transportation systems and goods being transported but also created

Haiphong railroad bridge complex.

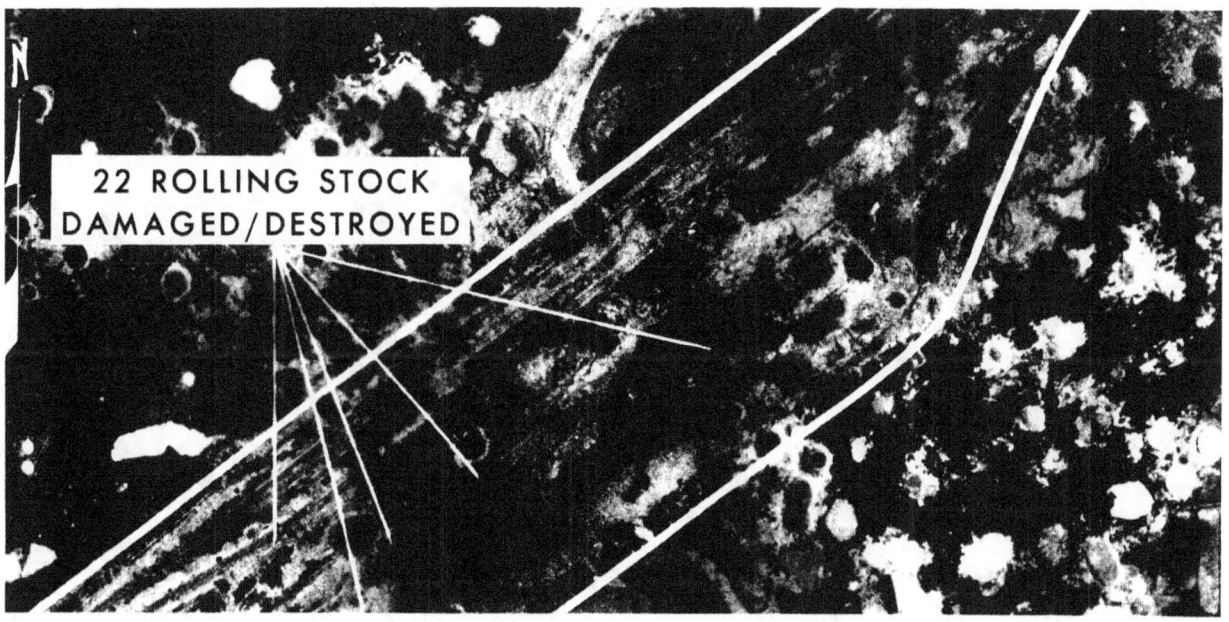

Kep Railroad Yard #2.

additional management, distribution, and manpower problems. The attacks caused a bottleneck at Haiphong where the inability to effectively move goods inland from the port resulted in congestion on the docks and a slowdown in unloading ships. By October road and rail interdictions had reduced the transportation clearance capacity at Haiphong to about 2,500 tons per day. An average of 4,000 tons per day of imports had arrived in Haiphong during the year.

Impeding Movement of Men and Material

Men and material needed for the level of combat prevailing in South Vietnam continued to flow despite our attacks on LOC's, but we made such movement increasingly costly. In the complementary naval gunfire program, our offensive operations involved 1,384 ship-days on station and contributed materially toward reducing enemy seaborne infiltration in southern North Vietnam and in the vicinity of the Demilitarized Zone.

During 1967 attacks against the North Vietnam transport system resulted in destruction of logistics carriers and their cargo as well as personnel casualties. Air attacks throughout North Vietnam destroyed or damaged over 5,260 motor vehicles, 2,500 pieces of railroad rolling stock, and 11,500 watercraft. Naval gunfire accounted for over 1,500 waterborne logistic craft destroyed or damaged. The enemy suffered additional material losses from destroyed rail lines, bridges, ferries, railroad yards and shops, storage areas, and truck parks. Some 3,700 land targets were struck by naval gunfire, including some 300 coastal defense and radar sites that were damaged or destroyed. Through assistance from other Communist countries the enemy was able to replace or rehabilitate many of the items damaged or destroyed, and logis-

Haiphong Cement Plant.

tics carrier inventories thus were roughly at the same level as they were at the beginning of the year. Nevertheless, construction problems and delays caused interruptions in the flow of men and supplies, caused a great loss of workhours, and restricted movement, particularly during daylight hours.

A major effect of our efforts to impede movement of the enemy was to force Hanoi to divert the efforts of 500,000 to 600,000 civilians to full-time and part-time war related activities, in particular for air defense and repair of the LOC's. This diverted manpower from other pursuits, particularly from agriculture. The estimated lower food production yields, coupled with an increase in food imports in 1967, indicated that agriculture had difficulty in adjusting to this smaller work force. (Imports in 1967 were some six times those of 1966, but an unusual drought was partly the reason.) The cost and difficulties of the war to Hanoi had sharply increased and only through the willingness of other Communist countries to provide maximum replacement of goods and material had North Vietnam managed to sustain its war effort.

Destroying in Depth the War-Making Resources in North Vietnam

Air attacks were authorized and executed by target systems for the first time in 1967, although the attacks were limited to specific targets within each system.

Strikes against authorized targets during the good weather period in 1967 resulted in damage to all target systems and decreased productivity. The Thai Nguyen iron and steel combine, which was North Vietnam's major plant located 30 miles north of Hanoi, and which had an estimated design production capacity of some 300,000 metric tons of pig iron annually, was first struck in the

Hanoi transformer station.

spring of 1967. By the end of June production of pig iron and coke had completely ceased as had the fabrication of bridge pontoons, barges, oil storage tanks, and other steel products utilized in supporting the war effort. The status of this industry when combined with the unserviceability of the Haiphong Cement Plant pointed to the drastically reduced North Vietnamese capabilities for construction and repair of LOC's. To compensate for these losses North Vietnam had to look to either the inefficient production of the many small shops of the handicraft industries or to additional imports from Communist China, the USSR, or the Eastern European countries. Either adjustment brought additional problems of distribution and management. The requirement for additional imports reduced shipping space normally allocated to other war supplies and added to the congestion at the ports as more ships were required to meet the added requirements.

Strikes against power plants in the crucial northeast area continued during the good weather period for 1967, including the Hanoi Thermal Power Plant which was struck for the first time in May. By mid-November some 85 percent of the North Vietnamese power system had been rendered unserviceable, affecting industrial, government, and consumer needs.

It is of vital importance, however, in viewing results achieved by ROLLING THUNDER operations during 1967, to bear in mind that the objective of applying continuing and steadily increasing pressure over an extended period of time was not attained. The objective was approached briefly during the summer months and it was during that period that the air campaign began to have its greatest impact—to make the pressure felt by the enemy. The pressure period was foreshortened, even as the enemy began to hurt.

HOLIDAY STAND-DOWNS

Prior to 1967 three cease-fires were observed in South Vietnam: Christmas 1965—30 hours; *Tet* 1966—over four days; and Christmas 1966—48 hours. Bombing of North Vietnam had been suspended for even longer periods. On 22 November 1966 the Joint Chiefs of Staff informed the Sec-

Haiphong Thermal Power Plant.

retary of Defense that they opposed any stand-downs in military operations during the holiday seasons. The Joint Chiefs of Staff indicated that if a cease-fire were directed, bombing stand-downs should be limited to a maximum of 48 hours in order to minimize the military advantages to the enemy, and that, if there was no indication of North Vietnam's willingness to negotiate, we should be allowed to strike unusual military targets in North Vietnam which might develop. This action by the Joint Chiefs of Staff supported CINCPAC's position on this matter.

During 1967 four stand-downs were observed: New Years—48 hours, *Tet*—over five days, Buddha's Birthday—24 hours, and Christmas—24 hours. As in the case of all previous stand-downs, those in 1967 were beneficial to the enemy. He took full advantage of the opportunity to conduct major resupply operations and to reconstitute and replenish his forces, all of which cost the United States and other Free World forces greater casualties.

Intensive photographic reconnaissance conducted over North Vietnam during the period of *Tet* in 1967, supplemented by visual sightings from ships and aircraft, revealed significant logistic movement of materiel by water, truck, and rail transport. As a result of this reconnaissance we estimated that North Vietnam moved between 22,300 and 25,100 tons of supplies from the north into the area below 19° North in the period 8 to 12 February.

Evidence indicated that the North Vietnamese had anticipated and calculated in their planning the probability of a bombing pause during *Tet* and took full advantage of the situation.

On Buddha's Birthday, 23 May 1967, another stand-down was observed. This time we were authorized to conduct both naval gunfire operations and air strikes against any observed substantial military resupply activity in North Vietnam south of 20° North.

No official United States position had been announced concerning a Christmas or New Year stand-down by 18 November 1967 when a Hanoi radio broadcast stated that the National Liberation Front was ordering a suspension of military attacks from 23 to 26 December 1967 for Christmas, from 29 December 1967 to 1 January 1968 for the New Year, and from 26 January to 2 February for *Tet*.

On 9 December the Joint Chiefs of Staff noted that the United States would be prepared to institute stand-downs of military activity for 24 hours at Christmas and New Years and 48 hours at *Tet*. They recommended to the Secretary of Defense a modification of the rules of engagement promulgated in 1966 to provide authority to counter major resupply and infiltration activities detected during the stand-down period.

On 15 December 1967 the South Vietnamese government announced a 24-hour Christmas stand-down for the Allied forces, which went into effect as announced.

On 30 December the South Vietnamese government announced that a New Year cease-fire would be in effect from 31 December 1967 to 2 January 1968. The cease-fire period included a 12-hour extension which the South Vietnamese government had added in response to the appeal made by Pope Paul VI to make 1 January 1968 a "day of peace." The same instructions governing military cease-fire activities at Christmas were observed during the New Year cease-fire.

Prior to the 24-hour Christmas and 36-hour New Year stand-downs there were many indications the enemy planned to take full advantage of these periods. Later events proved that he conducted a massive and well organized resupply of his forces. Pilot sightings and photographic coverage recorded over 3,000 trucks moving in the Panhandle area of North Vietnam during the two stand-downs, the great majority heading south. Almost 1,300 trucks were noted during Christmas and about 1,800 during the slightly longer New Year stand-down. This compared with a daily average of about 170 for the other days between 22 December 1967 and 4 January 1968. A minimum of about

NORTH VIETNAM
TARGET ELEMENT SUMMARY
1967

TARGET CATEGORY	DESTROYED	DAMAGED	TOTAL DESTROYED & DAMAGED
AAA/AW SITES	450	1,479	1,929
SAM SITES	33	196	229
COMMUNICATIONS SITES	19	121	140
MILITARY AREAS	194	614	808
POL AREAS	2	130	132
STAGING/SUPPLY AREAS	27	1,545	1,572
BUILDINGS	2,354	1,193	3,547
LOC's	813	5,684	6,497
PORTS	13	75	88
POWER PLANTS	2	28	30
RAILROAD YARDS	3	176	179
MOTOR VEHICLES	2,929	2,658	5,587
RAILROAD VEHICLES	1,077	1,434	2,511
WATER VEHICLES	4,396	7,367	11,763
TOTAL	12,312	22,700	35,012

NOTE: SOME FIXED TARGETS WERE RESTRUCK NUMEROUS TIMES AND DAMAGE TO THEM MAY BE REPORTED ABOVE MORE THAN ONCE.

5,000 tons was moved by the enemy toward forces in the Demilitarized Zone and Laos. It should be noted that almost all of these sightings were during daylight. Poor weather undoubtedly precluded numerous additional sightings. The trucks sighted were almost ten times those sighted during the same holidays in 1966–67 when two 48-hour truces were observed. If these activities had been only for internal defense, there would have been little cause for concern. However, they were undertaken chiefly to support the external aggressive operations of North Vietnamese and Viet Cong troops against South Vietnam. The intent was purely hostile and aggressive.

ROLLING THUNDER OPERATIONS JANUARY THROUGH MARCH 1968

The effort in North Vietnam during the first three months of 1968 was drastically curtailed due to the northeast monsoon. During all three months, weather was worse than predicted. In the northern Route Packages there was an average of only three days per month on which visual strikes could be accomplished. The weather during February was the poorest experienced during any month since the beginning of ROLLING THUNDER.

The damage level to the fixed targets in the northern sectors of North Vietnam remained relatively unchanged through the end of March. Nearly all strikes required the use of all-weather bombing techniques. Weather inhibited drastically our post-strike assessment and we were unable to evaluate the effectiveness of much of our effort.

ROLLING THUNDER 57 remained in effect through June 1968. Nine new targets were added to the basic target list during 1968; of these seven were attacked.

EFFECTS, JANUARY THROUGH MARCH

Bombing operations against North Vietnam continued into 1968 with the aim of isolating the port of Haiphong from the rest of the country to prevent the distribution within the country of material being imported. This concerted campaign against LOC's around Haiphong forced the North Vietnamese to adopt extraordinary efforts to maintain a flow of material over existing lines. Distribution problems for Hanoi were further aggravated by the arrival of a near-record number of foreign ships in Haiphong in January and again in March when over 40 ships arrived each month for off-loading. The port of Hon Gai was used in February as an off-loading point for a Soviet and a British ship, probably in an effort to reduce the pressure on Haiphong. This port normally served the nearby coal mining area and did not contribute significantly to the flow of imports into the country.

Expansion of the road transportation net continued as North Vietnam sought to gain greater flexibility by the addition of bypasses and the construction of entirely new road segments. Of particular significance was the new route being built to connect the Ning-Ming area of Communist China with the Haiphong-Cam Pha region of North Vietnam, a development which would add an estimated 1,000 metric tons per day capacity to the cross-border capability between the two countries. Repair efforts elsewhere in the country were vigorously pursued. The Paul Doumer Bridge located immediately north of Hanoi was the object of numerous air attacks and suffered heavy damage. Concurrent with construction activity at the Doumer Bridge, several bridge bypasses and ferry landings were built elsewhere along the banks of the Red River near the bridge, attesting to the importance of the route in the movement of material from Communist China and inland from Haiphong.

Rolling stock attrition on Railroad #7.

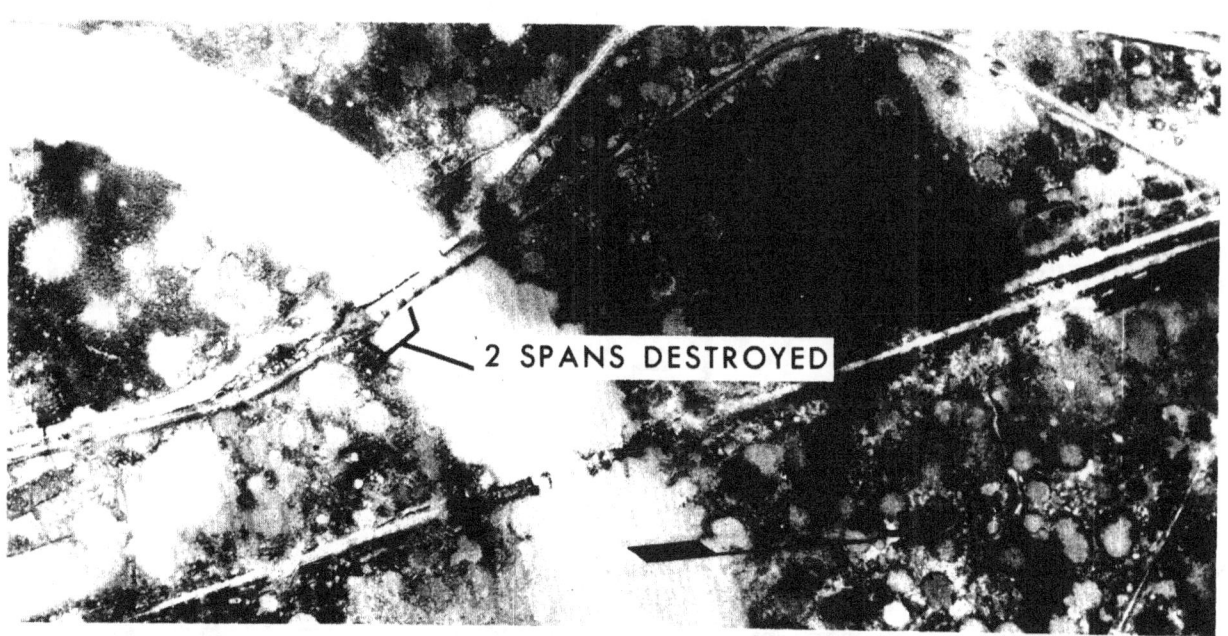

Tam Da Railroad Bypass #2.

NORTH VIETNAM TARGET ELEMENT SUMMARY 1968

TARGET CATEGORY	DESTROYED	DAMAGED	TOTAL DESTROYED & DAMAGED
AAA/AW SITES	143	333	476
SAM SITES	14	76	90
COMMUNICATIONS SITES	18	70	88
MILITARY AREAS	25	142	167
POL AREAS	34	180	214
STAGING/SUPPLY AREAS	54	479	533
BUILDINGS	532	232	764
LOC's	199	2,533	2,732
PORTS	3	10	13
POWER PLANTS	1	5	6
RAILROAD YARDS	0	6	6
MOTOR VEHICLES	2,234	2,470	4,704
RAILROAD VEHICLES	139	209	348
WATER VEHICLES	1,200	1,515	2,715
TOTAL	4,596	8,260	12,856

NOTE: SOME FIXED TARGETS WERE RESTRUCK NUMEROUS TIMES AND DAMAGE TO THEM MAY BE REPORTED ABOVE MORE THAN ONCE.

CURTAILMENT OF ROLLING THUNDER OPERATIONS

On 1 April in a further attempt to get Hanoi to the peace conference table, the President of the United States stopped bombing attacks over the principal populated and food producing areas of North Vietnam except in the area north of the Demilitarized Zone where enemy actions directly threatened United States and Free World forces in South Vietnam. Because ROLLING THUNDER was thus limited, primary strike emphasis was directed against truck parks, storage areas, and military complexes. Armed reconnaissance strikes were directed against logistic vehicles and interdiction points along the main LOC's.

NORTH VIETNAM'S ACTIVITY DURING THE PARTIAL BOMBING CESSATION

Intelligence sources reported extensive repair and improvements to North Vietnam's LOC's underway or completed since the bombing cessation. The roads between Hanoi, Haiphong, and Hon Gai were reported to be well maintained. Bridges between Hanoi and Haiphong had been repaired and traffic flowed smoothly during day and night hours.

Limited aerial reconnaissance provided evidence of large rolling stock inventories in Hanoi and Haiphong but coverage was too infrequent to determine a buildup or increased movement. In view of the bombing limitations and apparent repairs, it is logical to assume that Hanoi moved maximum tonnages over LOC's in the northern part of the country.

South of 19° North there was evidence to indicate that intensive air strikes had resulted in shifting traffic patterns. There appeared to be a concerted effort to keep cargo moving through the use of inland and secondary routes.

Reports since the 1 April bombing limitation indicated that off-loaded cargo at Haiphong was

Burning trucks in the Demilitarized Zone area.

not being stacked but was being loaded directly onto trucks which immediately departed the wharf area. Photos revealed extensive storage throughout the port area but stockpiles did not remain static, suggesting that cargo flowed unrestricted. The labor supply at the docks was reported as adequate and efficient and the morale of the stevedores was reported as high.

Once the presence of United States aircraft over the northern portion of the country was stopped, North Vietnam took maximum advantage of the freedom of action by increasing training activities of all elements of the air defense system.

As of the date of this report, there are no indications that Hanoi is ready to negotiate an acceptable peace at Paris. The North Vietnamese delegation gives the impression that it is prepared for long drawn-out discussions. In the meantime, Hanoi continues to try to give the impression that the Communist forces in South Vietnam are strong everywhere. The offensive against Saigon begun in late May sought to undermine popular support of South Vietnam and to strengthen Hanoi's hand in the peace talks in Paris.

NORTH VIETNAM'S AIR DEFENSE SYSTEM MID-1968

The deployment and increase in the number of AAA weapons was rapid after the Gulf of Tonkin incidents. In mid-February 1965 the AAA order of battle had increased by some 1,400 weapons to a total of more than 2,100. In May 1965 searchlights were identified for the first time, and in July 1965 the introduction of 100-mm AAA enhanced the enemy air defenses by providing a gun capability against aircraft flying at altitudes up to nearly 40,000 feet. By April 1968 there were 8,000 AAA weapons, the majority of which were light AAA and automatic weapons.

In 1966, 1967, and the first half of 1968, early warning equipment continued to be modernized and increased to provide extensive overlapping coverage of all of North Vietnam and into Laos in the west and over the Gulf of Tonkin to the south and east. Altitude discrimination was enhanced by the addition of height finders. The radar net was evaluated as having the capability to detect and track aircraft above 1,500 to 2,000 feet and the net was also probably sufficiently sophisticated to maintain continuity of tracking and coordinate air defense even under pressure of multiple penetrations. GCI radars provided control for jet operations in the Haiphong-Hanoi-Thai Nguyen areas, and, for a time, in the southern Panhandle in early 1968. A total of more than 350 radars was carried in North Vietnam's inventory at the end of April 1968. Fire-control radar was believed to be increasing in the southern Panhandle following the limitation on bombing.

The concentration of our strikes in the Panhandle in April 1968 led to apparent attempts by North Vietnam's Air Force to establish a fighter capability again at Vinh, but our strikes at that airfield in May left it unserviceable. Construction continued at Yen Bai; and the airfield was capable of supporting limited operations by May 1968, thus extending the North Vietnamese air defense capability to the northwest. The bombing limitation permitted airfields to be repaired and construction projects to be resumed.

In the first months of 1968 the overall level of MIG reactions was low. However, continued individual MIG flights into the area south of 20° North demonstrated an increasing aggressiveness and refinement of tactics. Air engagements resulted in the downing of nine MIG's and eight of our aircraft. The North Vietnamese fighter aircraft inventory remained at about 20 to 25, primarily based at Phuc Yen and Gia Lam.

Observed SAM activity was relatively light because of limited United States air activity in SAM-defended areas. At the end of April the number of SAM sites identified since the beginning of the war totaled almost 300. SAM effectiveness continued its downward trend between January and April when the ratio of SAM's fired to aircraft downed was 67 to 1. As the bombing pause continued, it was expected that North Vietnam likely would move SAM units and other air defense resources to the areas south of the restricted zone.

NAVAL SURFACE OPERATIONS

Our ROLLING THUNDER air campaign was not the only means by which we took the war to the enemy in North Vietnam. Our naval surface forces also conducted a vigorous and unremitting campaign against logistic craft in North Vietnamese waters and against land targets within the range of their guns.

On 14 May 1965 the use of naval gunfire in support of friendly forces in South Vietnam had been authorized. The results that were obtained proved the value of such support.

To augment ROLLING THUNDER operations, particularly during periods of adverse weather and reduced visibility, we believed that naval gunfire could be employed effectively against North Vietnam as well. There were significant Navy resources with such capability already in the Gulf of Tonkin. These were engaged in missions of early warning and search and rescue, and they supported our aircraft carrier operations. Except for defensive action, however, this capability had not yet been exploited against North Vietnam.

CINCPAC suggested that naval gunfire could divert and dilute some of North Vietnam's defensive efforts, which were concentrated on air defense, and thereby aid in reducing pilot and aircraft exposure and attrition. On 13 May 1966 therefore, the Joint Chiefs of Staff recommended to the Secretary of Defense that naval gunfire be authorized against targets ashore and in the coastal waters of North Vietnam in the area 17° to 20° North.

Authority was received on 15 October to conduct surface ship operations against waterborne traffic in the coastal waters south of 17°30′ North, but shore bombardment was only authorized in self-defense. Attacks on watercraft engaged in fishing or in nonmilitary pursuits were prohibited.

These operations, conducted under the nickname SEA DRAGON were initiated on 25 October by the destroyers *Mansfield* and *Hanson*. Both ships proceeded to the assigned interdiction zone, which was limited to a 12-mile belt of water extending from the Demilitarized Zone to 17°30′ North. During the first day of operations both ships came under fire from North Vietnamese shore batteries, which they returned.

During the short period of their employment in October, SEA DRAGON forces fired 1,354 rounds of five-inch ammunition against enemy watercraft destroying 101 and damaging 94 others. Counter-battery fire totaled 426 rounds.

The Demilitarized Zone was a secure sanctuary for the enemy during the first half of 1966, not because of a lack of friendly firepower capability, but because of United States restraint. But on 20 July, the Joint Chiefs of Staff authorized limited United States actions to counter the serious threat posed by North Vietnamese Army infiltrees through the Demilitarized Zone. Thereafter, our comanders could conduct air strikes and artillery fire (land and naval) against clearly defined military activity in the area south of the Demarcation Line.

As late as 24 November 1966, however, the rules of engagement prohibited employment of artillery and naval gunfire against even clearly defined military activity in the Demilitarized Zone north of the Demarcation Line. This facilitated the establishment of extensive enemy field fortifications with particular emphasis on antiaircraft artillery.

On 11 November in connection with implementation of ROLLING THUNDER 52, the

SEA DRAGON OPERATION AREAS

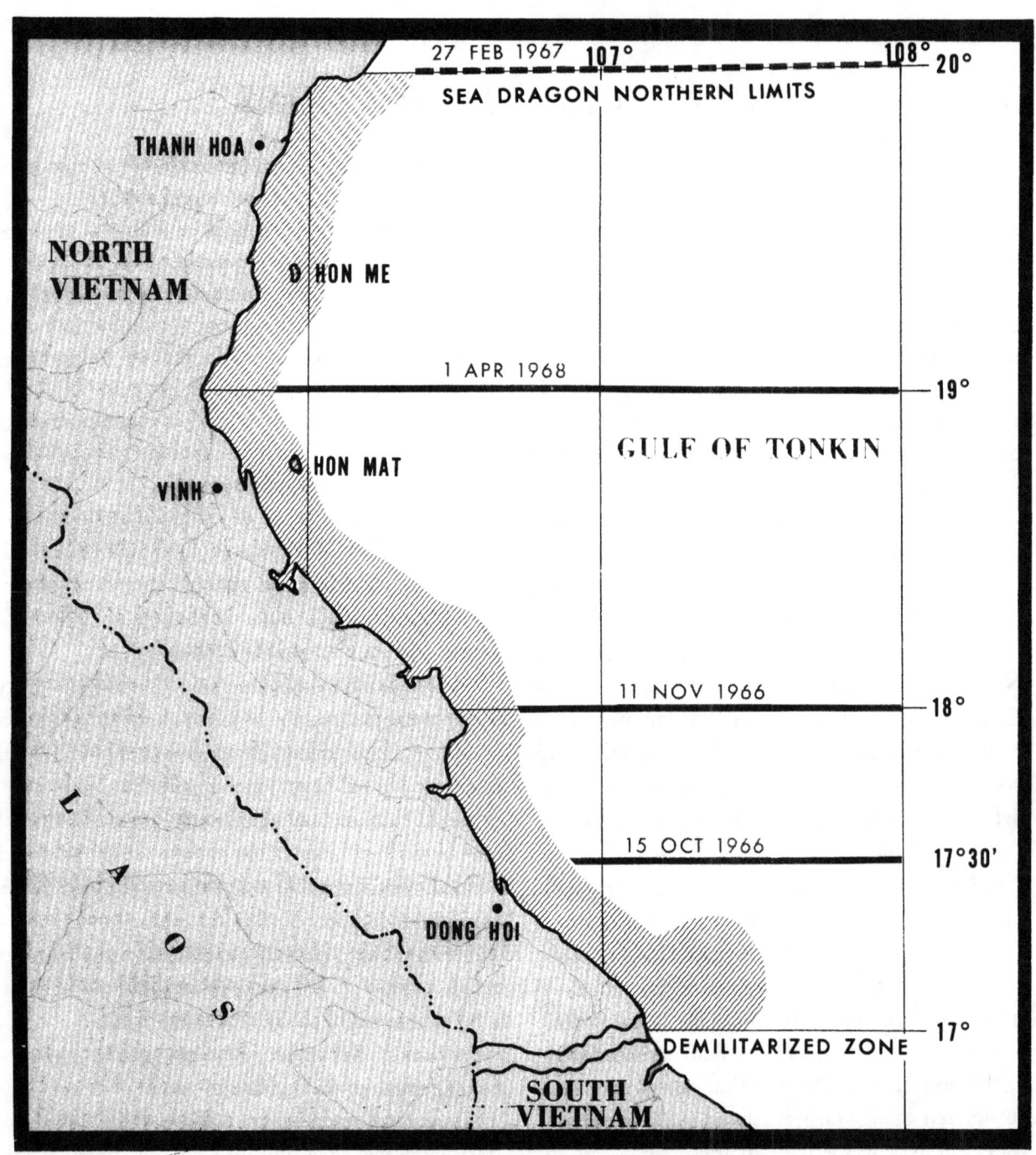

northern boundary of the SEA DRAGON area was extended northward to 18° North.

By the end of 1966 SEA DRAGON forces, consisting of two destroyers on station at a time, had destroyed 382 waterborne logistic craft (a collective term for the small watercraft used to transport men and supplies) and damaged another 325, destroyed five shore batteries and damaged two, and destroyed two radar sites and damaged two more. Equally significant, SEA DRAGON had forced the bulk of the logistic movement that had been seaborne back into the crowded land routes or into the inland waterways where it was subject to attrition from the air.

By the end of the year, it appeared that the enemy had concentrated his coastal defense batteries in the SEA DRAGON area. CINCPAC proposed to the Joint Chiefs of Staff that naval surface operations in 1967 should be extended northward. Diluting the enemy's defenses would reduce the threat to friendly forces. Since the naval gunfire effort against coastal waterborne logistic traffic in 1966 proved to be an effective complement to ROLLING THUNDER operations, its extension northward would also compound the enemy's logistic problems by forcing him to transport additional materials over already overtaxed land lines of communication.

Early in 1967 the SEA DRAGON effort was enhanced by the assignment of the first Australian destroyer to the task force. Since that time an Australian ship has been on station off Vietnam either as part of the SEA DRAGON force or providing naval gunfire support to our forces in South Vietnam.

On 27 February with ROLLING THUNDER 54, the area of operation was extended to 20° North. At the same time, naval gunfire against military and logistic targets ashore was also authorized. To more effectively complement ROLLING THUNDER operations, SEA DRAGON forces were increased to one cruiser and four destroyers composing two separate task units. Attendant with the increase in ships, there was a decrease in waterborne logistic craft traffic during the first quarter of 1967.

SEA DRAGON forces continued to apply pressure on waterborne logistic craft, lines of communication, radar and antiaircraft artillery sites, and other military targets along the coastline of North Vietnam between 17° and 20° North. In May the greatest number of waterborne logistic craft detected during the SEA DRAGON campaign was encountered—635 craft. We destroyed or damaged 257 of them. On 22 May alone, elements of SEA DRAGON forces, in coordination with Seventh Air Force ROLLING THUNDER operations, struck the Quang Khe Ferry Complex in the southern portion of North Vietnam and destroyed at least 40 waterborne logistic craft.

June 1967 saw a decline in watercraft detected, and July an even greater decrease. The reduction may have been due to a decrease in availability of or a reluctance on the part of the enemy to expose the craft available to him. On the other hand there was a significant increase in the number of land targets struck in July, 518 as compared to the previous monthly high of 374 in March. SEA DRAGON forces tripled the July figure in August when 245 logistic craft were damaged or destroyed. Over 1,000 fixed or moving targets were taken under fire.

In September SEA DRAGON forces continued patrolling between 17° and 20° North. The number of waterborne logistic craft sighted decreased considerably over the previous month. SEA DRAGON forces were then moved to the Demilitarized Zone area to provide naval gunfire support for our land forces. During their absence, late in September, a marked increase in waterborne logistic craft and truck activity was observed and the SEA DRAGON forces were returned to their regular missions.

During the fourth quarter of 1967 there was a 62 percent decrease in the number of waterborne logistic craft detected compared to the third quarter. This decrease could be attributed to a combination of poor weather and the continued deterrent of SEA DRAGON forces. In the same period, however, 1,707 land targets were struck as compared to 1,258 in the third quarter, a 36 percent increase.

During 1967 the number of ships assigned to SEA DRAGON at any one time fluctuated. In one instance there were eight ships assigned, but normal force composition was five ships, a cruiser and four destroyers, operating in two task units.

CINCPAC recommended that a battleship be made available to take advantage of its greater firepower. As a result, in August, the Department of Defense approved the reactivation and refitting of the mothballed *New Jersey,* with deployment scheduled for the fall of 1968.

Damage to our ships from North Vietnamese coastal defense artillery was light in comparison to the damage and destruction they caused. Although the accuracy of North Vietnamese gun crews improved throughout the year, it appeared that evasive action and other tactics employed by our ships offset the improved accuracy of coastal batteries.

After one full year of operations, SEA DRAGON ships had destroyed or damaged over 2,000 waterborne logistic craft, attacked over 3,300 selected shore targets, and engaged in over 150 duels with enemy shore batteries. They significantly reduced the movement of supplies in the coastal waters and assisted in the interdiction of land routes within their gun range.

Seaborne infiltration of enemy personnel and supplies from North Vietnam was considered by this time to be making a relatively small contribution toward meeting requirements. Naval surface operations had reduced this enemy capability. As in the ground war, however, the enemy appeared willing to accept high losses and continued his attempts to resupply in certain hard-pressed combat areas.

During the first three months of 1968 the enemy increased pressure along the Demilitarized Zone and stepped up logistic movement in the southern portion of North Vietnam. SEA DRAGON ships were shifted southward to provide increased naval gunfire support for our forces in the general area of the Demilitarized Zone. Only two destroyers patrolled the southern SEA DRAGON area, yet 34 percent of the detected waterborne logistic craft were destroyed or damaged. Land targets taken under attack remained high, but the poor weather precluded adequate assessment of results. The April 1968 decision to limit attacks on North Vietnam to the area below 19° North further reduced the SEA DRAGON interdiction zone by one-third, but in the area where operations were permitted our ships continued to distinguish themselves.

EFFECTS OF ROLLING THUNDER

Despite operational restrictions, weather cycles, and a resourceful enemy, ROLLING THUNDER operations had a profound effect on North Vietnam. By April 1968 when air operations over the northern areas were stopped, North Vietnam was faced with numerous and serious problems. The cumulative effects of air operations and the demands of the war in South Vietnam resulted in unprecedented stresses and strains on the North Vietnamese economy, production and distribution systems, the life of the people, and the political control apparatus. Conditions may have been sufficiently serious to have induced North Vietnam to use the tactic of "negotiation" to gain a period of relief in order to rectify its more pressing problems, and to reinvigorate support of the war in South Vietnam.

Perhaps the most significant manpower drain was caused by the rapid expansion of the armed forces to supply replacements for the war in the south and to man air and coastal defenses in the north. In addition, workers were needed to repair and maintain the vital lines of communication. This included the repair of roads and rail lines, and reconstruction of bridges and ferry crossings damaged or destroyed by our air campaign. Another important manpower requirement was for the rapidly expanded air defense system. Workers were needed for site construction and as laborers at the many hastily built radar, antiaircraft artillery, and surface-to-air missile sites. Most of these people came from agriculture; and women, children, and old people were forced to fill the manpower gap in the economy.

In addition to the manpower problems, air operations affected farm schedules and compounded problems caused by bad weather, resulting in a reduced output of food. ROLLING THUNDER also complicated the government's collection and distribution of food and impacted on the narrow margins of agricultural sufficiency.

Air operations destroyed most of North Vietnam's heavy industry and power generating capability. Hanoi was forced into a defensive posture marked by frustrations and delayed aspirations. Transportation and industry were forced to disperse, thereby creating problems dealing with the redistribution of labor, allocation of raw materials, and control of output. The attendant managerial problems were immense.

North Vietnam's exports drastically declined from the 1966 average of 100,000 metric tons per month to tonnages on the order of 20,000 per month. This decline was attributed to the bomb destruction of industry, interdiction of lines of communication, and the disruption of port operations.

The air operations caused a decline in the standard of living, particularly for the urban dweller but also for the rural peasant. Dislocation of people, interdiction of transportation, destruction of goods, and more stringent rationing of all commodities including food and clothing impacted adversely on the people and were in varying degrees attributable to ROLLING THUNDER. Shortages of food, particularly rice, affected the cities, but imports continued to provide marginally sufficient food. Food consumption levels continued to be stringent and caloric intake appeared to drop to levels that threatened the effectiveness of the working force.

The impact of ROLLING THUNDER on morale in North Vietnam was a difficult matter to assess. Prior to the more intense air operations, the morale of the people had not been an overriding concern of their government. Under the intensified air attacks, morale appeared to have slipped, particularly in the urban centers, as the people tended increasingly to question the propaganda concerning their ultimate victory.

All of these economic and sociological problems were in varying degrees a result of air operations. The stresses they created contributed to an increased divergence between the authoritarian ideals and objectives of the government and its actual capability to control and manage. As air operations intensified, North Vietnam responded with increased concern for internal security, particularly as it related to control of the people during air raids. The physical relocation of governmment offices and ministries from the capital and the interdiction of transportation and communications introduced confusion and even greater inefficiencies.

Cessation of bombing has allowed a reconstitution of lines of communication and a return to a more normal pattern of living. The North Vietnamese had long demonstrated extreme resourcefulness at repairing damage caused by ROLLING THUNDER. With the fear of air raids eliminated in most areas, they have worked vigorously at repair and rebuilding, particularly of their lines of communication.

Perhaps the most important measure of the effects of the bombing, however, would be the consideration of the situation if there had been no bombing at all. The uninhibited flow of men, weapons, and supplies through North Vietnam to confront our forces in South Vietnam could have had only one result for the United States and its allies—considerably heavier casualties at a smaller cost to the enemy. Since this alternative was unacceptable, the bombing of North Vietnam, as an essential element of the overall strategy, was clearly successful in fulfilling its purposes.

PACIFIC COMMAND-WIDE EFFORTS IN SUPPORT OF THE WAR

LOGISTICS

A significant aspect of the war in Vietnam has been the continuous provision of effective logistics support to United States and other Free World forces without mobilization of our national economy. The technology of modern logistics has been given a severe test. Responsive and timely logistics support by all of the Services and application of modern airlift combined with a large fleet of freighters have been the keys to success. Computer-aided procedures were used to predict logistics requirements, to test the feasibility of supporting incremental troop strength increases, and to plan the buildup of the logistics base.

Logistics support workloads were assigned to adapt to Service needs and capabilities. Primary logistics functions in the northernmost Combat Tactical Zone in South Vietnam, for example, were given to the Commander in Chief of the Pacific Fleet because the combat forces in that zone were predominantly Marines. The Army was assigned those functions in the other three zones.

The lack of sufficient logistical support units was compensated for by the use of civilian contractors in this limited war environment. The unprecedented amounts of munitions and petroleum that were required were successfully moved over some of the longest resupply routes ever utilized by our forces.

The war in Vietnam fostered a gradual change in the character of logistics management at the Headquarters of the Commander in Chief, Pacific. Far greater emphasis was placed upon the control of transportation assets, munitions resupply, construction programs, and critical items. It became apparent that the Unified Commander must control the allocation of limited services and materiel to those multi-Service theater needs of highest priority.

MUNITIONS

The intensified Southeast Asia air operations of mid-1965 caused a significant drawdown of the limited resources of air munitions. The air munitions inventory reached a low point in June 1966. Because of the production lag it was necessary to ship directly from the various production lines to oversea destinations. Therefore, it often happened that bombs were available but not usable without essential parts such as fins or fuzes, which had been shipped separately.

In April 1966 CINCPAC received authority to control all air munitions within the Pacific Command. Immediate action was taken to draw from all available stocks and redistribute critical munitions without regard for Service ownership. Higher authority took action to increase production and to redistribute munitions from worldwide stocks, especially from Air Force and Navy depots in the United States.

By the end of 1966 the problems of specific shortages and incomplete rounds were fairly well resolved.

In December 1966 the Joint Chiefs of Staff identified certain ground munitions in critical short supply and requested CINCPAC to provide the Department of the Army a desired allocation of these items for the subsequent six-month period.

This was accomplished and in July 1967 the allocation of ground munitions was taken over by the newly established Military Services Ammunition Allocation Board.

Through careful management of assets, a steady flow of air and ground munitions was maintained through the pipeline to Southeast Asia, even as the war tempo increased. To balance requirements of all users, CINCPAC adjusted Pacific Command inventories and redistributed theater assets whenever necessary.

PETROLEUM

The evolution of petroleum, oil, and lubricants (POL) support of the war in Southeast Asia since the Tonkin Gulf incident was marked by a 300 percent increase in consumption throughout the Pacific Command, the construction of over ten million barrels of new tankage, and the establishment of new distribution systems and methods. In Vietnam, there was a transition from a strictly commercial POL supply system to a combined civilian-military system, using newly established POL ports of entry, tank farms, pipelines, and distribution methods. Floating POL storage and shuttle tanker and coastal tanker delivery systems were also established. These actions, plus adherence to a policy of keeping all POL tanks as full as possible, assured adequate POL support to all types of air, sea, and ground operations.

When the Arab-Israeli frontier war broke out in June 1967, quick action was taken to prevent a potential POL shortage. Most of the POL requirements in the Pacific Command, including those for Southeast Asia operations, were being provided from the Middle East. When that source of supply was substantially cut off, it became necessary to draw from various POL inventories in the theater and to increase the use of Western Hemisphere oil. As a result, actual shortages did not develop in either Southeast Asia or the key island bases supporting combat operations.

CRITICAL ITEMS SUPPORT

Intensive logistics management alleviated problems in supply and maintenance.

Lightweight utility uniforms and direct-molded-sole tropical boots, both highly desirable items in a hot, wet climate, were newly developed and still in short supply when the Southeast Asia buildup began. CINCPAC established a system of issue priorities so that the supply that was available would go to the forces that needed them the most. Contractor schedules were accelerated by the Defense Supply Agency and factory deliveries were airshipped to Southeast Asia. Deficiencies of these items were overcome by May 1967.

In 1965 friendly combat units not equipped with the new M16/M16A1 rifles were often outgunned in short range engagements. Issue of this weapon had been authorized to United States, South Vietnamese, and other Free World forces, but sufficient production had not been attained to supply the demand. CINCPAC recommended and received priority allocation to the Pacific Command of whatever M16/M16A1 rifles were available in order to place firepower where it was most critical.

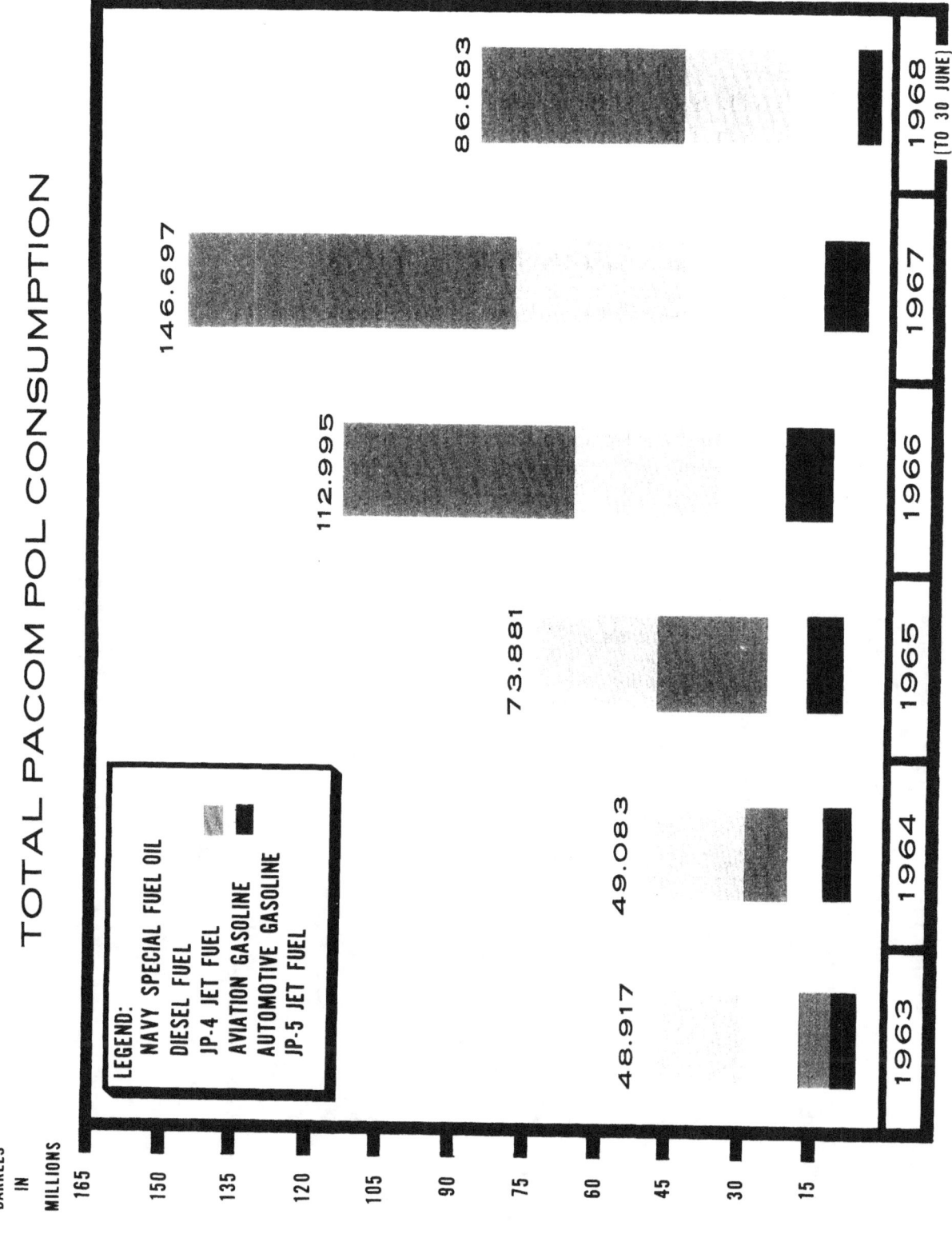

Consistent with armed forces procurement regulations and gold flow considerations, supply responsiveness was improved with the procurement of selected items in friendly Asian and Pacific countries to augment the normal flow from the United States. Certain construction materials and foodstuffs were procured in this manner.

Facilities in Japan, Okinawa, Taiwan, and the Philippines were developed to meet requirements for repairing or rebuilding equipment from Vietnam. The time required for these services was thus reduced for such items as armored personnel carriers, wheeled vehicles, material handling equipment, and harbor craft.

CONSTRUCTION

In early 1965 a massive construction program was undertaken to provide the base facilities necessary for the support of Allied forces in Vietnam. For the first time in United States military history a major part of the construction effort in an active combat theater was accomplished by civilian contractors. In 1965 South Vietnam had one major port, which was located at Saigon. By 1968 there were seven deep-water ports with 32 berths and many smaller ports for shallowdraft ships. Where once there were three jet runways at three small bases, by 1968 there were 15 jet runways at eight major airbases. In addition, there were more than 200 smaller airfields and almost 200 heliports. Major bases were built for complete tactical units. Major construction of storage depots, hospitals, communications sites, roads, and bridges was being completed in record time.

Phan Rang Airbase, South Vietnam.

MILITARY CONSTRUCTION VIETNAM
PROGRAMS THROUGH 30 JUNE 1968
$ IN MILLIONS

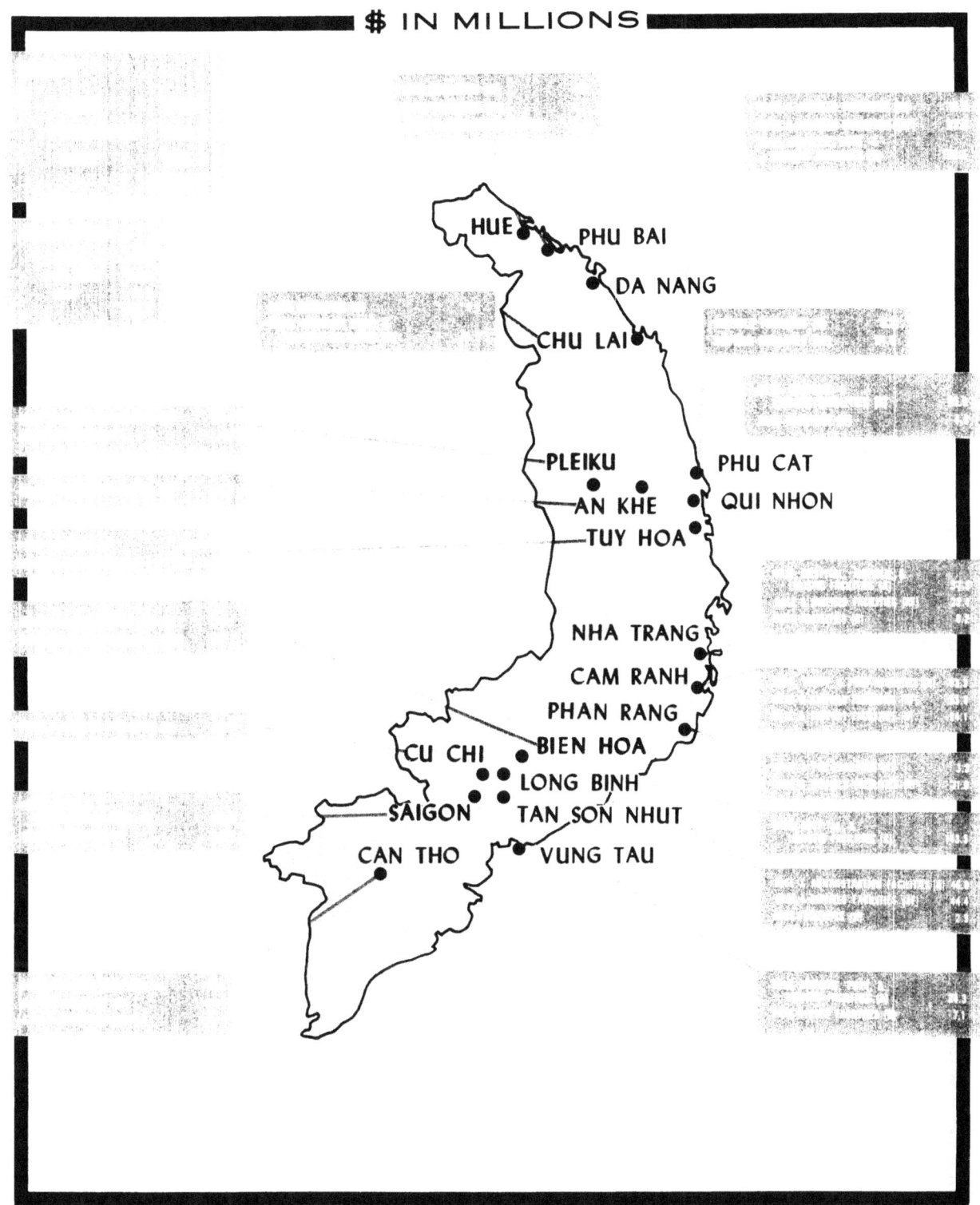

MILITARY CONSTRUCTION THAILAND
PROGRAMS THROUGH 30 JUNE 1968
$ IN MILLIONS

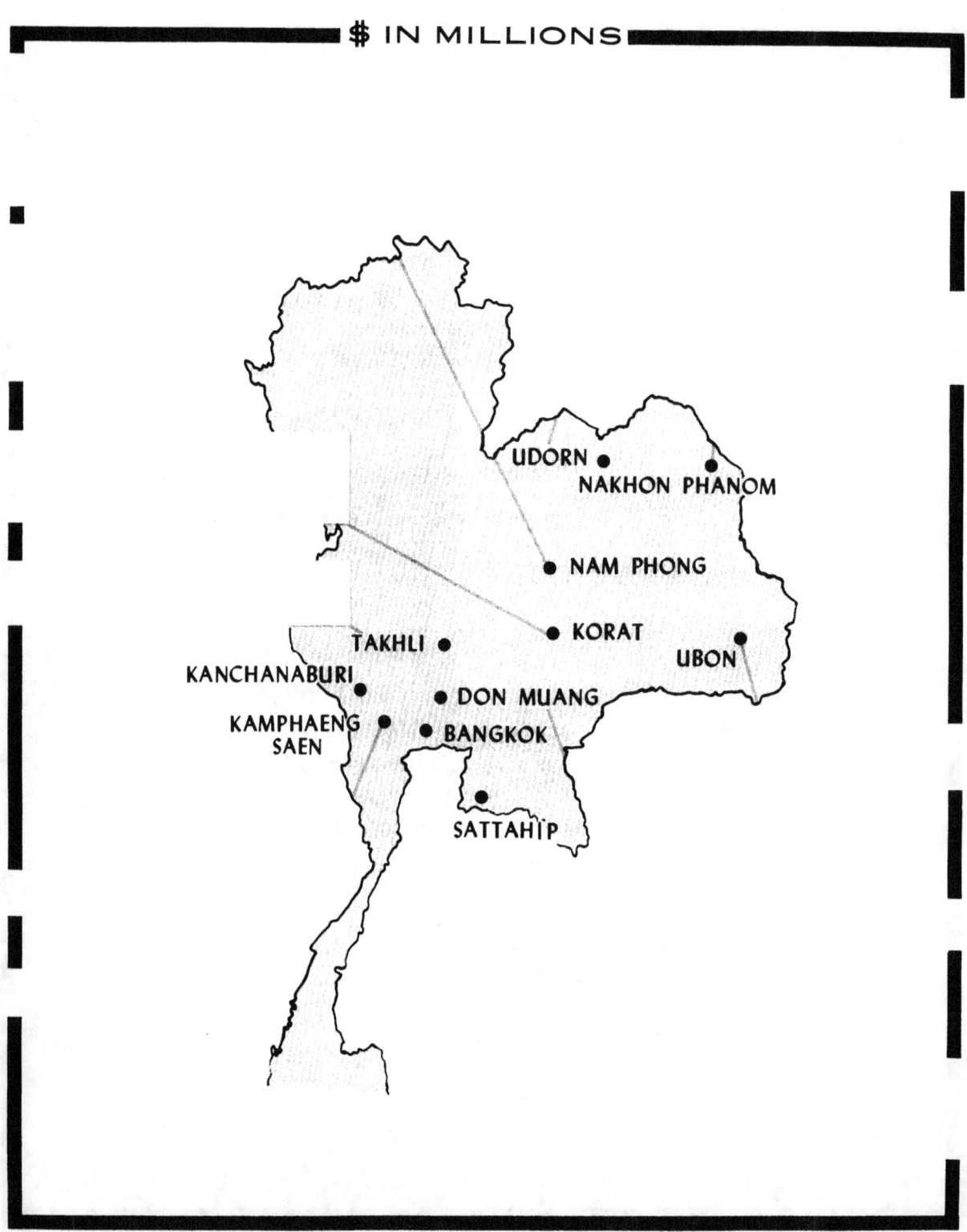

The $1.6 billion construction program nearing completion in South Vietnam in 1968 was executed by civilian contractors and 44 battalion-size military construction units. In support of Southeast Asia operations, civilian contractors and troop units in Thailand at the same time neared completion of a $400 million construction program. This included a major deep-water port at Sattahip; a new operational airbase at U-Tapao; communications, storage areas, and major expansion of six Royal Thai airbases.

COMMUNICATIONS—ELECTRONICS

With the buildup of forces in Southeast Asia, Pacific Command communications and electronics facilities underwent major expansion, upgrading, and reorientation. High quality communications were required not only in Southeast Asia and to deployed combat forces in the Western Pacific, but also to those support elements scattered throughout the command. The result was the establishment of an integrated communications system in support of Southeast Asia operations extending from Hawaii to Korea in the north, to Vietnam and Thailand in the south, and along the island chain from the Philippines to Japan.

The buildup in the Pacific since 1964 resulted in a dramatic increase in communications operations. Teletype message traffic at the CINCPAC Communications Center at Camp Smith, Hawaii, rose from 29,000 to 60,000 per month. Message traffic in the command at large increased from approximately 12 million messages in 1964 to over 18 million in 1967. Telephone calls through the Joint Overseas Switchboard in Hawaii increased from 27,000 to 150,000 a month.

To meet this vastly increased traffic load and provide the needed quality for passing secure voice and high speed data stream communications between the highest levels of government and tactical units in the field, the primary Pacific Command communications network evolved from narrowband, high frequency radio to wide-band, cable, tropospheric, and microwave radio for regional distribution. The number of circuits in the Defense Communications System in the theater increased from 3,500 to 13,900. At the same time, conversion to automatic message switching centers and telephone exchanges was well underway.

Support of Southeast Asia operations also required a major expansion of air traffic control, flight following, and navigation facilities. Surveillance and warning systems were expanded and improved. Automated command and control facilities and their supporting communications were developed to meet the quick reaction times required of forces in the field.

Pacific Command radio frequency management requirements kept pace with the increased tempo of operations. The number of radio frequencies in use in the Pacific climbed from 12,000 to 21,000.

The major communications problem stemmed from the long lead time involved in the processing and implementation of major telecommunications requirements. CINCPAC had developed and submitted a plan for long-haul communications in Southeast Asia before the buildup of United States forces began. The plan was restudied and approved for implementation when the decisions were made to deploy forces. Pacific Command communications capability, however, has lagged behind the requirements ever since. Considering the long lead times required to obtain operating systems, the availability of the basic plan was most important. Without it as a place to start, the situation would have been almost impossible. By mid-1968 we were on our third expansion of that basic plan but had not yet caught up with the snowballing requirements which resulted from force expansion in Southeast Asia.

CINCPAC believed from the outset that the

cost of engineering for future expansions and a moderate initial capability in excess of minimum requirements was both reasonable and cost effective, and experience has proven this view correct.

While there has been no positive indication that a lack of long-lines communications has been a limiting factor in the planning or conduct of operations, or in the management of material or personnel, the approved and funded programs are not totally adequate, and efforts to improve Pacific Command communications capabilities should be continued.

TRANSPORTATION

The fluid combat situation in South Vietnam, the lack of sufficient ground lines of communication, and the vulnerability of the existing meager ground LOC's placed unprecedented demands upon airlift. With increased requirements for air transportation throughout the Pacific Command the need for a CINCPAC agency to supervise the use of intratheater airlift became apparent. To fill this need the Western Pacific Transportation Office was established at Tachikawa, Japan. As the co-ordinator between users of airlift and the airlift operating units, the Western Pacific Transportation Office has played a vital role. In the early phases of the war, airlift in Vietnam was provided by the 315th Air Division, headquartered in Japan. The tactical situation demanded command and control within South Vietnam of all airlift resources. To meet the need, the 834th Air Division was activated in October 1966 to operate the tactical airlift system for the Seventh Air Force. Assets included C-123 and C-7A aircraft, augmented by C-130's of the 315th Air Division. The latter were rotated to Vietnam from off-shore locations and were under operational control of the 834th Air Division while in South Vietnam.

By early 1968, 96 C-130's were operating in South Vietnam. New records of airlift accomplishments included 137,000 tons lifted in March 1968 and 4,939 sorties in support of emergency requests in February 1968. Hundreds of unit moves in direct support of ground operations were completed. Air support alone sustained the garrison under siege at Khe Sanh where 12,430 tons of cargo were delivered by air between 31 January and 8 April 1968.

Saigon was the original aerial port in Vietnam. To meet the increased airlift movement from the United States to Vietnam, new aerial ports were opened at Cam Ranh Bay, Da Nang, Bien Hoa, and Phu Cat. By 1968, 1,000 tons of high priority cargo were received each day in Vietnam through these ports and Tan Son Nhut. About 200 aircraft, most of which were long-range jets, were committed to this task. A dramatic display of our strategic airlift capability was the deployment of two brigades of the 101st Airborne Division from Fort Campbell, Kentucky to Vietnam in December 1967. Military Airlift Command C-141 Starlifters and C-133 Cargomasters, flying nearly 400 missions, moved almost 10,000 troops and over 5,000 tons of cargo. The main body, consisting of 8,500 troops and 4,000 tons of equipment, moved from their original base to the combat zone in less than 18 days.

In late 1965 surface shipments began to overwhelm the receiving capability of Saigon, the only established port in South Vietnam. CINCPAC assigned priority to port construction. This led to the rapid development of four new major ports and numerous over-the-beach operation sites. By July 1968 almost 98 percent of the dry cargo as well as all bulk petroleum products were being moved to South Vietnam by ship. Tonnages delivered by surface transport have multiplied more than six times since early 1965. Over 250 military controlled cargo ships supported the Pacific Command. On a typical day, 30 ships were being loaded at United States ports for Vietnam, 55 ships were in Vietnam ports, 150 were at sea, and 25 were working in and between other Pacific Command ports.

Above, The site for Newport, near Saigon, before construction began. *Below,* The completed port in operation.

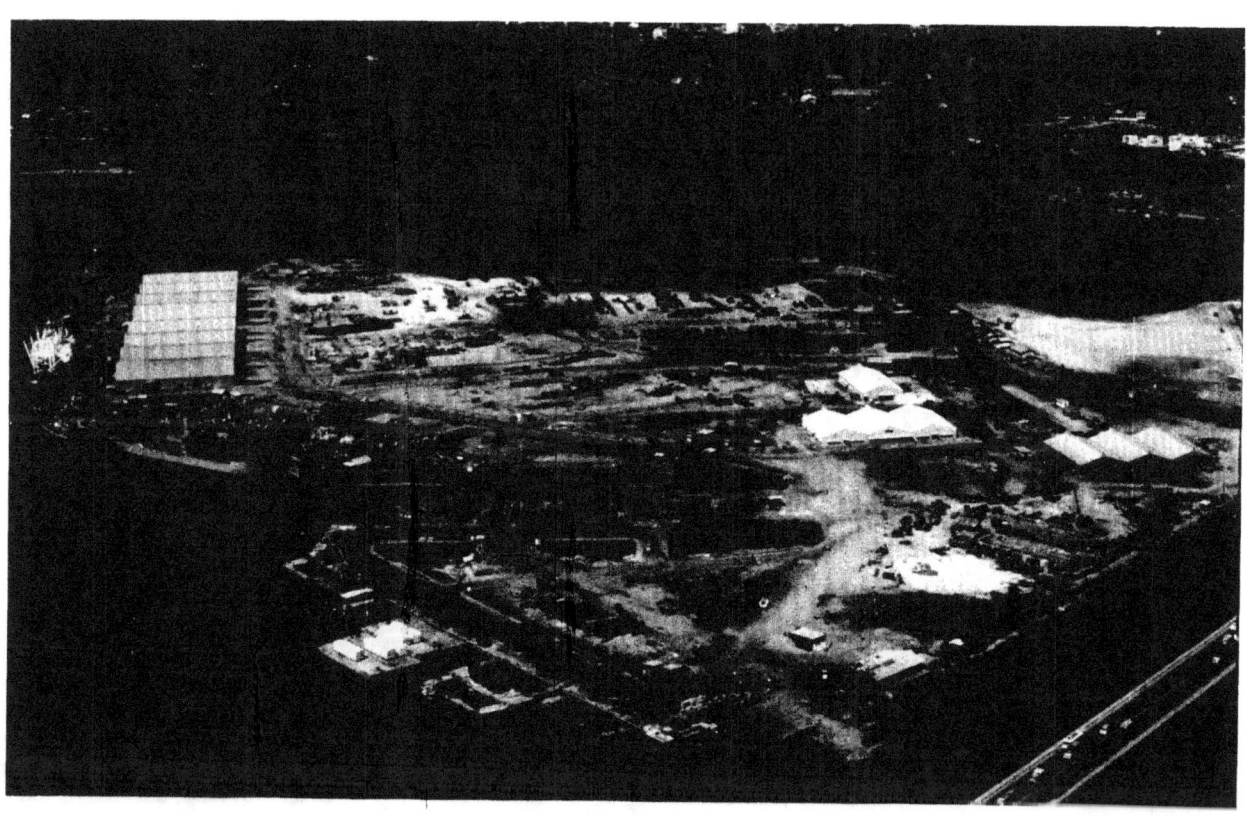

Below, Port facilities at Dong Tam, South Vietnam in the Delta region. *Above*, A view of the area before construction began.

Sattahip, Thailand, *Above,* Before construction began. *Below,* The port after development.

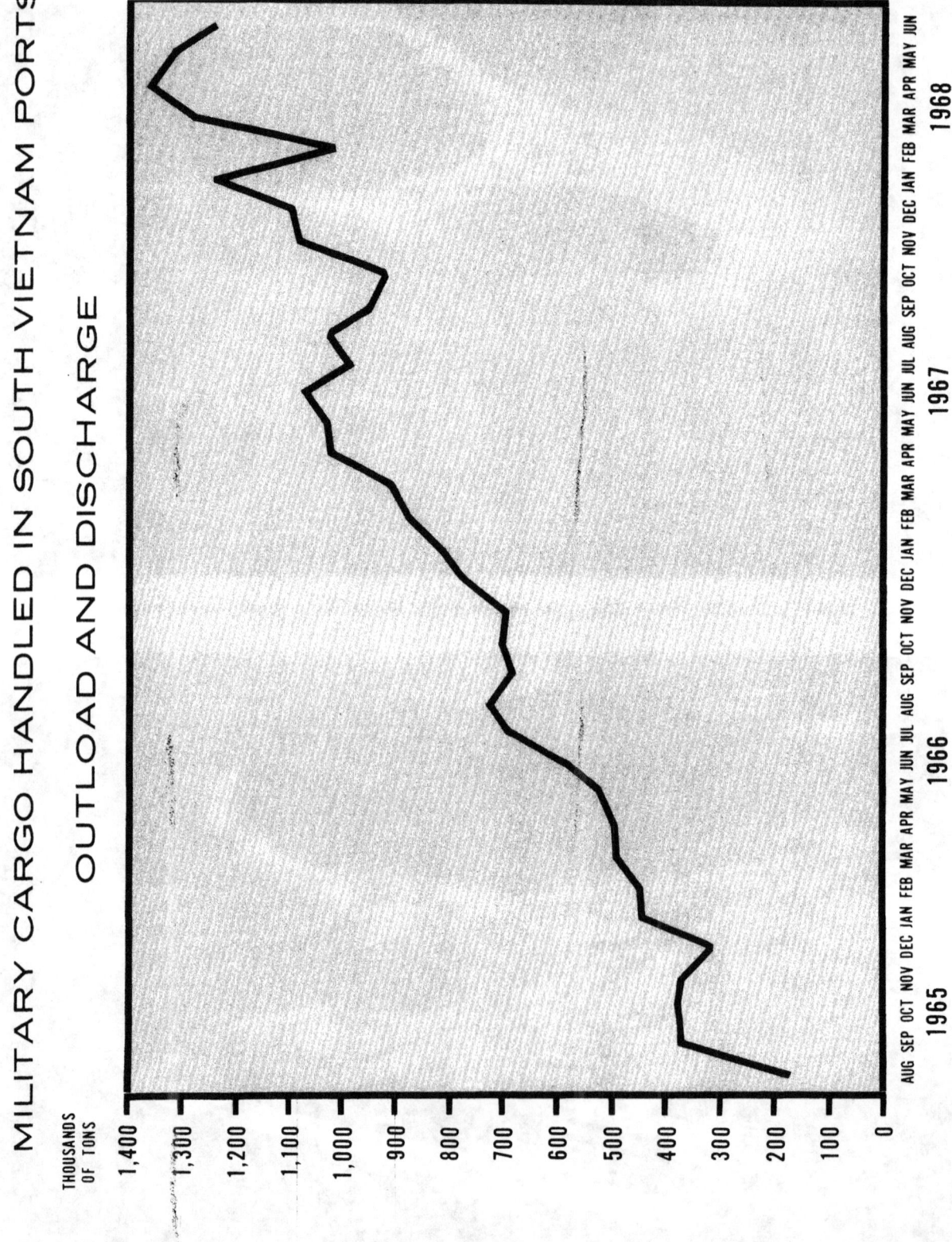

CINCPAC also established two movement control agencies, a branch of the Western Pacific Transportation Office at Yokohama, Japan, and the Pacific Command Movements Priority Agency at Oakland, California, to control the flow of cargo to South Vietnam from Pacific Command and United States ports. These agencies assured that urgently required cargoes were transported promptly and that the number of ships awaiting discharge in South Vietnam was held to a minimum.

A CINCPAC recommendation that ships be loaded in the United States for a single port of discharge in Vietnam was a major factor in expediting ship turnarounds. Faster and more efficient handling of supplies in port areas also came with the introduction of roll-on/roll-off ships, which loaded or unloaded their cargo in one day. In 1966 of the time taken by conventional ships. Another improvement was the use of container ships, which loaded or unloaded their cargo in one day. In 1966 the Pacific Command Joint Transportation Board became operational to assist the CINCPAC in the control of transportation activities, resolution of transportation problems, and establishment of overall priorities for the allocation of transportation resources.

MILITARY ASSISTANCE, SERVICE FUNDED

By early 1966 it became apparent that Military Assistance Program funding and procedures were not adequate for, nor compatible with, the expanded operational role which had been imposed upon Free World forces fighting in Vietnam. The Military Assistance Program was designed to provide deterrence and a capacity for initial defense against aggression, not to underwrite sustained military operations. Consequently, in 1966 the responsibility for the support of Vietnamese and other Free World forces was transferred from the Military Assistance Program to the military services. The transfer progressed smoothly, with no degradation of support. Under the revised system, plans and programs for the support of forces in Vietnam were developed by the Commander of the Military Assistance Command, Vietnam. After review and approval by the CINCPAC and the Service Component Commanders, they were forwarded to the military departments for approval and funding action.

MEDICAL SUPPORT

The United States military medical effort in Vietnam required the backup support of an extensive system of hospitals in the Pacific Command. These hospitals of the three Services have provided definitive surgical care second to none in the world. From 1963 to May 1968, of the wounded surviving to reach a hospital, only three percent died. From 40 to 45 percent of the patients evacuated to hospitals outside of Vietnam were later returned to duty within the command.

This excellent hospital system was developed under conditions of time urgency and fund limitation. These factors made it necessary to modify nonhospital buildings already in United States possession, though some were not in ideal locations. From a total of 1,448 beds in January 1965, bed capacity had been increased to nearly 9,000 beds by June 1968.

The joint medical regulating system guided the evacuation of 80,000 patients from Vietnam; 62,000 going to hospitals in the Pacific Command and the remainder to the continental United States. The transportation of these casualties was accomplished by Pacific Air Force and Military Airlift Command aircraft with medical flight crews.

Under the auspices of the CINCPAC, a series of War Surgery Conferences was held at which surgeons of all Services formulated professional guidance for care of casualties based on the latest evolving experience. Proceedings of these conferences have been made available to each military medical service.

PRISONERS OF WAR

The treatment of United States prisoners of war was of constant concern. The International Committee of the Red Cross (ICRC) was the main point of contact on these matters. The ICRC, through State Department and military efforts, constantly encouraged North Vietnamese compliance with the Geneva Convention concerning treatment of prisoners, relief packages, mail, repatriation of sick and wounded, and exchange of prisoner lists. All efforts, however, have been to little avail and the actual number of United States personnel held and the treatment they received is still not precisely known.

South Vietnam, on the other hand, cooperated with the ICRC and fulfilled all requirements for Viet Cong and North Vietnamese personnel held as prisoners of war. South Vietnam maintained custody of all prisoners of war captured in South Vietnam, including those taken by allied forces.

MORALE OF FORCES

The morale of United States forces involved in the war in Vietnam was consistently high. This condition could be attributed to a belief in the mission of the United States in Vietnam, pride in accomplishing this mission, esprit de corps within units, the one-year tour, and the Rest and Recuperation (R&R) Program. The one-year tour length allowed a serviceman to know from the beginning of his tour the day he would return home. This was considered to be the single greatest morale factor for our forces. The R&R Program allowed each man to have one respite of five or six-day duration from the combat zone during his tour. Ten sites, ranging from Tokyo to Sydney and from Hawaii to Singapore, were offered. This program moved approximately 400,000 troops to R&R sites between July 1967 and June 1968. Other important factors in maintaining the high morale included exceptional medical care, a responsive awards and decorations policy, free mail, combat pay, income tax benefits, and excellent food service.

REPORT ON OPERATIONS IN SOUTH VIETNAM

JANUARY 1964 — JUNE 1968

BY
GENERAL W. C. WESTMORELAND
COMMANDER
U.S. MILITARY ASSISTANCE COMMAND
VIETNAM

PREFACE

In April 1968 the President asked me to prepare a report on my four and a half years of duty in South Vietnam. My official report describing problems, decisions, innovations, and operations was submitted to Admiral U. S. G. Sharp, the Commander in Chief, Pacific (CINCPAC). The letter of transmittal to CINCPAC is included in Appendix M. Hastily prepared in the press of business, the report was couched in military terms which could be confusing to the general reader.

Believing that each American deserves a clear understanding of our great effort in Vietnam, I have redrafted my original report in a form which I hope will be more understandable and useful to all who may be interested.

Certain parts of the report have been expanded to clarify and explain concepts and practices that may not be well known to the general public. Some material that was inadvertently omitted or previously prohibited from public release because of security classification has also been added.

The report is organized chronologically. Except for an introductory chapter covering the period 1954–1963, there is a chapter for each successive year. I have attempted to provide an overview of each year by describing only the most important events and considerations relating to actions by both sides. This is followed—except in the introductory chapter covering a period when I was not in Vietnam—by a section setting forth my observations on selected problems, developments, and decisions. Finally, each chapter contains a chronology of major events. Necessarily, this chronology duplicates some of the material in the overview. My views covering the entire period are summarized at the end of the report, and a series of appendices elaborate on areas of particular importance and interest.

One aspect of the report needs a word of prior explanation. Frequent reference is made throughout to changes in the government in Saigon and to political problems and disruptions which arose from time to time. The fact of the matter is that these events were as important and in some cases more important than the unfolding of the tactical situation on the ground. If any generalization can be made about the war in South Vietnam it is that the U.S. effort, both military and political, prospered to the extent that the government of Vietnam was strong, coherent, and active. The corollary, of course, is that none of our efforts had any chance of success in the periods during which the government was weak, divided, and thus ineffective. Upon my arrival in Vietnam, this strong and direct connection between military and political problems was quickly impressed upon me. This, I hope, will explain why I have included those major political events which in my opinion and experience bore so heavily upon the course of the war and on both our successes and our frustrations.

These successes and frustrations were not, of course, mine alone. They were shared with literally millions of others—individuals, each of whom, in his own way, contributed to the success of our efforts—and to whom I am deeply grateful.

First and foremost, I express my respect and warm feelings for the Vietnamese people at all levels from the highest national leadership to the individual farmer and volunteer soldier who has fought, sacrificed, and died in a long and cruel war. Our combined effort was made immeasurably less difficult through the contributions of other nations who offered support to help overcome the threat to South Vietnam. While each of the national contributions varied in nature, size, and activity, the unity of the effort against a common foe gave us heart and hope in times of adversity.

My task was eased by the magnificent support and understanding which I received from my superiors, both military and civilian—the Commander in Chief, Secretaries of Defense, the Joint Chiefs of Staff, and Commander in Chief, Pacific. I valued most highly the assistance and support afforded by General Earle G. Wheeler, the Chairman of the Joint Chiefs of Staff, and Admiral U. S. G. Sharp, CINCPAC, both of whom served in those highly responsible positions throughout the entire period of my service in Vietnam. To the wholly dedicated and competent representatives of the other departments and agencies of our government working in Vietnam, I owe a large measure of appreciation. Ambassadors Henry Cabot Lodge, Maxwell D. Taylor, and Ellsworth Bunker provided wise counsel and meaningful direction to our activities. During the period of this report the Ambassador was ably assisted by a Deputy Ambassador who in each case provided valuable support to the Military Assistance Command, Vietnam (MACV). These highly competent officials were, in order, U. Alexis Johnson, William J. Porter, Eugene M. Locke, and Samuel D. Berger.

To my wife, who lived for three and one-half years without her husband, who made a home for our children, and who somehow found time to work several days a week at a military hospital attending wounded men from the battlefield, I owe my deepest gratitude.

Lastly, and most importantly, I lived for almost four and one-half years with an acute daily awareness of the sacrifices that the men of the armed services of the United States were making in effort and in blood.

No words can express my admiration for these valiant Americans or convey my respect for their accomplishments. It is to them that I humbly dedicate this report.

W. C. WESTMORELAND
General, United States Army

CONTENTS

	Page
Preface	71
Chapter I—The Advisory Years (1954–1963)	75
Chapter II—The Year of Crisis (1964)	83
Chapter III—The Year of Military Commitment (1965)	97
Chapter IV—The Year of Development (1966)	113
Chapter V—The Year of the Offensive (1967)	131
Chapter VI—The Year of Decision (1968)	157
Conclusions	189
Appendix A—Enemy Organization for the Conduct of the War in South Vietnam	203
Appendix B—Republic of Vietnam Armed Forces	209
Appendix C—Free World Assistance	221
Appendix D—Pacification	229
Appendix E—Psychological Operations/Civic Action	237
Appendix F—The State of the Command	241
Appendix G—Logistics and Base Development	253
Appendix H—Medical	267
Appendix I—Press	273
Appendix J—Major United States and Free World Military Units in Vietnam	275
Appendix K—Commanders of Major United States and Free World Military Assistance Forces in Vietnam	279
Appendix L—List of Major Operations	281
Appendix M—Original Letter of Transmittal	291
Photographs	295
Glossary	347

References in this document to the operations of allied and enemy forces are based upon contemporary reports received at MACV. In some instances these reports were not clear or complete. The narrative of operations in full and accurate detail will be more adequately written by historians after the war has ended and a more complete record is available.

Illustrations

	Page.
1. Major Battles and Significant Localities 1954–63	Faces 82
2. Major Battles and Significant Localities 1964	Faces 96
3. Military Assistance Command Vietnam Organization	102
4. Major Battles and Significant Localities 1965	Faces 112
5. Major Battles and Significant Localities 1966	Faces 130
6. Typical Viet Cong Tunnel System	150
7. Typical Enemy Camouflaged Tunnel Entrance	151
8. Concealed Tunnel Entrance by River Bank	151
9. Major Battles and Significant Localities 1967	Faces 156
10. Opposing Maneuver Battalions by Corps Tactical Zone as of 25 Jan 1968	176
11. Allied Combat Battalion Locations as of 25 Jan 1968	177
12. Opposing Maneuver Battalions by Corps Tactical Zone as of 13 Mar 1968	178
13. Allied Combat Battalion Locations as of 13 Mar 1968	179
14. Opposing Maneuver Battalions by Corps Tactical Zone as of 19 Jun 1968	180
15. Allied Combat Battalion Locations as of 19 Jun 1968	181
16. Major Battles and Significant Localities 1968	Faces 188
17. Ratio of Enemy to Allied Casualties	191
18. Ratio of Enemy to Allied Weapons Losses	193
19. North Vietnamese Army and Viet Cong Combat Battalions in South Vietnam	195
20. Vietnamese and Allied Forces in South Vietnam	197
21. Population Status in South Vietnam	199
22. Communist Party Dominance in Enemy Organization	205
23. Typical Province Communist Organization in South Vietnam	206
24. Typical Village Administrative Liberation Association in South Vietnam	207
25. Ports, Land Lines of Communications, and Major Logistic Commands	259
26. Tactical Airfields, South Vietnam—1968	262
27. Topographic Map of South Vietnam	Faces 348
28. Political Boundaries of South Vietnam	Faces 348

Chapter I

THE ADVISORY YEARS—1954-1963

OVERVIEW

From the Geneva settlement of the Indochina War in 1954 until late 1963, the United States progressively expanded its support and assistance to the new government of Vietnam under President Ngo Dinh Diem and his successors. After the French withdrawal, the U.S. helped to organize and train the military forces of the new nation. In late 1961 the U.S. expanded this effort to include field advisors with tactical units and began to provide increased aircraft and communications support to the beleaguered South Vietnamese government.

The Geneva Accords, agreed to jointly by France and the Democratic Republic of Vietnam (North Vietnam), divided Vietnam at the 17th parallel, provided for a withdrawal of Communist forces from the south, and created a number of limitations or prohibitions on the introduction of foreign military personnel and materiel. The final declaration of the Geneva Conference associated the United Kingdom, the Union of Soviet Socialist Republics, and the People's Republic of China with these settlements. The United States, while not joining in the declaration, stated that it would abide by the spirit of the accords so long as the Communists did so.

In keeping with one of the provisos of the Geneva Accords, during the 1954-55 period approximately 100,000 Vietnamese elected to go to North Vietnam from the south, while close to one million persons living in the area that became the Communist Democratic Republic of Vietnam went south. (Over 65,000 of those who went north were to return to South Vietnam as "regroupees" and as cadre for enemy units.)

Originally—and in light of our experience in Korea—the emphasis was placed on developing South Vietnamese forces capable of meeting an overt thrust across the Demilitarized Zone (DMZ). While the danger of such an event did not disappear, it became increasingly clear that the principal threat was one of externally supported internal subversion and insurgency.

Events in South Vietnam clearly indicated that the Hanoi leaders planned to re-create the circumstances of their earlier triumph—that is, to follow the path which had proved so successful in the Indochina War. Subversion, espionage, and terror would be followed by gradually intensifying guerrilla warfare. The process would culminate in the decisive employment of large heavily-armed military units.

Not only was the scenario to mirror that of the earlier conflict but the Hanoi-controlled political-military organization was also designed to parallel that which had helped the Viet Minh to oust the French. The groundwork for the open resumption of the insurgency was laid by members of the southern branch of the North Vietnamese Communist Party—the Lao Dong (Vietnamese Worker's) Party.

The symptoms of early insurgency were clearly present in South Vietnam in 1959. Reports increasingly drew attention to an elaborate, carefully planned campaign of violence and subversive pressures aimed at undermining the stability and institutions of the Diem government. Assassinations and kidnappings of officials and government supporters in rural areas were increasing sharply—killings alone doubled in a year. Infiltration, from Laos, across the DMZ, and from the sea jumped sharply upward in 1959–1960, establishing a pattern that was to persist throughout the mid-sixties. In fact, this pattern was clearly drawn from the classic three-step prescription of Mao Tse-tung:

Step One (Creation of Bases)

Secretly establish control of the rural people by the use of selective terrorism (murder) and propaganda.

Gradually eliminate government influence by the assassination of village chiefs and other notables.

Establish a political and military base among the people through force and persuasion.

Conduct guerrilla operations against the forces of law and order.

Step Two (Equilibrium)

Form squads, platoons, companies, and battalions from among the controlled population.

Increase guerrilla operations against remaining forces of law and order.

Expand the military and political base in order to build forces as strong as the government forces and in order to:

—Destroy isolated government forces;
—Extend political control of the people.

Step Three (Counteroffensive)

Create large military formations capable of attacking and destroying the government forces.

Extend political control over the entire population, eliminating by execution those who resist.

Attack and destroy the remaining forces of law and order.

In January of 1961 Radio Hanoi announced the formation of the National Liberation Front (NLF), patterned after a similar organization which had operated with great success in the last years of the Indochina War. This earlier Lien Viet or "Fatherland Front" had managed to enlist the cooperation and participation of a broad range of nationalist elements outside the Communist Party. The NLF, later dubbed the "political arm" of the Viet Cong, was specifically designed to emulate this earlier success and to create a sense of nationalistic continuity between itself and the Lien Viet.

The southern branch of the Lao Dong Party was renamed the People's Revolutionary Party on 1 January 1962. Although it claimed to be separate and distinct from the Lao Dong, the People's Revolutionary Party was what it had always been—the southern branch of the party in the north. As such, it continued to receive its instructions from Hanoi while it masqueraded as the organ of a nationalistic movement in the south.

The People's Revolutionary Party was organized on lines paralleling the NLF's hierarchical structure. Beginning with cells at the hamlet level, its structure rose through village, district, and provincial chapters to regional headquarters embracing several provinces. It culminated in a central committee—the Central Office for South Vietnam (COSVN).

Thus, the People's Revolutionary Party was organized so that it could transmit orders and monitor activities at every level down to the squad and hamlet. On the political side, its successive layers permitted it to control all levels of the NLF which served as a "shadow government." Similarly, it exercised indirect control over so-called Viet Cong military formations—main forces, local forces, and guerrillas. The Hanoi-dominated party overarched and controlled a coordinated political-military war effort. Although the term Viet Cong (VC) is usually associated with the military effort, its meaning (Vietnamese Communists) includes the entire political-military apparatus composed of South Vietnamese, as opposed to the North Vietnamese Army and individuals. (A more detailed discussion of this organization may be found in Appendix A.)

The VC, who numbered only 4,000 men in April of 1960, had grown to 5,500 by the end of that year and soared to over 25,000 in 1961. In 1962 they increased to over 33,000 and in 1963 to 35,000. By this time the political infrastructure involved more than 40,000, of which increasing numbers of influential cadre had come from the north.

The Viet Cong conducted their first battalion-size attacks in 1960. These attacks increased in frequency and expanded to multi-battalion size in 1961. The structure of the South Vietnamese government was attacked directly by assassinations and abductions. Assassinations rose from 239 in 1959 to 1,400 in 1960. Abductions doubled during the same period. By 1962 over 1,000 persons a month were killed or abducted—most of them government officials.

In an attempt to counter this rapidly expanding insurgency, the Vietnamese government increased its regular military forces, its paramilitary units, and its pacification efforts. Regular military forces grew from 148,000 at the end of 1960 to 216,000 at the end of 1963. Provincial and district paramilitary forces (precursors to the present Regional and Popular Forces) increased during the same period from fewer than 100,000 to more than 180,000. The arms and training of these forces were improved with U.S. assistance. Civilian Irregular Defense Groups (CIDG) were formed in 1961 amongst the primitive Montagnard tribes in the Central Highlands. By the end of 1963, CIDG strength had risen to 18,000. In late 1961 the Diem government began to formulate a Strategic Hamlet Program to provide local security against insurgent terrorists and guerrillas. Announced early in 1962, the program was intended to provide the means by which the pacified area would be consolidated as it expanded. This program was inspired by, and patterned after, the British experience in Malaya.

In a series of decisions in late 1961 and early 1962, the U.S. decided to increase sharply its assistance to the hard-pressed government of South Vietnam. The authorized number of U.S. military advisors was increased from 746 to over 3,400. Most of these newly authorized advisors were in Vietnam by June 1962. U.S. tactical aircraft were provided to the Vietnamese Air Force and U.S. Army helicopter units were sent to Vietnam to support and train the government's forces.

The U.S. Military Assistance Command, Vietnam (USMACV) was formed in February 1962, to direct the expanding U.S. effort. General Paul D. Harkins became its first commander.

Notwithstanding this combined U.S.-South Vietnamese effort, Viet Cong successes continued to mount. Although it seemed that the tide of battle was beginning to shift by late in 1962, this encouraging period was short-lived. In the spring of 1963, President Diem was accused of provoking an adverse reaction among the people, particularly the Buddhists, which led first to demonstrations, then spectacular Buddhist immolations, and finally general turmoil and the overthrow and assassination of Diem.

Following the assassination of Diem, the government of Vietnam was shaken by a series of coups and power struggles among various military and religious factions. In this unstable political environment, the enemy made quick and widespread political and military gains. The depth of the problem was not completely apparent in late 1963, but it became only too evident in the year of crisis—1964.

CHRONOLOGY OF MAJOR EVENTS—1954–1963

1954

The Geneva Accords were signed on 20 July 1954. At the request of the South Vietnamese government, the United States offered military materiel and equipment to the Republic of Vietnam Armed Forces under the so-called pentalateral agreement with France and the Protocol States—Vietnam, Cambodia, and Laos. A Military Assistance Advisory Group (MAAG), Vietnam was established to supervise and coordinate this logistical support program.

1955

In February the Joint Chiefs of Staff expanded the mission of the MAAG, giving it authority to organize and train as well as equip the armed forces of South Vietnam.

1956–1957

The Communist organization in South Vietnam, the Viet Cong, initiated its campaign of terror to undermine the authority of the central government. The prime targets of this campaign were government officials and backers who provided essential public services and symbolized governmental authority in the rural areas of the country. Some 15 to 20 per month were being assassinated as the terror campaign gained intensity.

1958–1959

It became clear that the Viet Cong were being reinforced by cadre sent from North Vietnam. Nearly all of the infiltration from 1958 until early 1964 consisted of the so-called "regroupees," Vietnamese Communists who had elected to go to North Vietnam after the 1954 Geneva settlement. After intensive political and military training, these regroupees were infiltrated back into South Vietnam, mostly into leadership positions.

Assassinations and kidnappings of government officials and supporters by the Viet Cong continued to increase. Killings rose from 193 in 1958 to 239 in 1959, while kidnappings jumped to 344, up from 236 the preceding year.

1960

Regroupee infiltration reached a new high as over 4,500 persons entered South Vietnam. Most of these infiltrators were officers, noncommissioned officers, and political cadre. At least half of them were members of the Communist Lao Dong (Vietnamese Worker's Party). The influence upon Viet Cong leadership by these infiltrators became increasingly evident; within four years the regroupees would be clearly dominant.

During this year, some Viet Cong forces were organized into units as large as battalions. The first battalion-size attacks occurred against isolated government posts and small towns. These attacks created conditions of security and morale which permitted and encouraged accelerated growth by the Communist political organization, further eroding the authority of the central government in some rural areas.

Statistics for 1960 on assassinations and kidnappings of government workers, primarily in the rural areas, gave dramatic proof of the increasing tempo and scope of the VC terror campaign. Compared to the previous year, assassinations increased sixfold, from 239 to 1,400, and kidnappings doubled, rising from 344 to almost 700.

In September the Third Congress of the Lao Dong Party in Hanoi set the "liberation" of South Vietnam as one of its primary strategic tasks. The Congress called upon the people of the South to form a united front and to struggle against the "U.S.-Diem clique" for the unification of the fatherland.

1961

In January Radio Hanoi announced the creation of the National Liberation Front in South Vietnam.

Enemy local and main force units continued to grow rapidly. The year-end strength of 26,700 was almost five times that at the beginning of the year. Viet Cong military activity was conducted increasingly by larger units; three attacks of 1,000 men each occurred in September alone.

On 13 May Vice President Lyndon B. Johnson and President Diem issued a joint communiqué announcing that the U.S. defense and economic development programs with Vietnam would be expanded in response to the worsening situation.

Near the end of the year, President John F. Kennedy decided to enlarge the U.S. support for the South Vietnamese. The United States agreed to support an increase in South Vietnamese regular forces to about 200,000 with commensurate increases in the Civil Guard (later, Regional Forces) and Self Defense Corps (later, Popular Forces). U.S. military advisors would, under this decision, be assigned for the first time to operational Vietnamese units in the field.

On 11 December two U.S. Army helicopter companies were deployed to South Vietnam to provide operational support for the Army of the Republic of Vietnam (ARVN) and to train Vietnamese helicopter units for the future. Their arrival brought the total of American military personnel in Vietnam to slightly over 3,000 at the year's end.

The People's Revolutionary Party, announced in January of 1962, was formed in December 1961 and portrayed itself as an indigenous South Vietnamese political party independent of the Communist Lao Dong Party of North Vietnam. Captured documents indicated otherwise, however, revealing the People's Revolutionary Party to be nothing more than the subordinate southern element of the Lao Dong. The purpose of this subterfuge was to deceive non-Communist nationalists in South Vietnam and to confuse the U.S. and other nations concerning the true source of direction for the insurgency.

1962

In January the U.S. installed a tactical air control system in Vietnam and furnished 16 C–123 "Provider" aircraft for combat and logistical airlift support. Airlift within the country became increasingly important as Viet Cong attacks made movement by road and rail more hazardous and costly.

Early in the year, Viet Cong strength reached 30,000 regular forces and the infrastructure or "shadow government" was reported to have between 20,000 and 30,000 members.

Infiltration by all means continued to rise. Available evidence showed a 100 percent increase during the year from 6,295 ("confirmed" and "probable" infiltrators) in 1961 to 12,857 in 1962. These continued to be mainly regroupees, but there were clear indications that this source of manpower for the NLF and VC in the south was nearly exhausted.

On 8 February the United States Military Assistance Command, Vietnam, was established with General Paul D. Harkins as commander.

A Strategic Hamlet Program was announced by the South Vietnamese government in February. The program was designed to provide security to the populace in rural areas, usually by grouping them in fortified hamlets. The expanded Civil Guard and Self Defense Corps were progressively to take over from the ARVN the task of providing local security. The regular forces would thus be freed for mobile operations against the VC main forces. The pacified area could, in this fashion, be continuously expanded on a rational and secure base.

The Strategic Hamlet Program was launched in March during Operation SUNRISE in Binh Duong Province, immediately north of Saigon. The operation involved forced relocation of rural peasants, notwithstanding their strong attachment to their ancestral plots of land. Moreover, the first experiment, in Ben Cat District, was made in an area which had long been under strong Viet Cong influence.

During 1962 and 1963 the government was to construct well over a thousand Strategic Hamlets. Their quality varied widely, as did the extent of population relocation (in some areas there was little or none), and the wisdom with which sites were chosen.

In May a second squadron of C-123's arrived in Vietnam with 21 aircraft. With the addition of smaller U.S. Army and Air Force aviation units, this brought the total of U.S. aircraft of all types in Vietnam to 124, including four helicopter companies.

In July the nations which had participated in the 1954 Geneva Conference—joined by Thailand, Burma, Canada, India, and Poland—met again in Geneva to discuss Laos. The participants agreed to recognize and respect the independence, unity, territorial integrity, and neutrality of Laos.

By the end of 1962 airmobile operations were conducted frequently by Vietnamese Army forces transported in U.S. Army helicopters. These helicopters were placed under the operational control of the U.S. advisors with Vietnamese tactical units. Particularly in the Mekong Delta area, a number of bold operations were conducted that initially threw the enemy off balance.

Control of the rural areas was hotly contested, with Viet Cong terrorism a persistent problem. In 1962 the Communists killed or abducted 1,000 civilians each month, most of whom were government officials and teachers. The government of Vietnam was being bled to death by these gruesome and despicable measures.

As the year ended, there were approximately 11,000 U.S. advisory and support personnel in South Vietnam. These included 26 Special Forces "A" detachments of 12 men each and 3 modified "B" detachments to provide command and control. Overall control was exercised by U.S. Army Special Forces Command, Vietnam (Provisional). These teams operated initially under the control of the U.S. Embassy, but it was decided during this year to switch them back to U.S. Army control during 1963.

1963

Since the introduction of American helicopters to provide added mobility to the ARVN, Viet Cong units had generally refused to stand and fight when South Vietnamese forces were airlifted into close proximity. But in January, at Ap Bac in the Delta, a Viet Cong force engaged a superior ARVN force attempting to surround it by using heliborne assault tactics in conjunction with conventional ground movement. Five American helicopters were destroyed and nine damaged. The VC inflicted heavy casualties and later withdrew. The ARVN forces did not close the trap they had set and failed to take aggressive advantage of their superiority. The results of this battle increased the Viet Cong's confidence in their ability to fight successfully against government forces with superior equipment.

In April President Ngo Dinh Diem proclaimed a sweeping *Chieu Hoi* (Open Arms) campaign, promising clemency, financial aid, and family reunions to guerrillas who stopped fighting and returned to live under government authority.

The new UH-1B helicopters were first used on ARVN operations with considerable success in June. The increased speed and maneuverability of these aircraft compared with CH-21's was a welcome improvement.

Growing tension between South Vietnam's various factions led to a riot in Hue early in May. Tensions increased and martial law was imposed in Hue in June.

Also in June a Buddhist monk, Thich Quang Duc, committed suicide by burning himself in public. Within several days, riots broke out in Saigon and were forcibly put down by South Vietnamese troops. As the Buddhist crisis persisted, martial law was extended throughout the entire nation in August. However, intermittent rioting continued.

On 18 August the showplace strategic hamlet of Ben Tuong—the first-built of all strategic hamlets in Operation SUNRISE—was overrun by the Viet Cong. Also in August, armed government police and troops raided the Buddhist Xa Loi pagoda in Saigon. Incidents such as these, plus periodic self-immolations by Buddhist monks and resignations from the South Vietnamese government (both to protest discrimination against Buddhists and to protest government moves to alleviate tension), kept feelings at a high pitch.

On 24 October in response to an earlier invitation from President Diem, a United Nations fact-finding mission arrived in Saigon to investigate charges that the government was suppressing Buddhists. (The fact-finding mission reported to the United Nations 24 hours before Diem was assassinated that the charges were unfounded.) The following day, another monk burned himself to death in public, the seventh such suicide in four months.

By October the U.S. Army Special Forces working with the Civilian Irregular Defense Group Forces totalled 31 "A" detachments, 4 "B" detachments (one for each corps zone), and one "C" detachment to provide overall command and control.

On 1 November a military coup, organized by key officers of the armed forces, deposed President Diem. Diem and his brother, Ngo Dinh Nhu, were later killed. A provisional military government was established under the leadership of Maj. Gen. Duong Van "Big" Minh.

President Kennedy was assassinated on 22 November. Two days later, the new U.S. President, Lyndon B. Johnson, publicly proclaimed his determination to continue support for South Vietnam's efforts to defeat the insurgency.

By year's end it was clear that the November coup had proved costly in the countryside. Many strategic hamlets were overrun or revealed to be Communist-controlled. Weapons losses to the Viet Cong increased sharply. Many local paramilitary units simply melted away into the population. It was unclear at this time whether the new government would be able to heal the internal wounds and provide the leadership required to reverse the course of the struggle.

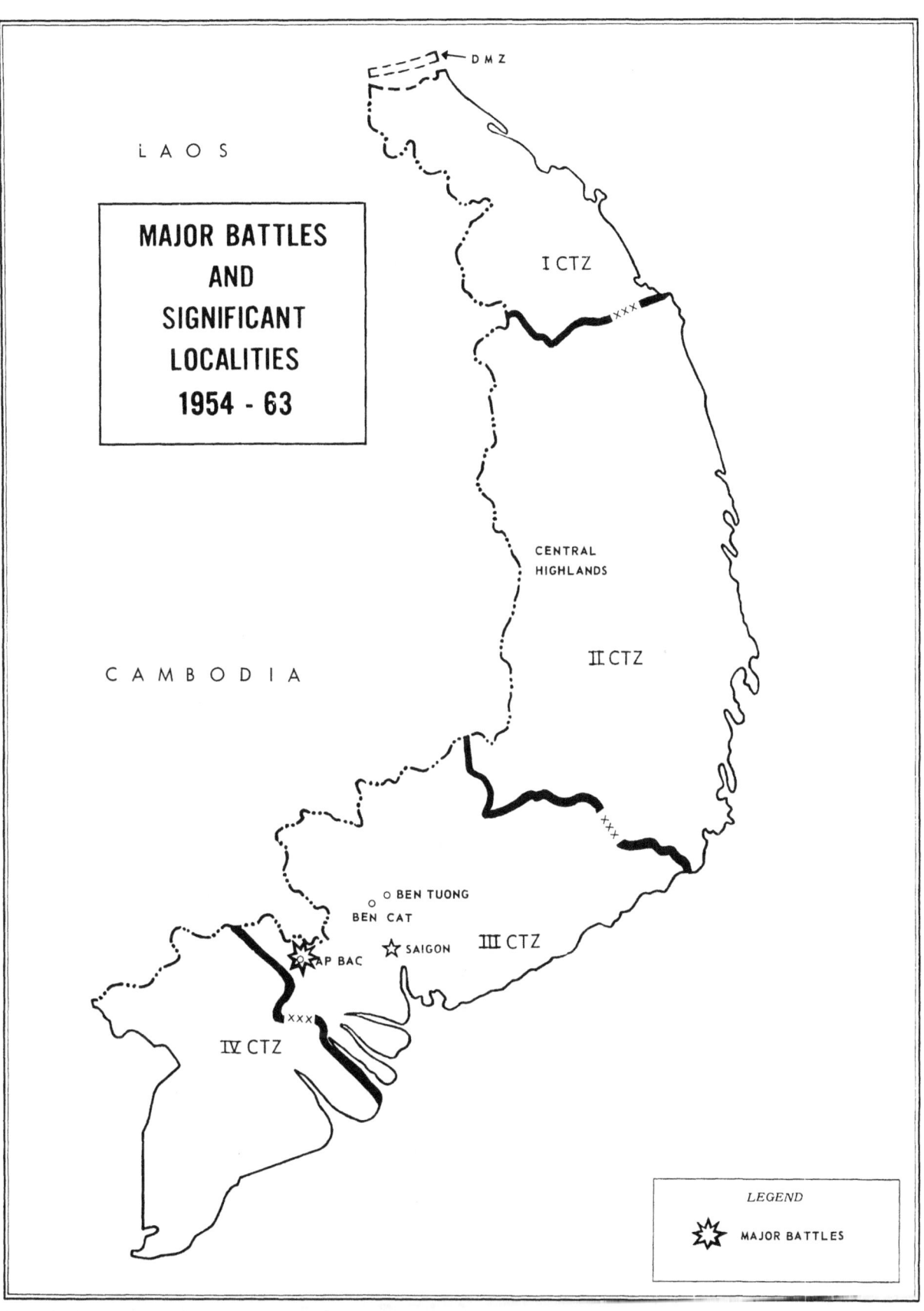

Chapter II

THE YEAR OF CRISIS—1964

OVERVIEW

I arrived in Saigon on 27 January 1964 and assumed duties as principal assistant to General Harkins with the title of Deputy Commander, U.S. Military Assistance Command, Vietnam.

Three days after my arrival, Maj. Gen. Nguyen Khanh led a bloodless coup which overthrew the government headed by General Minh. General Khanh installed himself as Premier. This was the second major political upheaval in three months. Unfortunately, it presaged a long period of the worst kind of political instability. Over the next year and a half, a series of coups, attempted coups, and counter-coups followed one another in rapid and alarming succession. Government effectiveness steadily declined throughout this entire period. South Vietnamese civil servants became dispirited and inactive in the face of this continued political instability. Institutions of government formed during the regime of President Diem progressively deteriorated and in some instances, particularly elements of the intelligence and police forces, disappeared altogether. The gains which had been made so slowly and laboriously in the previous eight years were steadily vanishing.

Since all but one of the province chiefs and most of the district chiefs were military officers, and in view of the fact that each ARVN corps commander exercised civil authority as the "government delegate" in the provinces embraced by his corps zone, instability in Saigon was reflected downward through each successive echelon of political authority. The effects could be seen in many ways. For instance, the impetus behind the Strategic Hamlet Program quickly disappeared. In many outlying areas—and especially in the Delta—local government officials reached tacit agreements with the Viet Cong and Communist infrastructure to "live and let live." The same was true of many Regional and Popular Force commanders in remote outposts.

Although the Vietnamese Army and paramilitary forces increased during the year by 117,000 men to a total strength of over 514,000, the overall effectiveness of these forces decreased markedly. Indeed, the increases in size were accomplished in the face of a large decrease in voluntary enlistments. The overburdened draft system faltered. South Vietnamese units were almost without exception below authorized strength, a problem compounded by desertions. Vietnamese forces scored a number of isolated victories throughout the year, but these were the exception.

The same instability which plagued the government's political structure also permeated the military forces. Poorly-motivated South Vietnamese units were no match for the well-disciplined Viet Cong forces. As a consequence, government forces seldom chose to close with the enemy. Patrolling to enhance population security virtually ceased. Offensive operations were timid and of short duration. Vietnamese troops depended almost wholly on air and artillery support, which usually came too late to prevent the VC from disengaging after inflicting heavy losses on South Vietnamese forces.

This lack of aggressiveness on the part of South Vietnamese military units reflected the extent to which leadership was thinly spread and the degree to which lowered morale damaged unit performance. It did not reflect adversely on the innate ability of the individual South Vietnamese soldier. He was then—as he is now—a hardy, willing, and capable individual. Given aggressive, professional leadership and even modest support, he will perform admirably. The support we were able to provide him in 1964 was exceedingly modest. The basic problems were those of weak leadership and its effect on morale.

As the government of Vietnam's position deteriorated, that of the Viet Cong grew stronger. The Viet Cong continued their military tactic of building their force from the lowest level upward. Additional companies were formed at district level, thus permitting the formation of new battalions in many provinces. This increase, in turn, allowed battalions of the main forces to expand into regiments. By the end of the year, a Viet Cong division was organized and committed to combat.

At the beginning of the year the Viet Cong were not equipped with standardized weapons. Their armament included a great variety of old French arms, U.S. weapons captured from the South Vietnamese, and several models of Communist-manufactured arms. This created an acute problem in ammunition and weapons resupply as Viet Cong forces increased in size.

Consequently, the Hanoi high command decided to convert the Viet Cong forces progressively to a standard family of small arms using one caliber of ammunition and to provide them more modern supporting arms. This decision increased Viet Cong firepower and simplified battlefield supply of both arms and ammunition. However, it complicated the overall logistic problem in that the newly-introduced automatic weapons (especially the AK–47 assault rifle) required larger tonnages for resupply. Thus Hanoi had taken an important decision. It was obliged thereafter to send large quantities of arms and ammunition south on a continuing basis over the long infiltration system, by sea or through Laos and Cambodia.

It was this process of quantitative and qualitative growth during 1964 that culminated in the formation of the Viet Cong 9th Division, comprising at first the 271st and 272d Regiments, which had been formed the previous year in War Zones C and D—long-developed Viet Cong base areas located, respectively, in Tay Ninh Province near the Cambodian border and in the vast jungle north of Bien Hoa. Much of the manpower to fill these units came from the Delta. This division attacked the Catholic village of Binh Gia, 40 miles east of Saigon, on 28 December. In the course of battle it ambushed and virtually destroyed the 33d Ranger Battalion and the 4th Marine Battalion. VC troops remained on the field of battle for four days rather than following their usual hit-and-run tactic.

During the same month, regular units of the North Vietnamese Army (NVA) were en route to join the battle in South Vietnam. The enemy had clearly decided—following General Giap's adaptation from Mao's earlier formulation of doctrine—to move from guerrilla warfare to a more conventionally organized general offensive. Hanoi had determined that the time was ripe to begin the final and decisive "mobile" phase of the war, which would lead to the collapse of the government and a complete Communist victory. This, unmistakably, is the significance of the enemy decisions in 1964 to begin to form Viet Cong divisions and to start the southward deployment of regular NVA forces.

The enemy's assessment was based on political as well as military evidence. During 1964 political infrastructure was installed in hamlets previously controlled by the government and existing infrastructure was greatly strengthened. Capitalizing on disorder and demoralization in the government, the enemy revitalized his Administrative Liberation Associations at hamlet and village level and renamed them Autonomous Administrative Committees. As an example of this Communist political resurgence, a captured document indicated that the Viet Cong province chief in Tay Ninh Province reported to his superiors in 1964 that 46 of the 48 villages in the province had been satisfactorily organized from both a political and military standpoint.

This is a somber, though realistic, background against which to describe U.S. efforts to assist the South Vietnamese during 1964.

In June General Harkins was reassigned and I assumed command. I believed from the beginning that the key to the effectiveness of the Vietnamese Army lay in improving leadership at all levels and in improving the training of the small infantry units, and in providing them with adequate weapons and equipment. Programs to accomplish this objective were devised and initiated at all levels. However, the modernization of equipment involved long leadtimes and high costs. Advisors were instructed to concentrate on these basic matters and also to do their utmost to encourage commanders of Vietnamese forces to move back into the countryside to patrol, to attack, and to regain the initiative.

To help strengthen the military province and district chiefs in their roles as sector and subsector military commanders, we also decided to expand the U.S. advisory effort to district level and to increase the number of advisors at province level. This step was first started in key provinces around Saigon and gradually expanded to include most of the areas in which government organization existed.

During the year, the U.S. Army's 5th Special Forces Group was deployed to Vietnam in order to recruit and train irregular forces for the defense of border areas. A number of fortified camps and patrol bases were organized amongst the Montagnard populated areas of the Central Highlands.

This effort and the Special Forces' influence among the Montagnard tribes probably averted a massive defection from the government of Vietnam in September of 1964 when a serious uprising occurred.

As U.S. strength and activities increased, we had determined in May to combine the U.S. MAAG and MACV. Our growing support organization was thus combined with our advisory effort under unified direction.

At the beginning of 1964 the U.S. had 388 aircraft in Vietnam, including 248 helicopters, too few to accommodate the expanding advisory effort and increased Vietnamese Army operations. Over the year this inventory gradually grew to 561, including 327 helicopters. This made it possible to place a U.S. Army aviation company or U.S. Marine Corps aviation squadron in support of each Vietnamese Army division, with additional aviation supporting each corps. Part of the increase in U.S. jet aircraft was directly attributable to our concern arising from the incidents in the Tonkin Gulf in early August.

The Tonkin Gulf incidents and the U.S. response in early August represented a crucial psychological turning point in the course of the Vietnam War. The fleeting engagements at sea and the retaliatory strikes against the North Vietnamese coast marked the first direct confrontation between North Vietnamese and U.S. forces. The naval and air forces involved were under the operational control of CINCPAC. The decisions taken were at the national level on the basis of CINCPAC recommendations. Our actions to protect the major air bases at Bien Hoa and Da Nang from possible North Vietnamese attacks were rapid and positive.

The psychological impact of these events upon everyone was tremendous. It gave us clear indication of the aggressive intentions of Hanoi; it crystallized allied determination and resolve; and it provided solid evidence of our resolute support to the South Vietnamese.

By late summer it was also evident that the Viet Cong posed an immediate threat to Saigon. They were extremely active in the critical provinces around the capital city and had even penetrated in strength into Gia Dinh Province, which constitutes the immediate environs of Saigon. It was obvious to all of us that the seat of government had to be held at all costs.

Political instability in the Saigon government notwithstanding, we urged upon the South Vietnamese government a coordinated political-military pacification effort radiating outward from Saigon. A combined U.S.-Vietnamese group, embracing a broad array of government ministries, planned this operation. Named HOP TAC, it was launched in September. Frankly, it did not accomplish all that we had hoped it would. Even though the concept was sound, the relative strengths were too disparate, governmental coordination too demanding under the circumstances, and execution of the plan too weak. However, I believe that HOP TAC—in spite of its many shortcomings—probably saved Saigon from enemy control.

With the appearance of the Viet Cong 9th Division on the battlefield of Binh Gia and North Vietnamese regulars moving toward South Vietnam, 1964 ended on a clearly ominous note.

OBSERVATIONS—1964

Viet Cong Operations

A grasp of enemy organization and doctrine is essential to an understanding of events as they unfolded in Vietnam during 1964. Basically, the Communist organization featured parallel and mutually supporting military and political structures, which were controlled by the overarching Communist Party. Appendix A discusses this organization in greater detail.

The military side of this integrated political-military structure featured village and hamlet guerrilla units and part-time self-defense forces. The part-time forces, under the direction of lower level political cells in their communities, worked to insure adequate control over the local population and to enlist its active support. Local force companies were organized in districts and local force battalions were formed at province level. These military units protected the local guerrillas and assisted them in their operations against government units. Also at the regional (inter-province) level, main force battalions, regiments, and later, divisions, were created. Their mission was initially to assist local forces; eventually they were to conduct large-scale mobile operations against the government and allied forces. Finally, commencing in late 1964, numerous elements of the North Vietnamese Army started their southward movement to augment and strengthen these main and local force groups.

The Communists appreciated the great importance of gaining both political and military dominance in an area. They demonstrated a keen understanding of the interaction between the two. Once they were organized politically, areas were used as lucrative recruiting sources. Conversely, political organizing went forward quickly in regions where there were successful enemy military operations.

The political and military substructures interfaced in other ways. When government forces threatened local guerrillas or political units (the two events usually occurred simultaneously), the hamlet and village party organizations requested military assistance from the district or province echelons. If the province forces proved inadequate, main forces would be brought in to meet the government threat and to restore an environment where Communist recruiting and organizational efforts could proceed.

The local VC-NLF organizations at each echelon provided numerous services for main force units in their areas. These included providing intelligence, food and shelter, guides, couriers, and liaison agents. Transient main force units thereby obtained the advantages of all the local knowledge available to the indigenous forces. Local guerrillas and civilian labor also built fortifications, transported arms and ammunition, furnished aid stations, evacuated wounded, and collected money for the larger main forces.

This system of mutual support and reinforcement flourished following the assassination of President Diem, reaching its peak effectiveness in 1964 and 1965. However, as the enemy's numbers and operations dramatically increased, the logistical burden outstripped local capability and the Viet Cong became increasingly dependent upon an extensive formal North Vietnamese logistical system oriented upon the infiltration routes by sea and through Laos and Cambodia.

Rearming the Viet Cong

In 1964 the enemy began to convert from weapons of various calibers and origins to a standard family of small arms using a single caliber (7.62-mm). Prior to this time, the VC were armed with weapons captured from government forces and by World War II stocks remaining at the close of the Indochina War. Combat itself was a lucrative source; the Viet Cong were consistently capturing more weapons on the battlefield than they lost.

Units were rearmed according to a rough criterion of combat priority: main force units first, local units next, and guerrillas last.

The most important of the new weapons was the Soviet assault rifle, the AK–47. In the early days of the conversion most of the AK–47's were Chinese copies of the Soviet model. In addition to this excellent automatic rifle, the rearmament included 7.62-mm machine guns, an excellent rocket launcher firing a shaped charge (the RPG–2), 82-mm Soviet and Chinese mortars, and 57- and 75-mm recoilless rifles (mostly manufactured in China). Progressively larger and more modern weapons—including heavy mortars, rockets, and antiaircraft weapons—followed the initial infusions.

Rearmament of the Viet Cong 9th Division in the early fall of 1964 provides a typical example of the upgrading process. The division moved from War Zones C and D to Xuyen Moc in eastern Phuoc Tuy Province where it rendezvoused with seaborne deliveries of the new family of light infantry weapons. After familiarization training on the weapons, the division was first committed in the December attack on Binh Gia.

The most economical and direct route of supply for Viet Cong forces was by sea to points on the long, lightly-guarded coast. The major points of entry were the tip of the Cau Mau Peninsula, the swamps of Kien Hoa Province in the northern part of the Mekong Delta, the eastern part of Phuoc Tuy Province near Xuyen Moc, the coastal areas of Khanh Hoa and Phu Yen Province near Vung Ro Bay, the Chu Lai area of northern Quang Ngai, and all along the infamous "Street Without Joy," a portion of Highway 1, in Thua Thien and Quang Tri Provinces.

Binh Dinh Crisis

Events in Binh Dinh Province in November 1964 dramatized the interrelationship of the main forces, regional forces, and guerrillas. Furthermore, they provided clear evidence of what the enemy's powerful combination of better arms, larger units, and skillful and energetic political terrorism could produce if it was not checked.

Prior to the crisis I had persuaded the ARVN leaders to decentralize control of their units to province and district chiefs. We also persuaded them that saturation patrolling in their areas offered the best prospects of increasing local security so essential for pacification. The enemy responded to the initial success of this tactic by requesting main force reinforcements. These arrived in November when two VC regiments mounted a general offensive in the province, defeating the ARVN, Regional Force, and Popular Force units there and driving them into fortified camps. This created the ideal climate for the VC to strengthen their infrastructure, to recruit local guerrillas, and to organize larger military formations in this crucial coastal province.

We had to take action, using our meager resources, to salvage this chaotic situation. I decided to request temporary deployment from Okinawa to Binh Dinh of a U.S. Army Special Forces ("Green Berets") "B" Detachment with several subordinate "A" Detachments. These Special Forces teams were distributed in key district towns along the coast to work with the local Regional and Popular Forces. Despite formidable handicaps, the Special Forces teams were able to rally the remnants of these forces and to restore their morale. After a short period of training and resupply these Regional and Popular Forces took the field once more—re-establishing islands of government control which still existed when U.S. and Free World Forces entered the area in 1966 and 1967.

South Vietnamese Organization and Equipment

The country was divided into four corps tactical zones, each under a corps commander. The I Corps encompassed the northern five provinces, the II Corps the bulk of the central region, the III Corps generally the provinces surrounding Saigon, and the IV Corps the Mekong Delta. Divisions and separate regiments normally operated under corps control, as did the Ranger battalions, which served as a corps reserve. An airborne brigade and several

Marine battalions constituted the general reserve under the direct control of the Vietnamese Joint General Staff.

Regular Vietnamese forces were equipped with standard U.S. World War II weapons, such as the M1 rifle, the Browning automatic rifle, and the Browning light machine gun. The Regional and Popular Forces were more lightly armed, principally with the semiautomatic U.S. carbine.

U.S. Organization

In the months prior to General Harkins' departure in June, I had strongly encouraged consolidation of the Military Assistance Advisory Group and the Military Assistance Command. In my view this change would eliminate duplication, facilitate coordination, economize on personnel, and simplify the coordination and performance of advisory efforts with the Vietnamese. This was accomplished in May, shortly before my assumption of command. However, I quickly realized that although the formal organizational problem was solved, the problem of refining and preparing the new command for its inevitable future challenges still lay ahead.

One such refinement occurred in late 1964. We responded to the heightened emphasis on pacification by creating a special staff agency, entitled the Revolutionary Development Division, within MACV headquarters. This new division was to coordinate the military support of the pacification program directed by the Embassy. As the pacification effort expanded and assumed increased importance, a general officer was assigned to head this new staff division.

The Mission Council

In July 1964 the senior officials of the civil and military elements of the U.S. Mission in Saigon began to meet formally in a body known as the Mission Council. The council was a policy-formulating body, chaired by Ambassador Taylor, who retained overall responsibility for all U.S. activities in Vietnam. The council provided a mechanism for high level coordination and discussion of the increasingly complex multi-agency activities in Vietnam. Meetings of the group enabled the Ambassador to hear frank and complete discussion of proposals and problems across the entire range of functional activities. New programs were often first proposed to Vietnamese government officials when they met periodically with the Mission Council. As the U.S. military commander, I provided the council with military advice relating to the development of mission policies and kept the other members of the council abreast of military developments and plans. Other members of the Mission Council included the chiefs of the economic and political sections in the Embassy, the country directors of the U.S. Agency for International Development and the U.S. Information Service, and the Special Assistant to the Ambassador.

HOP TAC

I have already noted the challenging and crucial nature of the HOP TAC operation around Saigon in 1964. It required the most extensive and meticulous coordination between agencies of both governments performing military, economic, political, and social functions.

In HOP TAC, government control was to be pushed outward from the capital until the nearby six provinces (Gia Dinh, Bien Hoa, Binh Duong, Hau Nghia, Long An, and Phuoc Tuy) were firmly under government influence. Operations were directed toward eliminating Viet Cong influence and establishing security for the population. Once a modicum of security was guaranteed, I hoped the joint efforts of the ministries and agencies of our governments could provide the populace of the HOP TAC area with a standard of living perceptibly higher than the VC could reasonably provide. To this end, we programmed resources to build schools, dispensaries, and other community development projects.

The HOP TAC plan envisaged a sequence of operations conducted throughout four roughly concentric lettered zones (A, B, C, D) emanating from the Saigon-Cholon hub. Zone A, predominantly urban and closest to the center, would be secured while Zone B, further out, was being cleared. Simultaneously, search and destroy operations would be conducted in the two outermost zones, C and D. As military operations progressively cleared each zone, the local defense forces—the Regional and Popular Forces, the National Police, and the hamlet militia—were to move in, root out the infrastructure, and provide local continuing security. Behind the outer ring of Vietnamese Army operations and an inner ring of security provided by the Regional and Popular Forces, civilian officials were to direct the needed community projects.

Coordination of the civilian and military agencies in HOP TAC was the task of a special national control group which included officials of the III Corps, the Capital Military District, the commander of the Rung Sat Special Zone (a VC-infested area of swamps southeast of Saigon), and representatives of the Ministry of Interior, the National Police, and the Vietnamese Central Intelligence Organization, along with their U.S. counterparts. During the planning and execution phases we continually stressed (to Vietnamese and U.S. alike) that the U.S. civilian and military role was solely to advise and provide commodity support. The Vietnamese government had control of the program.

The Vietnamese airborne and Marine brigades and the ARVN 5th Division were the clearing forces. I induced the Vietnamese to move their 25th Division (less one of its regiments) south from the II Corps zone to provide security in Hau Nghia Province where the VC had almost complete control. I also suggested that Long An Province be shifted from IV Corps to III Corps to facilitate coordination of military and civic operations near the Capital Military District.

HOP TAC, which lasted from September until mid-1965, never achieved the objective we envisioned—true pacification failed to materialize. In my view, there were three prime causes for this failure. First, there were simply not enough competent police and local forces to keep pace with the security mission. Once Vietnamese Army units cleared an area, immediate security operations were essential to prevent the reemergence of the VC infrastructure and the re-creation of a political base. The police lacked the necessary numbers of trained units, and the VC quickly appeared from hiding to reassert their authority.

Secondly, the civilian agencies, in the main, failed to produce the schools, dispensaries, and other facilities promised by the Vietnamese Army units as they cleared an area. This failure reflected an inability to coordinate and implement plans and projects among ministries, rather than a lack of willingness to produce. To these basic technical problems were added the continuing changes of government. This created a paralyzing sense of insecurity among officials charged with making crucial decisions throughout the operation. New leaders, unfamiliar with HOP TAC, were suspicious, believing it to be an American-dominated and sponsored program.

Finally, the performance of the Vietnamese Army was disappointing. Some senior leaders were not aggressive, preferring to conduct static defensive operations instead of the more effective (and difficult) offensive operations required to clear and hold an insurgency-ridden area successfully. Troop shortages, aggravated by an unrealistic prohibition against recruiting men under age 20, further hamstrung ARVN activities. Even an increased desertion rate became a problem in the newly-relocated Vietnamese 25th Division. Many soldiers wanted to rejoin their families in the II Corps area where the division had long been stationed and from whence most of the soldiers had been recruited. Transfers and the movement of dependent families eventually reduced the magnitude of this problem, but in the future attempts were made to avoid moving ARVN divisions great distances from their home bases. When reinforcements were called for, we tried to use the Vietnamese general reserve—airborne and Marine troops based near Saigon, or Ranger battalions stationed in each corps area.

Special Forces Operations

The mission of the 5th Special Forces Group (Airborne) was to advise and assist the Vietnamese government in the organization, training, equipping, and employment of the Civilian Irregular Defense Group forces.

The first Civilian Irregular Defense Group camp had been built near Ban Me Thuot in 1961. At the beginning of 1964, there were 25 of these border camps, a figure which would double by the end of the year. This network of strategically located fortified camps, each with an airstrip, proved invaluable reconnaissance and fire support bases for Vietnamese forces fighting the enemy main forces in the remote border areas.

Operational Terminology

In 1964 we adopted three terms to describe the basic missions performed by the Vietnamese military forces. These terms were intended to be doctrinal teaching points—concise, standard expressions to describe military operations and to relate them to the pacification effort.

A balance between each of these three types of operations was essential, but emphasis would shift from one type of operation to another depending upon enemy intelligence, the availability and training of troops, support available (such as helicopters), weather, and terrain.

The first operational term was "search and destroy." Operations of this type were designed to find, fix in place, fight, and destroy (or neutralize) enemy forces and their base areas and supply caches. This was essentially the traditional attack mission of the infantry.

The second term was "clearing operations." The objective of a "clearing operation" was to drive large enemy units out of a populated area so that pacification efforts could proceed. The "cleared" areas were not completely secure, for the local guerrilla threat persisted, but "clearing" removed the graver threat to pacification posed by large enemy main force units. Frequently "clearing operations" would be reported as "search and destroy" and many could properly be so classified.

The third term was "securing operations." These operations were designed to protect pacification teams, to attack (and eliminate) local guerrilla units, and to uproot enemy political infrastructure in areas undergoing pacification. This type of operation logically followed on the heels of clearing operations and was conducted by the Regional and Popular Forces and the police.

The urgent requirement for such operational terminology became evident during the preliminary planning for HOP TAC. We needed a set of clear mission definitions so that all the forces involved would understand their tasks and the differences between various tasks. The tasks were familiar military ones. However, the usual military terminology was unfamiliar to many of the civilians in HOP TAC. Thus the terms served as instructional tools or teaching points for these civilians and standardized operational terminology in the Vietnamese Army and the Regional and Popular Forces.

Unfortunately, the term "search and destroy operations" was distorted in later years. Somehow, it was equated in the public mind with aimless searches in the jungle and the destruction of property. Because of this misunderstanding, the term "search and destroy" was eventually dropped and more conventional terms were used to report the same type operation. These substitute terms were: combat or offensive sweep, reconnaissance in force, and spoiling attack.

Regardless of what offensive operations were called, we had learned from our experience in Binh Dinh and several other places that we had to take the fight to the enemy if pacification was ever to succeed. In particular, we at least had to neutralize the enemy's main forces—to take them off the backs of the local security troops. Once we had located the enemy we wanted to attack him by fire and maneuver. Further, we realized that eventually we had to locate and destroy his base areas and supply caches. These were formidable tasks that in the main would have to await the availability of stronger and more professional forces led by aggressive commanders.

CHRONOLOGY OF MAJOR EVENTS—1964

January

On 2 January a Vietnamese Army force in the Delta region seized a huge cache of Communist Chinese-manufactured equipment including mortars, 300,000 rounds of small arms ammunition, and recoilless rifle ammunition.

On 18 January 115 helicopters—the largest airlift of the war—carried 1,100 Vietnamese troops into the critical War Zone D region north of Bien Hoa. Despite the magnitude of this action, no enemy contact was made and the operation produced no significant tactical results.

On 27 January I assumed duties as Deputy Commander, United States Military Assistance Command, Vietnam.

In late January there were persistent rumors of impending political upheaval. These reports were borne out when on 30 January, General Khanh ousted the government of General Minh.

February

The modest tactical successes achieved in January were offset by a wave of Viet Cong terrorism and victories. Violence first erupted in the vicinity of Kontum City on 3 February when enemy forces attacked the compound of the U.S. Military Assistance Advisory Group. During the period 3–6 February Viet Cong forces launched a major offensive in Tay Ninh Province and in the Mekong Delta. In both areas, government forces suffered heavy casualties.

On 7 February the enemy initiated a series of bombing attacks in Saigon. Three U.S. personnel were killed and 50 wounded by a Viet Cong bomb explosion in the Capital-Kinh Do Theater at a time when it was occupied primarily by American personnel and their dependents.

Continuing his reorganization of the government, General Khanh assumed control of the nation by naming himself Premier and appointing General Minh as Chief of State on 10 February.

March

On 3 and 4 March Vietnamese forces achieved an encouraging victory. Vietnamese airborne and mechanized troops operating in the Plain of Reeds along the Cambodian border killed over 100 and captured 300 of the enemy. In the course of mop-up operations, Vietnamese units inadvertently intruded into Cambodia in the vicinity of the village of Chantrea, precipitating a sharp exchange of diplomatic notes with that nation.

In an effort to consolidate his political control, General Khanh, on 6 March, replaced three of the incumbent South Vietnamese Army corps commanders and five of the nine division commanders. This purge of the military high command was followed by the wholesale replacement of province and district chiefs over the next several months. Due to the weakness of the central government, these corps commanders had enjoyed autonomy approaching that of the traditional "war lord." They were not only responsible for military operations within their corps areas but also had been assigned the additional role of the so-called "government delegate," which embraced civil and administrative powers. Each time the command structure of the Vietnamese Army was altered by the power struggle in Saigon, mass changes in provincial and district leadership occurred automatically. As much as any other factor, this turbulence in the administrative structure of the nation contributed to the deterioration of the government's credibility and concurrently increased the prestige and power of the enemy's position among the people.

In contradiction to the chaotic state of the nation's political affairs, the Vietnamese Army in the Plain of Reeds provided a second gratifying victory over the enemy on 23 March, trapping a Viet Cong battalion in a fortified village and killing 120 of the enemy.

Although the general morale and efficiency of the Vietnamese Armed Forces was poor, there were isolated examples of great valor and aggressiveness on the part of some commanders. By and large, the airborne and Marine troops, the armored units, and some of the Ranger battalions acquitted themselves well. These examples were enough to confirm our conviction that the major problem within the armed forces was poor leadership. This leadership problem started with the central government and permeated the entire civil and military system.

April

The growing aggressiveness of the enemy around the capital city and indications of a possible counter-coup prompted General Khanh on 7 April to create a special military zone around Saigon.

Less than a week later, the district capital of Kien Long in the southern tip of the Mekong Delta was overrun by the enemy. Apart from the great concern which resulted from the loss of a major political center, the Vietnamese Army suffered over 300 killed while 200 civilians also were killed or wounded.

May

On 2 May a Viet Cong underwater demolition team sank the helicopter-carrying USNS *Card* while it was at berth in the port of Saigon. Terrorism continued unabated, including an abortive Viet Cong attempt to mine a bridge along Secretary of Defense Robert S. McNamara's route into Saigon on the 10th.

A major reorganization of the U.S. command took place on 15 May. The Military Assistance Advisory Group was abolished and its functions integrated with the MACV structure, facilitating and simplifying coordination, eliminating duplication of effort, and achieving a significant economy in U.S. personnel.

June

As General Harkins departed Vietnam on 20 June, I assumed command of USMACV. Ambassador Lodge, who resigned on 23 June, was replaced by General Maxwell D. Taylor early in July. Mr. U. Alexis Johnson was appointed as the Deputy Ambassador.

Two successful Vietnamese operations were conducted on the 24th and 25th. In the first, Vietnamese forces again scored a victory over the enemy in the Plain of Reeds, killing 99 of the Viet Cong. A day later, the Vietnamese Army attacked a Viet Cong training camp in Quang Ngai Province and killed 50 of the enemy.

June also marked the beginning of a growing tide of Free World assistance to the Republic of Vietnam. On 29 June a New Zealand Army Engineer detachment arrived to assist government officials in developing priority civic action projects.

July

Viet Cong operations against the relatively isolated Special Forces camps located along the borders of Vietnam intensified during July. Attacking boldly, the enemy imposed increasing losses on the South Vietnamese. On 4 July an enemy force of regimental size overran the Special Forces camp at Polei Krong in Pleiku Province, killing 50 Civilian Irregular Defense Group troops. Two days later, the enemy attacked and partially overran the Nam Dong Special Forces camp in the northern part of the nation, killing 55 South Vietnamese, two U.S. Special Forces soldiers, and one Australian advisor.

It was also during this month that we received the first tentative reports of some type of participation by the North Vietnamese Army in Viet Cong operations. The participation appeared to be in the form of individual officers or cadre serving with Viet Cong units.

On 27 July we announced that several thousand additional military advisors would be sent to Vietnam. Our plan was to strengthen our advisory effort at province level and to expand it to the district level.

August

One of the crucial months of the year, August marked the first open confrontation between North Vietnamese and United States forces. On 2 August North Vietnamese naval forces attacked the U.S. Navy Destroyer *Maddox* in the Tonkin Gulf, followed by a second attack on 4 August against the *Maddox* and the U.S. destroyer *C. Turner Joy*. The American response to these unprovoked attacks was prompt and determined:

aircraft from U.S. carriers in the Tonkin Gulf on the following day struck PT boat bases and fuel storage areas along the coast of North Vietnam.

In the wake of these actions, the U.S. Congress on 7 August adopted a Joint Resolution which affirmed that the United States would support the Republic of Vietnam and "take all necessary measures to repel any armed attack against the forces of the United States."

As U.S. involvement in the international aspects of the struggle expanded, the government of Vietnam underwent another traumatic change in political leadership. General Khanh removed General Minh as the Chief of State and assumed the role of President on 16 August. Beset with factionalism and an internal power struggle, he resigned his position ten days later. On the 27th, a military triumvirate was established, consisting of General Khanh, General Minh, and Maj. Gen. Tran Thien Khiem. The triumvirate two days later appointed Dr. Nguyen Xuan Oanh as Premier.

Against the possibility of North Vietnamese retaliatory air raids on U.S. and Vietnamese bases, U.S. tactical aircraft arrived in Vietnam in mid-August. By the end of the month, ten RF–101 jet reconnaissance planes and six F–102 jet air defense interceptors were located at Da Nang and one squadron of B–57 "Canberra" bombers at Bien Hoa. Plans were made to dispatch two Marine Corps Hawk antiaircraft missile batteries to the vicinity of Da Nang.

September

The military triumvirate soon proved ineffective, and on 3 September it was replaced by a 15-man committee which was to elect a temporary Chief of State and Prime Minister.

The problems of establishing a viable governing organization were complicated by growing religious strife throughout the nation. Riots, self-immolations, and protest parades became common, indicative of a deep-seated resentment and bitterness existing among the various religious orders. On 6 September 150,000 Buddhists paraded in Saigon at a funeral for victims of a Buddhist-Catholic riot.

The decisions of the 15-man leadership committee were made known on 8 September. General Khanh became Premier with General Minh designated as Chairman of the Leadership Committee. However, the decisions of the committee failed to end the power struggle; within less than a week dissident Army officers staged an abortive coup. General Khanh reacted by arresting the leaders, including Maj. Gen. Duong Van Duc, Brig. Gen. Lam Van Phat, and the head of the influential Vietnamese Worker's Confederation, Tran Qua Buu.

On the international scene, U.S. and North Vietnamese relations further deteriorated as a result of a second series of torpedo-boat attacks against the U.S. destroyers *Edwards* and *Morton* on 18 September.

During the remainder of the month, a new and serious problem for the government of Vietnam emerged. Under the banner of the United Front for the Struggle of Oppressed Races (FULRO), U.S.-trained Montagnard irregular troops staged a major uprising in the Central Highlands and marched on the city of Ban Me Thuot with the objective of creating an autonomous Montagnard state. U.S. officials attempted to mediate the dispute but achieved only limited success. On 27 September U.S. Special Forces and helicopters terminated the active phase of the rebellion when they successfully rescued the district chief, over 60 other Vietnamese hostages, and a number of hostages held by FULRO troops in the Special Forces camp at Bon Sar Pa in Quang Duc Province.

October

During the first week of the month, rioting and further disorders again erupted in Saigon. It was significant that these disturbances were not motivated by religious differences but were organized by labor movements within the city.

On 11 October three Viet Cong battalions engaged Vietnamese Army forces along Highway 1 in Tay Ninh Province and inflicted heavy casualties on the government units. A week later, government troops partially compensated for this defeat by destroying 123 of the enemy along the border between Ba Xuyen and Bac Lieu Provinces.

It appeared that a major step toward establishing governmental stability had occurred on 20 October when a new Vietnamese constitution was adopted and the Khanh government gave way to civilian rule. On 24 October Phan Khac Suu was chosen to become the Chief of State by the Vietnamese National High Council and within a week had designated Tran Van Huong as Premier. The High Council confirmed Huong's appointment on 31 October.

Throughout the month, elements of the 1,300-man 5th U.S. Special Forces Group arrived in Vietnam with the mission of assisting the Vietnamese government in developing its Civilian Irregular Defense Group program in remote border areas.

November

On 1 November the enemy mortared the major U.S. air base at Bien Hoa, killing two U.S. and four Vietnamese soldiers.

Enemy action throughout the month centered on Binh Dinh Province where two enemy regiments mounted a sustained and highly effective offensive throughout that heavily populated central coastal province. In a series of attacks and ambushes, government forces in the area were either overrun, destroyed, or driven back into their fortified camps. Control over the countryside was lost and military initiative passed to the enemy. By the end of the month, most of this second largest province in Vietnam was under the domination of the Viet Cong, and government presence was limited to a few district towns and the capital city of Qui Nhon.

December

The apparent progress achieved in the political situation in October and November was shown by December to be illusory. Internal wrangling and General Khanh's reluctance to provide full support to the Prime Minister drastically reduced the ability of the government to cope with its multitudinous problems.

On 5 December Air Vice Marshal Nguyen Cao Ky, then commanding the Vietnamese Air Force, issued an ultimatum to General Khanh to support Prime Minister Huong or to face removal. After a long debate and much maneuvering, the High National Council was dissolved on 20 December in another bloodless coup.

American personnel again became the target of terrorism on Christmas Eve when, in Saigon, the Viet Cong detonated a 300-pound explosive charge under the U.S. Bachelor Officers' Quarters in the Brink Hotel. Two Americans were killed and over 100 wounded.

On 28 December the ARVN 21st Division in Ba Xuyen Province attacked three Viet Cong battalions, killing 87 and making the largest capture of enemy weapons in the war up to that point, including two 75-mm recoilless rifles and four .50-caliber antiaircraft machine guns. However, on this same day, the VC 9th Division with two regiments seized the Catholic village of Binh Gia. Over the next four days the enemy ambushed and virtually destroyed the Vietnamese 33d Ranger Battalion and the 4th Marine Battalion and inflicted heavy casualties on other relieving armored and mechanized forces. This was the first time that enemy forces remained on the battlefield and met government forces in sustained combat. The battle was regarded as a major event in the war by both contestants. To the enemy, it marked the beginning of the classic and final "mobile" phase of the war. To the South Vietnamese government, it meant the beginning of an intensive military challenge which the Vietnamese government could not meet within its own resources.

To add to the foreboding which accompanied the close of the year, reports were received that at least three regular North Vietnamese regiments—the 95th, 32d, and 101st—had left their bases in North Vietnam and were moving south for possible commitment in South Vietnam.

At the end of the year, U.S. military strength in Vietnam stood at about 23,000. Infiltration from North Vietnam during the year totalled nearly 12,500, a significant increase over the previous year.

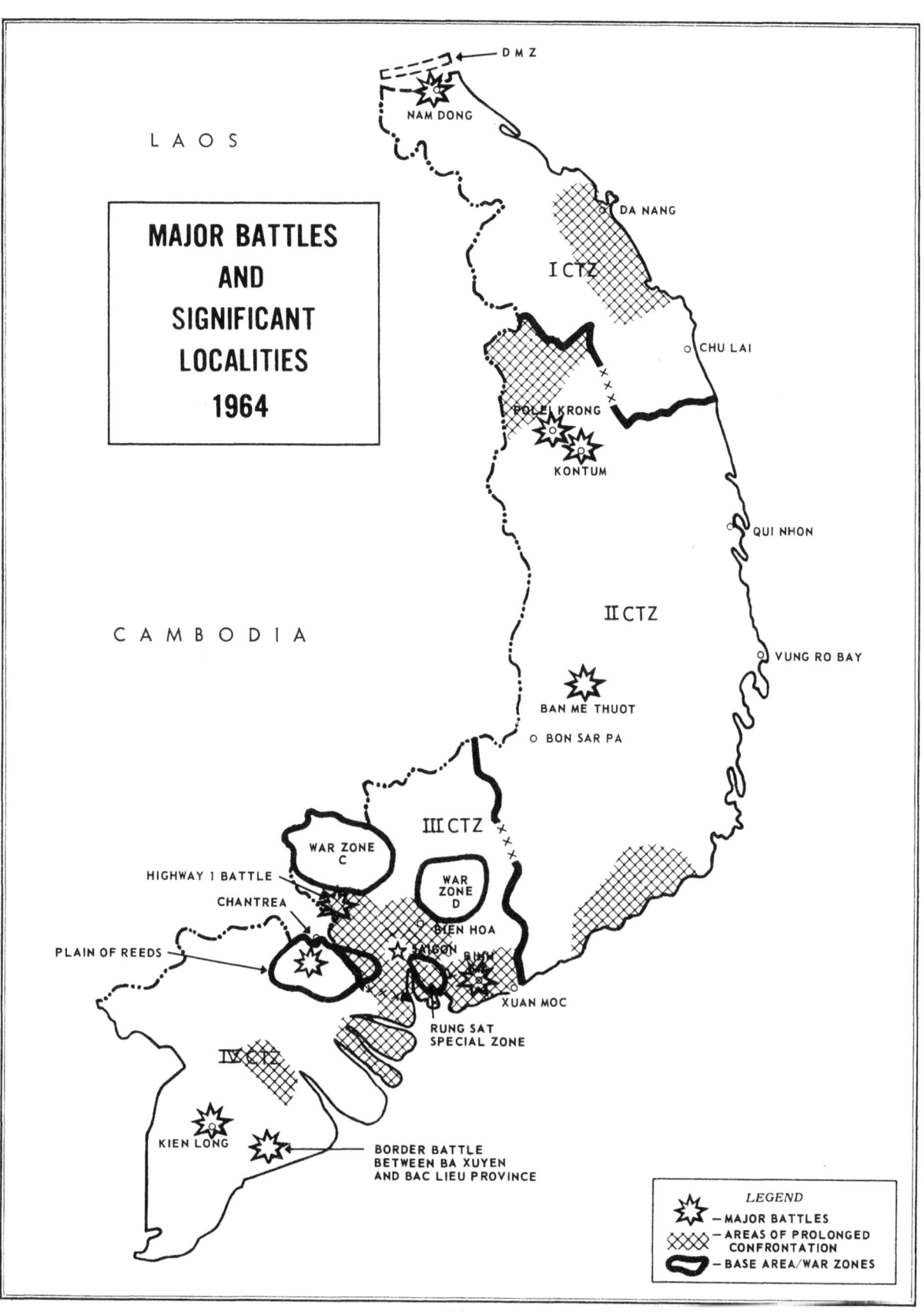

Chapter III
THE YEAR OF MILITARY COMMITMENT—1965

OVERVIEW

The year 1965 was one of momentous decisions and of commitment. It started on an uneasy note. In the closing days of 1964, 40 miles east of Saigon, the enemy launched the first division-sized attack against the South Vietnamese Army. The battle carried over into 1965. We now believe that this battle at Binh Gia—described in the preceding chapter—was regarded by the High Command in Hanoi, and in particular by General Vo Nguyen Giap, North Vietnam's Defense Minister and commander of North Vietnamese Armed Forces, as the beginning of the final phase of the war. At the same time, the first commitment of regular North Vietnamese Army Forces had taken place near Dak To in the Central Highlands north of Kontum. Capitalizing on the political disorder which afflicted the Saigon government, upon the weakness of government administration throughout the country, and upon deteriorating morale in the Vietnamese Armed Forces, the North Vietnamese and their southern affiliates were moving in for the kill. Additional North Vietnamese forces were on the move south through Laos. We did not believe that the armed forces of South Vietnam could contain this expanding enemy military force.

The government of Vietnam had been seriously weakened by a series of coups and upheavals following the 1963 overthrow of President Diem. These upheavals continued throughout the first half of 1965. The weakness of the government stemmed in part from the fact that since 1962 there had been over 6,000 assassinations and 30,000 kidnappings among the civilian population. A total of 436 government officials had been assassinated and an additional 1,131 had been kidnapped in 1964 alone. The overthrow of President Diem had left the country without a constitution and without the institutions of legal government. The pacification of the countryside had been nearly stopped and the enemy was everywhere resurgent. We now know that decisions were taken in mid-1964 in Hanoi to employ large elements of the North Vietnamese Home Army to hasten the process of total Communist victory.

Flushed with success, the Lao Dong Party in Hanoi and its South Vietnamese regional branch—the People's Revolutionary Party—moved quickly in 1964 and 1965 to establish a political structure which could seize the reins of power upon the collapse of the South Vietnamese government. At hamlet and village level this shadow government consisted of Autonomous Administrative Committees supervised and directed by the Communist People's Revolutionary Party. In its weakened condition and with its fragmented organization, the South Vietnamese government could not cope successfully with this political offensive. By mid-1965 the government controlled the cities and major towns while the enemy controlled most of the countryside.

In February, after a number of terrorist attacks against Vietnamese and U.S. installations, and with North Vietnamese regular army units appearing on southern battlefields in increasing numbers, the U.S. began a limited bombardment of North Vietnam by air and naval forces. This bombardment was under CINCPAC control. My interest in the bombing of North Vietnam was centered in the destruction of war-supporting activities which would assist us directly in the prosecution of the ground battle in the south. In March at Da Nang, and near Saigon in May, the U.S. deployed limited numbers of Marines, Army airborne troops, and Hawk surface-to-air missiles, to defend our airbases against possible enemy retaliation prompted by our bombing of North Vietnam.

Earlier, in January, I had requested and received authority to conduct jet air strikes to support Vietnamese troops under emergency conditions. I was also granted authority to employ U.S. jets to strike targets in remote areas which could not be attacked effectively by the Vietnamese Air Force. The first jet strike against enemy forces took place on 19 February. Later in the same month we used jet strikes to help extract a Vietnamese force surrounded by the enemy. In this instance, aerial firepower helped turn a potential disaster into a victory.

But, while tactical jet aircraft were indispensable for close support, they could neither deliver sufficient numbers of large bombs in sudden surprise attacks nor cover large enough areas at one time. However, the Strategic Air Command's big B–52 bombers could do both. Upon my request, B–52's based on Guam were employed for the first time on 18 June to strike a well-entrenched enemy base in War Zone D, 40 miles northeast of Saigon. The results were so impressive that I began thereafter to request and employ B–52 strikes on a continuing basis.

Measures such as these made the insurgency more costly to the enemy but they were not sufficient to reverse the course of the war. By late spring of 1965 the South Vietnamese Army was losing almost one infantry battalion a week to enemy action. Additionally, the enemy was gaining control of at least one district capital town each week. It was my estimate that the government of Vietnam could not survive this mounting enemy military and political offensive for more than six months unless the United States chose to increase its military commitment. Substantial numbers of U.S. ground combat forces were required.

I realized, as did Ambassadors Taylor and Johnson, that the U.S. was faced with a momentous and far-reaching decision. In making my recommendations in the spring and early summer of 1965, as indeed in the case of later recommendations, I was mindful of the stated U.S. objective with respect to Vietnam: "To defeat aggression so that the people of South Vietnam will be free to shape their own destiny." It was my judgment that this end could not be achieved without the deployment of U.S. forces. With the concurrence of Ambassador Taylor, I so recommended.

Starting in July, substantial numbers of U.S. Army and Marine ground forces, together with supporting air and naval forces, began their deployment to South Vietnam and into adjacent waters. As these U.S. forces arrived, they were committed at the points of maximum peril on a "fire brigade" basis.

The evidence strongly suggests that in 1965 the enemy intended to cut South Vietnam in half along a line from Pleiku in the highlands to Qui Nhon on the central coast. The initial commitment of North Vietnamese Army forces was in this area and the threat was real and immediate. In order to counter this threat, the decision was made to deploy the 1st Cavalry Division (Airmobile) in the Central Highlands at An Khe, located between Pleiku and Qui Nhon. Its mission was, initially, to open—and to hold open—Route 19, the major artery along this same axis.

The South Vietnamese concurred in the decision to commit the 1st Cavalry Division in the Central

Highlands. In fact, they suggested that all deploying U.S. combat forces be concentrated in this comparatively remote area in order to minimize the impact upon the South Vietnamese economy and populace. I recognized the necessity to guard against unintended adverse effects stemming from the presence of U.S. combat forces, but I regarded it as essential to U.S.-Vietnamese success that U.S. units be available to reinforce and stiffen South Vietnamese forces in the critical areas of high population density. Consequently, I planned to build up U.S. forces in an arc around Saigon and in the populous coastal areas and not to restrict U.S. troops to the Central Highlands.

Although the U.S. military services had acquired considerable experience and knowledge about enemy tactics and techniques during the advisory years, it was not until 1965 that American troop units engaged the enemy on the ground in direct and close combat. It was to be expected that great significance would be attached to the outcome of the first battles. This was especially true since some of the first major battles would probably be fought by the newest Army division (1st Cavalry Division), embodying for the first time the full-blown airmobile concept.

The first major battle, Operation STARLIGHT, was fought by the Marines just south of Chu Lai in August. In this battle, the 3d Marine Division detected and engaged the Viet Cong 2d Regiment, which had exposed itself in the coastal lowlands of Quang Ngai Province. The Marines pinned this force against the sea and inflicted over 700 enemy casualties in a period of two days of intense man-to-man combat. The supreme confidence and élan with which the Marines entered battle was fully borne out by their valiant and professional performance.

In October the North Vietnamese concentrated three regiments of their best troops in the Central Highlands in an area between the Cambodian border and the Special Forces camp at Plei Me. After the enemy attacked Plei Me, I decided to commit the 1st Cavalry Division to its first combat, not without considerable anguish, for the troops and the airmobile concept were untested in battle, and no more inhospitable terrain could be imagined for a first test than the trackless jungle near Plei Me. Failure in our first big test would have sharp repercussions on our self-confidence and morale and on the American people. An American defeat would have been disastrous to South Vietnamese morale, undermining South Vietnamese confidence in our ability to defeat the Viet Cong.

The bloody and classic campaign of the Ia Drang Valley followed, allaying my concern, proving the soundness of our tactics and training, and demonstrating the valor of our troops. The ability of Americans to meet and defeat the best troops the enemy could put on the field of battle was once more demonstrated beyond any possible doubt, as was the validity of the Army's airmobile concept.

Although the first commitment of U.S. troops to combat drew the most attention in 1965, my concern as the commander was equally centered on the development of a logistical system to sustain and support the combat elements. As late as March 1965, no decisions had been taken on U.S. intervention with ground forces other than the limited Marine security force deployed to protect the Da Nang airfield. Consequently, there was no logistic system in being and no development of secure logistic bases except the totally inadequate installations associated with South Vietnamese forces. There were inadequate ports and airfields, no logistic organization, and no supply, transportation, or maintenance troops. Nonetheless, in the face of the grave tactical situation, I decided to accept combat troops as rapidly as they could be made available and to improvise their logistic support. That this calculated gamble paid off is a tribute to the imagination, determination, and energy of those officers and men in all the services who were charged with this almost impossible task.

The decision to enter the war with large U.S. forces having been taken, the strategy for their deployment was modified and refined as experience was gained and as the balance of forces changed in our favor. My initial concept visualized a three-phase sustained campaign.

The first phase involved arresting the losing trend, stifling the enemy initiative, protecting the deployment of our forces, and providing security to populated areas to the extent possible. I estimated that this phase would carry through to the end of 1965. In the second phase, U.S. and allied forces would mount major offensive actions to seize the initiative in order to destroy both the guerrilla and organized enemy forces, thus improving the security of the population. This phase would be concluded when the enemy had been worn down, thrown on the defensive, and driven well back from the major populated areas. The third phase would involve the final destruction of the enemy's guerrilla structure and main force units remaining in remote base areas.

A basic objective in each of the three phases was to cut off the enemy from his sources of supply—food, manpower, and munitions. Simultaneously, pressure would have to be maintained against all echelons of the enemy's organization—main forces, local forces, guerrillas, terrorist organizations, and political infrastructure.

As the deployment of major U.S. forces began, I made the decision to commit the Marine Corps units farthest north (in the zone of the South Vietnamese I Corps) and U.S. Army forces in the Central Highlands and adjacent coastal areas (II Corps) and in the area around Saigon (III Corps). These deployments met the immediate threat, permitted a simple command structure, and utilized fully the ability of the Marines to supply themselves over the beaches in an area of few ports and airfields. At this time we did not consider it necessary to commit U.S. troops to the zone of the IV Corps, in the Mekong Delta. One important consideration was that no North Vietnamese Army units had thus far been deployed that far south. Furthermore, Viet Cong operations in the Delta remained at a lower level of intensity and thus offered a lesser immediate threat. Therefore, we had reason to expect that the three ARVN divisions already in the Delta could hold their own and, hopefully, make some modest progress.

By year's end the emergency phase of the war was passing. Along with our allies, we had deployed to South Vietnam and positioned forces equivalent to more than five combat divisions. We had secured and started to build the necessary logistic and administrative bases. U.S. strength had risen to 184,000. Our presence had materially improved the security of a number of populated areas. Our ground attacks had blunted the enemy's initiative and had made incursions into his base areas. We had defeated a concentrated North Vietnamese effort to cut the country in two. Our air strikes had taken the war to the enemy base areas and, together with artillery and naval gunfire, had continually harassed him. We had developed confidence in our ability to operate successfully in the guerrilla environment of Vietnam and had gained the confidence of the South Vietnamese and earned in battle the respect of the enemy.

Although set back by our military commitment and determination, the enemy had redoubled his efforts. Over 26,000 North Vietnamese had infiltrated into South Vietnam during the year, including some eight North Vietnamese regiments. At year's end the enemy was infiltrating forces at the rate of 12 battalions a month. Although the North Vietnamese and Viet Cong had lost some 35,000 men killed and more than 6,000 captured during the year, their combined strength—including main forces, local forces, and guerrillas—had risen to 221,000 by the end of 1965.

OBSERVATIONS—1965

Command, Control, and Organization

Overall U.S. authority in South Vietnam was vested in the U.S. Ambassador. In 1965 the Embassy was directly responsible for the U.S. side of the pacification effort as well as for advising the Vietnamese government on political, economic, and social problems. Pacification activities were coordinated by the Mission Liaison Group. MACV provided appropriate support in many fields. As a practical matter, military operations were handled by MACV and political matters by the Embassy. When one impinged upon the other, decisions were made in close consultation, usually in the forum of the Mission Council. That this arrangement worked smoothly is a tribute to the succession of prominent and talented ambassadors who have been appointed to the post in Saigon.

As the U.S. force buildup in South Vietnam began in 1965, MACV continued to operate as a joint U.S. Military Command, directly subordinate to the Commander in Chief, Pacific (CINCPAC), Admiral U. S. Grant Sharp, with headquarters in Hawaii. As the U.S. commander in Vietnam, I now had two missions. I continued to be responsible for our advisory effort and for support of the armed forces of the Republic of Vietnam. In addition, as operational forces deployed, I became responsible for the combat operations of all American Armed Forces within South Vietnam.

In order to satisfy these dual responsibilities, I organized commands and duties as follows: I exercised operational control over Air Force, Marine, and Navy forces through their senior commanders. On the Army side, I established a new headquarters, U.S. Army, Vietnam (USARV), primarily for logistic, administrative, and support functions. I was Commander, USARV, but designated a Deputy USARV Commander to concentrate on these functions.

To insure that continuing detailed attention was focused on the advisory effort, I assigned my MACV Deputy—Lt. Gen. John L. Throckmorton, and later, Lt. Gen. John A. Heintges—to undertake, as his principal concern, the vital task of insuring continued proper attention to the advisory structure and to all forms of support for Vietnamese forces. At the same time, I continued to devote a large portion of my own time to consultation with my counterpart, General Cao Van Vien, Chief of the Vietnamese Joint General Staff, on these same important matters and to make frequent visits to the Vietnamese corps, divisions, and subordinate troop units, as well as to the paramilitary forces of the provinces and districts.

Thus, although the lines of authority ran to me in several different ways, I was able to provide unity of command for the entire American military effort in South Vietnam, and also to give my personal attention to the entire range of advisory, combat, and support activities embraced by our commitment to South Vietnam.

Air operations against North Vietnam were conducted by CINCPAC through the Commander, Pacific Air Forces, and the Commander, Pacific Fleet. This was a fully-workable division of responsibilities and authorities because air assets of various kinds were employed against North Vietnam in connection with our operations there. This meant, of course, that the Seventh Air Force and the Seventh Fleet divided their efforts between the air war in the north and support of the ground war in the south. The Commander, Seventh Fleet, also provided naval gunfire support for allied troops in South Vietnam and later for coastal bombardment of North Vietnam. Similarly, the Commander, Seventh Air Force, received his orders or missions from two sources. He received directions for the air war in the north from CINCPAC through the Commander, Pacific Air Forces, and for support of the ground war in the south through me.

On the surface, this would seem to be a complicated arrangement fraught with potential difficulties. In practice, however, the system worked well

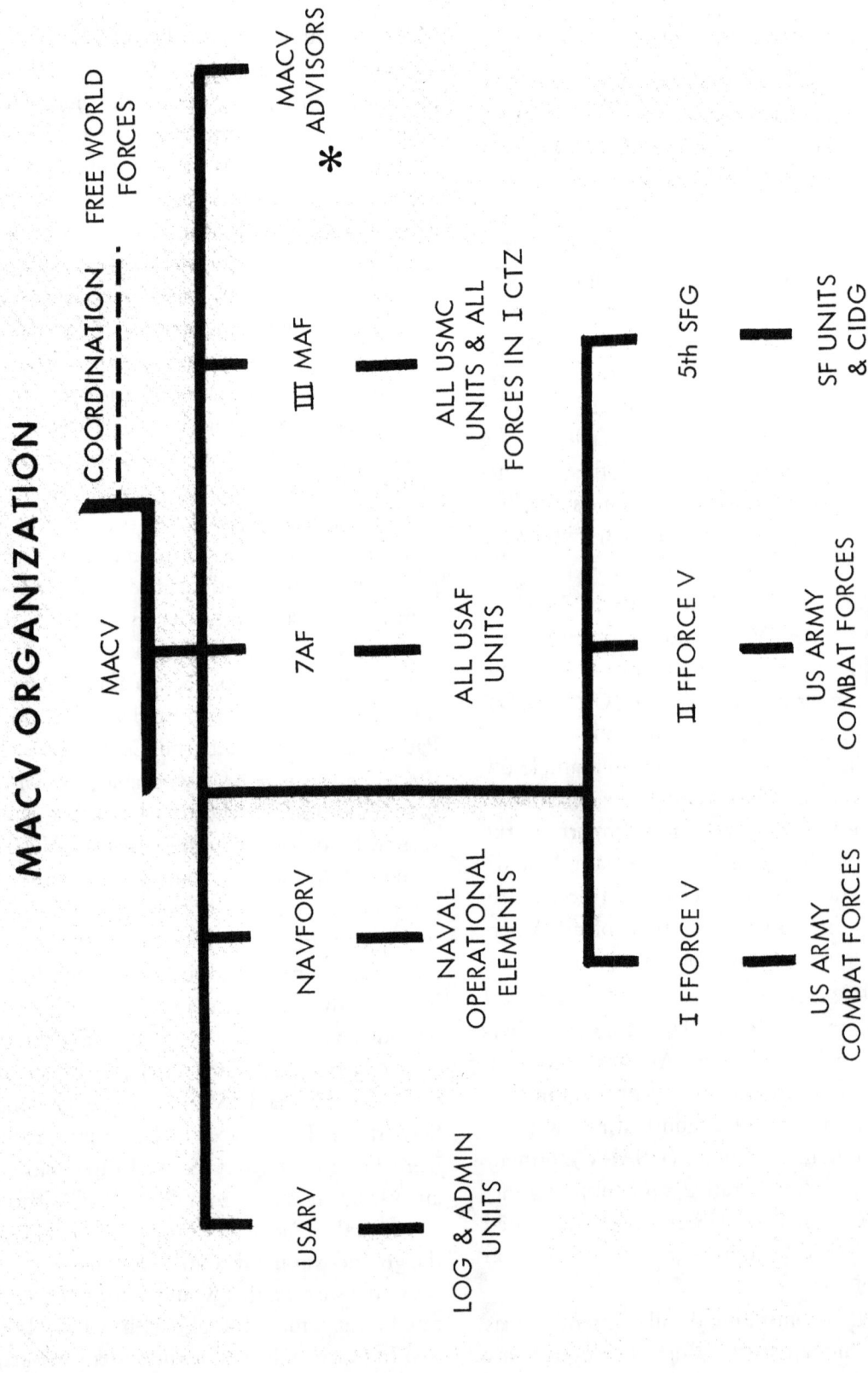

* EXCEPT THOSE MACV ADVISORS WHO DOUBLE AS COMMANDERS OF U.S. TROOP UNITS

principally because of the judicious and skillful assignment of priorities by Admiral Sharp, Commander in Chief, Pacific. Throughout the four and one-half years of my service in Vietnam, Admiral Sharp provided counsel and support which were invaluable to me and to the war effort. His management and direction of complex and interrelated air and naval operations were made vastly easier and more effective by the high professional competence of the successive naval and air commanders involved.

In an emergency and upon my request, CINCPAC would divert all necessary air and naval capabilities to priority targets selected by me. When the enemy mounted a major offensive in the area of the DMZ, Admiral Sharp passed to my control all air operations in the southern panhandle of North Vietnam, because this area was in fact part of the extended battlefield. On many occasions aircraft of the Seventh Fleet were diverted from North Vietnam to targets in South Vietnam at my request. On other occasions air operations in South Vietnam were curtailed for short periods in order to add to the weight of the effort against high priority targets in the north. This arrangement permitted full and effective use of our air and naval capabilities.

Heavy Aerial Bombardment

Another welcome capability provided from resources outside Vietnam was the B-52 effort. The strategic bombers of the 3d Air Division of the Strategic Air Command on Guam flew at a very high altitude and struck the enemy without warning. They could be neither seen nor heard. They struck with as many as 100 bombs each, in day or at night, in any kind of weather, and with an accuracy which is phenomenal. The effectiveness of their strikes has been attested to by prisoners who have revealed that the "silent, sudden death" from the big bombers has been one of our enemy's foremost fears. The use of this weapon in mass has won many battles and made it unnecessary to fight many more. The skillful crews of the Strategic Air Command made a tremendous contribution to our combat efforts in Vietnam.

Tactical Control

To control our ground field operations in 1965, we established at Nha Trang a headquarters designated initially as "Task Force Alpha" and shortly thereafter as "Field Force Vietnam." Initially, this tactical headquarters operated under MACV control for operations in the II and III Vietnamese Corps areas.

We elected to adopt the field force concept rather than organize a normal corps headquarters for two primary reasons. First, since we intended to organize and operate in conformance with the South Vietnamese corps zones, it would have been confusing to introduce another corps designation into those zones. Second, a corps headquarters is somewhat fixed in organization. We needed to tailor an organization precisely to the missions to be performed. The field force headquarters was, therefore, designed to control Army units of all sizes as the situation demanded—initially brigades and later divisions. I foresaw the time when, as our buildup increased, we might be required to inject a corps headquarters below field force level to control several divisions—an eventuality which did occur in 1968.

We were to establish a second field force headquarters in the spring of 1966, as our buildup continued. The final command arrangement was the I Field Force in the II Corps zone, the II Field Force in the III Corps zone, and the III Marine Amphibious Force as the equivalent command in the I Corps zone. Since I contemplated no early U.S. commitment in the IV Corps, the task of coordinating and controlling U.S. advisors and support troops there was assumed by the senior U.S. advisor to the Vietnamese IV Corps commander.

U.S.-Vietnamese Military Cooperation

The three U.S. field forces and the respective South Vietnamese corps were co-equal commands which operated in a spirit of mutual cooperation. A similar arrangement existed with the largest contingent of Free World forces, those from the Republic of Korea. As I was the military advisor to the commander of the Vietnamese forces on all matters ranging from the administrative to the tactical, so the field force and III Marine Amphibious Force commanders served as senior advisors to the ARVN corps commanders. I found both South Vietnamese and Free World commanders completely receptive and responsive to my advice and recommendations. At no time did an irreconcilable problem of command or coordination occur. In the field our troops and the South Vietnamese fought side by side—from division level to the smallest unit—in close coordination and cooperation. They supported one another as dictated by the tactical situation. As we gained experience by working and fighting together, our combined efforts grew in effectiveness.

At all command levels, we planned operations in close coordination with the Republic of Vietnam's Armed Forces. In the fall of 1965 we developed jointly our first Combined Campaign Plan in order to coordinate the total military effort as well as set forth our objectives, policies, relationships, and points of coordination for 1966. The plan was equally binding on all military forces.

I consistently resisted suggestions that a single, combined command could more efficiently prosecute the war. I believed that subordinating the Vietnamese forces to U.S. control would stifle the growth of leadership and acceptance of responsibility essential to the development of Vietnamese Armed Forces capable eventually of defending their country. Moreover, such a step would be counter to our basic objective of assisting Vietnam in a time of emergency and of leaving a strong, independent country at the time of our withdrawal. Subordination also might have given credence to the enemy's absurd claim that the United States was no more than a colonial power. I was also fully aware of the practical problems of forming and operating a headquarters with an international staff.

Combined Intelligence

Only in the critical area of intelligence did we establish a combined or integrated U.S.-Vietnamese activity. In order to take advantage of all U.S. and Vietnamese talents, resources, and information, we pooled U.S. and Vietnamese intelligence resources in the Combined Intelligence Center. This center had four major functions: interrogation of prisoners, exploitation of captured enemy material, exploitation of captured enemy documents, and the preparation of intelligence reports for both U.S. and Vietnamese commands. As our troop strength increased and our operations became more extensive, more documents and prisoners were captured and ralliers attracted. Thus, our intelligence technicians had more with which to work. U.S. and Vietnamese intelligence specialists worked side by side and kept pace with the demands placed upon them. Throughout the war the timely intelligence developed by this agency has been a key factor in battlefield success.

One aspect of our combined intelligence effort posed a particularly difficult challenge. This was the problem of identifying appropriate enemy targets for air and artillery strikes—and particularly for our B-52 heavy bombers. At the very beginning, our targeting for B-52 strikes was, frankly, somewhat primitive. With time and effort, however, this technique and process has become increasingly refined and vastly more effective. By combining intelligence from agents, prisoners, defectors, and the civilian population, with radar, infrared, and other photography, and other information, we have progressively increased the quality of our targeting and thus the effectiveness of these air strikes.

Tours of Duty

Early in the buildup of American forces, the question arose of the appropriate length of tour in

Vietnam for U.S. servicemen. Aware of the possibility that our involvement would extend over a long period of time, I wanted to build a well-balanced command of such size and composition that it would have high, stable morale and could be sustained for an indefinite period without resort to general mobilization. In the belief that high morale and fresh enthusiasm would offset problems of continuity and experience, I insisted on a standard tour of one year except for general officers. Of course, one could volunteer to extend—and many did.

Civic Action

Even before the military buildup, I became concerned about the effect of a massive U.S. presence on the civilian population. Lest friction develop between our forces and the very people we were trying to help, I directed that all U.S. units undertake an active, concentrated civic action program in the vicinity of their unit bases and, where possible, in areas of combat operations. U.S. Navy Seabees and Army engineers had begun such a program in 1964, digging wells and building bridges, small dams, schools, and other community facilities. Medical and dental care for civilians became an integral part of the program. Soon every operations plan included plans for civic action.

As our men arrived in Vietnam, they were thoroughly informed about the country and the people and received detailed instructions on the standards of conduct they were expected to maintain in their relationship with Vietnamese civilians. Each man was issued a pocket-size card listing "Nine Rules of Conduct," which made clear our aim to demonstrate to the people that we came as helpers. To forestall the inflationary impact of our presence on the economy, commanders restricted purchases of local goods and services and arranged fixed prices with the local authorities for those purchases which were necessary and unavoidable.

Our field advisors meanwhile attempted to orient the Vietnamese forces on their civic action responsibilities. On a national level the central government was urged to play a vital role in civic action by demonstrating a genuine intent to respond to the needs of the people.

Pacification

The U.S. Mission's efforts to support pacification during 1965 continued to be hindered by political instability. Vietnamese planning and coordination at the national level remained inadequate. Clarification of policies was slow and not enough qualified personnel were available to expand pacification efforts into all areas that had been cleared by military operations. However, hope for an improved political climate and better performance emerged in June with establishment of a government by the National Leadership Committee with Nguyen Van Thieu as Chairman and Nguyen Cao Ky as Premier.

But while the pacification effort fell short of its established goals, we nevertheless made some modest progress in a few places. The introduction of U.S. forces provided an added measure of security to portions of the South Vietnamese populace. This added security was reflected in a rise in the number of people who were able to live under government control. Notwithstanding the problems stemming from weakness at the top, a number of imaginative experiments were underway which developed techniques and organizations that later proved to be very useful. I have in mind the People's Action Teams, the Census Grievance Program, and the Armed Propaganda Program.

By year's end, about one-half of the South Vietnamese population was living under government control. Since the gains were from among those previously listed as "contested," the amount of the population under VC control remained at approximately 26 percent.

Measures of Progress

Since specific terrain features have less importance in the area-type war fought in Vietnam than in conventional war and since the usual gauge of progress—the location of the front lines—was missing, we had to turn to other indicators if we were to measure progress. The damage inflicted upon the enemy was one indicator. The health and condition of the South Vietnamese government and its armed forces was another. However imperfect a substitute for the usual indices, these had to suffice.

By actually counting the number of enemy dead—a practice instituted by the South Vietnamese prior to the American buildup—we gained some knowledge of the degree of damage done the enemy without the gross inaccuracy that would have resulted from mere estimates of enemy killed. The number of enemy weapons captured was an indication not only of the armament lost by the enemy but also of the state of enemy morale and battlefield competence. The number of villages and hamlets pacified, the percentage of the population under government control, the number of miles of waterways and highways opened to traffic, proficiency tests of South Vietnamese military units— all these provided some if not full measure of the progress we were making in pacification and building effective South Vietnamese Armed Forces.

Information Policy

In regard to the information media—press, radio, and television—we early studied very carefully the advisability and practicality of imposing some form of censorship such as that practiced in World War II. In the end, I decided that under the particular conditions prevailing in Vietnam, censorship would be unenforceable and that greater benefits might be derived from a policy of maximum candor in keeping with the fact that objective and responsible coverage of such a complex war was indispensable to an understanding of it in the United States and elsewhere. Within the limits of genuine security restrictions, we made every effort to cooperate with newsmen and to provide them facilities to cover the war. Whenever available, we provided helicopter and aircraft transportation to enable them to move about the country. A set of ground rules required each newsman to act as his own censor in deleting information of value to the enemy.

CHRONOLOGY OF MAJOR EVENTS—1965

January

The first North Vietnamese Army regiment to enter South Vietnam, the 95th, arrived in Kontum Province in December 1964 and was joined within the first two months of 1965 by the 32d and 101st Regiments. During the same period the North Vietnamese 6th Regiment was being activated in Quang Tri Province. The infiltration rate at this time was something over 1,000 men per month. North Vietnam also provided Viet Cong forces with an addition to their arsenal—the 12.7-mm antiaircraft gun.

As the year opened, a major portion of South Vietnam's military force was tied down in static security missions. Most efforts at large-scale offensive operations had proved ineffective and had been abandoned. This lack of military activity reflected low morale and indecision which stemmed in large part from political upheavals and uncertainty in the minds of the Vietnamese regarding the future of the country. In January the Tran Van Huong government was ousted and a military/civilian government established by the Armed Forces Council. On 9 February General Khanh, who dominated the Council, nominated Dr. Oanh as the acting Premier.

The unhappy battle of Binh Gia made it clear that Vietnamese forces urgently needed additional firepower and support to cope with the heavily armed enemy regiments. Helicopter gunships performed magnificently, but even heavier ordnance was needed. Consequently, in late January, MACV requested and obtained approval to use U.S. jet aircraft against the enemy in support of Vietnamese troops under emergency conditions. COMUSMACV also requested authority to conduct jet air strikes in remote areas against VC concentrations which had been confirmed by reliable intelligence and were beyond the capability of the Vietnamese Air Force to handle effectively. This authority was granted with the understanding that COMUSMACV would personally make each employment decision on a case by case basis.

February

On 7 February the U.S. advisory compound and the airfield at Camp Holloway near Pleiku were attacked with mortar fire and by demolitions teams. Eight U.S. personnel were killed and 109 wounded while five aircraft were destroyed and 15 were damaged. In response to this attack and numerous earlier incidents of terror, the U.S. on the same day launched a retaliatory air strike on the Dong Hoi military barracks in North Vietnam. Three days later, however, the Viet Cong detonated a large explosive device which destroyed an American enlisted men's billet in the city of Qui Nhon, killing 23 Americans and wounding 21.

On 15 February the Armed Forces Council announced that the government of Prime Minister Oanh was being replaced by that of Dr. Phan Huy Quat. Two days later, Vietnamese Army and Marine Corps units staged a bloodless coup in Saigon and ousted the head of the Armed Forces Council, General Khanh. By 21 February General Khanh had accepted the demands of the council for his resignation and expatriation.

In mid-February a Viet Cong regiment was reported to be concentrated deep in the jungles of Phuoc Tuy Province, not far from the scene of the bloody fighting around Binh Gia in January. On the 19th, after necessary clearance had been obtained from South Vietnamese officials, 24 U.S. B–57 "Canberra" bombers attacked this target— the first jet strike of the war against enemy forces in South Vietnam.

On 24 February a company of Vietnamese Rangers and a company of Civilian Irregular Defense Group troops with a U.S. Army Special Forces team became entrapped in an enemy ambush near the Mang Yang Pass on Route 19 between An Khe and Pleiku. (This was the same area in which the Viet Minh had destroyed the French Group Mobile 100 in 1954.) In this case I exercised the emergency authority which had been granted to me in January for the employment of U.S. jet aircraft. Twenty-four F–100's along with B–57 "Canberras" and helicopter gunships attacked the ambush site while Army troop-carrying helicopters extracted the beleaguered force without the loss of a man. The enemy lost 150 killed. Thereafter, under procedures developed by the 2d Air Division, then commanded by Maj. Gen. Joseph H. Moore, the use of U.S. jets to support the South Vietnamese Army when heavily engaged became standard practice.

After the successful extraction from the Mang Yang Pass area we deployed another CIDG force, composed of Montagnards of the Rhade tribe, into this area. Within several weeks the Montagnard soldiers had become homesick for their families and began to return overland to their homes near Ban Me Thuot—a considerable distance. We learned from this experience that only regular forces could be counted upon for mobile operations away from their normal base area.

A 600-man Republic of Korea engineer unit arrived on 25 February as part of the Free World military effort to assist the South Vietnamese. This unit, with its own security force attached, was known as the Korean "Dove Force." It engaged in civic action projects of an engineering nature, such as road and bridge repair and construction.

March-April

On 8 March the 9th Marine Expeditionary Brigade (later redesignated Amphibious Brigade) arrived from Okinawa and was positioned in Da Nang to provide security for the important airbase there. The U.S. Army's 716th Military Police Battalion arrived in the Saigon area on 21 March and assumed security duties for selected U.S. installations.

On 30 March a truck loaded with several hundred pounds of plastic explosives was detonated outside the U.S. Embassy in Saigon, causing heavy damage and killing two Americans and 11 Vietnamese. Deputy Ambassador Johnson was among those wounded.

May

The 173d Airborne Brigade, comprising two battalions of infantry and one of artillery, arrived by air from Okinawa to provide security for the major air base at Bien Hoa and, initially, the airfield at Vung Tau.

By the end of the month, U.S. forces in South Vietnam had passed the 50,000 mark (22,500 Army; 16,000 Marine Corps; 10,000 Air Force; 3,000 Navy).

June

The 1st Battalion of the Royal Australian Regiment arrived at Vung Tau in June and began operating with the U.S. 173d Airborne Brigade near Ba Ria in Phuoc Tuy Province.

During the same month, the Marines began to develop a major base at Chu Lai in Quang Tin Province.

In addition to its sheltered anchorage, Chu Lai was selected as the site of the second jet-capable airfield in the northern provinces. The existing airfield at Da Nang was overloaded with Marine and Air Force tactical fighters and transport aircraft. In a remarkable performance, the III Marine Amphibious Force built an expeditionary jet airfield at Chu Lai in 30 days by using advanced techniques and light weight aluminum planking. The early occupancy of this airfield was a necessity in view of the overall military situation.

Off-shore, the MACV naval component command augmented the Vietnamese coastal surveillance and anti-infiltration operation with radar surveillance ships, small craft, and aerial patrols. This reinforcement provided sorely needed assistance in the effort to block the steadily growing North Vietnamese seaborne supply effort. Further off-shore, the U.S. Seventh Fleet Task Force 77, composed of aircraft carriers, destroyers and cruisers took up station in the South China Sea to provide air and naval gunfire support for allied ground forces. The Navy could provide accurate fire, day and night and in any kind of weather, with weapons up to 8-inch guns striking as deep as 16 miles inland. This support was particularly valuable in the zones of the I and II Corps where critical operations most often took place in the narrow coastal lowlands.

In May and June the Vietnamese Army suffered two major reverses. In a four day battle at Dong Xoai, the VC 9th Division, for the first time with three full regiments, overran the Special Forces camp and then ambushed relieving Vietnamese forces. One battalion of the ARVN 7th Regiment and the Vietnamese 6th Airborne Battalion were largely destroyed in this battle. The South Vietnamese lost 650 killed or wounded. In the northern province of Quang Ngai, in the battle of Ba Gia, the Viet Cong 1st and 2d Regiments decimated the 39th Ranger Battalion and badly mauled relieving South Vietnamese forces.

By the end of June, Prime Minister Quat decided to hand back to the Armed Forces Council the reins of government. At the same time, General Nguyen Van Thieu was proclaimed Chief of State as Chairman of the Vietnamese National Leadership Committee. Air Vice Marshal Ky was installed as Premier. The inauguration of this government marked the end of a long debilitating period of political turmoil. The Thieu-Ky government was destined to remain in power until the general elections and adoption of a new constitution in 1967.

Upon my request, on 18 June B-52 bombers from the Strategic Air Command's Third Air Division on Guam were employed for the first time to strike a well entrenched enemy base in War Zone D. The results were sufficiently impressive so that B-52 strikes were requested and employed thereafter on a continuing basis.

At the end of June, troops of the 173d Airborne Brigade launched the first U.S. ground offensive operation into War Zone D north of Bien Hoa Airbase. Several sharp engagements ensued in which the airborne troops killed many enemy and uncovered a large enemy base in the jungle, acquitting themselves with distinction.

July

July marked the beginning of the accelerated U.S. force buildup. The 2d Brigade of the 1st Infantry Division arrived at Long Binh, near Bien Hoa, and the 1st Brigade, 101st Airborne Division, deployed to Cam Ranh Bay. Two more Marine battalions also arrived in July. One was positioned at Da Nang and the other assigned a security mission at Qui Nhon.

With the area secured by U.S. combat forces, work began on the major logistic bases at Cam Ranh Bay, Qui Nhon, and Da Nang. The fourth logistic effort was at Saigon where the existing port facilities were to be improved and where we planned to build a new port for the exclusive use of U.S. forces.

On 28 July President Johnson announced that our forces in Vietnam would be raised from 75,000 to 125,000 and that additional forces would be sent as requested.

August

The first major battle involving U.S. forces occurred in August. The III Marine Amphibious Force, commanded by Maj. Gen. Lewis Walt, discovered and engaged the Viet Cong 2d Regiment on the Batangan Peninsula just south of the new Marine base at Chu Lai. The Marines surrounded the Viet Cong unit and pinned it against the sea. In a bitter fight, much of it hand-to-hand, the Marines killed 700 of the entrapped force in Operation STARLIGHT. This battle proved beyond any doubt what the Marines had been sure of all along—that they could meet and defeat any Viet Cong or North Vietnamese force they might encounter.

The tactical picture in the Central Highlands during this same period was not encouraging. On 18–19 August, a battalion-sized VC force overran the U.S. Special Forces camp located at the district capital of Dak Sut. Of the 250 CIDG troops stationed there, only 50 escaped along with 8 of their U.S. advisors. Although not confirmed, it was suspected that the attack had been supported by elements of the NVA 101st Regiment.

September

U.S. military strength in South Vietnam rose above 119,000. The 1st Cavalry Division (Airmobile) arrived at Qui Nhon and An Khe in September. In anticipation of the 1st Cavalry Division's arrival, and to facilitate its initial deployment, the

1st Brigade of the 101st Airborne Division cleared the An Khe area and secured, along with Vietnamese forces, Highway 19 leading from Qui Nhon to the new base at An Khe. The brigade killed 226 Viet Cong in the process of clearing the area.

At Qui Nhon in September the 2d Battalion, 7th Marines (which had arrived there in July to secure the port and logistic complex under development) first employed the riot control agent "CS." This effective type of tear gas has a temporary incapacitating effect. It assisted allied troops in gaining control of an area with minimum use of firepower and, thus, to avoid civilian casualties. This technique also proved very effective in clearing underground tunnels and caves.

October

In October the North Vietnamese Army began a major operation in the Central Highlands. By this time the enemy had assembled three North Vietnamese Army regiments in western Pleiku Province and in adjacent Cambodia—the 32d, 33d and 66th. We believed this action to be part of his plan to cut South Vietnam in two. In addition, there is reason to believe that he welcomed the opportunity to spoil the debut of the U.S. ground forces in this area; the 1st Cavalry Division, which now stood in his path, was as yet untested in battle.

On 19 October the enemy opened his campaign with an attack on the Plei Me Special Forces camp 25 miles southwest of Pleiku. He attacked the fortified camp with one regiment while holding the bulk of his division-size force in reserve. The Vietnamese Army countered this attack with the assistance of concentrated tactical air strikes. One brigade of the 1st Cavalry Division was moved into the area south and west of Pleiku to block any further enemy advance and to stand in readiness as a reaction force.

On 27 October I directed the 1st Cavalry Division to seek out and destroy the enemy force in western Pleiku Province. Thus began the month-long campaign known as the battle of the Ia Drang Valley. The principal engagements in the campaign were fought during the period 14–19 November around the base of Chu Pong mountain. The performance of the 1st Cavalry Division was magnificent. In extended combat against a skillful and determined foe, it demonstrated the great effectiveness of the airmobile division concept and opened a new chapter in the history of land warfare.

As the enemy withdrew his assault regiment from Plei Me, the regiment incurred severe casualties from air strikes and pursuing air cavalry. However, when the cavalry division put a blocking force behind the withdrawing enemy and only a few miles from the Cambodian border, the North Vietnamese commander committed his remaining two regiments in an attempt to redeem his earlier failure at Plei Me and to destroy a major U.S. unit. The 3d Brigade, 1st Cavalry Division—barely 30 days in Vietnam—was the target. This gallant brigade decisively defeated each enemy regiment in turn. Altogether, 1st Cavalry Division and ARVN troops killed an estimated 1,800 North Vietnamese. Despite our troops' inexperience, the division's tactical leadership, training, tactical mobility, firepower, and flexible doctrine enabled it to gain an impressive victory. This timely victory produced a sharp upturn in the morale of the South Vietnamese government and its armed forces.

The Plei Me/Ia Drang campaign also proved the worth of the lightweight, rapid-firing M16 rifle in battlefield competition with the Communist AK–47 assault rifle. Up to this point, only a few U.S. units had these weapons. At this time, I strongly recommended equipping all U.S., Free World, and Vietnamese forces with the M16 as soon as possible.

The Korean Capital (Tiger) Division arrived and assumed the mission of providing security in the area of Qui Nhon and adjacent areas in Binh Dinh Province. The Korean 2d Marine (Dragon) Brigade also arrived to assume a similar mission at Cam Ranh Bay. Within a very short period both units had established well-earned reputations for combat prowess.

On the 23d, U.S. military strength in Vietnam reached a total of 148,300 (89,000 Army; 8,000

Navy; 37,000 Marines; 14,000 Air Force; 300 Coast Guard).

November

In November the South Vietnamese suffered a major defeat. The ARVN 7th Regiment, operating in the Michelin Plantation northwest of Saigon, was engaged by the Viet Cong 271st Regiment. The South Vietnamese regiment inflicted a heavy defeat on this VC unit. However, five days later a companion regiment of the Viet Cong 9th Division (the 272d Regiment) overran the South Vietnamese troops, inflicting very heavy casualties and rendering the regiment ineffective. The Vietnamese regimental commander was killed during the battle.

December

A 30-hour Christmas truce was agreed to by both sides. The U.S. suspended all offensive acts and also suspended its air strikes in North Vietnam during this truce. Upon the expiration of the 30-hour cease-fire, U.S. and allied troops were ordered to maintain their defensive positions and not to fire unless fired upon or attacked. As Viet Cong and North Vietnamese attacks grew in number and intensity, we were forced to resume offensive operations late on 26 December. However, the suspension of air attacks on North Vietnam remained in effect.

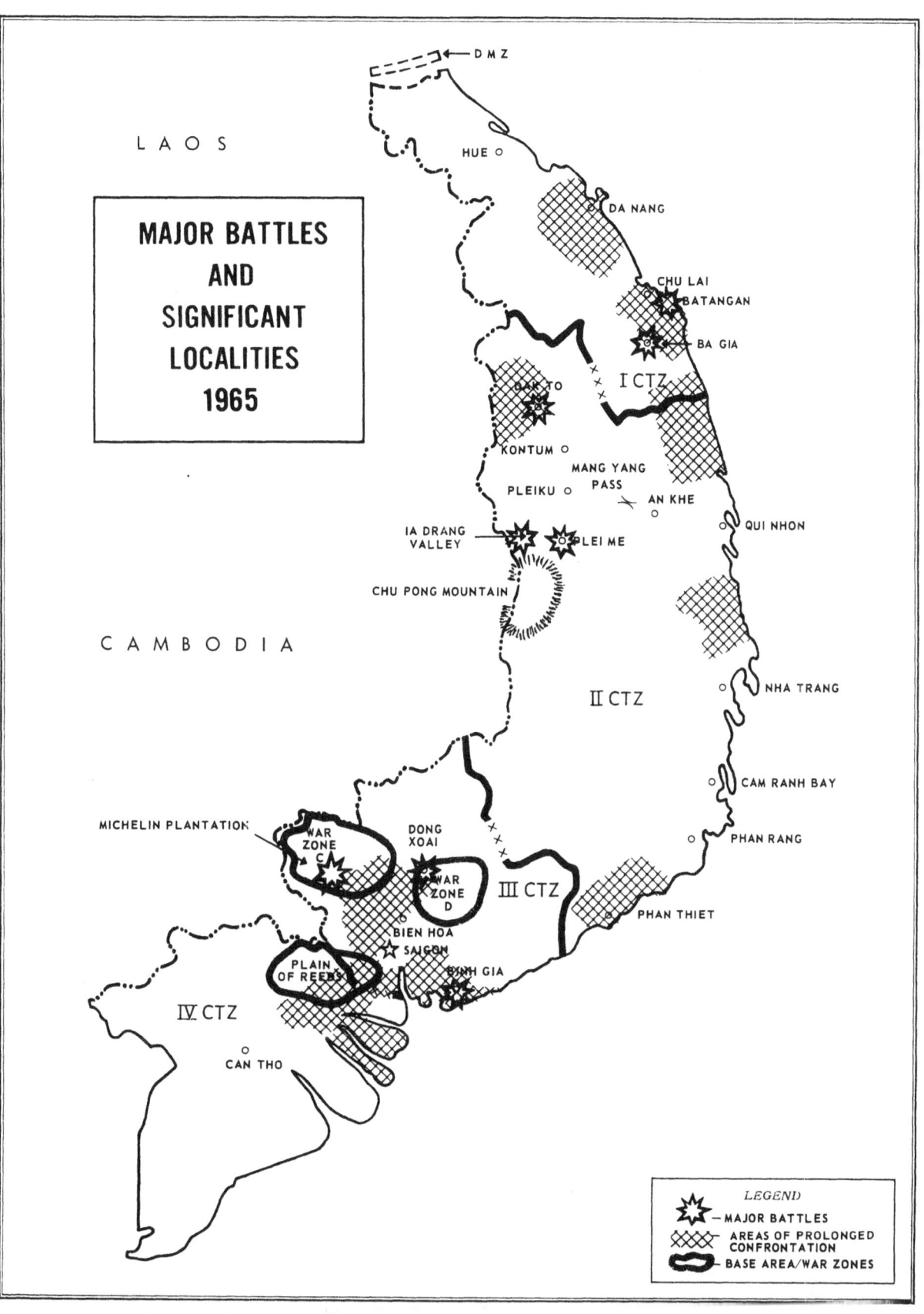

Chapter IV

THE YEAR OF DEVELOPMENT—1966

OVERVIEW

From the U.S. standpoint, the year 1966 was one of accelerated buildup and development and the beginning of major offensive operations. To the government of Vietnam it was a year during which a serious challenge to political stability was successfully weathered and some gains achieved in pacification. Further, the Vietnamese Armed Forces began to regain confidence and slowly to resume an offensive posture. It was also the year in which the enemy began to have misgivings about his strategy and his tactics.

In January of 1966 General Giap published an article in *Nhan Dan*—a government newspaper in Hanoi. He was exhorting his troops to greater effort and assuring them that the introduction of U.S. troops would pose no problem. He made a number of points of which the following are salient:

(1) The U.S. would not be able to put into South Vietnam the number of troops required.

(2) U.S. forces would antagonize the Vietnamese people as time went on.

(3) Pressure against the war would grow in the U.S. and throughout the world and the costs of the war would be very high.

(4) The morale of South Vietnamese forces would decline.

(5) U.S. weapons and equipment were not suited for this kind of war, geography, or climate.

(6) U.S. troops were then being encircled so they could not move about freely.

(7) U.S. troops were demoralized.

(8) U.S. infantry was weak and cowardly.

(9) U.S. commanders were incompetent.

(10) U.S. tactics were ineffective.

I will address these points again in my conclusions.

The military tasks which confronted us at the beginning of the year were many and varied: first, the protection of the government and the people; second, the protection and development of our installations and logistic bases to keep pace with the continuing deployment of major U.S. troop units; third, the qualitative and quantitative improvement of the South Vietnamese Armed Forces. We found it necessary on numerous occasions to mount quick spoiling attacks against increasingly large enemy main force units building up in the border areas, which posed a constant and growing threat to all of our programs and objectives.

We could not accomplish all of these tasks with equal emphasis everywhere at once. Therefore, we concentrated our efforts in the most vital areas. Elsewhere we applied the military principle of economy of force. I judged that the critical regions requiring first attention were the populated area around Saigon in the III Corps and the coastal lowlands in the I and II Corps. The more important of these regions was that around the capital city. To the north, the central coastal provinces of Binh Dinh and Phu Yen were most critical. Not only were these provinces heavily populated and a prime source of VC support, but enemy forces there threatened to sever the country by linking up with North Vietnamese units operating in the Central Highlands. With these priorities and considerations in mind, I deployed the bulk of our reinforcements into these areas.

For example, the remainder of the U.S. 1st Infantry Division was deployed north of Saigon and the 25th Infantry Division was positioned just northwest of Saigon astride a major access route to the city. Specific troop dispositions were designed not only to provide a defensive shield for the densely populated areas but also to secure selected installations of value to the Vietnamese economy, such as rubber plantations. A new Vietnamese division, the 10th (later to be designated the 18th) was organized and positioned northeast of Saigon. The Republic of Korea 9th Infantry Division was deployed into the critical coastal areas of II Corps and the U.S. 1st Marine Division occupied the heavily populated southern provinces of the I Corps. Although one brigade of the U.S. 4th Infantry Division was initially positioned in the coastal area of Phu Yen Province, the entire division was eventually deployed to the Central Highlands to counter the steady buildup of North Vietnamese units in that region.

These deployments, which moved us beyond the "fire brigade" approach we had taken out of necessity in 1965, again affirmed my conviction that the combined U.S.-South Vietnamese military effort must begin in the critical areas in which the population was concentrated. Secretary McNamara, on a visit to Saigon, supported me in my opposition to yet another South Vietnamese suggestion that U.S. forces be deployed only to remote areas such as the Central Highlands.

The enemy's view of the critical areas was much the same as ours. As a consequence, the major battles of the year developed in these critical areas.

The largest battle, involving 22,000 American and South Vietnamese troops, took place northwest of Saigon in Operation ATTLEBORO where the Viet Cong 9th Division, reinforced by a North Vietnamese regiment, was soundly defeated and driven back to the Cambodian border. In a series of savage battles, the 1st Cavalry Division, Korean units, and ARVN forces cleared the northern half of Binh Dinh Province on the central coast, in Operation MASHER/WHITEWING/THANG PHONG II. In the process they decimated the Sao Vang Division which was later to be designated the North Vietnamese 3d Division. U.S. Marines of the 3d Division were progressively moved into the area of the northern two provinces and in conjunction with South Vietnamese Army and other Marine Corps units conducted a highly successful campaign (Operation HASTINGS) against enemy forces infiltrating across the DMZ.

By year's end our strength in Vietnam had increased by over 200,000 men, including additional helicopter, infantry, and artillery units and a substantial augmentation in tactical fighter squadrons and a substantial growth in naval forces. Understandably, this very rapid buildup placed heavy strains on the logistic system, which was barely able to keep up with mounting supply, maintenance, and transportation requirements. The monthly tonnage of arriving supplies rose from 390,000 in December 1965 to over 600,000 a year later.

In these early days before sufficient forces were available to open and maintain the road and highway system, our combat forces were almost wholly dependent upon aerial resupply, especially when they operated any distance away from the coastal bases. Therefore, 59 additional airfields were constructed during the year, raising the total number of fields able to handle transport aircraft to 73.

Enemy forces also increased rapidly. During the year at least 58,000 men had infiltrated from North Vietnam—equivalent to 5 divisions. The enemy's total combat strength at the end of the year was over 282,000 total plus an estimated 80,000 political cadre. North Vietnamese officers, non-commissioned officers, and political cadre began to assume leadership positions in many Viet Cong units. In 1965 individual replacements for Viet Cong units had been drawn primarily from the populous IV Corps area. Increasing reliance on North Vietnamese replacements reflected problems of recruitment which began to plague the Viet Cong by late 1966.

As enemy forces increased, so too did the quality of enemy arms. The most significant addition of the year was a marked increase in numbers of the lightweight rocket launcher, the RPG-2, first employed in 1964. In attacks against the Special Forces camp at Khe Sanh and the Da Nang airfield in the month of January, 120-mm mortars were employed for the first time. The range of this weapon almost doubled the distance from which the enemy could conduct mortar attacks against our installations, thereby sharply increasing our base defense problem. Viet Cong local and guerrilla forces began to appear with AK-47 assault rifles.

Although the enemy's forces continued to grow in size, to improve in armament, and to reflect an increasingly large North Vietnamese commitment, the high command in Hanoi made no change in strategy to meet the additional U.S. deployments. The Communist leaders apparently retained their faith in the interaction between political and military organizations. They continued to rely on the concept of mutual support between VC guerrilla and local forces, on the one hand, and the VC and NVA main forces on the other—arrangements which had paid off handsomely in 1964 and 1965.

By the last half of 1966—and extending into 1967—this military strategy of mutual support encountered increasing difficulties. Evidence of these difficulties is most clearly provided by the fact that main force units were almost exclusively employed in remote border areas and along the DMZ or in difficult mountain or jungle terrain. Isolated outposts were attacked with relative frequency but major attacks were confined to Con Thien and Gio Linh near the DMZ, to Dak To and Duc Co in the Central Highlands, and to Song Be and Loc Ninh along the Cambodian border north of Saigon. In fact, during most of 1966 (and extending into 1967) main force enemy units, in areas other than the Delta, generally failed to bring their weight to bear in the populated areas in support of enemy local and guerrilla forces and the enemy political apparatus. For a period of some 15 months, for example, no main force unit of the enemy's 5th, 7th, or 9th Divisions entered the populated area around Saigon. The commander of enemy forces in the south apparently thought that he could not afford to engage his growing main force units at greater distances from their border sanctuaries without exposing them to destruction by the firepower of the highly mobile allied forces.

By the summer of 1966, the commander in the south, General Nguyen Chi Thanh, revealed to Hanoi his reluctance to pursue the earlier strategy in the face of battlefield realities. In an exchange of views with the high command in Hanoi—published in the Hanoi press and broadcast over the Hanoi and "Liberation" radios—General Thanh appeared to resist the urgings of General Giap to press on with the strategy of 1964-65.

No apparent decision emerged from this exchange. In any event, it was overtaken by the advent of the northeast monsoon, which brought clear skies and dry weather to the southern regions of South Vietnam. These conditions favored allied operations; the enemy soon found himself heavily engaged by the 1966-67 allied dry season campaign.

Although the enemy made no change in basic strategy, he did open a new front just south of the DMZ in the late winter and early spring. Moreover, he did so with great vigor and determination, and in a region so separated from the rest of the country as to make allied reaction more difficult. This region—the two northernmost provinces of Quang Tri and Thua Thien—is isolated by a mountain spur that runs to the sea just north of Da Nang. The highway over this obstacle is narrow, winding, and vulnerable. No all-weather ports existed north of the pass. The imperial city of Hue in Thua Thien Province is politically and psychologically important to all Vietnamese. The populated coastal strip in this region is very narrow and difficult to defend. Enemy lines of communication, on the other hand, are shorter than those required to support operations in any other area in South Vietnam. Furthermore, the enemy was able to use, to his great advantage, the sanctuary just across the DMZ. This enemy buildup in the north was met by the U.S. 3d Marine Division and by Vietnamese Army and Vietnamese Marine Corps units in Operation HASTINGS, the second largest engagement of the year.

I believe that the enemy opened this new front in order to divert our forces from the area that has always been his preferred objective—the heavily populated region around Saigon. At the same time, we suspected that the enemy might try to seize and hold this northern area and establish there a "liberation" government. Such a development would have had obvious and serious effects. At this early date I was concerned that we would have to confront major North Vietnamese forces in the extreme northern area or abandon the region to the enemy.

The threat in the north continued to mount during 1967—and during 1968, as well. The fact that we were able to meet this formidable threat of five to six enemy divisions in the far north without giving up any positions of real value farther south is, to me, the major military feat of the war. It was the product of logistic flexibility and the momentum provided by our planning prior to the event.

South Vietnamese government control of this northern area was also challenged by internal elements in Hue and Da Nang. From March until midsummer, the government went through a serious political crisis when the Buddhist and Student Struggle Movement led to riots and civil disorders throughout the country, but primarily in the areas of Hue and Da Nang. The eventual suppression by the Ky government of this near-revolt increased the government's strength and confidence. These, in turn, enabled progress toward free elections and the drafting of a new constitution.

Pacification continued to be a disappointment albeit with some minor progress. A Revolutionary Development Program, introduced by the South Vietnamese government in November, showed some promise. The most important development of the year was the opening of the Pacification Cadre School at Vung Tau and the deployment of 59-man Revolutionary Development teams into contested hamlets. The government's *Chieu Hoi* program, which welcomed disillusioned Viet Cong back to government loyalty, made impressive gains—20,242 returnees in 1966—almost double the preceding year's total of 11,124. Largely because of the presence of more U.S. forces, the percentage of the population able to live in reasonable security increased from slightly more than 50 percent in January to approximately 60 percent at year's end. As in 1965 these gains were made almost entirely in previously contested areas.

By mutual agreement, South Vietnamese forces, which could better identify the local guerrillas and infrastructure, concentrated on area security; U.S. and Free World forces conducted most of the major offensives against Viet Cong main forces and the North Vietnamese. At this stage of development, the task of eliminating the infrastructure was the particular responsibility of the National Police.

The coastal surveillance program by the United States and Vietnamese Navies began to reach a high state of effectiveness in stopping enemy seaborne movements. Tactical air support procedures were refined and U.S. ground forces received superb support from the Seventh Air Force, the 1st Marine Air Wing, and the Seventh Fleet. Additional Korean, Australian, New Zealand, and Thai troops arrived and added a major and professional component to the growing allied force.

By the end of 1966 sufficient forces had been deployed, together with their logistic support, so that the total allied military establishment was in a position for the first time to go over to the offensive on a broad and sustained basis in 1967.

OBSERVATIONS—1966

Offensive Combat Operations

During 1966 our offensive combat operations expanded and intensified. Throughout 1965 our modest troop strength and relatively scarce firepower had forced us to conduct spoiling attacks on an emergency or "fire brigade" basis. However, in 1966 increased numbers of troops, helicopters, and tactical fighter aircraft, buttressed by an increased allocation of B–52's, permitted us to plan these operations more deliberately.

Although all our operations fell into one of three broad categories (security—clearing—search and destroy) the nature of the tactical situation nevertheless varied widely between corps zones. The war took on a different and changing complexion in each zone and the three types of operations received varying emphasis.

Attacks by air and artillery fire constituted the bulk of our offensive operations in early 1966 until our ground strength reached appropriate and effective levels. Reconnaissance in force operations and spoiling attacks by ground units were reserved for those enemy forces and installations which constituted an immediate and grave threat. These ground offensive operations paid multiple dividends. They disrupted enemy activity of all types, deprived the enemy of the initiative, and placed him on the defensive. They forced the enemy to move continuously to avoid destruction or engagement on markedly unfavorable terms. This movement in itself disrupted his plans, forestalled his operations, and frequently induced high casualties from our firepower. Massive attacks by firepower alone were launched against more remote, less threatening targets. Our improved and broadened intelligence capability, whose growth corresponded with that of our strike forces, greatly enhanced the effectiveness of these attacks by providing us more and better defined targets.

Weakening (in some cases destroying) and driving back enemy main force units not only removed a major threat to the populace, but also seriously impaired the offensive capability of local guerrillas who were dependent upon the main force units for support. Our active operations against main force units adversely affected local guerrilla strength in yet another way. The Viet Cong replacement system prescribed that local guerrilla units provide replacements to main force units. As we inflicted increasing losses upon the enemy main force units, guerrilla groups experienced an immediate and serious manpower drain. They were drawn upon to restore main force troop strength and suffered accordingly.

Operations Against Base Areas

The number of enemy reported killed in our attacks against enemy base areas sometimes made the operations against these objectives appear inconsequential. This was misleading. The enemy frequently abandoned his base areas, refused battle and evaded, thereby minimizing his personnel losses. But the supplies and materiel we captured or destroyed in these base areas were vital to the enemy; the base complexes themselves represented a capital investment difficult to replace. Loss of the supplies and destruction of base area facilities sharply limited the enemy's ability to fight and created an immediate (and eventually chronic) disruption of his operations.

Increased intelligence was another vital dividend resulting from attacks on main force units in base areas. We captured copies of the enemy's campaign and battle plans, strategic guidance, tactical doctrine, attack orders, standing operating policies and procedures, personnel rosters, medical and casualty reports, equipment, supply, and weapons reports, along with evaluations of his own weaknesses and our strengths and plans to overcome both. These operations also resulted in the capture of a number of the enemy and provided an opportunity for disillusioned VC to rally to the government side. Prisoners and defectors provided additional insight into enemy plans and reactions to our methods.

Combat Intelligence

Our expanding Combined Intelligence Center quickly exploited this hard, comprehensive intelligence, which could be gained only through major penetrations into base areas. Our possession of this information created a dilemma for the enemy: he could pursue plans we were prepared to counter or delay his actions to develop new plans. The time required by the enemy to change plans and replace lost supplies was often several months, usually a delay that he could ill afford.

To enhance our intelligence capability, I requested the early deployment to Vietnam of separate air cavalry squadrons. These units with the great mobility and extensive communications provided by their organic aircraft, could range throughout the country on both combat and reconnaissance missions. They proved to be especially useful in locating the enemy and developing the initial combat situation against enemy main force units so that larger and heavier forces could be more effectively employed in a reaction and exploitation role. Two of these squadrons were activated in the fall of 1966 and were to be sent by air at my request in the fall of 1967. Others would come later.

Special Forces Operations

Border Defense and Surveillance

Border defense and surveillance was another major type of operation during this period. This activity was based primarily on the fortified camps of the Civilian Irregular Defense Groups and their U.S. Army Special Forces advisors. These camps performed a valuable intelligence and surveillance function. They were purposely located astride major supply and infiltration routes. Patrols operating from them inhibited enemy movement and upon contact frequently brought down the wrath of our aerial firepower upon the enemy—often North Vietnamese regulars. Consequently, the enemy constantly sought to destroy or neutralize them. Once the enemy concentrated and moved into the open to strike these camps, we employed our superior mobility and firepower either to reinforce the threatened camp or to counterattack and destroy the exposed enemy units. To insure survival, these outposts were habitually backed up and supported by mobile ARVN, U.S., or other Free World units operating in the general area.

Mobile Guerrilla Force

In 1966 we refined the organization and employment of a multipurpose reaction force, at first known as the Mobile Guerrilla Force and later redesignated the Mobile Strike Force. Composed of company-size groups of 150 to 200 men, this force conducted sustained guerrilla operations against the enemy, employing guerrilla doctrine and using many techniques borrowed from the Viet Cong. Inserted clandestinely into an area of operations, the troops of the Mobile Guerrilla Force normally broke contact with their base and conducted mobile operations for periods as long as 45 days. To prevent compromising these units, resupply was also carried out clandestinely. These special operations were highly successful in penetrating isolated enemy bases, disrupting the enemy's lines of communications, attacking hidden logistical support bases, and gathering intelligence.

Reconnaissance Forces

The U.S. and Vietnamese Special Forces also created deep reconnaissance and reaction forces that operated throughout the country in response to MACV and the Vietnamese Joint General Staff. Striking into remote areas, these units gathered intelligence, conducted raids, and interdicted the enemy's lines of communication. They attacked the enemy by calling in air strikes and directing artillery fire. Occasionally these units guided Mobile Strike Forces into contact with enemy units. They also executed deception and photographic missions and performed post-strike assessments of bomb damage from our air strikes.

Other Special Forces Activities

Our Special Forces continued their valuable contribution in civic action and psychological operations. In remote areas of Vietnam they were frequently the only contact the local inhabitants had with the central government or the outside world. Their contributions to education and medicine in these areas were extensive; they built or sponsored over 300 schools and provided medical care for innumerable isolated small communities.

The overall value of our Special Forces and the Civilian Irregular Defense Groups can scarcely be overstated. The intelligence they furnished on enemy infiltration and operations in remote areas was vital. With minimum strength they maintained a measure of control in vast areas that otherwise might have gone to the enemy by default. They brought some 45,000 fighting men and a proportionate population under government control or influence, all of whom might otherwise have been recruited or dominated by the enemy.

Pacification

In November Ambassador Lodge announced the creation of the Office of Civil Operations (OCO), under Deputy Ambassador William J. Porter, a move designed to achieve some consolidation of the fragmented civilian pacification effort. Mr. L. Wade Lathram, an outstanding Foreign Service Officer with experience in the Saigon office of the Agency for International Development (AID), was named the first director. Under Mr. Lathram, OCO assumed responsibility for all civilian support of the South Vietnamese Revolutionary Development effort and all U.S. civil operations in the pacification field.

Concurrently, I elevated the MACV Revolutionary Development Division to a Directorate, thereby providing emphasis through a larger staff headed by a general officer. Although not responsible for the civilian advisory effort in support of pacification, I had long been concerned with developing means to assist and support it. There is no way to separate security considerations from pacification operations. Furthermore, MACV furnished the province and district advisors who were central to the pacification effort. Thus by mid-1966 the Military Assistance staff division of MACV began to work jointly for me and for Ambassador Porter. Our interests and responsibilities were so interlocked that this arrangement served us both well.

Inflation and its Impact

Fueled by the tremendous buying power of our troops, inflation posed a formidable and growing problem. In 1966 my staff and I directed considerable attention to it. We instituted programs to divert the buying power of our troops by encouraging savings and by increasing the number of post exchanges and the range of items offered in the exchanges. The Rest and Recuperation (R&R) program for our troops was expanded to outside countries. These efforts, plus closer coordination with Vietnamese officials at all levels to encourage price control measures, kept the problem within manageable proportions. Conversely, the fear of inflation led to the imposition of piaster expenditure ceilings that restricted the rate of buildup of both United States and Vietnamese forces.

Republic of Vietnam Armed Forces

During the year I devoted the greater part of my time to the American buildup and our combat operations, while my able, combat-experienced deputy, General Heintges, continued to dedicate most of his time to our effort to build viable South Vietnamese forces. Each MACV headquarters staff section had major elements that worked on developing the Vietnamese Armed Forces and advising their Vietnamese counterparts in the Joint General Staff. I continued frequent contacts with the Chief of the Vietnamese Joint General Staff, General Vien, and often made visits to the Vietnamese corps and division headquarters and their field units.

The Republic's Armed Forces had expanded during the year, with ARVN absorbing the majority of a 20,000-man increase to the regular forces and the Regional and Popular Forces increasing by 30,000. At the end of 1966 Vietnamese forces of all types totalled approximately 623,000 men, of whom 329,000 were regulars. On 21 December 1966 the U.S. Mission Council completed a South Vietnamese manpower study. The document concluded that the maximum sustainable level of the armed forces should not exceed 622,000. In response to this judgment, I revised the projected force level downward from 633,645 to 622,153.

South Vietnamese Administrative Organization

The administrative organization of the Vietnamese forces continued to improve during 1966 with an expansion of existing training facilities and establishment of division training centers. With our advice and assistance the Joint General Staff formed a Command Leadership Committee. The committee took a number of forward looking actions that included procedures for improving the promotion system for officers and noncommissioned officers, enacting a merit promotion system for enlisted men, establishing criteria for selection to attend the Vietnamese Command and General Staff College, and improving the awards and decorations program.

Quarterly Reviews

During 1966 we instituted a system of quarterly reviews of progress. General Vien and I visited each of the corps every three months to meet with the senior Vietnamese and Allied commanders. During these visits we reviewed and evaluated progress in their areas in light of the Combined Campaign Plan. In the II Corps area, Lt. Gen. Chae Myung Shin, commander of the Republic of Korea forces, joined with us to review quarterly progress and to make appropriate decisions. This management system proved valuable in measuring our progress and adjusting our programs. It provided a timely method to collect the experiences and lessons learned in different areas by different units. These lessons were subsequently disseminated throughout the command, thereby broadly improving the quality of our tactics and operational procedures. I held frequent commanders' conferences, at sites away from my headquarters in Saigon, at which we exchanged information on tactical innovations and other new ideas. Also, several times each week I visited individual commanders in the field to see at first hand their problems, to review with them their situation, to determine their views, to give them guidance, and to visit their troops.

Tactical Experimentation and Innovation

In 1966 we were progressively developing our ability to fight an elusive enemy on an area battlefield while improving our troop and logistical capability. It was a year of learning: old tactics had to be modified, new tactics and techniques explored. New equipment had to be developed and new skills acquired. We had to learn the enemy's tactics and how to deal with them, how to detect and defeat his attacks and ambushes, and how to locate and destroy his forces.

One innovation prompted by the basic fluidity of the area battlefield was the system of interlocking fire support bases and improved night defensive positions developed to provide effective and continuous all-around defense. This system was not unlike the all-around defense practiced during the American Indian Wars. Major emphasis was put on fire support; artillery was positioned so that any point in the area of operations could be reached by fire from at least one and usually two or more batteries. The batteries were mutually supporting in that they could fire in support of one another in case of an attack. The artillerymen organized their positions so that the guns could deliver fire in all directions. The great range of the 175-mm gun made it possible to deliver a heavy concentration of accurate fire to positions and patrols within 20 miles of the gun position, regardless of the weather. We also refined our fire support procedures for both air and artillery to insure prompt as well as reliable delivery of support. An elaborate system of firing checks and clearances was developed and instituted to guard against endangering civilians or adjacent units.

A valuable firepower innovation was the AC–47 gunship, dubbed "Puff the Magic Dragon" or "Spooky." This was a DC–3 transport aircraft with three "miniguns" mounted to fire out the left side. With each gun firing 6,000 rounds a minute, these aircraft were able to illuminate a target at night with flares and deliver upon it a devastating attack. The gunships maintained nightly airborne vigils and were frequently instrumental in disrupting enemy night attacks against our defensive perimeters, ARVN outposts, and Special Forces camps.

To counter the enemy's favored tactics of ambush and surprise attacks on small isolated units, we developed a system of providing every regular unit, convoy, and installation with instantly responsive fire support and an immediate reaction force. This not only required sophisticated communication and fire support procedures, but entailed development of highly coordinated counter-ambush techniques and tactics.

In our "Road Runner" operations we would conduct sudden dashes through possible ambush sites, reconnoitering by fire to pre-empt enemy initiation of contact. This and other counter-ambush tactics soon began to pay off. Attempted ambushes dropped perceptibly as enemy casualties in these operations mounted. In some cases we ourselves succeeded in luring the enemy into ambushes. By pooling helicopters and reinforcing between brigades or divisions, we were able to take advantage of firm enemy contacts by rapid reinforcement against their forces, blocking their routes of withdrawal, and if possible, surrounding them. We called this quick reinforcement technique "pile-on tactics."

In "cordon and search" and "County Fair" operations, developed first by the Marines and then adopted by all ground commands, our troops would encircle an area and provide welfare services for the civilians while South Vietnamese officials made a detailed search within the cordoned area for Viet Cong personnel, arms, and ammunition. We sought to interfere with the enemy's night movements by setting ambushes on his supply and movement routes under what was called the "Bushmaster" program.

Trained scout and sentry dogs, highly intelligent and loyal, served us well in a variety of assignments. As sentinels, they strengthened the security and perimeter defenses of our bases. Operating as scouts with tactical units, they provided early warning of the enemy's approach or presence. They could detect the enemy's entry into a prepared ambush site and were particularly useful in spotting booby traps, locating enemy tunnels and bunkers, and locating caches of weapons, supplies, and food.

Combat Tracker Teams were also formed. These were five-man teams using dogs chosen for endurance, color, stability and good nature rather than ferocity, as in the case of the canine sentries. The dog's sense of smell and the soldier's specialized scouting skills formed a powerful combination capable of tracking the enemy for miles and often leading to larger base camps, caches, or ambushes. In the Mekong Delta the tracker dogs were used to detect night movement of sampans on the rivers and canals. (By mid-1968 some 1,500 dogs would be used throughout Vietnam. Thirty-six were killed in action and 153 wounded.)

In September 1966 I instructed the 5th Special Forces Group at Nha Trang to organize a Recondo (reconnaissance-commando) School to train selected U.S. and Free World troops in the specialized techniques and skills of long-range patrolling. Instructors from the Australian Special Air Service Regiment provided invaluable assistance. The school was soon graduating some 35 men every two weeks, and we later helped the South Vietnamese to establish a similar school.

With graduates of the MACV Recondo School providing a nucleus, all major units organized Long Range Reconnaissance Patrols consisting of from four to eight men. These patrols penetrated deep into contested areas and obtained valuable information about the enemy's location and movement, often calling down air and artillery on enemy troop concentrations and concealed bases. The Australian troops were especially effective in this type operation.

During 1966 airmobile operations came of age. All maneuver battalions became skilled in the use of the helicopter for tactical transportation to achieve surprise and outmaneuver the enemy. We also perfected a technique of shifting our light and medium artillery pieces by helicopter to provide continuous fire support to units involved in rapidly shifting engagements.

Until this time there was considerable skepticism about the ability of the helicopter to survive in a combat environment. The craft actually proved to be a rugged vehicle and the inordinate losses some had predicted failed to materialize. We lost only one helicopter shot down every 3,600 flying hours. Most of these were repairable. In fact, helicopter losses (nonrepairable) to enemy fire occurred, on the average, only every 9,250 flying hours.

One technique used on airmobile operations in the jungle was to lower men with jungle clearing equipment from helicopters equipped with rope ladders. Once these men had cleared a landing zone, helicopters landed additional men and equipment for support of the particular operation. In order to speed up this laborious, time-consuming process, we submitted a requirement for a special type of bomb that could penetrate the heavy jungle canopy and blast a clear area sufficiently large for a helicopter landing zone. Steady progress was subsequently made in satisfying the requirement.

We found the armored personnel carrier a valuable tool for penetrating the enemy's jungle positions, both because of its mobility and because it could counter many of the innumerable mines, snares, and booby traps that the enemy used. In more open areas, we "married" tanks, armored personnel carriers, and helicopters in an effective team to fix and destroy the enemy. The "Road Runner" operations conducted by mobile armored units cleared and retained control of vital highways and considerably eased the strain on our airlift.

We had to develop individual and unit skills in the techniques of detecting, penetrating, and destroying the enemy's well-concealed bunker and tunnel complexes. The riot control chemical "CS" was extensively used to bring the enemy to the surface without jeopardizing unduly our men or the safety of numerous civilians whom the Viet Cong habitually held in the tunnels as workers, hostages, or as shields against our troops. We employed specially trained teams of men of small physical stature (who proudly referred to themselves as "tunnel rats") to search the tunnel complexes for prisoners, equipment, and documents. Once searched, the fortifications had to be destroyed. The sheer magnitude of the complexes created major logistics problems in providing sufficient amounts of explosives and thus taxed our ingenuity, but several systems of demolishing or flooding the tunnels were developed.

To prevent the enemy from reoccupying and rebuilding his base areas it was then necessary virtually to level vast stretches of the jungle. To meet this problem I ordered 56 "Rome Plows," specially equipped bulldozers capable of heavy duty land clearing. In September specially trained army engineer units operating the "Rome Plows" commenced a massive jungle clearing project that I named Operation PAUL BUNYAN. We also used the device to clear fields of fire around our base camps and a 200-yard strip along either side of main supply routes to eliminate potential ambush sites.

CHRONOLOGY OF MAJOR EVENTS—1966

January

On 15 January the South Vietnamese Premier, Air Vice Marshal Ky, pledged to hold, in October, a popular referendum on a new constitution as the first step toward "genuine democratic elections in 1967" leading to a civilian government.

A temporary cease-fire from 20 through 23 January marked the *Tet* holiday period. Although many minor clashes occurred, the enemy in general honored the truce. When the North Vietnamese gave no indication that the suspension of air attacks against North Vietnam, begun the preceding month and still in effect, might lead to meaningful negotiations, the United States resumed its bombing of military targets on 31 January, ending the 37-day suspension.

During the month allied forces began a series of spoiling attacks, radiating from the capital city of Saigon, to clear main roads, forestall enemy operations, and improve security. Saigon is not only the heart of the nation in political terms but about 40 percent of the population of South Vietnam and almost all of its industry lie within a radius of 50 kilometers of the city. The proximity to the capital of long-developed major enemy base areas (the "Iron Triangle," War Zones C and D, and the Rung Sat mangrove swamp) afforded the enemy jumping-off spots, logistic support bases, training centers, rest camps, and hospitals within striking distance of the most vital area in the country.

On 4 January the enemy attacked a Special Forces camp at Khe Sanh in Quang Tri Province with the heaviest weapons yet employed, 120-mm mortars.

During the first half of January, the 1st Brigade, 1st Cavalry Division, conducted Operation MATADOR to find and destroy the enemy in Pleiku and Kontum Provinces. At one point the air cavalrymen saw the enemy flee across the border into Cambodia and into base camps inside that country, confirming what we had already deduced—that the enemy had well-developed sanctuaries inside Cambodia.

On 19 January the 1st Brigade, 101st Airborne Division, the Korean 2d Marine Brigade, and the ARVN 47th Regiment began Operation VAN BUREN. This operation was to locate and destroy the NVA 95th Regiment, believed to be in the Tuy Hoa valley, and to protect the rice harvest in the coastal region. The success of this major combined operation can be measured in the 679 enemy killed, 49 captured, and 177 who defected; 4,700 inhabitants were relocated to safe areas and over 30,000 tons of rice were harvested.

Having begun to arrive in Vietnam during the last days of 1965, the 3d Brigade, 25th Infantry Division, assembled in the vicinity of the town of Pleiku. Key to the High Plateau, Pleiku was also the headquarters of the South Vietnamese II Corps.

February

On 6 February President Johnson and other senior American officials arrived in Hawaii to confer with Premier Ky and other representatives of the South Vietnamese government. When the conference adjourned on the 8th, Vice President Hubert H. Humphrey accompanied Premier Ky to Saigon for further discussions on South Vietnamese economic and social problems.

Beginning in February, the war in the northern provinces assumed a new and ominous aspect, as two North Vietnamese Army divisions—the 324B and 341st—threatened invasion across the Demilitarized Zone into the northernmost province of Quang Tri. By March infiltration of the enemy forces was well under way. At the same time, the enemy began to infiltrate through Laos into the next province to the south, Thua Thien, whose capital is the ancient imperial city of Hue. The two northernmost provinces are separated from the rest of the country by a precipitous mountain barrier extending to the sea and traversed only by the narrow Hai Van pass. At the time, only the Vietnamese 1st Division and a single U.S. Marine battalion were deployed in the two provinces.

In response to this imminent threat, we progressively shifted the bulk of the U.S. 3d Marine Division north of the Hai Van pass and also introduced the first U.S. Army combat units into the northern provinces: a battalion each of paratroopers of the 173d Airborne Brigade, 175-mm artillery, 105-mm self-propelled artillery, and 40-mm antiaircraft guns with a battery of mobile .50-caliber quadruple machine guns attached. The 175-mm guns could provide long range fire support all the way from their positions near the coast to Khe Sanh near the Laotian border. They could also fire into and across the Demilitarized Zone, which the enemy had turned into an invasion corridor.

Based on intelligence reports of enemy activity in the vicinity of Ban Me Thuot in Darlac Province, the headquarters and two battalions of the 3d Brigade, 25th Division, moved in late February to that provincial capital in a portion of the Highlands that had yet seen few American troops. In a series of offensive moves known as Operation GARFIELD and extending well into March, the battalions in their first combat experience ferreted out a number of enemy concentrations in the vicinity of the town. On one occasion helicopters airlifted a battalion to the vicinity of an enemy base and faked extraction the next day. That night the battalion moved unopposed on the Viet Cong base and killed 30 of the enemy.

March

During March the Republic of Korea announced plans to increase its commitment in Vietnam by another division and an additional regiment. Australia revealed plans to triple its force in Vietnam from 1,500 men to 4,500. By 2 March U.S. forces in South Vietnam reached a strength of 215,000 men, with 20,000 more en route.

During March we sustained the only significant setback of the year when the North Vietnamese 95B and 101C Regiments attacked a Special Forces Camp in the high and remote A Shau Valley. After three days of valiant and heavy fighting in the worst possible weather, the Civilian Irregular Defense Group forces and small detachments of U.S. and Vietnamese Special Forces found it necessary to abandon the camp. Men of the Special Forces Marine, Air Force, and Army helicopter units performed innumerable acts of bravery in supporting and extracting these troops.

After the abandonment of this camp, the North Vietnamese moved into the A Shau valley and began to develop a major logistical base and to construct roads into Laos to tie in with the extensive network of motorable routes leading from North Vietnam. Short of troops and helicopters and threatened by a major force along the Demilitarized Zone, I reluctantly decided against reinforcing or reoccupying the remote camp. Two years would pass before we would be in a position to return to this valley.

Early in March a political crisis arose in the I Corps when a militant Buddhist and student faction in Hue and Da Nang challenged the authority of the central government. After the South Vietnamese government removed the I Corps commander, Lt. Gen. Nguyen Chanh Thi, mass protests occurred, creating political turbulence which was destined to spread and to continue until midsummer. Later in the month, and again in early April, anti-government protests erupted in Saigon. Premier Ky flew to Da Nang in an effort to quell the rebellion there. From 12 to 14 April, a National Political Congress met in Saigon to adopt a program designed to meet Buddhist demands. Although the demonstrations ended on 14 April, not until 15 May would Vietnamese government troops regain control of Da Nang. Throughout the spring and summer, disorders flared in Saigon. Seizure by South Vietnamese troops, in late June, of the principal Buddhist center in Saigon marked the virtual end of this episode of political unrest. The power of the militant Buddhists was broken and the government of Vietnam emerged with increased confidence.

In late March the two battalions of the 3d Brigade, 25th Division, that had been operating in the vicinity of Ban Me Thuot, marched north along Route 14, repairing road and bridges as they moved in the first use of that highway in many months. Midway between Ban Me Thuot and Pleiku, the battalion occupied a Special Forces camp at Buon Brieng that had been abandoned a year and a half earlier. Meanwhile, the brigade's cavalry troop and tank company drove south down Route 14 from Pleiku. Upon link-up, infantry, cavalry, and tanks retraced Route 14 northward to its juncture with Route 19 and followed that road westward almost to the Cambodian frontier at Duc Co. In one of the first major U.S. road-clearing operations, the brigade made little contact with the enemy.

The continuing campaign to clear the enemy from the provinces surrounding Saigon met with heavy resistance in Hau Nghia Province, west of the capital. Because the enemy there posed a major threat to Saigon, and since the province contained major enemy supply routes linking the Mekong Delta with War Zones C and D and infiltration routes from Cambodia, I decided to deploy the incoming U.S. 25th Infantry Division directly to Hau Nghia Province. The division established its base camp along Highway 1 at Cu Chi and began operations extending throughout the province.

In March and early April the 1st Infantry Division and the First Australian Task Force launched Operation ABILENE, a spoiling operation to destroy base camps and caches established by the Viet Cong 5th Division east of Saigon in preparation for an enemy move against the capital. Although no major engagements ensued, the allied troops seized quantities of rice and other supplies and forced the Viet Cong division to abandon the area temporarily.

April

On 24 April the 1st Infantry Division entered War Zone C near the Cambodian border in Tay Ninh Province—the first major allied foray into that enemy stronghold since 1962. Known as Operation BIRMINGHAM, the move uncovered vast quantities of rice, clothing, medicine, and miscellaneous supplies just inside the frontier of South Vietnam. Judging from loading ramps observed on the Cambodian side of the river that marks the border, and unloading ramps on the Vietnamese side, the supplies quite obviously had come from Cambodia. Since Viet Cong main force units withdrew ahead of the 1st Division troops, all engagements were with security troops assigned to guard the enemy supplies.

In Operation AUSTIN VI, which began on 25 April and ended on 18 May, the 1st Brigade, 101st Airborne Division, killed 101 enemy and completely routed the NVA 3d Battalion, 141st Regiment, forcing that unit to retreat to its Cambodian sanctuary. In and around Bu Gia Map airstrip, the brigade successfully employed its famous "checkerboard" tactics.

May

Through the spring and early summer, the U.S. Marines in the I Corps zone concentrated their operations along the coastal plain of Quang Nam, Quang Tin, and Quang Ngai Provinces. In conjunction with South Vietnamese forces, the Marines radiated out from secure base areas to bring large portions of the coastal region back under government control.

In the course of these operations, the III Marine Amphibious Force developed an imaginative and effective program to reinforce Vietnamese territorial security forces. Once a hamlet had been cleared of major enemy units, a Marine squad would join the Popular Force platoon defending the hamlet. Thereafter, the Marines stayed permanently with the territorial unit as part of what was called a Combined Action Platoon. The Vietnamese troops were afforded training, improved communications, and access to U.S. fire support, when needed. The Marines who lived and fought with their Popular Forces counterparts have contributed greatly to the allied effort and deserve the greatest credit and admiration.

June

On 2 June the 1st Brigade, 101st Airborne Division, and ARVN units launched Operation HAW-

THORNE, a classic spoiling attack that would carry these forces to Tou Morong, Tan Canh, and eventually to Dak To. In 19 days of vicious combat, the enemy lost 531 killed and the NVA 24th Regiment was rendered ineffective as a fighting unit.

On 6 June South Vietnam's ruling National Leadership Committee, composed of ten general officers, expanded its membership to include ten prominent civilians. A fortnight later Premier Ky signed a decree setting 11 September as the date for election of a constituent assembly to draft a new constitution.

The date of 17 June marked the end of the first year of B–52 bomber strikes in South Vietnam, during which the B–52's had flown 3,715 sorties. We employed the B–52's increasingly *en masse* against large enemy forces and bases that were located through an ever-improving combined intelligence effort. On 6 July the B–52's were to operate for the first time with a "combat sky spot" bombing system, whereby ground radar control directed the big bombers over the target and also indicated the moment of bomb release. The system reduced planning time and added a flexibility that made it possible to divert the bombers to targets of opportunity. Also on 6 July we began to employ the Strategic Air Command's "Quick Run" reaction force, which consisted of six B–52's on continuous alert on Guam. Within a few hours of a field commander's request, we could use this force against enemy forces in direct contact with our ground troops. The B–52's were so valuable that I personally dealt with requests from field commanders, reviewed the targets, and normally allocated the available bomber resources on a daily basis. I also continued to urge that action be taken to substantially increase B–52 sorties.

In June and July the U.S. 1st Infantry Division and the Vietnamese 5th Division mounted a series of operations along the eastern flank of War Zone C. Their objectives were to open Route 13 from Saigon to major rubber plantations in Binh Long Province and to attack and destroy major elements of the Viet Cong 9th Division that were massing for an attempt to seize and hold the province capital of An Loc and several district capitals, including Loc Ninh. Known as EL PASO II, the operation involved five major engagements against all three regiments of the Viet Cong division. In the operation's latter stages, American and South Vietnamese troops developed highly effective counter-ambush tactics based on the firepower capability of armored cavalry units and rapid reaction of helicopter-borne infantrymen. Leaving behind over 850 dead, the Viet Cong division withdrew into sanctuaries along the Cambodian border deep in War Zone C.

July

In July with political stability returning, the Vietnamese government turned its attention back to the problems of pacification. To provide the vitality, the emphasis, and the central direction that had been lacking in earlier efforts, in February Premier Ky gave the Minister of Rural Construction directional authority over the newly formed Revolutionary Development cadre teams built around the concept and personnel of the earlier People's Action Teams. The People's Action Teams had been trained in military, political, economic, and social processes and had begun to carry out the rudimentary aspects of these processes at the hamlet level in 1965. To provide security to the hamlet, all members of the new Revolutionary Development teams were trained and armed. Team members established a hamlet government, conducted a census, and listened to grievances. Another vital function was the identification and elimination of the members of the local VC political and military organization. In 1967 and 1968 this program expanded enormously.

Attention also was given to expanding the chain of border surveillance camps in the critical tri-border area of the Central Highlands. A new CIDG camp was established at Dak Seang to replace the Dak Sut installation which had been overrun and destroyed by the enemy in August

1965, while a second camp was slated for construction at New Plei Djereng to control the southern exit of the Plei Trap valley—a major route of enemy infiltration. During July U.S. and Vietnamese Marines and the Vietnamese airborne division conducted Operation HASTINGS against the North Vietnamese 324B Division in Quang Tri Province. In intense fighting immediately south of the Demilitarized Zone, constituting the second largest engagement of the year, the enemy lost 882 killed. By late July the North Vietnamese division was withdrawing northward into the sanctuary of the Demilitarized Zone.

During the month the Department of Defense announced that U.S. forces in Southeast Asia had increased above 350,000 men and that additional troops would be provided as needed. Free World Forces were also to increase as the Republic of the Philippines authorized dispatch to Vietnam of a 2,000-man civic action group (engineers). A Filipino medical team arrived on 23 July, and the next day the Royal Thai Air Force deployed a training team to Vietnam.

August

With arrival of the 196th Light Infantry Brigade on 14 August, total U.S. strength in Vietnam rose to approximately 300,000.

On 18 August the 1st Australian Task Force annihilated a Viet Cong battalion in Operation SMITHFIELD in Phuoc Tuy Province for the largest Australian victory up to that time.

September

Last contingents of the U.S. 11th Armored Cavalry Regiment arrived at Vung Tau on 7 September. The Republic of Korea's 9th Infantry (White Horse) Division arrived to assume responsibility for an area of operations in Khanh Hoa, Ninh Thuan, and Phu Yen Provinces in the II Corps. Highly professional, tough, and aggressive, the Korean troops provided security for the logistic and air bases at Cam Ranh Bay, Phan Rang, and Tuy Hoa, while at the same time conducting some of the most imaginative and effective pacification operations of the entire war.

On 11 September 81 percent of eligible South Vietnamese voters elected a 117-member constituent assembly to draft a new constitution and prepare for restoration of civilian government during the next year. That a nationwide election could be held in a country torn by a war was a tribute to the organizational ability of Premier Ky's administration and an even greater tribute to the willingness of the individual voter to participate in the elective process in the face of personal danger.

At this stage, the war in the sprawling Mekong Delta, where neither North Vietnamese nor U.S. ground troops were yet engaged, was in something of a stalemate. However, I was increasingly concerned about enemy activity in Long An Province, immediately south of Saigon. The province had long provided routes for Viet Cong access to Saigon. It was one of three or four provinces in the country over which the Viet Cong had exercised a high level of control for many years. Despite some apprehension in the U.S. Mission and in Washington that the population would resent American presence in the Delta and that American troops would upset the economy of that rice-rich land, I decided to introduce limited U.S. forces into Long An Province. Earlier concern proved unfounded when, in early September, a battalion of the U.S. 25th Infantry Division moved into the province. Well received by the people, the U.S. troops demonstrated that American units could operate effectively in that region of canals, swamps, and inundated rice paddies.

The U.S. Navy component command also entered the Delta waterways in Operation GAME WARDEN designated to thwart Viet Cong use of the waterways as supply and infiltration routes and to reduce Viet Cong tax collection in the same area. The GAME WARDEN forces employed fiberglas boats—propelled by water jets and armed with .50-caliber machine guns—which could move with such speed and had such a shallow draft that they could easily outrun and outmaneuver enemy junks and sampans. By the end of the year, GAME WARDEN forces supported by armed Army helicopters (later replaced by Navy helicopters) were teaming with river assault groups of the Vietnamese Navy in the slow process of reasserting government control over the principal lines of communication in the Delta, heretofore used by the Viet Cong with impunity.

To take advantage of floods on the Mekong and Bassac Rivers, the South Vietnamese Army, Special Forces, and Regional and Popular Forces began a series of attacks in the Plain of Reeds in the northwestern part of the IV Corps. At that time of the year, the water reached depths as great as 15 to 20 feet and the Viet Cong were forced to move in sampans and to live on the few islands of dry ground. This made them highly vulnerable to attack. Using helicopters, Navy patrol boats, air-cushion vehicles, sampans, and tactical aircraft, the South Vietnamese killed and captured over 600 of the enemy.

By the fall of 1966, Operation MARKET TIME, designed to seal the coast of South Vietnam against infiltration of enemy troops and supplies, had become highly effective. The MARKET TIME barrier consisted of two belts formed by some 115 ships and support craft. High speed aluminum-hulled "Swift" boats and 82-foot Coast Guard cutters patrolled an inner belt. Further offshore, but within the 12-mile zone contiguous to South Vietnam, Navy destroyer escorts and minesweepers formed a second belt. Overhead, U.S. Navy patrol aircraft conducted visual and photographic reconnaissance. Working in conjunction with the Vietnamese Navy's coastal force, MARKET TIME units in 1966 detected an estimated 90 percent of all the steel-hulled trawlers operating along the South Vietnamese coast and reduced enemy maritime infiltration to a trickle. Before 1965, we estimated that the enemy had received about 70 percent of his supplies by sea; by the end of 1966, our best guess was that not more than 10 percent of his requirements arrived by that route. This forced the enemy to greater reliance on the long, torturous route through southeastern Laos.

Adjacent to the Delta, south and east of Saigon, lies one of the most unusual pieces of terrain in the world—a 50-square-mile region known as the Rung Sat. Through a vast, partly-inundated mangrove swamp wind thousands of serpentine waterways subject to six-foot tidal variations. These waterways include tributaries of the Saigon River, which provide the main ship channels to Saigon. The region afforded an improbable, but effective base for Viet Cong sapper and light infantry units, which made periodic attacks on shipping proceeding to and from the Saigon port. U.S. Marines, contingents of the U.S. 1st Infantry Division, GAME WARDEN patrols, and U.S. Navy SEAL (Sea, Air, Land) Teams began a series of operations to eliminate this harassment. So effective were the SEAL Teams that their numbers were expanded and their operations extended into the Mekong Delta. Vietnamese Navy SEAL Teams were trained and combined with U.S. teams.

October

On 24 October Chairman Thieu and Premier Ky joined President Johnson and other officials for the "Manila Conference," and on the 26th the President paid a surprise visit to Cam Ranh Bay, where he toured a hospital, met commanders and troops, and decorated a number of officers and men.

During the month, the 2,000-man Philippine Civic Action Group, consisting of engineers and medical teams supported and protected by a security force, arrived in Vietnam. Deployed to Tay Ninh Province, this force worked closely with local Vietnamese authorities in refugee relief, medical service, construction, and general assistance. This contribution by the Republic of the Philippines was a most welcome and valuable addition to the Free World Forces.

At Manila the United States and five other nations assisting South Vietnam—the Republic of Korea, Thailand, Australia, the Philippines, and New Zealand—pledged that their military forces in Vietnam "shall be withdrawn, after close consultation, as the other side withdraws its forces to the north, ceases infiltration, and the level of violence thus subsides." They would be withdrawn, the pledge continued, "as soon as possible and not later than six months after the above conditions have been fulfilled."

On 5 and 12 October the 1st and 3d Brigades of the 4th Infantry Division arrived in Vietnam, completing deployment of the division.

In late October the Viet Cong 9th Division deployed its three regiments, together with the North Vietnamese 101st Regiment, into central Tay Ninh Province with the objective of attacking the Special Forces camp at Sui Da. The enemy's plan was to lure allied forces into the area in response to an attack on the camp by one regiment, and then to destroy the relieving forces through ambushes and counterattacks with the other three regiments. The 196th Light Infantry Brigade discovered the enemy's presence south of Sui Da while searching for rice and other enemy supplies. When four companies of the U.S. 5th Special Forces Group's Mobile Strike Force were inserted into landing zones north and east of Sui Da, they immediately became heavily engaged. So great was the enemy strength that one company was overrun and the others had either to withdraw in small groups or to be extracted by helicopters.

Conscious that a very large enemy force was involved, we met the threat by committing the 1st Infantry Division, contingents of the 4th and 25th Infantry Divisions, and the 173d Airborne Brigade. The battle that ensued—known as Operation ATTLEBORO—rapidly developed into the largest fought to that time, with over 22,000 U.S. and allied troops participating. In a series of engagements extending into early November, allied forces killed well over 1,100 enemy and captured huge quantities of weapons, ammunition, and supplies. So badly whipped was the Viet Cong 9th Division that it would not reappear in combat until the spring of 1967.

November

The Vietnamese Minister of Defense announced that in 1967, in accordance with the Combined Campaign Plan, much of the South Vietnamese Army was to be employed in support of the pacification program. Some 50 to 60 Vietnamese battalions were to provide security for the pacification effort in selected priority areas. Since South Vietnamese troops faced no linguistic or cultural disadvantages, they were well suited for local security and for ferreting out the Viet Cong political organization. American, Korean, and Australian forces, along with Vietnamese airborne, Marine, and Ranger battalions were to carry the war to the ever-growing enemy main forces.

On 25 November the Viet Cong announced a 48-hour truce to be observed both at Christmas and the New Year. Five days later the South Vietnamese government announced similar truces and added a four-day period over the Lunar New Year.

On 28 November the advance party of the 199th Light Infantry Brigade arrived at Bien Hoa Airbase.

December

The Australian Prime Minister announced that Australian strength in South Vietnam would be increased from 4,500 to 6,300.

On 19 December advance contingents of the U.S. 9th Infantry Division arrived at Vung Tau.

As of 31 December U.S. military forces in South Vietnam totalled 385,000 men.

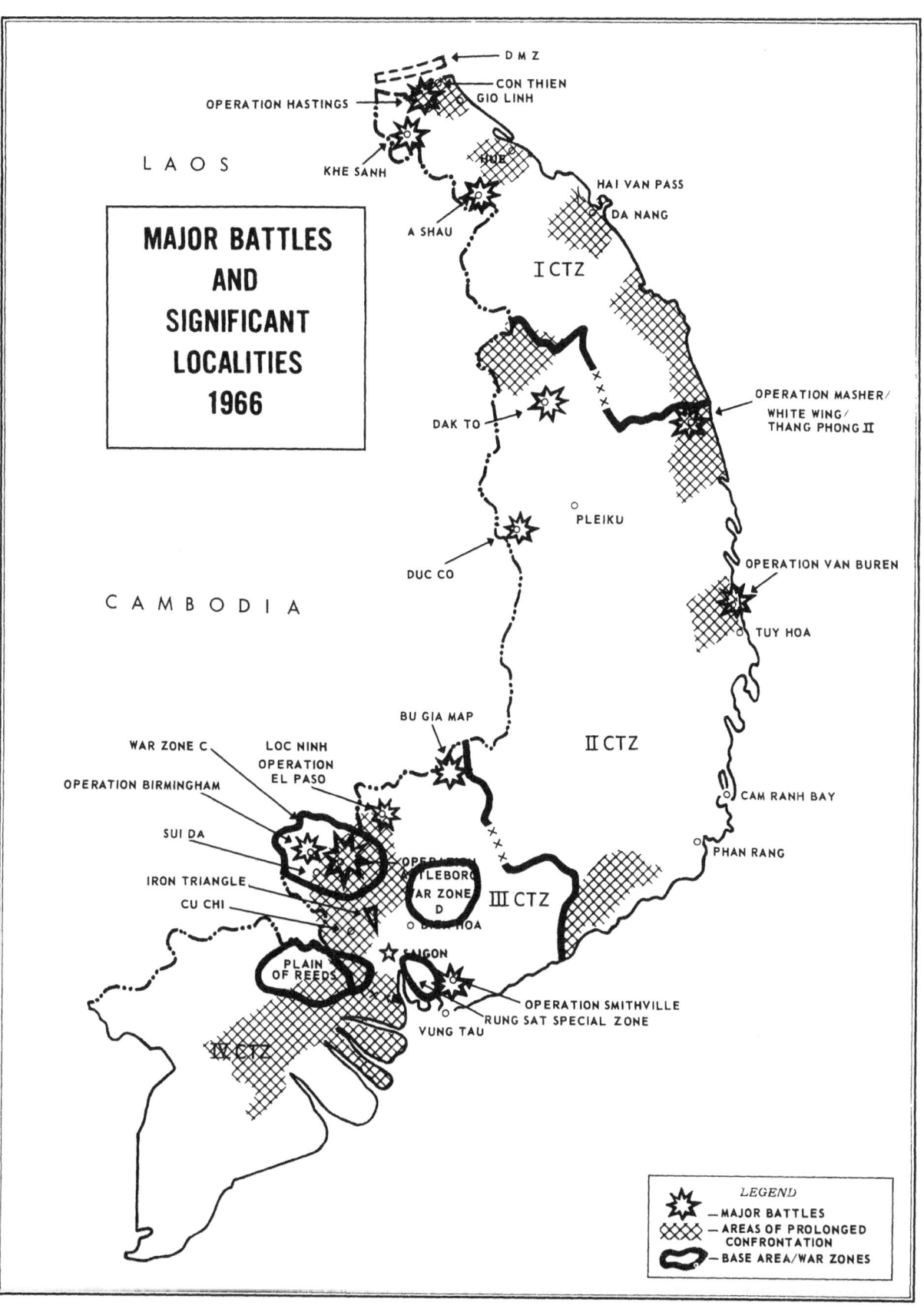

Chapter V

THE YEAR OF THE OFFENSIVE—1967

OVERVIEW

The momentum gained by the end of 1966 carried over into 1967. Additional troops and other available resources enabled the scope and pace of our offensive operations to increase steadily throughout the year. During this period, U.S. strength increased from 385,000 to 486,000. The number of maneuver battalions available to allied forces rose from 256 to 278. By year's end 28 tactical fighter squadrons were on hand to provide close air support and assist in the interdiction campaign. Over 3,000 helicopters of all types were organized into 107 units (Army companies and Marine squadrons), up from 68 units the previous year. The number of B-52 sorties increased sharply from 725 to 1,200.

The Mekong Delta Mobile Riverine Force was established at Dong Tam as a joint Army-Navy force. The 2d Brigade, 9th Infantry Division, was combined with two Navy River Assault Squadrons of 50 boats each. Two barrack ships housed the brigade between ground operations. The Navy's River Patrol Forces reached a high level of effectiveness with 125 ships, boats, and supporting craft. Equally important, the logistic system was filled out so that for the first time, U.S. and allied forces were operating from a fully adequate and flexible support system.

With these larger forces, added firepower, and improved mobility, we carried the battle to the enemy on a sustained basis throughout the year. Concurrently, we planned to intensify and expand the pacification effort. The Joint Vietnamese-U.S. Combined Campaign Plan for 1967 assigned to the Vietnamese Armed Forces the primary role in pacification and specified the priority areas for their employment. The same plan provided that U.S. combat forces would carry the bulk of the offensive effort against Viet Cong and North Vietnamese Army main force units.

As I said in a speech on 24 April to the Associated Press Managing Editors, we had to carry forward several tasks simultaneously:

> At one and the same time, we must fight the enemy, protect the people, and help them build a nation in the pattern of their choice.
>
> The real objective of the war is the people. If the enemy could take Saigon, or the heavily populated areas of the Delta, or both, the war would be over—without negotiation or conference. He lost this chance two years ago, and I can promise you that his military tactics alone will not win him another opportunity. Yet, despite his staggering combat losses, he clings to the belief that he will defeat us. And through a clever combination of psychological and political warfare—both here and abroad—he has gained support which gives him hope that he can win politically that which he cannot accomplish militarily.

Four days later I expanded on this point in my address before a joint session of the Congress:

> This is the enemy—this has been the challenge. The only strategy which can defeat such an organization is one of unrelenting but discriminating military, political, and psychological pressure on his whole structure—at all levels.

It was precisely to the establishment of such unrelenting military pressure at all levels that the Combined Campaign Plan for 1967 was directed.

The U.S. concentration on the enemy's main forces did not imply an emphasis at the expense of the pacification effort. Its purpose was complementary—to drive the enemy main forces away from the priority pacification area. Moreover, numerous U.S. units would assist and reinforce Vietnamese units in pacification just as Vietnamese Marines, airborne units, Ranger battalions, and other selected Army units would help to prosecute the offensive against the main forces. In fact, we anticipated that over half of the U.S. combat forces would continue to be employed in close proximity to the heavily populated areas of the country, targeted against the guerrillas and local forces—and over half were so employed throughout 1967.

The reasoning behind the partial differentiation of functions embodied in our Combined Campaign Plan for 1967 made good sense then as it does today. The highly-mobile U.S. forces could concentrate and disperse more quickly than could most of the other allied forces in South Vietnam. In addition to their larger airmobile capability, their extensive communications and flexible logistic support systems were well suited to the task. Above all, their tremendous firepower made it vastly more desirable that they fight in remote, unpopulated areas if the enemy would give battle there. This would enable the full U.S. firepower potential to be employed without the danger of civilian casualties. It would also minimize the impact of U.S. forces and operations on the Vietnamese civilian economy.

Many Vietnamese units, on the other hand, had only a modest mobility capability. Troops were accustomed to a decentralized system of sustenance which depended on local markets. However, most important of all, the soldiers understood the language, customs, problems, and aspirations of the Vietnamese people—for they were part of this people. They were much better suited to measures requiring some degree of population control than U.S. soldiers would have been. On the other hand, numerous U.S. battalions were in constant contact with local Vietnamese officials.

Widespread recognition of the fact that the pacification effort and the main force war were essentially inseparable—opposite sides of the same coin—was one of the reasons why responsibility for the entire U.S. pacification support effort was placed under MACV control in May of 1967. I had objected strongly to the "two war" thesis then popular in some circles. To direct these civil programs we formed within the command the office of the Assistant Chief of Staff for Civil Operations and Revolutionary Development Support (CORDS) and Ambassador Robert W. Komer arrived to serve as my deputy in the entire pacification area.

With the U.S. side of the pacification effort given unified direction and the relative roles of U.S. and Vietnamese forces agreed to, we had to determine where to concentrate and where to conserve in our campaign against the enemy's main forces. We decided to intensify our efforts in the III Corps zone, to begin our expansion into the IV Corps area, to continue our expansion in the populous southern region of the I Corps while continuing to guard the DMZ with minimum forces, and to conserve forces in the II Corps area.

At the beginning of the year the enemy still enjoyed relative security in the huge War Zones in the III Corps, and our use of roads was generally restricted to Saigon and the immediate vicinity. Even our vital water links on the Long Tau and Dong Ngai shipping channels connecting the Saigon area with the sea were never totally secure. With the exception of Operation ATTLEBORO in late 1966, we had not yet entered these enemy areas on large-scale offensive operations, so that many of them were still largely untouched.

In the northern part of the I Corps, our objectives for 1967 were to meet and defeat North Vietnam's invasion through the DMZ and Laos, to interdict the enemy's infiltration routes in South Vietnam, and to neutralize his base areas near the coastal plain, which provided his guerrilla forces much of their support. Equally important in the southern portion of the corps zone was the protection of our base areas and the lines of communication that enabled the government to extend its control. Having largely denied to the enemy the rice-producing coastal regions of the II Corps and much of the Quang Nam Province of the I Corps in 1966, we intended to link those areas and expand our control into Quang Ngai and Quang Tin Provinces.

In the Central Highlands we intended to screen the Cambodian border with light forces and send reinforcements to the area only when North Vietnamese regiments undertook to cross the border and mount offensive operations. This saved us troops for more important tasks.

In the IV Corps, major allied objectives during 1967 were to increase government pressure on the enemy, enhance security for Revolutionary Development teams, and upgrade the security of major roads, particularly Route 4—the lifeline of the Delta. The biggest change in the tactical picture was the introduction of the U.S. Mobile Riverine Force (a Navy task force and troops of the 9th Infantry Division), the first major U.S. combat unit to operate as far south as the Mekong and Bassac Rivers.

Throughout 1967 I continued to be acutely aware of the conflicting demands on U.S. forces. I knew that it was necessary to strike out against the very formidable forces assembling in the border sanctuaries and remote base areas in order to prevent them from planning and executing deliberate attacks against the populated areas and against government centers. At the same time, I was aware of the necessity to protect the pacification effort, whose success or failure would, in the long run, determine the fate of South Vietnam.

To explain the interrelationship between these two important missions to our troops and to our Vietnamese allies, I drew on a simple analogy. A boxer faces problems of both defense and attack. As he jabs and probes with one hand, he keeps his defense up with the other. Only when he sees a clear opportunity does he attack with both fists. When he does use both offensively, he accepts a calculated risk by leaving himself momentarily uncovered. Conversely, if he uses both hands defensively for too long—covered up, as a boxer would say—he surrenders all initiative to his opponent. He cannot win by defensive measures alone.

Our problem was similar to that facing the boxer. So, too, was the dilemma posed to the leaders in Hanoi. Before describing their problem and eventual decision, I would like to give an example from 1967 to illustrate how we used the troops available to us to increase our offensive against the enemy's main forces while we continued defensive measures to enhance local security.

In the III Corps area we started the year with a large clearing operation, CEDAR FALLS, in the "Iron Triangle" area just north of Saigon. This area had for many years been under development as a Viet Cong logistic center and as the headquarters for Military Region IV, which controlled enemy activity in and around Saigon. We captured huge caches of rice and other foodstuffs, destroyed a mammoth and deep system of tunnels, seized many documents of significant intelligence value, killed 720 enemy, and captured 213. This operation permitted a speedup in the pacification area close to Saigon.

In February the same U.S. forces that had been engaged in this clearing operation were committed, along with other units, against the enemy's main forces in the largest allied operation of the war to that time, JUNCTION CITY, in War Zone C. Over 22 U.S. and 4 ARVN battalions engaged the enemy, killing 2,728. Additionally, we constructed three airfields capable of handling C-130's, erected a bridge entering the zone on its eastern edge, cleared innumerable helicopter landing zones, and fortified two camps in which Special Forces teams with CIDG garrisons remained as we withdrew. Henceforth, we would be able to enter this important but difficult area with relative ease and with much smaller forces, as we have done many times since.

As Operation JUNCTION CITY ended, elements of the U.S. 1st and 25th Infantry Divisions, the 11th Armored Cavalry Regiment, and ARVN forces swung back toward Saigon and conducted yet another clearing operation, MANHATTAN, in the Long Nguyen base area just north of the previously cleared "Iron Triangle." Later in the year we improved the security of the "Iron Triangle" by scraping away its remaining jungle cover with the "Rome Plows." (Explained under Observations—1966.)

Using this technique of expanding offensive strikes while continuing clearing operations, we were able during the first half of 1967 to execute our plans essentially as we had intended, not only in the III Corps but in other areas as well. By June we had initiated our offensive operations in the Mekong Delta area of the IV Corps and had succeeded in restricting enemy activity in the II Corps zone.

In northern I Corps, our offensive operations took a heavy toll of the enemy and met what was very nearly a conventional invasion. However, the North Vietnamese continued to turn their half of the Demilitarized Zone into a vast armed camp. In April we shifted Army forces from further south to the populated areas of southern I Corps and to the enemy's base areas in the foothills. To accomplish this I formed Task Force OREGON as a provisional division. This later became the 23d (Americal) Division. Contingency plans for this task force had been prepared well in advance and component combat and service units had been earmarked and alerted. This shift freed Marines in southern I Corps to reinforce in the area southwest of Da Nang and near the DMZ where the enemy threat continued to grow in size and intensity throughout the year.

Based on our intelligence, I foresaw an even higher level of enemy effort in the far northern provinces in the future. Consequently, I set in motion a number of actions to increase our logistical capability in the area. A major step was the construction of the Quang Tri Airfield because the airfield at Dong Ha farther north was in range of enemy artillery north of the DMZ. Additionally, we increased the number of LST landing ramps and began planning for additional port facilities. In the actual event these preparatory measures paid off in that we were able to deploy very large forces into this area just before and after the *Tet* offensive and to supply and support them adequately.

In order to free the Marines near the DMZ for mobile operations, we also made plans in concert with the Vietnamese Army to increase the size of one ARVN regiment in the DMZ area. We tailored its forces so that they could man and hold the strong point system, canalize enemy infiltration and secure fire support bases in that area. Additionally, the Vietnamese agreed to increase their armored cavalry forces in northern I Corps as a reaction force and we initiated steps to obtain the necessary equipment for this increase.

Thus, while we continued to gain momentum in both our clearing operations and strikes against the enemy's main forces, we were compelled either to build up our forces near the DMZ or to lose the northernmost provinces to increasingly large North Vietnamese forces.

The leaders in Hanoi were by this time faced with a very serious problem of strategy and tactics. I mentioned in my Overview for 1966 that they had begun an exchange of views on this problem during that year. In 1967 they made the momentous decision to change their basic tactics in an attempt to score a knockout blow. Generally, we had forced enemy main force units toward the remote areas and into jungle sanctuaries. This separated his main forces from his local forces and guerrilla units. It disrupted the mutual support practices which had earlier proved so rewarding to the Communist forces.

The analogy to boxing may help to explain the Hanoi leaders' basic dilemma. By remaining "covered up" with his main forces in the remote areas, the enemy could not attack the South Vietnamese population centers. As long as the enemy attacked only small outposts and towns near the border in an attempt to achieve psychological impact by an isolated victory, we were able to reinforce quickly and to defeat him. This was conclusively demonstrated late in the year by allied victories at Dak To and Loc Ninh. If, on the other hand, he decided to attack the large population centers, he would have to let his guard down—to leave his remote base areas and his secure sanctuaries in Laos and Cambodia and expose his forces to destruction by allied firepower.

Frankly, those of us who had been in Vietnam for a long period of time found it hard to believe that the enemy would expose his forces to almost certain decimation by engaging us frontally at great distances from his base areas and border sanctuaries. He would have to expose his forces to attack the population because we had, by 1967, destroyed or neutralized most of his large close-in bases. However, in 1968 this is exactly what he did—and in doing it he lost the cream of his army.

General Giap, in a statement in September of 1967, forecast very heavy fighting ahead for American and Communist forces. He also forecast victory. But he did so in the context of a border strategy which he claimed had drawn U.S. troops into the remote areas so that Communist guerrillas and local forces could press toward victory in the heavily populated zones. This is simply not what was really happening, since most of our forces were in the populated areas and we reinforced the border areas only to the extent necessary to counter the enemy's initiatives. Many of his planned attacks were pre-empted by the massive use of B-52's. Furthermore, his guerrillas were taking heavy losses.

General Giap was making a virtue out of a necessity. He was putting the best possible face on a strategy which had proved so unproductive that he and his colleagues in Hanoi were finally compelled to change it in late 1967. I can only conclude that he intended to deceive us as to his intentions and, at the same time, to conceal his dilemma.

This was neither a successful nor a productive time for the enemy. North Vietnamese and Viet Cong fortunes deteriorated as those of the South Vietnamese improved. The Autonomous Administrative Committees, constituting the shadow government which he had formed in 1964 and 1965 to inherit political control of the country, were languishing. Allied forces began picking up for the first time significant numbers of civilian specialists heading for positions in the Viet Cong infrastructure—suggesting that the Communist political apparatus needed beefing up. The strength of Viet Cong forces was slowly diminishing and the North Vietnamese were assuming an ever increasing share of the war. In January North Vietnamese forces represented about 43 percent of the enemy in organized combat units but by December they accounted for 50 percent.

In a series of elections from March—when the Constituent Assembly approved a new constitution—through September and October—when nationwide free elections were held—the South Vietnamese government established its legitimacy, selected its leaders, and organized its institutions and agencies. Newly-elected local governments also began to operate in the villages and hamlets. These marked momentous and far-reaching steps in the long quest of the South Vietnamese government for stability. I believe these elections to be one of the most important developments of this long war.

The improving political situation was reflected in other events. The South Vietnamese economy enjoyed an upswing as roads were opened and commerce began to flow. Consumer goods were penetrating the countryside for the first time. Life in the major cities and towns was increasingly prosperous. Government forces were increasing in size and effectiveness.

I had, by this time, refined my original concept of a three-phase war to one of four phases, two of which had already been completed. I envisioned 1968 to be the year of the third phase, in which we would continue to help strengthen the Vietnamese Armed Forces—turning over more of the war effort to increasingly capable and better armed forces. In the fourth—and decisive—phase I could see the U.S. presence becoming superfluous as infiltration slowed, the Communist infrastructure was cut up, and a stable government and capable Vietnamese Armed Forces carried their own war to a successful conclusion. These were the directions in which events pointed. The Communists had to do something to attempt to change this trend.

Thus, the combination of the enemy's inconclusive border strategy and growing South Vietnamese strength forced the leaders in Hanoi to change their tactics and their overall strategy. With long range trends running against them, they had no prospects except to see their chances for success continue to diminish. Furthermore, the North Vietnamese were not happy about the idea of several more years of U.S. bombing of their homeland. Thus it was that the leaders in Hanoi decided to bring their military power to bear directly on their main objective—the people and the government of South Vietnam—regardless of cost.

After the end of the southwest monsoon in October, they began to move their main forces into the populated areas throughout the entire country. We became aware of this movement in November and December through our intelligence, and as the number of incidents rose in the populated areas, the rate of ralliers returning to government authority fell off sharply, while pacification progress virtually stopped.

We now know that the enemy explained to his troops and cadres that the time had come for a herculean offensive effort and a general uprising. He probably had many things in mind—not the least of which was the necessity to do something dramatic to reverse his fortunes. He surely hoped that his dramatic change in strategy would have an impact on the United States similar to that which the battle of Dien Bien Phu had had on the government and people of France. In this way he might hope to bring about a halt of the U.S. effort and the withdrawal of U.S. forces.

OBSERVATIONS—1967

U.S. Operations

CEDAR FALLS and JUNCTION CITY deprived the enemy of enormous amounts of supplies, denied him unhampered use of vital communications centers near the urban areas, and partially eliminated his heretofore unchallenged sanctuaries within Vietnam. Several hundred thousand pages of enemy documents were captured—mostly from the headquarters of Military Region IV which controlled forces and operations in Saigon and the immediately surrounding provinces. CEDAR FALLS put this headquarters out of operation for six months and then it was broken down into five sub-regions. Even though the enemy failed to stand and defend his base areas, he suffered tremendous loss—the complexes which we destroyed in the "Iron Triangle" and War Zone C represented twenty years of work and a huge capital investment. The sustained pressure against this area caused 500 of the enemy to rally under the *Chieu Hoi* program in addition to over 200 who were captured and 700 killed.

In JUNCTION CITY we employed together for the first time all our different types of combat forces, including paratroopers and large armored and mechanized units. Four South Vietnamese battalions (two Army and two Marine) participating in the operation concentrated on securing the populated areas and supporting pacification. Military actions by U.S. troops kept the enemy so occupied that the Vietnamese forces experienced little interference from the enemy.

Although our strength was too limited to maintain enough troops in War Zone C to prevent the enemy from reentering it later, the three C-130 airfields which we constructed were designed to facilitate future operations in the vicinity, while the two Special Forces camps built nearby were to protect the airstrips and furnish continuing surveillance of the region. Although I had intended leaving the 196th Light Infantry Brigade in War Zone C as a "floating brigade" to conduct mobile operations against the enemy during the monsoon season, the ominous enemy developments in I Corps compelled me to withdraw the brigade in April. In addition to the destruction of enemy forces and supplies, JUNCTION CITY "prepared the battlefield" for easy reentry by allied forces.

Statements by several high level defectors a year later revealed the full impact of the enemy's loss in JUNCTION CITY. They commented—and captured documents confirmed—that the operation was essentially an enemy "disaster." According to these knowledgeable defectors, the loss of major base areas and the resulting deterioration of local forces in III Corps forced the enemy high command to make basic revisions in tactics. JUNCTION CITY convinced the enemy command that continuing to base main force units in close proximity to the key population areas would be increasingly foolhardy. From that time on the enemy made increasing use of Cambodian sanctuaries for his bases, hospitals, training centers, and supply depots.

Characteristically, General Giap portrayed JUNCTION CITY as a "big victory" rather than the serious defeat it was. The North Vietnamese continued to perpetuate the myth of crippling U.S. losses and defeat. This time, if anything, the reports were more exaggerated than usual. According to official North Vietnamese reports, 13,500 allied soldiers were killed in JUNCTION CITY; in reality U.S.-Free World forces lost 289 killed. The enemy claimed 993 vehicles destroyed (800 of them armored) and the destruction of 119 allied artillery pieces. We actually lost 21 armored personnel carriers, 3 tanks, 5 artillery pieces, and 9 trucks. Exaggeration of this magnitude was commonplace. Whether self-deception or carefully contrived myth, its existence played an important part in decisions the enemy was to make in 1968.

Early in the year enemy activity in I Corps intensified, reaching a critical level just as we were consolidating our successes from CEDAR FALLS and JUNCTION CITY. I clearly appreciated the need for a major reaction force to meet contingencies in the north, but the situations in both II and III Corps would not permit deployment of a division from either of those areas. I had to improvise a plan.

We developed a contingency plan for a task force known as Task Force OREGON, comprised of a provisional headquarters, division support troops borrowed from various U.S. Army units, and three brigades taken from areas where they could be spared at minimum risk. The brigades involved were the 196th Light Infantry Brigade from the III Corps area, and from the II Corps area the 1st Brigade of the 101st Airborne Division (which joined in May) and the 3d Brigade of the 25th Infantry Division (later to be designated the 3d Brigade of the 4th Infantry Division). My Chief of Staff, Maj. Gen. William B. Rosson, was to command the force.

Within weeks, the unabated enemy activity in the north prompted me to implement the plan. Task Force OREGON was quickly formed and deployed to Quang Ngai Province and the southern part of Quang Tin Province, where Viet Cong influence was strong. The arrival of Task Force OREGON permitted the Marines in Quang Ngai to move units further north to reinforce in the vicinity of the DMZ. The presence of this large force in the north also hastened the northward extension of the highly successful pacification support operations by the 1st Cavalry Division in the coastal area of Binh Dinh Province and the opening of Highway 1 to Da Nang. Task Force OREGON drove the enemy main force units from the area and then concentrated upon eliminating local forces and guerrillas. Later in the year we replaced two brigades (3d of the 25th Division and 1st of the 101st) with the 198th and 11th Light Infantry Brigades, just arriving in the country, and redesignated the task force as the 23d (Americal) Division.

The development and use of Task Force OREGON illustrates a common characteristic of our operations in Vietnam. Literally hundreds of comprehensive contingency plans were prepared to cope with changing situations or anticipated enemy movements. In many instances these plans were never implemented, but they were available should an appropriate situation develop.

In October and November the enemy effort shifted to the western border regions where at Song Be, Loc Ninh and Dak To, he hoped to achieve important psychological victories and to divert our attention from the urban areas and I Corps zone. The enemy realized we would face formidable logistical and operational problems in these areas, a prospect which heightened his confidence of success.

The first of these peripheral battles began in the early morning of 27 October near the village of Song Be in Phuoc Long Province when the North Vietnamese 88th Regiment attacked the command post of the 3d Battalion of the South Vietnamese 9th Regiment. The South Vietnamese repulsed every assault and inflicted heavy losses. Much the same happened in the second battle, which began two days later when elements of the Viet Cong 273d Regiment, 9th Division, attacked the small district town of Loc Ninh and a nearby rubber plantation eight miles south of the Cambodian border in Binh Long Province. Although U.S. troops were required to reinforce the position, by the time the enemy broke off the battle on 8 November, he had sustained severe casualties. The excellent performance by Vietnamese forces in both these engagements was an indication of a new strength and determination that they were to demonstrate consistently over the coming months.

In November the pivotal battle of the last quarter of 1967 occurred in the northwestern portion of the II Corps near the district seat of Dak To in Kontum Province. Since Dak To, like Song Be and Loc Ninh, is but a few miles from the Laotian and Cambodian borders, the enemy could take advantage of the nearby sanctuaries and short lines of communication to plan carefully and strike with speed and strength.

Dak To lies astride a natural infiltration route into Kontum and Pleiku Provinces. It was normally garrisoned by CIDG companies with Special Forces advisors and supported by a nearby ARVN battalion. In late October a battalion of the 4th U.S. Division happened to be in the area providing security for construction of a new Special Forces camp at Ben Het, west of Dak To. When reconnaissance confirmed movement of four North Vietnamese regiments into the area we deployed an additional battalion and a brigade headquarters of the 4th Division, and alerted a battalion of the 173d Airborne Brigade. Before the enemy could launch a coordinated attack, we had concentrated a brigade of three battalions, established artillery fire support bases, and fixed two of the enemy regiments by assault on their forward bases. We beat the enemy to the punch and he never regained the initiative. Before the battle ended, we had temporarily reinforced to a strength of three U.S. brigades including nine U.S. battalions, plus six South Vietnamese battalions. To support this array of forces we massed B–52 and tactical air strikes, using targets located by intelligence from long-range patrols.

Close air support and B–52 strikes were not the only ways in which airpower supported our ground operations. The Seventh Air Force had worked assiduously to improve its interdiction techniques. The skill and determination with which the interdiction campaign was pursued meant that many enemy infiltrators never reached the southern battlefields, that those who did so had been forced to expend additional energy and time infiltrating into South Vietnam, and that the flow of necessary enemy supplies required much larger numbers of enemy support troops.

The enemy paid a terrible price with little to show for his effort. U.S. and ARVN units decisively defeated the North Vietnamese 24th, 32d, 66th, and 174th Regiments, killing more than 1,600 of the enemy in an engagement exceeding in numbers, enemy losses, and ferocity even the Ia Drang Valley campaign of 1965.

In all three frontier battles we had soundly defeated the enemy without unduly sacrificing operations in other areas. The enemy return was nil. In the words of a ranking Communist officer who defected the following spring, the border battles had been both "useless and bloody."

South Vietnamese Operations

Throughout the country the tempo of Vietnamese operations increased during the year. The General Reserve was more active, participating in a larger number of sustained offensive operations, while the Vietnamese Navy relieved U.S. units of responsibility for several MARKET TIME stations. The Vietnamese Air Force flew 25 percent of all allied sorties flown within South Vietnam during the year.

As they became more active, the much criticized Vietnamese Armed Forces also grew more capable. Since improvement of these forces was a prime part of our mission, I placed strong emphasis on upgrading them in all respects—manpower, weapons, equipment, training, administration, and leadership. When General Abrams became my deputy on 1 June, I assigned him, as I had General Heintges, the principal mission of supervising the advisory and support effort to improve the Vietnamese forces. Under his aggressive and able supervision, the state of training and combat readiness of the Vietnamese units showed marked improvement by the end of the year.

The efforts to modernize and improve the effectiveness of the Vietnamese Armed Forces covered a wide range of activities from advising and recommending to the provision of military hardware. A major effort was exerted to improve overall military leadership through the expansion of military schools and the establishment of a more effective manpower management system. The concept of "battlefield promotions" was encouraged to insure recognition of outstanding junior leaders. Actions were taken to improve the training and use of tactical and support units throughout the country. Training Centers were expanded and programs accelerated. We also adopted a highly-successful program of ARVN on-the-job training with U.S. units.

Concurrently, our attention also was focused on the problem of expanding and improving the operational capabilities of the Regional and Popular Force units, so essential in providing the local security necessary for the revolutionary development program. With our assistance the Vietnamese government attacked many of the problems which had so long plagued these forces. Measures were taken to improve their logistic system and a complete revision of the command structure was undertaken to increase the responsiveness of the government to their requirements. To provide technical and tactical assistance, we decided to expand the U.S. advisory effort by more than 3,100 U.S. military personnel.

Our policy at all levels was to expand the role of the Vietnamese Armed Forces in the war, and I seized every opportunity to give them increased responsibility. In November, for example, a regiment of the ARVN 1st Division relieved U.S. forces defending a sector of the defenses facing the Demilitarized Zone. For this assignment, beginning in September we supplemented the ARVN division's firepower, adding crew-served weapons, 106-mm recoilless rifles, 60- and 81-mm mortars, and issuing the more modern M60 machine gun. This division was further strengthened by the issue of M16 rifles late in the year, following the priority issue of this excellent weapon to the General Reserve.

The ARVN 1st Division was given priority in the issue of this equipment in order to increase its firepower so that we could minimize the number of reinforcing units we would need in the northern I Corps, where the intensity of the war continued to increase. The new weapons—and especially the M16 rifle—also resulted in a noticeable increase in the morale of the division, as they did in the ARVN 2d Division when that unit received new equipment in January 1968.

In Binh Duong the keystone of the arch of provinces north of Saigon, a pacification support operation (LAM SON), jointly conducted by elements of the U.S. 1st Division and the ARVN 5th Division, proceeded to attack enemy guerrillas and to eliminate the political infrastructure. Similar operations by elements of the U.S. 25th Division and the ARVN 25th Division were carried out in Hau Nghia and Long An Provinces.

In Operation FAIRFAX (begun in November 1966) we continued combined U.S.-ARVN territorial security operations around Saigon through all of 1967. The operation was characterized by extensive small unit patrols, night ambushes, river ambushes, and cordon and search actions. While these actions helped to improve the security of the Saigon area, Operation FAIRFAX also served as a valuable training exercise for the ARVN units involved. The U.S. 199th Light Infantry Brigade and an ARVN group of three Ranger battalions worked together at all command levels from squad to group and brigade. In this way we hoped the South Vietnamese would learn our tactics and techniques more quickly and in time be prepared to assume an expanded and more effective operational role.

I decided to shift responsibility for the security of the FAIRFAX operational area from the U.S. brigade to the Vietnamese Rangers by the end of the year. According to a carefully developed program for the transfer, the 5th Ranger Group was augmented by a newly-organized artillery battalion and logistical support organization. Further, I equipped the Rangers with M16 rifles and modern field radios on a priority basis. The II Field Force conducted special training for the Regional and Popular Forces that would be operating in the area. In the event the 5th Ranger Group required assistance, uncommitted units of the ARVN airborne division and Marine brigade of the General Reserve were close at hand. Nearby U.S. combat units operating in III Corps could also be made available in a matter of hours.

I asked General Abrams to give the transition his personal attention and he continuously reviewed the process, making frequent visits to the Capital Military District to evaluate the progress of the turnover. By 15 December the 5th Ranger Group and Regional and Popular Forces under the commander of the Capital Military District had full responsibility for the defense of their capital. The Vietnamese accepted the mission with pride. The National Police cooperated in the assignment, but they were not under control of the military commander, an undesirable command situation primarily the product of political complications.

During 1967 it became apparent that the Vietnamese 9th Division in the Delta was overextended. The division was responsible for a wide area embracing the highly-populated central and central coastal sectors of the IV Corps, plus several less critical inland provinces along the Cambodian border. To conserve our forces for operations in the more productive and heavily populated provinces to the east and south, I urged the Vietnamese to establish a special zone in the northern portion of the Delta. In adopting my suggestion, they established the 44th Special Zone, including Chau Doc, Kien Phong, and Kien Tuong Provinces, an area which they manned with a special force of Civilian Irregular Defense Group companies and Regional and Popular Forces. Kien Giang Province was shifted to the responsibility of the ARVN 21st Division. This realignment prevented the enemy from taking refuge along the old Chuong Thien-Kien Giang provincial boundary, which prior to the change was also the boundary between two Vietnamese divisions and a frequent haven for enemy units.

During the year the Vietnamese Special Forces assumed responsibility for several Special Forces camps and for the CIDG companies manning them. In each case all of the U.S. advisors withdrew, leaving the Vietnamese in full command. The Vietnamese handled the responsibility well. As one of our Special Forces sergeants aptly put it, "We had succeeded in working our way out of a job." That was, of course, the ultimate objective of our entire advisory effort—in fact, the philosophy underlying our national commitment.

The South Vietnamese conducted several major operations during the last part of the year, and in spite of Viet Cong attempts to avoid battle, achieved a significantly increased number of contacts. ARVN small unit actions became more aggressive and fruitful. The three ARVN divisions in the Delta and the Regional and Popular Forces there scored a number of signal victories in late 1967.

The Vietnamese Armed Forces also showed great improvement administratively. With our advice, they modernized their military financial management system, established an Inspector General organization, created an Adjutant General staff, and instituted a modern personnel accounting system for the Regional Forces. They modernized their promotion system and improved their procedures for selecting officers to attend higher military schools. They adopted a more liberal leave and pass policy and built an extensive commissary system. With our urging they had provided a more precise definition of desertion in August 1966. Throughout 1967 they pursued measures to reduce the troublesome desertion rate. All of these improvements began to show returns as the desertion rate dropped 37 percent below that of the preceding year.

Despite the improvements, I remained convinced, as I had been for some time, that the Vietnamese would be unable to assume full responsibility for their own defense unless they greatly expanded their armed forces and placed the entire nation on a war footing. That would mean general mobilization. Since mobilization would affect every aspect of national life (of which the military was but one), I had as early as 1966 recommended that the problem be studied at U.S. Mission level. When Ambassador Bunker arrived in April, a joint U.S. civilian-military task force was established to study the problem and to develop basic data so that when the time for mobilization came, we might better assist the Vietnamese. In 1968 these efforts would be well rewarded.

General Vien and I continued to make joint quarterly reviews of the Combined Campaign Plan with our commanders in the field. These meetings provided a valuable clearing house for lessons learned. As the year drew to a close, we published our third annual Combined Campaign Plan, which for the first time brought together U.S. and Vietnamese civilian as well as military plans for pacification and nation building. With the assistance of the Vietnamese Joint General Staff, my staff had prepared the initial draft of the Combined Campaign Plans for 1966, 1967, and 1968. As we contemplated the 1969 plan, we agreed that the Vietnamese planners would prepare the initial draft. This was further evidence of progress and our confidence in the South Vietnamese.

Allies

The two Korean infantry divisions—the Capital and the 9th—conducted highly successful clearing operations in the central coastal plains. One of their largest, more important operations was OH JAC KYO I in March and April, in which the two divisions linked their areas of responsibility and secured a considerable portion of Route 1 along the coast. The Korean forces gradually assumed responsibility for most of the II Corps coastal area, releasing U.S. units there for other tasks.

The Korean troops were tangible proof of the nature of U.S. intentions in Vietnam. The Vietnamese realized that with the support of the United States, the Republic of Korea had successfully defeated a Communist attack and in the postwar period had established a viable economy, powerful armed forces, and a stable government. Dealing with fellow Asians, the Koreans were more effective than we were in explaining the aggressive character of communism and why U.S. and Free World troops were in Vietnam.

Organization

In May the Embassy's Office of Civil Operations and the MACV Revolutionary Development Support Directorate were combined to form the office of the Assistant Chief of Staff for Civil Operations and Revolutionary Development Support (CORDS) in MACV headquarters. There were similar consolidations at regional and provincial levels. Mr. Komer, who had a substantial background in pacification issues, was assigned as my Deputy for CORDS, with the personal rank of Ambassador.

This major and portentous change in the U.S. organization for pacification support was designed to provide better integration and coordination of effort by all U.S. agencies. Upon the creation of CORDS, MACV assumed operational responsibility for the entire spectrum (civilian and military) of U.S. support of the pacification program. The U.S. Embassy, which had heretofore administered the program with some support from MACV, retained responsibility for advising the Vietnamese government on political and economic matters at the national level. We were now organized to pursue a "one war" strategy.

By late 1967 our military assistance and support to the Vietnamese Armed Forces had grown so large and complex that we needed a special agency to coordinate and supervise matters which concerned nearly all portions of the MACV staff. The start of a major new program to expand and upgrade the territorial forces (Regional and Popular Forces)—a program demanding integrated staff action—emphasized this need for a focus of control and coordination. In November we created a principal MACV staff agency, Military Assistance, headed by a general officer and charged with responsibility for unifying the assistance efforts of the various staff divisions.

Airpower

Our tactical air requirements throughout Vietnam steadily increased, a demand spurred by our heightened ground activity, particularly in the area near the DMZ, and by our intensified interdiction campaign against the infiltration routes.

By the end of 1967 well over two thousand U.S. and Free World tactical jet aircraft were stationed in the Republic of Vietnam, in Thailand, or on U.S. Navy carriers in the Gulf of Tonkin. In addition, the immense firepower of the Strategic Air Command B-52's was also available for tactical use. In meeting the most pressing of the air requirements, that around Con Thien and Khe Sanh in I Corps south of the Demilitarized Zone, the massive use of B-52's played a major role.

Despite our spoiling operations, enemy activity in the DMZ intensified, as demonstrated by the intense shelling of the Marine base at Con Thien, a key position on commanding terrain south of the DMZ. The North Vietnamese apparently had two objectives in I Corps: first, to draw our troops into the region, thereby checking our success in other areas; and second, in the process of creating a major diversion, to achieve a significant military victory.

To counter this threat, in the fall we mounted Operation NEUTRALIZE, a massive concentration of air, artillery, and naval gunfire in support of the Marines at Con Thien. This particular kind of attack, which became known as a SLAM operation—for Seeking, Locating, Annihilating, and Monitoring—was refined over the months by General "Spike" Momyer, my deputy for Air Operations and commander of the Seventh Air Force. The SLAM concept used the entire spectrum of supporting fire, from B-52 strategic bombers (in a tactical role) to light artillery. After reconnaissance aircraft and intelligence gathering agencies fixed and defined the target, heavy bomber strikes by B-52's usually triggered the attack. Tactical air strikes and coordinated artillery and naval gunfire followed. During the attack, reconnaissance elements observed the target; later, specially trained long-range reconnaissance patrols entered the target area to assess bomb damage and to locate additional targets for the highly accurate tactical aircraft prepared to strike them.

SLAM operations became one of my most valuable and responsive tools. During the 49 days of the SLAM operation in support of Con Thien, we dislodged a firmly entrenched enemy, destroyed his prepositioned supplies, and forced him to withdraw at great loss—with massed firepower alone. At Con Thien we learned a lesson which proved to be of inestimable value later in the year at Khe Sanh.

The air effort in South Vietnam was primarily in direct support of ground operations such as CEDAR FALLS and JUNCTION CITY and in support of the Marine bases in the north. Over 100,000 sorties (not including B-52 strikes) were flown during the year in support of ground operations, with the I Corps receiving the major share. In one three-day period alone U.S. Air Force, Marine, and Navy aircraft flew more than 1,000 sorties over the I Corps. In CEDAR FALLS and JUNCTION CITY B-52 strikes were an integral and continuing part of the operation.

Logistics

For logistical support of northern I Corps we depended upon a hazardous coastal shipping system running north from the great deep water port of Da Nang to several shallower off-loading points in the vicinity of Hue and Dong Ha. The great quantities of construction material required to build fortifications south of the DMZ and plans for major operations in the A Shau Valley and other enemy base areas in the north during 1968 further taxed these overloaded facilities and resources. To meet all of these requirements we doubled the number of landing craft sites north of the Hai Van pass (to 18) and increased our tonnage capacity tenfold, from 540 tons per day to 5,500.

In the southern part of I Corps near Duc Pho and Sa Huynh in southeastern Quang Nam Province, Army engineer and transportation units developed during April an over-the-beach resupply system to support Operation MALHEUR, conducted by the 1st Brigade, 101st Airborne Division. When the northeast monsoon began in September, the engineers had completed a small sheltered coastal port at Sa Huynh and an all-weather airfield at Duc Pho capable of handling C-130 aircraft. Both developments helped ease the strain on the burdened supply network.

The big battle at Dak To in November stands as a tremendous tactical logistic effort, a prime example of successfully reinforcing an outpost in a remote border region by air with both troops and supplies. In addition to normal equipment and supplies, we had to replace a large amount of ammunition at Dak To after enemy shelling destroyed one of our dumps. Along with the gallantry and tenacity of our forces, our tremendously successful air logistics operation was the key to the victory.

During the year we conducted an extensive program to open and upgrade roads throughout the country. As military actions cleared new areas, we conducted "Road Runner" operations to secure the principal routes and applied substantial engineering effort to improve and maintain them. The expanded road network was both important militarily and vital to civilian trade and commerce. Mile after mile of road was opened. In the III Corps area the ARVN 18th Division, the Australians, Thais, and elements of the U.S. 9th Division opened and secured Route 15 connecting Saigon with the port and naval installations at Vung Tau. Route 20, extending from Saigon to the II Corps boundary where it ran eastward to Dalat, was opened by the U.S. 11th Armored Cavalry Regiment and ARVN 18th Division, then turned over to the Vietnamese public works ministry for maintenance. Route 13, closed for years, was cleared by the U.S. 1st Division, opening it for traffic from Saigon north to the Cambodian border.

In II Corps, we secured and improved Route 19, leading from the coast inland to Pleiku; Route 14, extending from Pleiku north into Kontum Province; and Route 20 from Dalat to the III Corps boundary. In the IV Corps, we devoted a major effort to safeguarding Route 4 connecting Saigon and the Mekong Delta.

Our most ambitious road project was opening coastal Route 1 all the way from Saigon north to the Demilitarized Zone. This involved a series of military and engineering operations by units stationed along the route, first to secure the road in the various tactical areas of operations, then to replace destroyed bridges and repair damaged sections of the route. A major section in the Da Nang area of Quang Nam Province (I Corps) had been secured in the spring of 1965 when the 1st Marine Division moved into the area. In the spring of 1967 the 3d Marine Division secured the section north of the Hai Van pass in Thua Thien and Quang Tri Provinces. In the southern provinces of I Corps, Task Force OREGON in May cleared the section running from northern Quang Ngai through Quang Tin and into the southern part of Quang Nam Province.

In the II Corps' Operation OH JAC KYO I during March and April, the Korean Capital and 9th Divisions opened the route from Phan Rang in Ninh Thuan Province to a point 40 miles north of Qui Nhon in Binh Dinh Province. The portion in northern Binh Thuan Province had already been cleared by the 1st Cavalry Division in Operation BYRD in August 1966. During Operation PERSHING in 1967, the same unit opened the remainder of the route through Binh Dinh Province.

To the south in III Corps during November and early December, in Operation SANTE FE, the U.S. 9th and ARVN 18th Divisions secured Route 1 in Long Khanh and Binh Tuy Provinces. The entire length of Route 1 and the other roads I have noted were open and operating as the year ended. The U.S. Army and Marine engineers, U.S. Navy Seabees, and ARVN engineers performed the herculean task of repairing and maintaining the hundreds of miles of roadway this net encompassed. The first convoy traveled the full length of Route 1 in January 1968, signalling the achievement of a long sought goal, one which facilitated both the nation's economic growth and the conduct of military operations.

Intelligence

The Combined Intelligence Center expanded to keep pace with the ever-increasing quantity of information coming from the field. Intelligence from the center provided the basis for our ground offensive operations and air strikes, and provided a reservoir of data about the enemy's infrastructure.

Operation CEDAR FALLS was the first large-scale operation to benefit from "pattern activity analysis," a system we had begun to develop in mid-1966. This procedure consisted of detailed plotting on maps of information on enemy activity obtained from a variety of sources over an extended period of time. As more data was plotted, patterns of activity and locations would emerge. We thereby could focus our prime attention on those areas of intensive or unusual activity.

Aerial observation and photography, sensors, patrol reports, infrared devices, sampan traffic counts, enemy probes of Regional and Popular Forces posts, agent reports, civilian movement reports, reports of increased antiaircraft fire, disclosures of caches (and the amount and nature of the material in them) and captured documents—these and more told us much about enemy intentions. Upsurges in road ambushes or bridge destruction usually meant that the VC intended to attack in a location where denial of the particular roads would aid the enemy. Something of the enemy's intent could be determined even by checking the amount of wood shipped into an area for the making of caskets or the number of civilians impressed as porters. The extent and nature of the enemy's own intelligence gathering revealed much about his intentions and even the size of the operation he was planning.

Assiduous plotting of all this information and careful analysis of the patterns enabled us to launch spoiling attacks both with ground troops and with massive air strikes. Where no pronounced pattern developed in an area, we concentrated our efforts elsewhere, thereby conserving our forces. Activity pattern analysis was invaluable in developing broad long-range direction of our military operations, while at other lower echelons it provided commanders with a basis for planning day-by-day operations.

We found extremely valuable intelligence when we overran major enemy base areas in JUNCTION CITY. We obtained maps, films, photographs, and two million pages of documents. The most important find was the enemy's complete plan of operations. A film of North Vietnam's second ranking officer, General Thanh, who was the senior commander in the south, inspecting Viet Cong troops in the field was particularly interesting.

The Strong Point System

One planned measure to decrease the massive infiltration across the Demilitarized Zone was to construct a strong point warning system just south of the zone. The system consisted of early-warning devices and some physical obstacles backed by carefully selected fortified positions on key terrain, manned as appropriate, and supported by artillery, airstrikes, and naval gunfire.

The line of fortified strong points eventually extended from the coast to the mountains west of Khe Sanh. The strong points served as observation posts, patrol bases, and fire support bases.

The entire system was designed as an economy of force measure. After the U.S. Marines had developed the system, I planned to turn the defense of the strong points over to the ARVN, thereby freeing our troops for mobile operations. We also hoped to cut down our costly search operations in the vicinity of the DMZ. The proximity of the enemy's sanctuary and his artillery and mortar fire made operations there particularly bloody. Furthermore, we hoped to enhance our reaction by fire to enemy incursions by canalizing his movement and detecting him at greater distances. It was an effort to counter both enemy infiltration and direct invasion by increasing the enemy's cost and minimizing our own. During the year, the intensity of the enemy's mortar, artillery, and rocket fire slowed down the development of the strong points and caused us to set aside the construction of obstacles and to restudy their practicability and useful location.

Riverine Operations

The Mobile Riverine Force, which we created in 1967, was composed of an Army infantry brigade and a Navy task force integrated at each level of command. An amphibious force operating entirely afloat, it was the first time the U.S. had used the technique since the Civil War, when similar Union Army forces operated on the Mississippi, Cumberland, and other rivers. The force was a complete package, independent of fixed support bases and with all of its normal fire support embarked or in tow. It provided great flexibility and markedly increased our operational capability in previously inaccessible areas.

The troops lived on barrack ships docked at the Mobile Riverine base anchorage. On tactical operations, Navy armored troop carrier boats, preceded by minesweeping craft and escorted by armored boats (nicknamed "Monitors"), transported the soldiers along the vast network of waterways in the Delta. The units debarked upon reaching the area of operations or upon enemy contact. As the Army troops engaged the enemy, the Navy boats provided close-in fire support with 40-mm guns, .30- and .50-caliber machine guns, 81-mm mortars and individual hand-held weapons. Artillery support was furnished by riverine artillery—Army 105-mm howitzers mounted on barges accompanying the force.

Although "immersion foot" was a restrictive factor in this kind of warfare, we minimized its effects by alternating units of the brigade in action. Fresh troops were brought into the battle every two or three days to sustain the attack while others were removed to "dry out" and refit.

The first element of the Mobile Riverine Force arrived in Vietnam in January and after shakedown training in the Rung Sat swamps, moved to its base near My Tho. Named Dong Tam (meaning "United Hearts and Minds"—a name my counterpart General Vien and I had agreed as appropriate), the base was a 600-acre "island" we had created among inundated rice paddies by dredging earth from the bottom of the Mekong River. The Mobile Riverine Force often operated with other units (GAME WARDEN units, SEAL teams, Vietnamese Marines, units of the ARVN 7th Division, and River Assault Groups) on reconnaissance, blocking, and pursuit operations. In five major operations during the year the Mobile Riverine Force killed over 1,000 enemy and by its presence gave encouragement to the populace and a new sense of confidence to ARVN units.

Enemy Rockets

The introduction of the portable Soviet-made 140-mm barrage rockets (8,000 meter range) by the enemy in February compounded our security problems, especially for our large airfields and logistical installations. Our concern heightened when a similar weapon with a range of 11,000 meters, the 122-mm rocket, appeared in July. To counter this increased enemy fire capability, we were forced to extend our search areas to provide local defense and warning for our installations.

To bolster local security, I directed construction of a number of high metal observation towers to ring our installations. These towers, some as high as 100 feet, were manned day and night by troops using flash-ranging devices, ground radar, or starlite scopes (night vision devices). The vantage points often enabled us to determine the location of the source of the enemy rocket or mortar fire and to direct counterfire before he could break off the attack and flee to safety. These towers were later available in quantity and served to improve greatly the security of Saigon and other important areas.

Operation MOOSE

My continuing concern about the effects of the massive U.S. presence upon the Vietnamese people and their economy prompted me to develop Operation MOOSE (Move Out of Saigon Expeditiously), designed to hasten the relocation of our units and installations from the urban areas, particularly Saigon where the military numbered 12,700 in early 1967. We implemented the program as facilities outside the city were completed.

Early in the year the headquarters of the U.S. Army, Vietnam (USARV), and the headquarters of the logistics command moved into a new prefabricated headquarters complex at Long Binh, 16 miles east of Saigon. During the summer my own headquarters moved into a new prefabricated facility near Tan Son Nhut Airbase.

The opening of our port facilities at Newport on the outskirts of the capital city permitted additional units to move and did much to reduce the congestion in downtown Saigon caused by supply convoys moving to and from the old commercial port. By the end of the year, we had reduced the U.S. military population in downtown Saigon to 8,500. By mid-1968 it would be down to 6,900. Similar moves away from populated areas were made throughout the country.

Economy Measures

As an extension of continuing efforts to hold down the costs of our effort in Vietnam without denying items needed by the individual soldier or in any way impeding combat operations, I decided in late 1967 to initiate a study of cost effectiveness and management procedures to aid in reducing costs and assuring the most efficient use of available supplies and personnel. Given the code name MACONOMY, the project was instituted both at MACV and at each of the component commands. Under MACONOMY, management at all levels undertook a continuing review of plans, programs, and methods with the goal of consolidating, substituting or reducing requirements, and eliminating nonessentials or simply maximizing our proficiency at the least cost.

Commanders in Vietnam embraced the program enthusiastically. Within a month MACV had received approximately 200 reports reflecting estimated savings in excess of $100 million. The Seventh Air Force, for example, conducted a survey to identify and distribute excess property at selected bases, resulting in savings of more than $70 million. In addition to these savings, the program provided a valuable tool for analyzing the efficiency of administrative and logistical operations.

Because of a constant effort to hold down the level of noncombat forces, the logisticians, who were responsible for receiving and supporting a very large force, were hard pressed from the beginning. On the one hand, the dispersed nature of our tactical operations, our support requirements to Free World military forces, and the consequences of the underdeveloped environment required that a major portion of our effort be spent in base development, construction, transportation improvement, and other equally important tasks. In the maintenance field alone, the size and extensive use of our helicopter forces created a staggering requirement for highly-skilled maintenance personnel and sophisticated facilities.

Our logisticians accepted the challenge of this situation and provided the highest quality of support ever received by combat forces in the field. Although logistic facilities were primitive and virtually nonexistent at the beginning of the troop buildup, tactical units were never restricted in their combat operations by a lack of support or supplies. Through the use of aerial evacuation techniques and mobile medical units, troops in the most remote areas were assured that comprehensive medical care was only minutes away. Combat units knew that mail from home would arrive on a scheduled basis and could be read while enjoying hot meals.

The level and responsiveness of logistic support in Vietnam is a tribute to the dedication, imagination, and initiative of our logisticians at all echelons. Even more remarkable is the fact that, as the quality and quantity of support increased, the proportionate strength of our support elements declined. By constantly analyzing requirements and capabilities, consolidating functions, and refining procedures, the support ratio was reduced from about 45 percent in 1966 to about 40 percent in 1967. This feat was accomplished during a period in which Free World military strength in Vietnam grew from 898,000 to over 1,300,000. Through the increased substitution of Vietnamese for U.S. support personnel and increased emphasis on local contracting, our support strength will continue to decline.

Resettlement Programs

Military considerations led us to undertake three major resettlement programs during 1967. The first one, at Ben Suc, was carried out in order to remove an important Viet Cong supply center near Saigon. The second, at Edap Enang, was designed to protect Montagnard tribesmen from Viet Cong terrorism and exploitation. Finally, we relocated a large number of local inhabitants from the DMZ battle area.

The Viet Cong fortified village of Ben Suc, long an enemy safe haven and supply center, was evacuated during Operation CEDAR FALLS. The central organization for the VC Long Nguyen secret base was located in—and operated from—Ben Suc. The people of the village were organized into four rear service companies. One company moved rice and other supplies in sampans on the Saigon River. A second company unloaded these supplies. The two remaining companies stored them in and around Ben Suc or in the jungles near the village.

When we entered Ben Suc we discovered up to three levels of carefully concealed storage rooms underneath the houses. In these and other nearby sites we found enough rice to feed a Viet Cong division for nearly a year. Just outside the village we found a large cache of enemy medical supplies, including surgical instruments and 800,000 vials of penicillin.

Thus, while we recognized that dislocating the families in Ben Suc would inevitably produce some resentment, it was a matter of military necessity that this enemy supply operation be brought to an end. Every effort was made to evacuate and resettle the people as humanely as possible. All their possessions, including farm animals, rice, and household furnishings, were loaded on boats and delivered to the resettlement center. There—near Phu Cuong—they were provided food, shelter, medical care, and water. Unfortunately, the resettlement phase was not as well planned or executed as the actual evacuation. For the first several days the families suffered unnecessary hardships. However, the government quickly rallied and built a new village.

The second resettlement program was in the Central Highlands. As the North Vietnamese Army intensified its infiltration of men and materiel into South Vietnam, it became obvious that large numbers of Montagnard villagers in the border regions were being terrorized and impressed into the enemy's service as laborers and porters. It was a matter of military necessity that the enemy be denied the use of this labor and that the border tribesmen be protected from intimidation by NVA troops. It was with these objectives in mind that the resettlement program at Edap Enang was initiated by the Vietnamese government in Pleiku Province in April at the urging of U.S. military authorities.

This program envisioned the relocation of some 8,000 Montagnard tribesmen from 18 villages along the Cambodian border into a central planned community near Pleiku City. The government designated one Vietnamese Ranger battalion to secure the new village and assigned over 200 revolutionary development cadremen to assist in resettlement of the population. The U.S. 4th Infantry Division provided support throughout all phases of the relocation, resettlement, and development of the village. This support included the provision of transport helicopters, cargo vehicles, land clearing equipment, and technical engineering advice.

By mid-July the community of Edap Enang consisted of some 7,000 inhabitants with nearly 600 acres of the projected 1,200 acres of farmland cleared. Market centers, a dispensary, a school, nearly 200 dwellings, and a series of lakes stocked with fish were either completed or under construction. Roads to the settlement were improved and a comprehensive defense system constructed around the community. A major civic action program was initiated by the 4th Division, in conjunction with the Vietnamese government, with the objective of improving the living standards of the inhabitants. Concurrently, representatives of the Vietnamese government embarked upon similar rehabilitation programs designed to better living conditions and enhance the government's image among the tribesmen.

Despite apparent initial success, a general population exodus from the settlement began in December 1967. By March 1968 the population had declined to about 2,200 people. The Montagnards were instinctively fearful of resettlement, but faulty planning regarding the provision of rice-growing farmland and the continuous deluge of VC propaganda denouncing the project as a "concentration camp" caused additional adverse effects. In fact, the tribesmen were free to leave the area—as many of them did.

The Vietnamese government, recognizing the seriousness of the situation, initiated high priority efforts to remedy food shortages and to reconstitute the community. By April 1968 the population trend had swung sharply upward and there were about 4,600 tribesmen in the settlement. This progress continued; by mid-1968 Edap Enang contained nearly 6,200 people. In spite of its shortcomings, the project had effectively separated a major section of the border population from the enemy and denied use of these tribesmen in support of the enemy's tactical operations.

In May a combined United States-Vietnamese operation near the Demilitarized Zone removed 10,000 local inhabitants from that intensive battle area where their safety could not be assured and resettled them in newly-expanded refugee villages at Cam Lo. The families were transported in ARVN and U.S. Marine trucks and in U.S. Navy landing craft to areas in which U.S. civilian agencies, Vietnamese provincial officials, and U.S. Marine engineers had built new homes, dug wells, and provided water storage tanks.

The resettled families were given inoculations by U.S. medics and instructed in basic public health measures. The status of their security and their opportunity to escape the effects of the intense fighting along the DMZ were thereby immensely improved. They were no longer subject to impressment by the growing NVA forces. In this instance there was, understandably, little or no effort on the part of the resettled Vietnamese to return to their homesites in the battle area.

At Edap Enang and Ben Suc, on the other hand, the process of dislocation and resettlement faced built-in obstacles. As in the earlier Strategic Hamlet Program under the Diem government, the separation of a rural people from their ancestral lands caused fear and resentment. Their usual reaction is to attempt to slip back as soon as the opportunity arises. Notwithstanding the efforts of the government to care for these unfortunate victims of a prolonged war, this pattern was repeated at Ben Suc and Edap Enang. Hopefully, these people will be able to return to their original lands when the war is over and the government can help them to rebuild.

TYPICAL VC TUNNEL SYSTEM

Typical Enemy Camouflaged Tunnel Entrance

Concealed Tunnel Entrance by River Bank

151

CHRONOLOGY OF MAJOR EVENTS—1967

January

On 1 January two brigades of the 4th Infantry Division, with contingents of the 25th Infantry Division attached, launched Operation SAM HOUSTON in Pleiku and Kontum Provinces, aimed at destroying the regiments of the North Vietnamese 1st Division operating in the two provinces from bases inside Cambodia. In 95 days the enemy lost 733 killed.

On 3 January Republic of Korea troops began Operation MAENG HO 8, a 60-day search and destroy operation in Phu Yen and Binh Dinh Provinces. The Koreans killed 211 Viet Cong and captured 403.

On 8 January the 1st Infantry Division, with the 173d Airborne Brigade and 11th Cavalry Regiment attached, and elements of the 25th Infantry Division, as well as ARVN units, launched Operation CEDAR FALLS just north of Saigon into the area of the "Iron Triangle," the Long Nguyen base area, and the Saigon River corridor northwest of Saigon. In a 19-day operation, 20 infantry and armored units under control of the II Field Force sealed off and thoroughly searched the region. Killing 720 enemy and capturing 213, the troops discovered a vast "underground city" beneath the jungle floor with chambers extending as far down as four levels and tunnel complexes several miles long. The headquarters of the enemy's Military Region IV was largely destroyed along with enough rice to feed 13,000 VC for a year. Over 500 Viet Cong took advantage of the disruption and the proximity of Allied forces to defect to the government side. Our troops also captured 490,000 pages of enemy documents, an invaluable intelligence find. It was in this operation that U.S. forces first made extensive use of the "Rome Plow" to clear the jungle and uncover the enemy's tunnel system.

Elements of the 9th Infantry Division established the first U.S. base in the Mekong Delta in Dinh Tuong Province in mid-January. Named Dong Tam (United Hearts and Minds), the base was a 600-acre "island" we created among inundated rice paddies by dredging earth from the bottom of the Mekong River. Occupying the base at Dong Tam was the first step toward creating the Mobile Riverine Force to operate on the waterways of the Delta.

Through the entire year the U.S. 199th Light Infantry Brigade provided security for Saigon with Operation FAIRFAX, an operation begun in November 1966. It operated in close conjunction with the ARVN 5th Ranger Group with the aim of training the South Vietnamese troops eventually to take responsibility for the security mission.

On the last day of the month, the U.S. 3d Marine Division terminated Operation PRAIRIE along the Demilitarized Zone. In 182 days the Marines had killed 1,397 enemy.

February

On 8 February allied forces began observing a four-day cease-fire over the period of *Tet*, the lunar New Year. The enemy marred the truce with 183 minor and 89 serious violations.

The 1st Cavalry Division, on 11 February, began Operation PERSHING in Binh Dinh Province, where the same division had conducted Operation THAYER the previous year. Designed to eliminate the enemy from that rice-rich coastal province, PERSHING was a long-range offensive that extended into 1968. In THAYER and PERSHING together, the air cavalrymen killed 7,500 of the enemy and helped establish effective government control over most of the province.

The largest operation of the year, JUNCTION CITY, began on 22 February, employing the 1st and 25th Infantry Divisions, the 173d Airborne Brigade, the 11th Armored Cavalry Regiment, the 196th Light Infantry Brigade, elements of the 4th and 9th Infantry Divisions, and South Vietnamese units against enemy bases in War Zone C in Tay Ninh Province. Three Vietnamese divisions and major elements of the Vietnamese airborne division and Marines remained near the populated areas to keep pressure on the guerrillas and local forces and to support revolutionary development.

On the 22d a battalion of the 173d Airborne Brigade made the first American parachute assault of the war, jumping into northern War Zone C to intercept enemy troops trying to escape into Cambodia. The operation continued until mid-May. Although the enemy at first avoided contact, he later began to engage our forces and lost 2,700 dead in comparison to 289 American and South Vietnamese killed. The enemy also lost over 600 weapons, vast amounts of ammunition, medical supplies, field equipment, and more than 800 tons of rice. During the operation U.S. forces built three airfields capable of handling the C–130 and established two new Special Forces camps to guard the airfields and provide continuing surveillance in the region. An inviolate Viet Cong stronghold for many years, War Zone C was now vulnerable to allied forces anytime we chose to enter.

On 28 February the Mekong Delta Mobile Riverine Force was activated under the Commander, Naval Forces, Vietnam.

March

During March, and extending into April, the Republic of Korea Capital and 9th Divisions conducted Operation OH JAC KYO I, which enabled the two divisions to link their areas of responsibility in the central coastal plains and secure a large portion of Highway 1.

On 15 March it was announced that Ambassador Ellsworth Bunker would succeed Ambassador Lodge.

The Constituent Assembly, on 18 March, voted unanimously approval of the new constitution for the Republic of Vietnam.

Elements of the U.S. 3d Marine Division launched Operation PRAIRIE FIRE III along the Demilitarized Zone and in the vicinity of Khe Sanh. Heavy fighting continued in the area through the entire year.

On 20 and 21 March officials of the South Vietnamese government met with President Johnson and other U.S. officials on Guam.

April

On 6 April two brigades of the 4th Infantry Division, with elements of the 25th Infantry Division attached, launched Operation FRANCIS MARION along the Cambodian border in Pleiku Province against the Viet Cong and the North Vietnamese 1st Division. In 190 days the Americans killed 1,200 of the enemy.

The White House, on 6 April, announced assignment of General Creighton W. Abrams, Jr., as Deputy Commander, U.S. Military Assistance Command, Vietnam.

On 12 April Task Force OREGON was established in the southern part of the I Corps as a provisional division-size organization, enabling U.S. Marine units to reinforce units in the northernmost provinces where enemy pressure continued to mount. The task force initially consisted of the 3d Brigade, 25th Infantry Division, and the 196th Infantry Brigade.

Eight Australian Canberra (B–57) bombers of Squadron No. 2, Royal Australian Air Force, arrived on 19 April at Phan Rang Airbase.

On 20 April the 7th Battalion, Royal Australian Regiment arrived to join the Australian Task Force in Phuoc Tuy Province.

The Commanding General, U.S. 1st Marine Division, turned over responsibility for the defense of the Chu Lai Airbase and logistics complex to the Commanding General of Task Force OREGON on 26 April.

In 984 villages throughout South Vietnam, 77 percent of the registered voters turned out on 29 April for local elections.

May

On 1 May U.S. military strength in South Vietnam reached 436,000 men.

Having started the preceding month, the North Vietnamese stepped up infiltration from Laos into the northwestern corner of South Vietnam and occupied hills dominating the airfield and Special Forces camp at Khe Sanh. U.S. Marines reacted by shifting two battalions to Khe Sanh and on 3 May, in some of the heaviest fighting of the war, seized Hill 881N, northwest of Khe Sanh, which afforded a dominating position overlooking the enemy's infiltration routes.

On 4 May General Abrams and Ambassador Komer arrived in Saigon to take up their duties as Deputy COMUSMACV and Deputy to COMUSMACV for Civil Operations and Revolutionary Development Support, respectively. On the 28th the Embassy's Office of Civil Operations and the MACV Revolutionary Development Support Directorate were combined into the Office of the Assistant Chief of Staff for Civil Operations and Revolutionary Development Support (CORDS) under MACV, with responsibility for both civil and military aspects of U.S. support of pacification falling to my command.

The 1st Brigade, 101st Airborne Division, was assigned to operational control of the III Marine Amphibious Force. In the brigade's first operation in the zone of the I Corps (Operation MALHEUR in Quang Ngai Province), the airborne troops killed 392 of the enemy.

From 14 May through 11 June, 4,612 hamlets throughout Vietnam conducted local elections.

Because of enemy shelling and ground attacks emanating from the Demilitarized Zone, U.S. Marine and ARVN units on 18 May entered and operated in the southern half of the zone for the first time. During a series of operations over an 11-day period, U.S. Marines and South Vietnamese troops supported by artillery, naval gunfire, tactical air, and massive B–52 strikes killed over 780 enemy and temporarily neutralized the enemy's offensive power in the southern half of the zone.

On 19 May President Thieu declared his candidacy for President of the Republic in upcoming national elections.

June

On the first day of June the 2d Brigade, 9th Infantry Division, and the Mobile Riverine Force launched the first major American operation in the Mekong Delta, Operation CORONADO in Dinh Tuong Province. In 54 days of offensive strikes centering on the vast waterways of the region, almost 500 Viet Cong were killed and 75 captured.

U.S. strength in Vietnam on 17 June approached 450,000. The total strength of the Vietnamese Armed Forces exceeded 600,000, and other Free World forces totalled 54,000. Intelligence estimates placed enemy strength at close to 260,000, including over 50,000 North Vietnamese regulars.

July

The Newport Marine Terminal facility near Saigon, designed to serve U.S. forces and relieve congestion in the Saigon port, officially opened on 11 July. Before the year ended almost all programmed military construction projects would be completed.

The enemy, on 15 July, fired 50 rounds of 122-mm rockets at the airbase at Da Nang, the first use of these long-range weapons. Ten aircraft were destroyed and 41 damaged.

Also on the 15th MARKET TIME coastal surveillance forces intercepted a North Vietnamese trawler heavily laden with arms and ammunition destined for Viet Cong operating in the vicinity of Chu Lai.

On 27 July Premier Ky announced that the Republic of Vietnam would increase its armed forces to 685,000 men.

August

President Johnson announced that American forces in South Vietnam would be increased to 525,000 men.

On 4 August MACV Headquarters moved from downtown Saigon to new headquarters at Ton Son Nhut Airbase on the outskirts of the city, part of a long-range program to relieve congestion in the capital.

In the Mekong Delta, two separate but mutually supporting naval operations helped drive Viet Cong tax collectors from the waterways. The U.S. Navy's GAME WARDEN patrols, cruising 24 hours a day, helped eliminate the tax collectors and keep commercial traffic moving, while River Assault Groups and the River Transport Escort Group of the Vietnamese Navy provided security for major rice and commodity convoys en route from the Delta to Saigon.

September

On 3 September 4.8 million voters, representing 81 percent of those registered, elected General Thieu as President of the Republic of Vietnam with 35 percent of the total vote. Air Vice Marshal Ky was elected Vice President. Members of the Upper House of the National Assembly were elected at the same time.

On 7 September the U.S. Secretary of Defense announced a decision to construct an anti-infiltration barrier just south of the Demilitarized Zone, consisting of strongpoints, obstacles, and electronic devices.

Task Force OREGON was redesignated on 22 September as the 23d (Americal) Division.

On 26 September HMAS *Perth* replaced HMAS *Hobart* to become the second Royal Australian Navy ship to operate with the U.S. Seventh Fleet, providing naval gunfire support to allied forces ashore.

On 29 September last contingents of the Royal Thai Army Volunteer Regiment, "the Queen's Cobras," arrived in Vietnam. The regiment began to conduct operations in Bien Hoa Province, just northeast of Saigon.

October

By 4 October a North Vietnamese siege of the U.S. Marine Corps base at Con Thien had been broken with severe losses to the enemy by a massive use of artillery, tactical aircraft, and B-52's.

On 8 October the new Huey COBRA (AH-1G) armed helicopter, especially designed for support of ground forces in South Vietnam, entered combat for the first time.

During the month the South Vietnamese conducted elections for the Lower House of the National Assembly.

On 27 October the North Vietnamese 88th Regiment attacked the command post of a battalion of the South Vietnamese 9th Regiment near the village of Song Be in Phuoc Long Province. Three times the North Vietnamese rushed the position but each time were repulsed. When the enemy began to fall back, the ARVN defenders left the safety of their position to pursue. The enemy lost 134 men killed to an ARVN loss of 13 in an engagement in which the defenders were outnumbered by at least 4 to 1.

On 29 October the Viet Cong 273d Regiment, 9th Division, attacked the town of Loc Ninh, near the Cambodian border in Binh Long Province. The area was defended by three CIDG companies, a Regional Force company, and a Popular Force platoon. As the fight developed over the next several days, ARVN units and the 1st Brigade of the 1st Infantry Division reinforced the position. By the time the enemy broke off the battle on 8 November, he had sustained severe casualties: over 850 killed at a cost of 50 dead among the defenders.

On 31 October President Thieu and Vice President Ky were inaugurated and the directorate dissolved. With installation of the Lower House, the constituent assembly passed out of existence. President Thieu appointed Nguyen Van Loc as Prime Minister.

November

During the month U.S. military strength in Vietnam reached 470,000.

Also during the course of the month the U.S. 3d Marine Division launched a series of operations in Quang Tri Province against growing enemy strength threatening Khe Sanh and Marine strongpoints at the "Rock Pile," Camp Carroll, Con Thien, and Gio Linh.

In mid-November reconnaissance revealed the presence near Dak To in Kontum Province of four North Vietnamese regiments. In addition to CIDG companies manning a Special Forces camp, a South Vietnamese battalion and a battalion of the 4th Infantry Division were in the vicinity. By reinforcing with one brigade each from the 4th Infantry and 1st Cavalry Divisions, the 173d Airborne Brigade, and six South Vietnamese battalions, we were able to attack and defeat the enemy before he could concentrate his forces. Massive air and B–52 strikes were made. More than 1,600 North Vietnamese were killed.

December

The enemy struck the Montagnard village of Dak Son in Phuoc Long Province on 5 December in a wanton attack constituting one of the most atrocious acts of terror in the entire war. Rampaging through the village with flamethrowers and hand grenades, the enemy troops systematically killed more than 200 of the civilian inhabitants, 70 percent of whom were women and children, and kidnapped some 400 tribesmen for use as forced laborers. The destruction left 1,382 people homeless.

On 8 December in the biggest single engagement yet to occur in the Mekong Delta, contingents of the South Vietnamese 21st Infantry Division trapped part of a Viet Cong main force battalion and a local force battalion along the Konh O Mon Canal, 100 miles southwest of Saigon. Helicopters lifted selected units into blocking positions while a battalion maneuvered up the canal from the southwest. Viet Cong dead numbered 365.

Also on 8 December leading elements of the remainder of the 101st Airborne Division arrived in Vietnam and located in the zone of the III Corps northeast of Saigon. Command elements of the division arrived on 13 December. Movement of the division involved the longest aerial combat deployment in the history of warfare. The 101st was not originally scheduled to arrive until early in 1968, but because of the ominous intelligence on enemy movements, I urgently requested its arrival before the end of the year.

The 199th Light Infantry Brigade and the Vietnamese 5th Ranger Group ended Operation FAIRFAX after having killed more than a thousand Viet Cong. Responsibility for the security of Saigon passed to the South Vietnamese force.

The 11th Light Infantry Brigade arrived in Vietnam on 24 December. Taking position in the southern part of the I Corps, the brigade became a part of the 23d (Americal) Division.

At the end of the year U.S. military strength in Vietnam totalled 486,000 (320,000 Army; 31,000 Navy; 78,000 Marine Corps; 56,000 Air Force; 1,200 Coast Guard). Free World strength was as follows: Australian, 6,812; Korean, 47,800; New Zealand, 516; The Philippines, 2,020; and Thailand, 2,205.

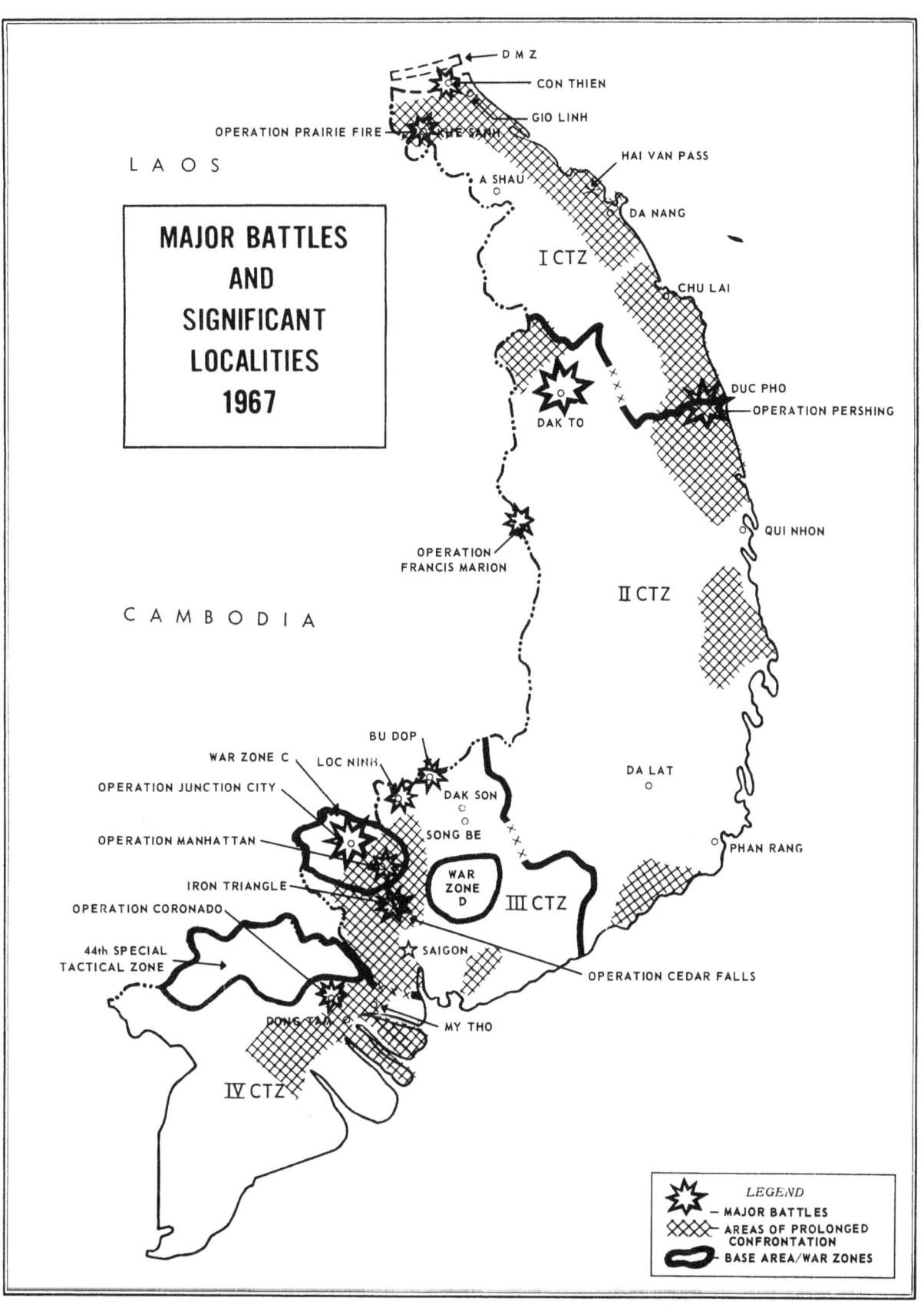

Chapter VI

THE YEAR OF DECISION—1968

OVERVIEW

In 1968 the war in Vietnam reached the decisive stage. In my Overview for 1967, I described the dilemma facing the enemy and the decision taken by Hanoi because of that dilemma. During early 1968 the enemy made a determined effort to execute the plans which flowed from this decision.

As the new year opened, I had planned to continue pursuing the enemy throughout the Republic, thereby improving conditions for the pacification program to proceed at an ever-increasing pace. I had also intended clearing remaining enemy base areas in zones of the I and III Corps and deploying the rest of the U.S. 9th Infantry Division and an air cavalry squadron to the Delta to reinforce the Mobile Riverine Force. I had prepared plans to shift the 1st Cavalry Division to the III Corps for operations along the Cambodian border during the dry season in that area (December to April) and to move the division north to the I Corps for operations, including a foray into the A Shau Valley, during the dry season in the northern provinces (May to September). The operations by the 1st Cavalry Division were to be in conjunction with planned operations by other U.S. and ARVN troops in the areas.

In December of 1967 information of massive enemy troop movements had prompted me to cancel these plans. As 1968 began events verified this intelligence, as the enemy continued the forward movement of his main forces toward Saigon, Da Nang, Hue, Khe Sanh, the DMZ, and a number of provincial and district capitals. Incidents rose sharply, as did enemy casualties. By January the enemy was well into the winter-spring campaign which he had started in October. During January we began to receive numerous reports about a major offensive to be undertaken just before or immediately after *Tet*. These reports came from agents and prisoners with increasing frequency and credibility.

Based on these reports, in January I modified previous plans to conduct major offensive operations into the enemy's well-established base areas in War Zones C and D and the enemy's huge Military Region 10 (MR 10) and directed Lt. Gen. Frederick C. Weyand, II Field Force commander, to strengthen U.S. forces in the area around Saigon by redeploying forces which had been targeted on the bases of the Viet Cong main forces and the North Vietnamese Army. Likewise, I discussed the situation with my counterpart, General Vien, Chief of the Joint General Staff, who directed troop readjustments in coordination with our actions. In response to this changed enemy situation, just before *Tet*, well over half of the maneuver battalions plus most of the Regional and Popular Forces in the III Corps were either defending the immediate approaches to Saigon, interdicting the corridors which lead to Saigon from War Zones C and D and the Plain of Reeds, or defending villages and hamlets. Even though by mid-January we were certain that a major offensive action was planned by the enemy at *Tet,* we did not surmise the true nature or the scope of the countrywide attack. Because of this uncertainty, a number of battalions were designated as emergency reserves for any contingency. It did not occur to us that the enemy would undertake suicidal attacks in the face of our power. But he did just that.

For the celebration of the lunar new year—*Tet*—the Republic of Vietnam had, after discussions between President Thieu, Ambassador Bunker, and myself, declared a 36-hour cease-fire to be effective from the evening of 29 January through the early morning of 31 January. Upon my advice an exception was made during the last week in the I Corps, the Demilitarized Zone, and nearby infiltration routes north of the DMZ, since the enemy activity seriously imperiled our positions in those regions. The Viet Cong announced a seven-day *Tet* truce to last from 27 January until the early morning of 3 February. Under cover of this premeditated subterfuge, the enemy launched attacks of unprecedented scope.

Several days before *Tet* U.S. troops were placed on full alert. Owing to an apparent mixup in coordination, the enemy attack was launched in I and II Corps 24 hours ahead of the attack in the remainder of the country. This gave us additional warning, but still did not reveal the nature of his plans in the Saigon area. The enemy main attack was launched late on the 30th and in early morning of the 31st of January, employing about 84,000 Viet Cong and North Vietnamese troops. In addition to Saigon, initial assaults were mounted against 36 of the 4 provincial capitals, 5 of the 6 autonomous cities, 64 of 242 district capitals, and 50 hamlets.

In preparation for the attacks, the enemy went to unprecedented lengths to assemble supplies and weapons and to infiltrate troops into the cities. After loss of his major base areas near Saigon in 1967, he made extensive use of Cambodia to establish secret bases and accumulate great quantities of arms, supplies, and troops. Along the Cambodian border north of Saigon he established Military Region 10 to coordinate the creation of a major logistics base. In the Plain of Reeds and in the "Eagle's Beak" section of Cambodia that projects southeastward to within 30 miles of the South Vietnamese capital, he established clandestine sanctuaries and undertook a long-range program to stockpile supplies for support of operations in the zone of the III and IV Corps. In preparation for the *Tet* offensive against Saigon and the larger cities of the Delta, the enemy smuggled munitions and weapons to forward sites hidden in isolated areas or to underground installations. He also returned temporarily to his earlier practice of drawing reinforcements from the Delta to support operations in the vicinity of Saigon.

Over a long period of time and especially before *Tet,* enemy troops in civilian dress, assisted by well-organized agents, slipped into the cities, particularly Hue and Saigon, among crowds of holiday travelers on public conveyances, on produce trucks, and in private vehicles. In Saigon they used funeral processions to smuggle weapons and ammunition. Other quantities of supplies arrived in market baskets and vegetable trucks, under lumber, or in false-bottom sampans. The Vietnamese National Police were ineffective in stopping or detecting the magnitude of the enemy's effort. The minds of the Vietnamese in Saigon and the other cities were preoccupied with the approaching *Tet* holiday, and our efforts to change this state of mind were only partially effective.

The enemy used primarily local forces rather than main force units to infiltrate the cities and conduct the first attacks. He held the larger main force units in reserve to exploit the anticipated popular uprisings. Some units had even planned victory parades in the cities.

In the areas around Saigon the terrain facilitated infiltration by large enemy units. Except for the few radial roads emanating from Saigon, the city is bounded to the north, west, and east by a combination of paddies, jungles, and swamps.

Notwithstanding efforts to increase the state of alert, large numbers of Vietnamese soldiers were on leave for *Tet* and their units were, in most cases, about half strength. The enemy penetrated in strength into Saigon, Quang Tri, Hue, Da Nang, Nha Trang, Qui Nhon, Kontum City, Ban Me Thuot, My Tho, Can Tho, and Ben Tre. In most cities, Regional and Popular Forces and the South Vietnamese Army threw back the enemy attacks within two to three days—in some cases, within hours. However, very heavy fighting continued for some time in Kontum City, Ban Me Thuot, Can Tho, and Ben Tre, and in Saigon and Hue the battle was protracted.

The Regional and Popular Forces demonstrated their growing tactical proficiency throughout this period. By their presence in the villages and hamlets they made it more difficult for the enemy to terrorize the people. Their contributions made it possible for U.S. and other allied forces to conduct mobile security operations rather than to be tied to static duties. This was particularly apparent in Quang Tri Province.

The enemy's attack in Saigon began with a sapper assault on the American Embassy, a move of dubious military value but psychologically important. Although the Viet Cong succeeded in blowing a hole in the Embassy wall, aggressive reaction by U.S. military police and Marine guards prevented the enemy from entering the Embassy building and by midmorning security was established in the area. The Viet Cong coordinated this abortive attack with assaults on the Tan Son Nhut Airbase complex, the Presidential Palace, the Vietnamese Joint General Staff compound, and other installations in Saigon. Nearby Bien Hoa Airbase also came under attack. In some instances the VC dressed in ARVN uniforms to gain initial entry into South Vietnamese bases—a tactic they had used earlier and have also employed since *Tet*.

Throughout Saigon the National Police, who in most cases absorbed the brunt of the attack, fought well. They successfully blocked enemy assaults on such important installations as the radio station and Presidential Palace. Both Vietnamese and U.S. troops reacted quickly. Within hours the quick deployment of Vietnamese Ranger, airborne, Marine, and Regional Force battalions had thrown the Viet Cong on the defensive. Reluctantly, I was forced by the urgency of the situation to put U.S. combat troops into the Vietnamese capital city, Saigon, for the first time. For political and psychological reasons I had hoped that the Vietnamese could defend their own cities and carry the heavy fighting in the populated areas as in the past. In view of the enemy's major effort, the risk involved in pursuing this policy became unacceptable, and I unhesitatingly set aside such a policy then and for the future. Therefore, American forces moved in behind the Vietnamese, the first units arriving at 6 a.m. By the end of the day, five U.S. battalions were in and about the city and two more moved in the next day. Many more U.S. battalions occupied positions along roads leading to the city in order to block enemy reinforcements which, according to our intelligence, were to exploit the success of the shock troops.

The enemy forces, consisting of elements of 11 local force battalions, failed to take any of their objectives except the undefended Phu Tho Race Track, which they briefly used as a base area. Except for breaching the wall and entering the grounds of the U.S. Embassy, the only successes against a government target were brief incursions into the rear of the Vietnamese Joint General Staff compound and into two remote areas of Tan Son Nhut Airbase.

At Hue the enemy had ready access to the city from his logistical base in the A Shau Valley, where we had no covering outpost like that at Khe Sanh. Under the concealment of low fog, enemy regular units consisting of eight battalions (made up of both Viet Cong and North Vietnamese) were able to infiltrate Hue with the help of accomplices inside the city. These troops quickly captured most of that portion of the city on the south bank of the

Perfume River. They later seized the bulk of the northern half, including the Imperial Citadel. U.S. Marines drove them from most of the south bank in the first few days, but the battle was fierce for the Imperial Citadel. Aided by very bad weather, the enemy was able to bring reinforcements from the Viet Cong 416th Battalion, NVA 5th Division, and NVA 324B Division, and to hold on until 25 February. Before the battle was over, some 16 North Vietnamese battalions had been identified in and around Hue.

The recapture of Hue was a bitter fight directly involving three U.S. Marine Corps and 11 Vietnamese battalions. The struggle at first involved house-to-house fighting and then a long arduous process of routing the enemy from the heavily walled ancient fortress of the Imperial City. This urban warfare against fortified positions was not unlike that in European cities during World War II.

Heavy damage to the city and to the Citadel inevitably resulted, and some 116,000 civilians were made homeless. It was a costly battle in human lives as well: the enemy lost over 5,000 killed in the city and an additional 3,000 to its immediate north—at least the equivalent of a full division—while U.S. and South Vietnamese units lost just over 500 men killed. During the time the enemy controlled the city he singled out and executed over 1,000 government officials, school teachers, and others of known government loyalty. This was a terrifying indication of what well might occur should the Communists succeed in gaining control of South Vietnam.

In anticipation of an enemy attack, I had moved the headquarters and two brigades of the 1st Cavalry Division northward from Binh Dinh Province in mid-January. At the time of the attack on Hue the 1st Brigade was near Quang Tri City and the 3d Brigade between Quang Tri City and Hue. Timely reinforcement of an ARVN regiment by the 1st Brigade brilliantly defeated an enemy attempt to capture Quang Tri City. Inflicting heavy casualties on the enemy, the air cavalrymen gave confidence to the ARVN and the local paramilitary forces, who fought well in this critical engagement.

The enemy's *Tet* offensive also envisioned the destruction of the Dak To-Tan Canh complex in the Central Highlands—the scene of the disastrous enemy defeat in November of 1967. The entire NVA 1st Division, consisting of three regiments supported by rocket artillery, was assigned this mission.

Between 15 January and *Tet,* two regiments of the division were detected en route to their attack positions and were engaged by the firepower of the 4th Infantry Division and U.S. Air Force light and heavy bombers. As a result of these attacks, three enemy battalions were incapacitated and the enemy's time schedule so disrupted that only one battalion was in its assigned assault position on the night the *Tet* offensive began.

From 15 January until 28 February the NVA 1st Division recklessly pursued its attempts to gain tactical positions around Dak To but was successfully countered and defeated by the combined forces of the ARVN 42d Regiment and the U.S. 4th Infantry Division. These actions constituted the heaviest concentration of enemy forces by the B-3 front during *Tet* and the longest sustained attack of the offensive. Since the total number of NVA battalions engaged in the operation was twice that of the combined U.S. and ARVN strength, the total defeat of the NVA 1st Division was a significant expression of the professionalism of American and South Vietnamese forces in the area.

Destruction from the countrywide attack was widespread, creating hundreds of thousands of refugees. When Vietnamese forces moved to the defense of province and district capitals, the enemy was able to move with great freedom in the rural areas and in the regions immediately surrounding the defended towns. Most of the battalions of the Vietnamese Army which had been providing security for the pacification effort also withdrew to the defense of government installations. They were often accompanied by the pacification cadre and in some cases by both Regional and Popular Forces, which withdrew from exposed outposts.

The *Tet* offensive was exceedingly costly to the enemy throughout the country. Between 29 January and 11 February the Communists lost some 32,000 men killed and 5,800 detained, out of an estimated force of 84,000 committed to the offensive. They also lost over 7,000 individual and almost 1,300 crew-served weapons (machine guns, mortars, etc.). Allied losses were 1,001 U.S. and 2,082 Vietnamese and Free World personnel. By the end of February the number of enemy killed had risen to more than 45,000. In the same period the enemy lost over 12,500 weapons.

This was only the initial price he paid for his new strategy and his efforts to foreshorten the war. The enemy told his troops and his political cadre that the time had come for the general offensive and a general uprising. It is not entirely clear whether the enemy expected to succeed with one mighty blow or whether *Tet* was simply the most dramatic episode of his 1968 offensive.

There is much evidence to support the first interpretation. In Hue, Kontum City, Ban Me Thuot, Qui Nhon, and Nha Trang, for example, the local VC political and administrative organization accompanied the assault troops and planned to occupy these provincial capitals and thereafter to operate from them as the Liberation or Revolutionary Government. In Hue, the enemy announced the formation of a Revolutionary Government and the New Alliance for National Democratic and Peace Forces designed to attract the participation of anti-government, but non-Communist elements. In each of these areas, the clandestine shadow government came out into the open and was largely destroyed.

It is difficult to believe that the enemy would have sacrificed these experienced and hard-core cadres if he had not expected to succeed. There is also some evidence, which has more recently become available, that the enemy tried seriously to seize the border areas and particularly the northern two provinces with the massive forces of about six divisions which he committed there. Another strong indication that he entertained high hopes for a decisive victory is the fact that throughout the country, and particularly in the Delta, he impressed into his military units very large numbers of untrained, local Vietnamese, many of whom were very young and others very old. This move had all the signs of a one-shot, go-for-broke attempt.

On the other side of the argument, however, is the fact that large North Vietnamese formations were not used initially in the attack in the III Corps area, particularly the North Vietnamese 7th Division, which was held out of the early decision stage of the battle. These may have been exploitation forces which were not committed because of the failure of the initial assaults. Indeed, in Hue the enemy reinforced his initial success. In Saigon and elsewhere there was really inadequate success to reinforce.

The government of Vietnam did not collapse under this blow. To the contrary, it rallied in the face of the threat with a unity and purpose greater than that which had ever been displayed up to that time. Perhaps the greatest blow to the enemy's hopes and plans was the fact that there was no evidence of significant participation by the population in support of the enemy. In other words, the general uprising simply did not occur.

To the contrary, following the *Tet* offensive, the Government showed a willingness to place arms for self-defense in the hands of civilian inhabitants of cities, towns and hamlets—a willingness it had never previously exhibited in my experience. Although the fight was touch-and-go in many places at the outset, no South Vietnamese military units were destroyed and their casualties were relatively low considering the heavy engagements they fought.

After a second flurry of attacks on 18 February, enemy activity fell off sharply, although enemy forces remained in forward deployments around the major cities and towns. These exposed forces continued to suffer heavy casualties. VC units had suffered the bulk of the casualties and this hastened the process of turning the war into more of a North Vietnamese affair. In October 1965 the North Vietnamese Army units had comprised about 25 percent of the combat maneuver forces in the south; but after the *Tet* and subsequent May offensive, that proportion increased to over 55 percent. Including North Vietnamese troops in Viet Cong units, the total percentage of North Vietnamese in combat maneuver forces had reached approximately 70 percent by June 1968.

Following the abortion of his February attacks, the enemy attempted to resupply some of his forces by landing along the coast four trawlers loaded with supplies, arms, and ammunition. The attempt was a disaster. U.S. and Vietnamese naval forces sank three of the trawlers. The fourth ship turned back before it entered South Vietnam's contiguous waters. In view of our well-organized coastal surveillance operations, this attempt to supply by sea was obviously a desperate measure.

Having sustained severe losses under the new tactics of a mobile war of decision, the Communists found themselves with a significant replacement problem. Even more than in the preceding year, they had to turn in 1968 to North Vietnam for manpower to fill their ranks—and the reservoir of trained manpower in North Vietnam was fast being depleted. The number of replacements infiltrated from North Vietnam rose from fewer than 4,000 in December 1967 to approximately 23,000 in January 1968, followed by some 19,000 a month until May when the number rose to approximately 30,000. The average monthly infiltration for the first half of 1968 was above 22,000. Most of these were raw draftees who had received only rudimentary training; many had not fired a weapon before being recklessly thrown into combat.

For example, in October of 1967, 82 percent of captured enemy prisoners revealed that they had served for more than six months; but by May of 1968 only 40 percent had been in the North Vietnamese Army for that long and 50 percent had less than three months total service, including the time consumed in southward infiltration. By May in the III Corps area the Communists were resorting to committing raw replacements into combat as a group, controlled and led by the escort detachment that had guided them south. Not only did enemy losses soar in this pathetic situation, but the enemy began more and more to leave his dead and weapons on the battlefield, a sure sign of plummeting combat effectiveness.

The degradation in the quality of enemy troops was also reflected in the ratio of the enemy's battlefield losses to those of the South Vietnamese, U.S., and Free World forces. In 1966 the ratio of killed in action was 3.3 Communists to 1 of our side; in 1967 it was 3.9 to 1; during the first half of 1968 it rose to almost 6 to 1.

While attention was centered on Saigon and Hue, the enemy increased his pressure on the Marine base at Khe Sanh. Located astride an east-west highway—Route 9—the Khe Sanh plateau commands the approaches from the west to Dong Ha and Quang Tri City and to the coastal corridor leading to Hue. Were we to relinquish the Khe Sanh area, the North Vietnamese would have had an unobstructed invasion route into the two northernmost provinces from which they might outflank our positions south of the Demilitarized Zone—positions which were blocking North Vietnamese attacks from the north.

Had we possessed greater strength, the Khe Sanh Airfield and nearby security base would have been less critical. We would have preferred to operate in this area with mobile forces, as we had done at Dak To and elsewhere; but at the time we had neither adequate troop resources in the north nor the logistical capacity to support them. In addition, another critical factor had to be considered—the weather. Poor visibility during the northeast monsoon in January, February, and March, because of low clouds and persistent ground fog, made helicopter movement hazardous if not impossible much of the time.

Lacking sufficient forces to counteract the enemy buildup with ground attacks, we had only two practical choices in regard to the Khe Sanh outpost:

to withdraw or to reinforce. Despite the importance of the outpost, there were strong arguments for withdrawal. We were in the midst of the northeast monsoon with no prospect of relief from bad weather until the end of March. This posed major problems for close air support and supply by air. Because Route 9 was closed from a combination of enemy sabotage and heavy rains, Khe Sanh would have to be maintained entirely by aircraft until the weather improved and we could open the highway. The enemy had the advantage of a short line of communications from a big logistical base he had built a few miles away across the border in Laos. Judging from the size of his buildup, and from his own statements, he was hoping to achieve a military-political victory similar to the one 14 years earlier at Dien Bien Phu.

On the other hand, adding to the importance of the Khe Sanh area from our viewpoint was the enemy's apparent determination to take it, which meant that by holding it we might tie down large North Vietnamese forces that otherwise would move against the populated areas. Furthermore, with the availability of artillery support—which was not hindered by weather—and our extensive capability for radar-controlled bombing, we were assured of a high level of fire support.

The question was whether we could afford the troops to reinforce, keep them supplied by air, and defeat an enemy far superior in numbers as we waited for the weather to clear, built forward bases, and made other preparations for an overland relief expedition. I believed we could do all of those things. With the concurrence of the III Marine Amphibious Force Commander, Lt. Gen. Robert E. Cushman, Jr., I made the decision to reinforce and hold the area while destroying the enemy with our massive firepower and to prepare for offensive operations when the weather became favorable. Because of our prior planning, we were able to solve the logistical problems in the north even during the height of the northeast monsoon. Ports, ramps, airfields, and roads were opened and put into use in record time.

In early January we had begun Operation NIAGARA I, an extensive reconnaissance program to obtain as much information as possible about the enemy. I reinforced the 3d Marine Division with special reconnaissance teams. Valuable intelligence was provided by a highly trained reconnaissance force of CIDG troops led by Vietnamese and U.S. Special Forces officers and men. Therefore, in mid-January we were prepared to initiate the firepower phase, NIAGARA II, which was to continue until late March. I instructed the Marines to dig in and to confine their patrols to those required for local security. Restricted ground maneuver would permit us the free use of massive supporting firepower without jeopardy to our troops and avoid risking the defeat of small elements by the larger enemy forces in the area. The supporting bombardment—placed in close proximity to our troops—was delivered by Marine artillery on the Khe Sanh plateau, by 16 U.S. Army 175-mm guns that were positioned so as to be in range, and by Marine, Air Force, and Navy tactical fighters. Farther from our defensive perimeter, we used the B–52's. However, on several occasions we put the big bombs from these planes within a thousand meters of Marine positions. The bombardment continued day and night. During this battle, I slept in my headquarters next to the combat operations center and personally decided where the B–52's would strike. To assist me in making these decisions, I met at least twice daily with my intelligence and operations officers.

At the beginning of the battle, two battalions of the U.S. 26th Marine Regiment held the position at Khe Sanh, located by an airfield just outside the village. The Marines flew in a third battalion from that regiment on 16 January from Phu Bai. Five days later the enemy attacked and overran the village of Khe Sanh, prompting our troops there and the villagers to withdraw to our defensive base near the airfield. The same day, the base itself and our outpost to the northwest on Hill 861 came under attack. From that time, this hill outpost and three others on Hills 558, 881 South, and 950 were resupplied, when possible, exclusively by helicopter.

On the 22d the base was further reinforced with the 1st Battalion, 9th Marine Regiment, from Gio Linh and four days later I persuaded the Vietnamese to reinforce with a Ranger battalion (the 37th) and to prepare to reinforce later with a second Ranger battalion if required. The 37th Ranger Battalion was deployed from the vicinity of Phu Loc. All together we had near the airstrip three Marine battalions, an ARVN Ranger battalion, and a U.S. Army Special Forces detachment together with a Civilian Irregular Defense Group company, and the vital aircraft-control radar detachments of the U.S. Air Force. Since the airstrip with its ground control devices was our lifeline, it had to be secured. A battalion and a reinforced company of Marines occupied the hilltop outposts. These allied forces faced an estimated two North Vietnamese Army divisions, some 15,000 to 20,000 strong, and one more enemy division within striking distance of our positions.

On 6 February concentrated artillery fire struck both the base at Khe Sanh and the Lang Vei Special Forces camp, a few miles to the southwest. During the night elements of the North Vietnamese 66th Regiment, 304th Division, attacked Lang Vei, employing heavy artillery, flamethrowers, mortars, and 9 Soviet PT-76 tanks (the Communists' first use of tanks in South Vietnam). In the face of overwhelming odds, most of the Special Forces and CIDG troops manning the camp fell back on the base at Khe Sanh. A few who held were soon trapped. The next day I directed a raid to retrieve the surrounded men. Under cover of artillery and air strikes, a rescue force of 10 U.S. Special Forces soldiers and 40 CIDG troops landed by Marine helicopter within a thousand yards of the camp and launched a ground attack to relieve the remaining defenders. When the rescuers were within 200 yards of the camp, the defenders broke out and joined the attackers. Helicopters evacuated the entire group.

During an 11-week period of heavy enemy bombardment, the Marine garrison at Khe Sanh, together with the Vietnamese Ranger battalion, resisted and threw back all attacks. On 23 February alone the base received 1,307 rounds of mortar, rocket, and artillery fire; but the enemy never penetrated beyond the barbed wire at the base's outer perimeter.

As the northeast monsoon waned, on 1 April we launched Operation PEGASUS-LAM SON 207 to reestablish land contact with Khe Sanh. Employing airmobile tactics, elements of the 1st Cavalry Division and three ARVN airborne battalions seized commanding positions to the east and south of Khe Sanh while U.S. Marines drove west from a base at Ca Lu along Route 9, clearing and repairing the road as they went. As the Marines neared the Khe Sanh base, the 26th Marines attacked from the base and linked up with the cavalrymen. None of our troops met much resistance, but they found ample evidence of the destruction our firepower had wrought, including over a thousand enemy dead and large quantities of abandoned supplies and equipment.

As the battle raged in February and early March emergency reinforcement plans for Vietnam were developed by the MACV staff in close coordination with the CINCPAC staff and the joint staff of the Joint Chiefs of Staff. As a matter of military prudence in the face of uncertainties regarding North Vietnamese intentions and capabilities in the northern area and the ability of the South Vietnamese to regain the initiative, I asked that additional forces be prepared for deployment. However, by the end of March, the uncertainty surrounding the *Tet* offensive had abated. The enemy had committed a major share of his forces and had been severely defeated, the government of Vietnam had held firm, South Vietnamese troops in general had fought well, and there had been no public uprising. Further, the government of Vietnam had issued a national mobilization decree on 24 October 1967 which, although delayed in implementation, was to have become effective on 1 January 1968. On 9 February 1968 the Vietnamese general assembly gave approval to the government's accelerated mobilization plan based on this decree. Thus, greatly increased military and pacification forces seemed in prospect.

Therefore, major additional U.S. forces were not required, but a decision was made to deploy 13,500 troops to provide necessary combat support and combat service support for the newly arrived 27th Marine Regimental Landing Team and 3d Brigade of the 82d Airborne Division that I had requested and received in February. The approval of this deployment raised our manpower authorization to 549,500. In addition, I received authority to hire 13,035 additional local civilians to augment selective logistic and construction units and thereby offset the need for additional U.S. military manpower. When it became known that the 27th Regimental Landing Team had to return to the United States, I requested as a replacement a brigade of the 5th Mechanized Division, consisting of one infantry battalion, one mechanized battalion, and one armored battalion. I asked for this highly mobile unit to operate in the coastal areas of Quang Tri and Thua Thien Provinces and in the area south of the Demilitarized Zone.

Meanwhile, to prevent the enemy from massing to launch further attacks in the vicinity of Hue and to take advantage of the short period of good weather in the region, we rapidly shifted the forces operating on the Khe Sanh plateau and mounted a reconnaissance in force into the A Shau Valley in westernmost Thua Thien Province. Our objective was the large logistics complex the North Vietnamese had been building since overrunning our Special Forces camp at the head of the valley in March of 1966. On 19 April two brigades of the 1st Cavalry Division and an ARVN infantry regiment conducted an airmobile assault into the valley. At the same time, the 101st Airborne Division, in conjunction with the ARVN 1st Division and an ARVN airborne task force, conducted extensive clearing operations around Hue and along Highway 547 leading to Hue from the A Shau Valley. This operation quickly turned into a counteroffensive against the enemy forces which were attempting to concentrate against Hue. Many arms, ammunition, and rice caches were located. The cordon and search and night operations by the 101st Airborne Division were particularly effective. Our troops performed magnificently in extremely rugged terrain.

After the linkup at Khe Sanh, I asked that the Provisional Corps—which I had introduced to assist in controlling the increased strength in the I Corps—make a study of possible redistribution of troops during the good weather of the next several months with emphasis on the Khe Sanh area and the DMZ. Lt. Gen. William B. Rosson, who commanded the corps, and General Cushman, Commanding General, III Marine Amphibious Force, subsequently recommended that the Khe Sanh base and airfield be abandoned and destroyed but that the Khe Sanh plateau, because of its tactical importance, be defended by airmobile troops supported from the new airfield and logistic base constructed by the 1st Cavalry Division at Ca Lu during Operation PEGASUS.

We now had greater flexibility because of the forward base at nearby Ca Lu, improved logistics in the northern area of the I Corps (and particularly just below the Demilitarized Zone), additional troops in the northern part of the I Corps, and greater availability of helicopters in the north. Of particular importance, we now had weather that would permit routine use of helicopters for supply, as opposed to fixed wing aircraft dependent upon larger airfields. I approved the plan advanced by Generals Rosson and Cushman in principle but deferred placing it into effect until the A Shau operation was completed and additional troops could again be deployed to the Khe Sanh plateau where they could consume the supplies stockpiled near the airfield. Furthermore, since I was scheduled to depart in a matter of weeks, I deferred the final decision to my successor.

With respect to the DMZ, commanders on the ground recommended modifications in the strong point obstacle system because the enemy's artillery and rocket fire had been so intense that the construction of the originally planned physical obstacles was not feasible. I approved a modified concept in principle but directed that a detailed plan be developed and presented for final decision.

In March, far to the south, Vietnamese Army units joined with elements of our 1st, 9th, and 25th Divisions in Operation QUYET THANG (Resolve to Win). Scouring the Capital Military District and six surrounding provinces, the combined force accounted for over 2,600 enemy killed and captured many arms caches during less than a month of operations. Again, numerous patrols and ambushes paid off for us.

In the IV Corps in March we launched Operation PEOPLE'S ROAD, aimed at reestablishing security and improving the condition of Route 4 from the III Corps boundary southward through Dinh Tuong Province to the Mekong River before the southeast monsoon. Both security and maintenance had suffered since the *Tet* offensive. While the 1st Brigade, 9th Infantry Division, provided security, two U.S. Army engineer companies made road and bridge repairs to include widening and surfacing the roadway. At the same time I insisted that the Vietnamese develop plans to assume complete responsibility for securing and maintaining this vital route. To this end, the Vietnamese proceeded to organize and train ten new Regional Force companies. By the end of June the operation was proceeding on schedule toward a planned completion date in the first part of August.

The 9th Division as a whole, but the 1st Brigade in particular, operated with great success and the highest professional competence in the southern approaches to Saigon for a number of months, destroying or decimating battalion after battalion of enemy troops. They developed to a fine point the exploitation of intelligence followed by large and sustained cordons.

Beginning in April U.S., Free World, and South Vietnamese forces everywhere moved to the offensive. Having met the challenge of the *Tet* offensive and the siege of Khe Sanh, we were prepared to exploit fully the dominant military position and high level of experience we had built up over the preceding three years. The operations ranged from the reconnaissance in force into the A Shau Valley to further forays by the Mobile Riverine Force in the Delta. In the III Corps, on 8 April, we launched a combined U.S.-ARVN campaign (TOAN THANG, or Complete Victory) employing 79 maneuver battalions, 42 U.S., and 37 Vietnamese. It was a highly decentralized operation since it consisted primarily of small search operations during the day and many ambushes at night, a continuation of our persistent security operations aimed at local forces, guerrillas, and infrastructure. When the operation came to a close on 31 May, the count of enemy killed had reached 7,600. Even more important, the operation had gone a long way toward disrupting Communist plans for a second-wave attack on Saigon.

In March and April the enemy replaced the bulk of his losses with North Vietnamese fillers and in May mounted the second major offensive of the year, timed to coincide with the opening of negotiations in Paris. This second offensive was to have been a slightly scaled down model of the *Tet* attack. However, it aborted badly in two important areas. The force which intended to attack Hue and nearby I Corps cities simply never got underway. North of the Hai Van pass the U.S. Army's 1st Cavalry and 101st Airborne Divisions had joined the 3d Marine Division in the Provisional Corps. These very aggressive forces anticipated the attack and spoiled the enemy's plans.

The North Vietnamese had also planned to mount a major offensive in the Pleiku and Kontum area with forces of their so-called B–3 Front, which maintained its headquarters in adjacent Cambodia. The actions of the 4th Infantry Division and reinforcements from the 173d Airborne Brigade, plus the massive use of B–52 strikes, caused the enemy to abandon his plans in this area and to withdraw into Cambodia.

However, the main attack occurred again in the Saigon area. In an effort to achieve better coordination than he had managed in the *Tet* offensive, the enemy relaxed the tight security measures he had employed in January and disseminated widely his May attack plans. Some of these plans fell into our hands and aided us in disposing our forces to meet the attacks. Our troops around Saigon were particularly well situated for blocking the enemy's approach. Aggressive patrols and ambushes intercepted and disrupted many of his units. By moving at night and approaching through jungles and swamps, the enemy was nevertheless able to bring units close to the capital before being detected.

Of the large force intended to attack Tan Son Nhut Airbase, less than one battalion reached the defensive perimeter. South Vietnamese units quickly drove off this force and then destroyed it in the nearby French cemetery. Otherwise, only small units survived to reach Saigon, principally from the west, and most of those were destroyed as they approached the outskirts.

As in February, the enemy employed artillery-type rockets in this attack. This prompted me to direct that the bulk of the metal observation towers we were constructing at Cam Ranh Bay be moved to Saigon, where they served a timely purpose in enabling us to spot enemy weapons and direct counterfire.

After a brief lull, the Communists launched another strike at Saigon on 7 May. This time the attack had no apparent military objective but was instead mounted strictly for political and psychological gain. For the most part, the Communists infiltrated small guerrilla bands and dispersed them over a wide area, primarily in the Cholon sector. Groups of four or five men holed up in buildings and fought suicidally against Vietnamese police and soldiers, who gradually rooted them out position by position. A few platoon-sized elements launched small but violent attacks, employing large volumes of random small arms fire. In a number of places the enemy deliberately set fires. The objective clearly was to try to establish an impression of "Saigon under siege," create terror, destruction, and refugees to overburden and embarrass the government, and achieve propaganda and psychological gain to influence discussions between the U.S. and North Vietnam that had begun in Paris.

In only one instance, in the vicinity of the "Y" Bridge over the Kinh Doi Canal along the southern edge of the city, did a force of any appreciable size manage to get into the outskirts of the city. The eventual outcome of the fighting was as inevitable there as elsewhere, but the Communists with their usual tenacity forced a fight continuing for several days before the last elements were eliminated. By 13 May all attempts to infiltrate the city had ceased. Although the fighting soon flickered out, enemy troops continued for several weeks to emerge from hiding and surrender. Most of these were North Vietnamese.

Earlier, on 10 May, a North Vietnamese battalion struck far to the north in the western portion of Quang Tin Province at a CIDG base serving as an outpost for a Special Forces camp at Kham Duc. Badly outnumbered, the CIDG tribesmen, reinforced by a U.S. Marine artillery battery, withdrew after almost 12 hours of heavy fighting. Since the Special Forces camp itself was apparently destined for attack, General Cushman of the III Marine Amphibious Force strengthened the defenders with a reinforced battalion of the Americal Division. One infantry company moved by helicopter from a position near Chu Lai and a battalion of the 196th Light Infantry Brigade with a battery of artillery moved by C–130 aircraft from Quang Tri airfield.

Before daylight on 12 May the North Vietnamese struck in regimental strength supported by rockets and mortars. The enemy overran our outposts on the surrounding high ground, thereby gaining commanding positions. General Cushman, with my approval, decided to evacuate the remote border post. During that afternoon planes and helicopters successfully evacuated our troops and Vietnamese dependents, but one C–130 aircraft was shot down with 150 Vietnamese passengers aboard, mostly civilian dependents of the Vietnamese garrison.

Enemy pressure and the speed of evacuation made it necessary to abandon and destroy large quantities of the unit's equipment and facilities of the camp. Over a period of several days—before, during, and after the evacuation—our total B-52 capability pounded enemy-held areas and suspected enemy locations, but marginal weather prevented assessment of the effectiveness of these massive strikes.

Also in May, after digesting the experiences of *Tet*, the enemy issued COSVN Resolution #6. The enemy's own statement of his strategic goals is interesting:

> *The Army and people as a whole must resolutely march forward and engage in a spontaneous uprising to drive out the Americans, overthrow the puppet regime, and turn over the reins of the Government to the people.*
>
> *Create conditions for Pacifist movements in the U.S.A. to expand, and the doves to assail the hawks, thus forcing the U.S.A. to radically change its VN policy.*

In their concerted drive to achieve these goals, the Communists had lost an estimated 120,000 men during the first six months of 1968. These losses were over one-half of their strength at the beginning of the year—or enough men to make more than 12 Communist divisions.

Also during the first half of 1968 the enemy lost some 37,000 small arms and crew-served weapons, enough to arm almost six of his divisions. The 180 tons of equipment we captured during the six-month period would have outfitted an enemy division operating in South Vietnam; the 856 tons of ammunition would have supported this division in combat for over five years; and the 2,841 tons of food we seized would have fed the same division for almost a year and a half.

By late spring even the enemy's hard-core cadre had begun to show signs of disillusionment, and for the first time a number of high level defections occurred. Particularly noteworthy were the defections of Lt. Col. Tram Van Dac, a political officer whose responsibilities were equivalent to those of a division commander, who defected on 19 April, and that of Lt. Col. Phan Viet Dung, commander of the North Vietnamese 165th Regiment, on 8 May. Dac saw the war as an impossible struggle which North Vietnam could not hope to win. Allied operations as far back as Operation JUNCTION CITY had convinced him of the hopelessness of the Communist cause. Colonel Dac was further discouraged when he attempted to fulfill his assigned task of contacting the Viet Cong political infrastructure to coordinate support for the enemy's May attack. He found the infrastructure so decimated that he could not perform his mission. Colonel Dung was no less emphatic. The situation was militarily hopeless, he told us, and continued fighting had no part in solving Vietnam's problems. The senseless manner in which North Vietnam was prosecuting the war had caused him to question the rightness of the cause.

Increasing numbers of lower ranking officers, including several unit surgeons, also surrendered. In each case, their rationale was much the same: the North Vietnamese could not win; still they were squandering the lives of their soldiers in hopeless attacks against unimportant yet unattainable objectives for the sole purpose of creating the impression of military strength. An experienced battalion commander who surrendered in the outskirts of Saigon in May stated that he could no longer lead men to certain death in illogical, futile attacks against inconsequential objectives—attacks which North Vietnam was ordering in order to provide a fulcrum for her diplomats in Paris.

Group surrenders began in May and continued at an increasing rate through June. The first took place on 1 May in Thua Thien Province when 95 enemy surrendered to troops of the 101st Airborne Division. On 4 June, 64 enemy (21 of whom were North Vietnamese) surrendered to a South Vietnamese unit in the same area, bringing most of their weapons with them. On 9 June the first organized group, a unit of 31 men led by their commander, surrendered near Saigon in Gia Dinh Province. Members of the Viet Cong 308th Main

Force and 6th Local Force Battalions volunteered that they surrendered because they knew they could not win. Small groups of men continued to give up during the month, the largest a 141-man company of the VC Quyet Thang Regiment that surrendered with weapons just north of Saigon on 18–19 June after absorbing a sound defeat from two Vietnamese Marine battalions. Aside from affording a commentary on the enemy's morale, the group surrenders pointed up the increased aggressiveness and effectiveness of South Vietnamese units.

As I left Vietnam in June the enemy was preparing for another attack. This attack, which occurred in mid-August when General Abrams was in command, was even less productive than previous efforts. The enemy achieved none of his offensive goals in Vietnam. Indiscriminate mortar and rocket attacks on populated centers and costly attacks on remote outposts were all he could show for his highly propagandized military efforts. The *Tet* offensive had the effect of a "Pearl Harbor"; the South Vietnamese government was intact and stronger; the armed forces were larger, more effective, and more confident; the people had rejected the idea of a general uprising; and enemy forces, particularly those of the Viet Cong, were much weaker.

OBSERVATIONS—1968

Political Effects of the TET Offensive

If imposing hardship on the civilian population was an objective of the enemy's *Tet* attacks, he was eminently successful. All of the larger cities and towns suffered extensive damage to homes, markets, and public buildings. By the first of March the fighting had created 800,000 evacuees, with over a third of these concentrated in and near Saigon. The widespread withdrawal of Vietnamese security forces from the countryside to defend the cities and towns—and the hardships the populace suffered at the hands of the enemy—dealt our pacification program a substantial setback. The pacification program did not regain its pre-*Tet* scope and effectiveness until the middle of 1968.

South Vietnamese Military Progress

During the enemy's *Tet* offensive and our own counterattacks that followed, the Vietnamese Armed Forces demonstrated their improved effectiveness and morale—improvement we saw as the tangible product of our years of effort. Their combat techniques and employment of supporting fires were excellent. Effective leadership emerged at all levels. The Battalion Commander's School, Command and General Staff College, improved basic training centers, good technical schools, and the indoctrination program to prepare the Vietnamese soldier for Revolutionary Development and civic action, all paid off at *Tet*. The Vietnamese Army stood fast—fought back—and came of age. The weapons modernization program had been especially effective—the combat performance of Vietnamese units equipped with the M16 was outstanding. With this gratifying performance in mind, I requested that modernization programs for the Vietnamese Army be accelerated.

The manpower problem that had long plagued the Vietnamese Armed Forces was gradually being resolved. President Thieu's general mobilization decree (supported with minor modification by the National Assembly) provided a realistic mobilization program, thus insuring an adequate supply of manpower for the Vietnamese forces in the uncertain times ahead. In March 19-year-olds became eligible for the draft, followed on 1 May by 18-year-olds. The false starts at mobilizing manpower in previous years were partly due to the weak and unstable nature of the central government. But in this critical time, the *Tet* offensive had further crystallized support for an already strengthened and stabilized government. This solidifying effect of *Tet* was, in my estimation, the single development which enabled the mobilization program to be successful. A marked wave of voluntary enlistments after *Tet*, together with the expanded draft, produced an increase of 122,000 in the Vietnamese Armed Forces during the first half of 1968.

During *Tet* we detected a serious weakness in the South Vietnamese command organization, one which hampered coordination and control of forces in the important capital area. The commander of III Corps held basic military responsibility for Saigon and its environs, yet the National Police, who bore responsibility for security of the city, were separately organized and under control of the Chief of National Police. During the *Tet* offensive, General Vien, the Chief of the Joint General Staff, had assumed command of all Vietnamese forces, including the National Police, within the Capital Military District.

The Vietnamese had not yet solved this relationship problem when the later attacks came in May, so we were forced once again to use an expedient. This time the III Corps commander, instead of the Chief of the Joint General Staff, took command of all the military and police forces protecting the city. This expedient worked somewhat better but the Vietnamese needed a permanent reorganization to insure the necessary planning and coordination between the police and military forces.

Since March I had persistently recommended that the Vietnamese authorities appoint a combat-worthy general officer to be permanent Military Governor of the Capital Military District. Internal political considerations prevented action on this recommendation until late May, when the Vietnamese government boldly shifted a number of senior officials. These changes cleared the way and in June, the government designated General Minh, the excellent combat commander of the ARVN 21st Division in the Delta, as the Military Governor of the Capital Military District. Operating under the III Corps commander, he controlled all Vietnamese Army, General Reserve, Regional and Popular Forces, National Police, and Military Police in the district.

A post of U.S. Senior Advisor to the Military Governor was created to parallel this significant organizational realignment by the Vietnamese. The general officer filling this post operated under II Field Force and exercised operational control of all U.S. advisors and forces involved in the security of the Capital Military District.

These two closely coordinated commands mustered an impressive force. On the Vietnamese side, there were 16 regular ARVN battalions, four Regional Force battalions, 26 separate Regional Force companies, 144 Popular Force platoons, and all the National Police in the area. U.S. forces consisted of a mechanized battalion, an armored cavalry troop, an air cavalry troop, and other U.S. reinforcements available on short notice.

The accomplishments of our overall advisory effort reflected in a sense the degree of political stability of the Vietnamese government. I have traced our slow progress in the early years. However, in 1966, as political stability increased, our advisory program gained momentum. By 1967 we were able to project a comprehensive development program for a Vietnamese Army of such size, quality, and balance that it could progressively assume a greater share of the fighting. The Vietnamese Army's successes against the foe's *Tet* attacks created a new sense of confidence. The national mobilization program was filling the ranks and easing the Army's expansion. Training had greatly improved, with particular attention being paid to security and fighting in the cities. The program for arming the Vietnamese forces with modern weapons and equipment had progressed rapidly in the prior six months and continued on schedule. Good military leadership began to emerge; leaders in all grades exhibited a promising independence and a continuous quest for responsibility.

Firepower

The key to our success at Khe Sanh was firepower, principally aerial firepower. For 77 days Air Force, Navy, and Marine aircraft provided round-the-clock, close-in support to the defending garrison and were controlled by airborne Forward Air Controllers or ground-based radar. Between 22 January and 31 March tactical aircraft flew an average of 300 sorties daily, close to one every five minutes, and expended 35,000 tons of bombs and rockets. At the same time, increasing numbers of the Strategic Air Command's B–52's were demonstrating their devastating ability to neutralize a large area. The B–52's flew 2,602 sorties and dropped over 75,000 tons of bombs during the siege and were instrumental in preventing the enemy from assembling in large formations. Marine and Army artillery fires supplemented this awesome quantity of aerial firepower. Marine howitzers within the combat base and sixteen Army long-range 175-mm artillery pieces located to the east fired over 100,000 rounds into the area during the siege, or nearly 1,500 shells per day.

This tremendous firepower prevented the two NVA divisions directly confronting Khe Sanh and a third in the immediate area from massing their forces to mount a major attack. Their supplies were destroyed, their troop formations shattered, and their antiaircraft fire rendered ineffective. The effect of our firepower upon the enemy's plans was dramatically demonstrated on 5 February when an enemy regiment attempted to launch an attack against a small Marine outpost on Hill 881 South. Our sensor devices detected the enemy unit as it moved forward to mount the attack. This information and our knowledge of enemy doctrine enabled us to locate accurately his staging areas and approach routes. As a consequence, just as the North Vietnamese completed their preparations and approached Hill 881, we struck them with a devastating air and artillery attack, killing or wounding large numbers of the 3,000-man force, scattering its units, and defeating the attack before it reached the jump-off position.

Logistics

As the fighting became heavier in the north, we realized how provident had been our logistical expansion along the northern coastal and river areas in 1967—particularly at Tan My east of Hue and the development of the Cua Viet channel and port facilities at Dong Ha. We were utterly dependent upon the sea logistical line. The enemy, recognizing this, consistently attacked our supply convoys and off-loading facilities, particularly along the Cua Viet, an estuary leading to Dong Ha. Tactical sweeps along the banks of the estuary by Marine and Army units and operations by some of the U.S. Navy's patrol and armored boats brought north from the Delta kept this tenuous line of communication open.

To the south of the Cua Viet in Quang Tri Province, the U.S. Army's 159th Transportation Battalion (Terminal) in March established an over-the-beach off-loading point, designated Wunder Beach, and the U.S. 14th Combat Engineer Battalion constructed a connecting road to Route 1. These facilities relieved the pressure of the increased volume of supplies passing through Hue and the Cua Viet. With the addition of Wunder Beach the logistical improvements we had made in the previous twelve months increased tenfold our seaborne cargo capability in northern I Corps.

The resupply of Khe Sanh stands as the premier air logistical feat of the war. This feat was made possible because of plans prepared for just such a contingency and troops made available in our programmed and balanced force structure. Despite low clouds, fog, and the poor visibility of the monsoon season, Marine and Seventh Air Force crews between 21 January and 8 April delivered about 13,000 tons of supplies to the isolated outpost. Approximately 65 percent of this tonnage was delivered by parachute from C–130 "Hercules" and C–123 "Provider" aircraft. In all, there were 679 parachute drops of supplies. Our airdrops were extremely accurate, chiefly due to an effective ground control station at the airstrip and the skill of the air crews. Fortunately, we had the trained parachute riggers, air crews, and ground control teams to make accurate parachute delivery of supplies and personnel. In addition, 455 aircraft landed on the Khe Sanh airstrip, many after the enemy had moved mortars and automatic weapons within range of the strip. During the first four months of the year three fixed-wing aircraft and two helicopters were destroyed by the enemy, and 49 helicopters were damaged in the Khe Sanh area. At no time during the siege did the defenders experience a serious supply shortage.

Organization

I responded to the command and control problems created by our buildup and the intensified action in I Corps area by opening a temporary headquarters known as MACV Forward. This forward headquarters was originally designed as a control element to supervise the combat force and logistical buildup in the area. Once MACV Forward became fully operational and established with adequate communication and staff support it would be converted to a tactical corps headquarters. Prior to that conversion, General Abrams, my deputy, operated from MACV Forward and exercised control in my name over the deployment of all joint combat and logistical forces involved—Army, Navy, Air Force, and Marine.

On 10 March I converted MACV Forward to a corps headquarters and simultaneously created the Provisional Corps, Vietnam, (later to be designated the U.S. Army XXIV Corps) commanded by General Rosson. The Provisional Corps functioned under the operational control of the III Marine Amphibious Force, with General Rosson exercising operational control over the 3d Marine Division, 1st Cavalry Division, 101st Airborne Division, and assigned corps troops. The new corps also worked closely with the ARVN 1st Division in the area.

As operations in the north expanded, I found it essential to make an important adjustment in the tactical aircraft control system in I Corps. The complex intermixture of U.S. Army, U.S. Marine, and Vietnamese ground forces had progressively complicated coordination and concentration of this indispensable air support provided by U.S. Air Force, U.S. Marine Corps, U.S. Navy, and Vietnamese Air Force tactical aircraft in addition to the B–52's of the 3d Air Division of the Strategic Air Command. In an effort to alleviate the problem, I introduced the concept of a "single manager" for tactical air. This action had the full approval of the Commander in Chief, Pacific. On 8 March my Deputy Commander for Air Operations assumed operational authority over all strike aircraft. My objective was to develop procedures that would combine into a single system the best features of both the Air Force and Marine tactical air support systems, and thereby provide more flexible, effective, and responsive aerial firepower support for our ground forces.

Intelligence

Many of the enemy rallying to the government's side provided valuable intelligence and frequently led our troops to arms caches and VC installations. Others served on propaganda teams working to encourage their former comrades to defect. Some defectors served with Revolutionary Development cadres. Beginning in 1966 the U.S. Marines in I Corps employed the ralliers as scouts—called "Kit Carson Scouts" after the American Indian fighter—and found them to be so effective that I encouraged all American units in the country to adopt the practice. By mid-1968 more than 700 former VC were serving as scouts for our troops.

Civic Action and Pacification

During early May General Vien, my counterpart, and I conceived a project to bring relief to Saigon inhabitants left homeless by the fighting and the enemy's destructive tactics. After discussions with President Thieu and Ambassador Bunker, the project was initiated on 20 May. The operation known as DONG TAM (United Hearts and Minds), was the largest civic action program to date. U.S. Army engineers, detachments from Navy Construction Battalions (Seabees), Air Force construction troops, and Vietnamese Army engineers working with the people cleared the rubble, established ten housing areas, and built some 1,500 family housing units complete with utilities and interior roads. The construction units were supported by medical civic action teams and psychological warfare teams that explained the project to the people. By the end of June Operation DONG TAM was well advanced with completion scheduled in September. The interest and concern for the civilian population manifested by the Vietnamese Armed Forces was a significant and gratifying aspect of this program.

At the time of my departure, the pacification effort was progressing under the able direction of Ambassador Komer. Since MACV assumed responsibility for the program in mid-1967, I believe we have aided the Vietnamese in adopting some simpler but more effective pacification procedures. An organized, countrywide attack on the Viet Cong infrastructure was proceeding to eliminate the Communist subversive threat. Such a campaign against the infrastructure would have promised little chance of success had we not dealt the enemy such heavy military blows during the earlier years and in the *Tet* offensive. The various political and military elements of the enemy's organization were so interwoven and mutually reinforcing that the political structure stood relatively inviolate until its military security was stripped away and defeated. Our increasingly successful military operations in the past three years had left the infrastructure more exposed and more susceptible to elimination.

Combat Force Dispositions

A number of considerations determine the disposition of allied forces at any give time. First and foremost is the continuing requirement to provide security for government centers and for the major population concentrations. To the extent that Vietnamese forces of all types could fulfill this requirement, U.S. forces could be used offensively. Secondly, our dispositions were necessarily adjusted to the location and level of activity of major enemy forces. For obvious reasons, I wanted to engage enemy forces as far as possible from populated areas. Except for the cities and towns, the areas of high population density, and certain invasion or infiltration corridors, terrain as such was of only temporary tactical importance. This was unlike the situation in wars of the past.

In early 1968—before *Tet*—the vast bulk of the total allied force was in or near the heavily populated areas. However, the Demilitarized Zone area presented a major exception. Enemy activity around the DMZ had, by early 1968, increased to such a level that we were faced with a major invasion. For example, three North Vietnamese divisions were on or near the Khe Sanh plateau and over three more were operating from the DMZ to the vicinity of Hue. If we had not engaged these very large enemy concentrations in the relatively remote northern area, we would have had to fight them in other, perhaps more populated, regions of South Vietnam or face the distinct likelihood that the two northernmost provinces—Quang Tri and Thua Thien—would be lost to the North Vietnamese forces. We now have intelligence indicating that the enemy was, in fact, readying a "liberation government" for these provinces.

It was politically unacceptable to surrender any part of South Vietnam to the enemy. For this reason we reinforced north of the Hai Van pass both before and after *Tet*. After the *Tet* offensive started, we increased the forces in the northern two provinces, but it was not necessary to make any wholesale shifts of units from one corps area to another. The additional units deployed from the United States gave us the necessary flexibility.

In the II Corps area, we were able to practice some economy of force, as the enemy had been progressively weakened over a long period of time. In the III and IV Corps, our forces moved closer to the populated areas since the enemy remained exposed in forward positions until after his abortive May offensive.

The following maps and charts illustrate the gradual changes from late January, just prior to *Tet*, to mid-June. The mid-March illustration depicts the situation at the height of the battle of Khe Sanh.

For each of these three dates, field locations of all allied combat battalions are shown. This portrayal understates the total numbers of forces of all kinds in the populated areas. More than 95,000 Regional Force and almost 140,000 Popular Force troops are not shown. Nor do these charts depict the Vietnamese police forces, Revolutionary Development cadres, Provincial Reconnaissance Units, and People's Self-Defense Forces. The total strength of all of these paramilitary forces exceeded 300,000. In addition to these Vietnamese forces, the maps and bar charts do not include the significant U.S. and allied support organizations and fixed bases, most of which are located close to population centers.

Although the battalions reflected in the bar charts are not of equal size, these charts show the ratio, by corps areas, between enemy and allied combat battalions. The maps portray the manner in which allied forces were disposed throughout the period.

SEQUENCE OF ILLUSTRATIONS DEPICTING COMBAT FORCE DISPOSITIONS

	Page
1. Opposing Maneuver Battalions by Corps Tactical Zone as of 25 Jan 68.	176
2. Allied Combat Battalions Locations as of 25 Jan 68.	177
3. Opposing Maneuver Battalions by Corps Tactical Zone as of 13 Mar 68.	178
4. Allied Combat Battalions Locations as of 13 Mar 68.	179
5. Opposing Maneuver Battalions by Corps Tactical Zone as of 19 Jun 68.	180
6. Allied Combat Battalions Locations as of 19 Jun 68.	181

OPPOSING MANEUVER BATTALIONS BY CORPS TACTICAL ZONE
As of 25 Jan 68

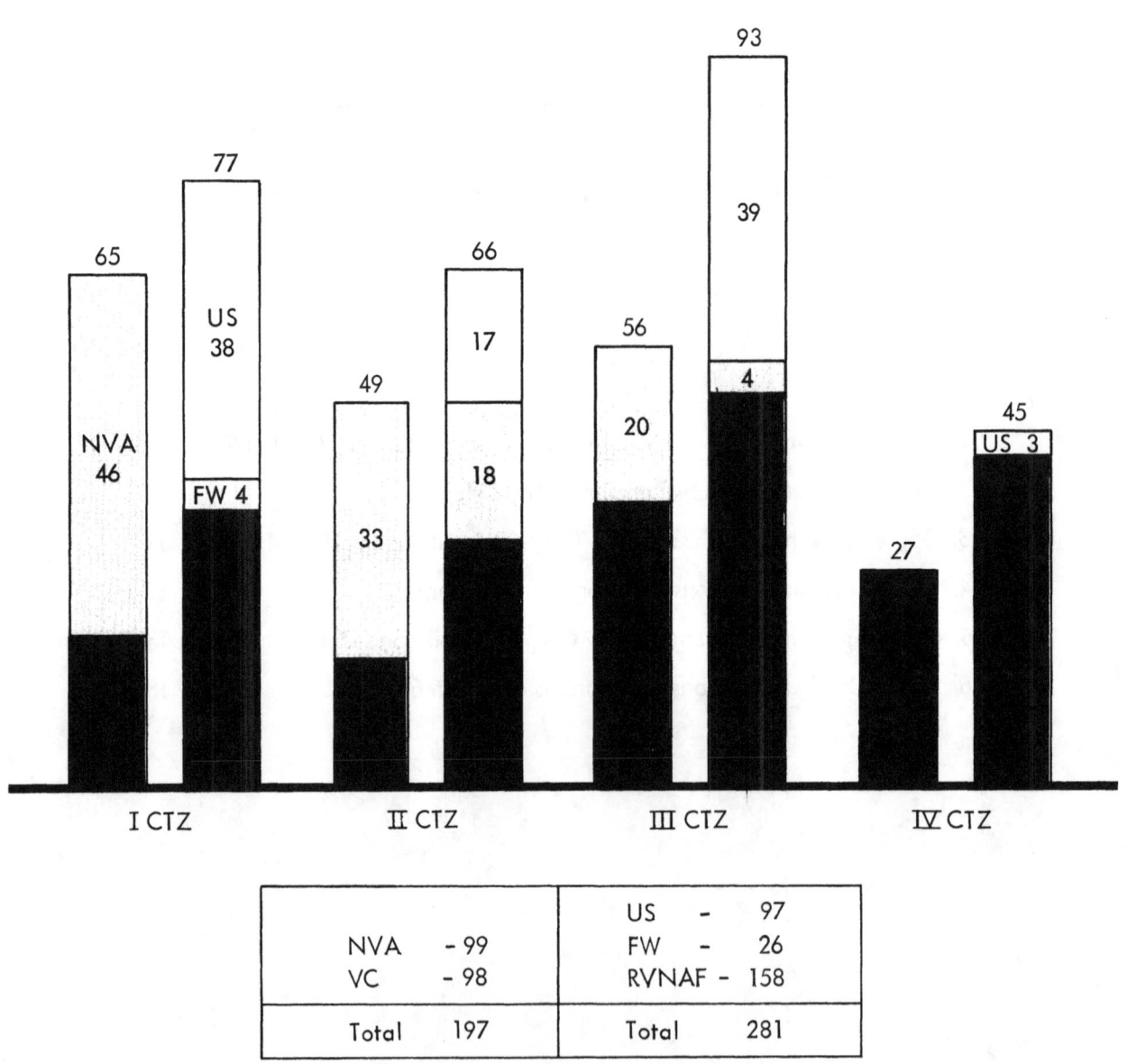

NOTE:
1. Illustration does not include over 300,000 Regional and Popular Forces, police forces, and Peoples Self Defense forces, most of which are located in the densely populated areas.
2. No adjustment has been made to compensate for the fact that US battalions are considerably larger than ARVN, VC, and NVA battalions.

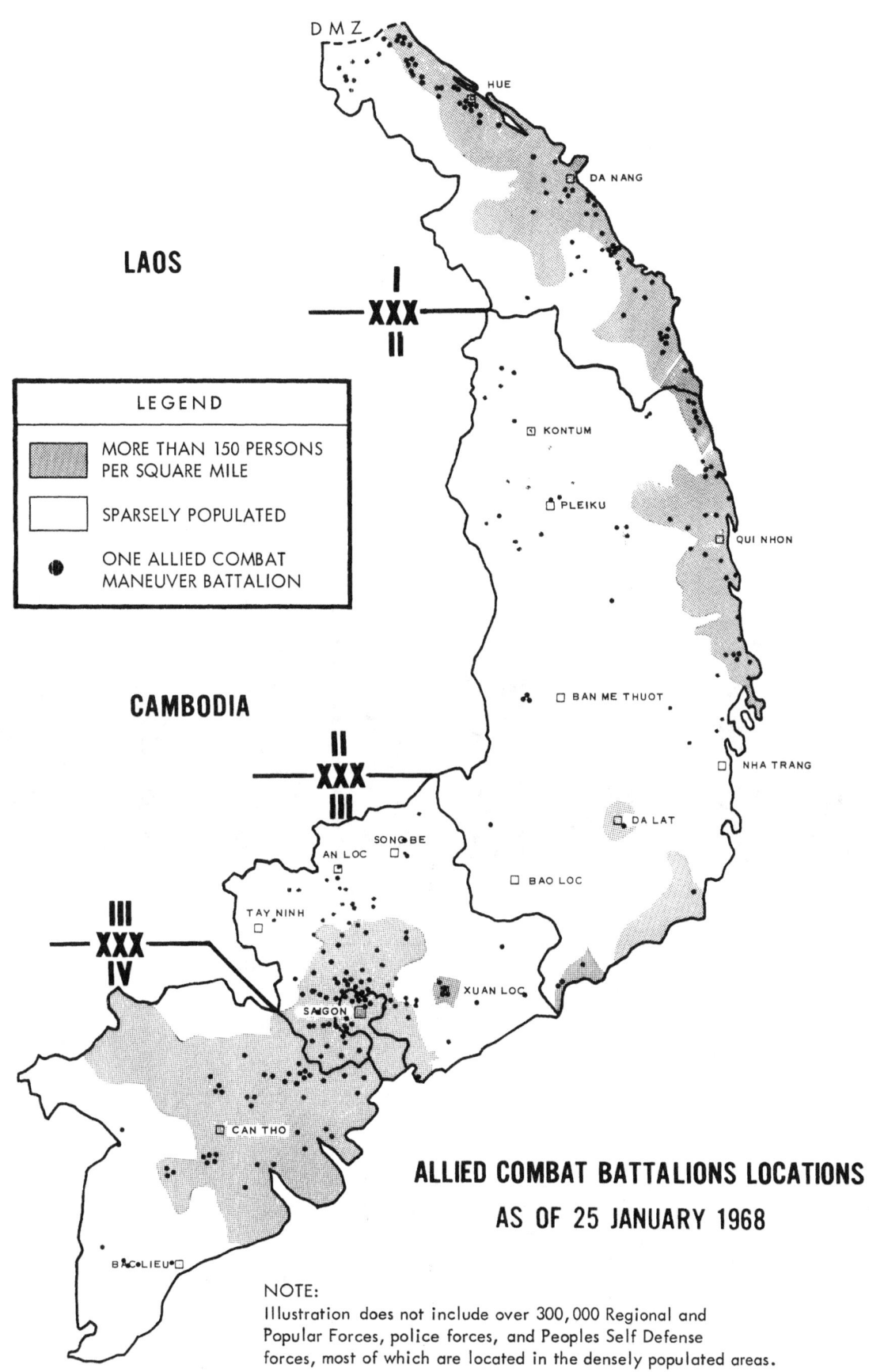

ALLIED COMBAT BATTALIONS LOCATIONS AS OF 25 JANUARY 1968

OPPOSING MANEUVER BATTALIONS BY CORPS TACTICAL ZONE
As of 13 Mar 68

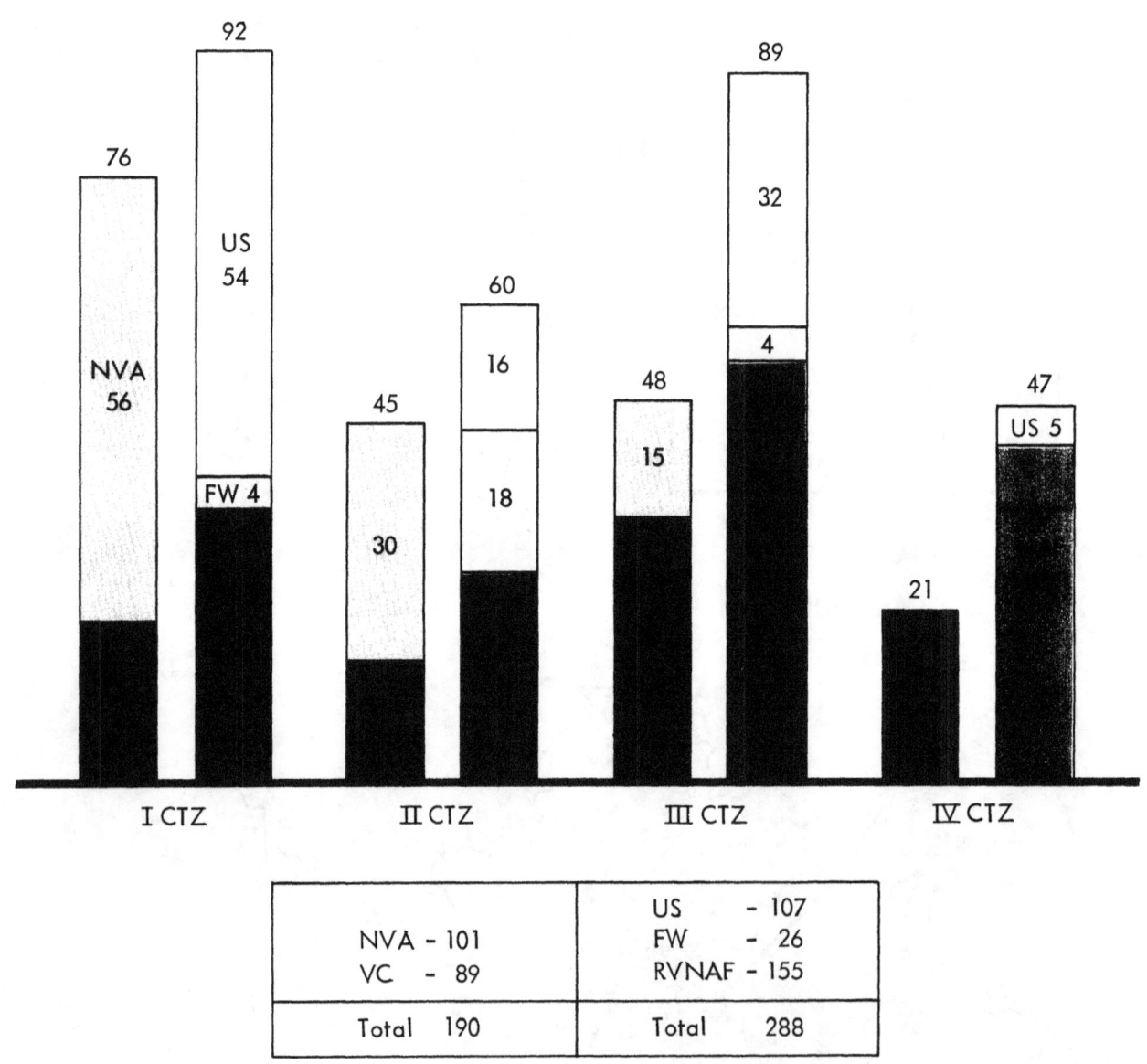

NVA - 101 VC - 89	US - 107 FW - 26 RVNAF - 155
Total 190	Total 288

NOTE:
1. Illustration does not include over 300,000 Regional and Popular Forces, police forces, and Peoples Self Defense Forces, most of which are located in the densely populated areas.
2. No adjustment has been made to compensate for the fact that US battalions are considerably larger than ARVN, VC, and NVA battalions. Nor does this chart reflect the fact that VC and NVA battalions grew progressively smaller during this period as losses were not replaced promptly.

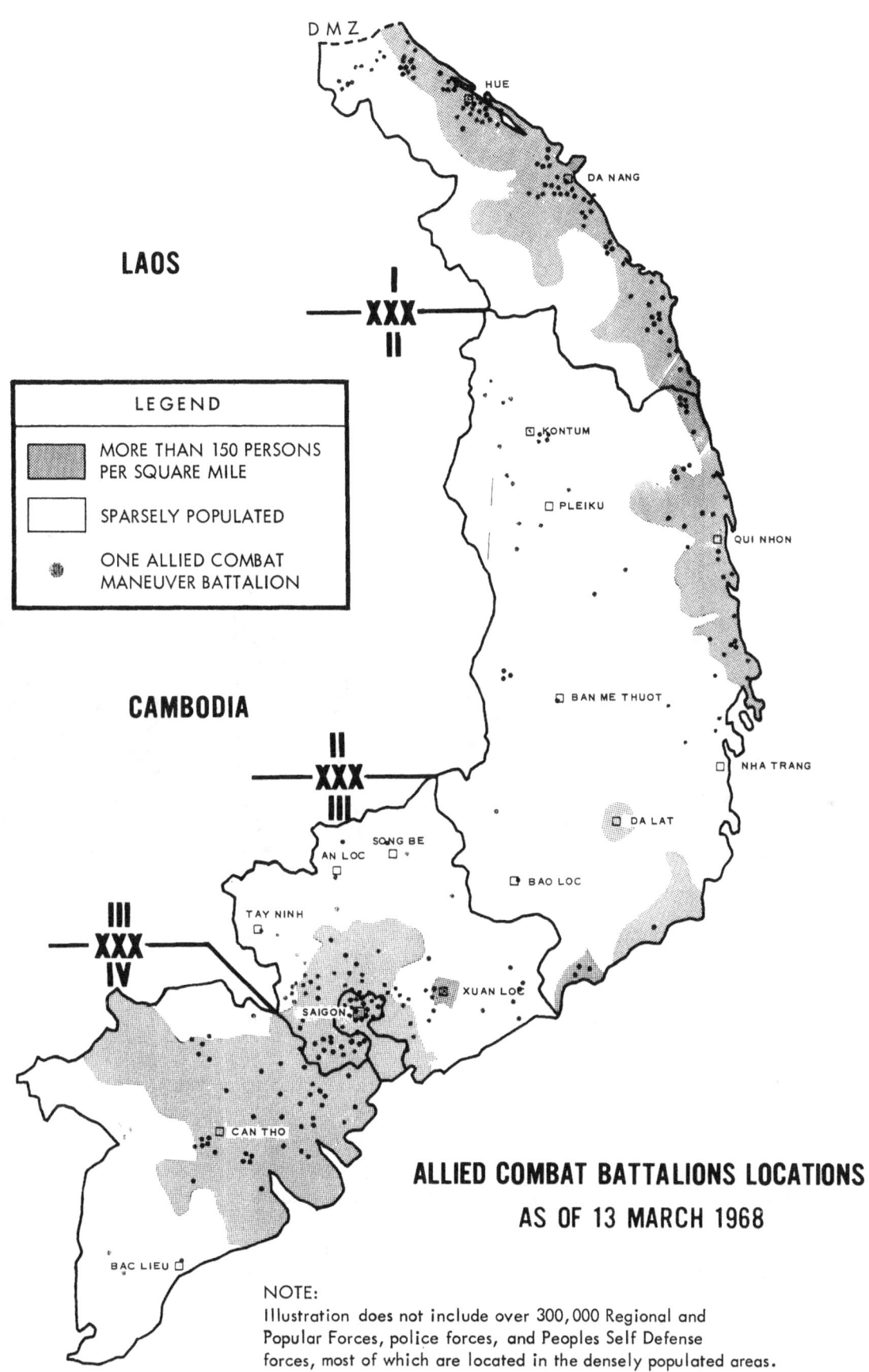

OPPOSING MANEUVER BATTALIONS BY CORPS TACTICAL ZONE
As of 19 Jun 68

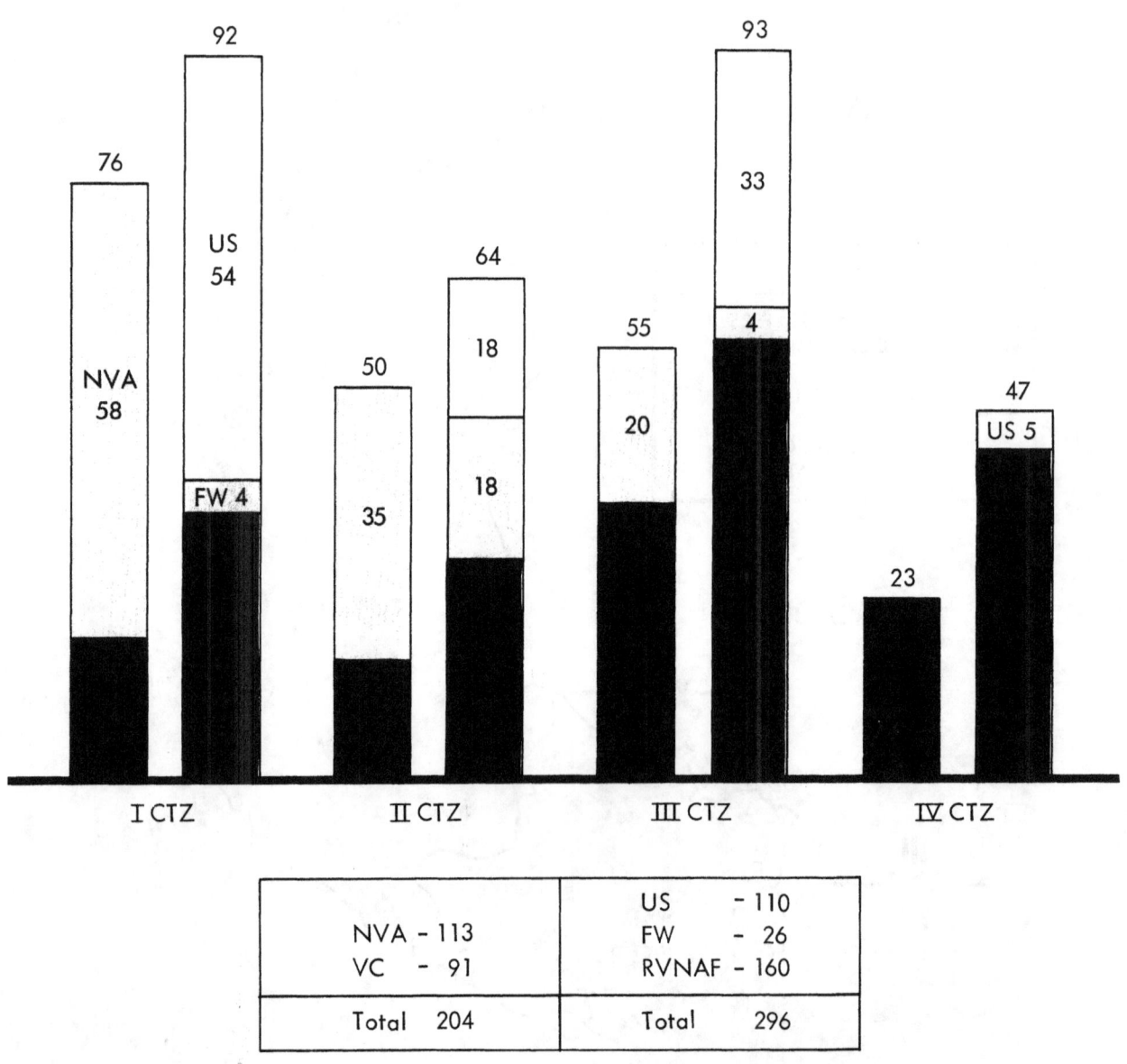

NOTE:
1. Illustration does not include over 300,000 Regional and Popular Forces, police forces, and Peoples Self Defense forces, most of which are located in the densely populated areas.
2. No adjustment has been made to compensate for the fact that US battalions are considerably larger than ARVN, VC, and NVA battalions. Nor does this chart reflect the fact that VC and NVA battalions grew progressively smaller during this period as losses were not replaced promptly.

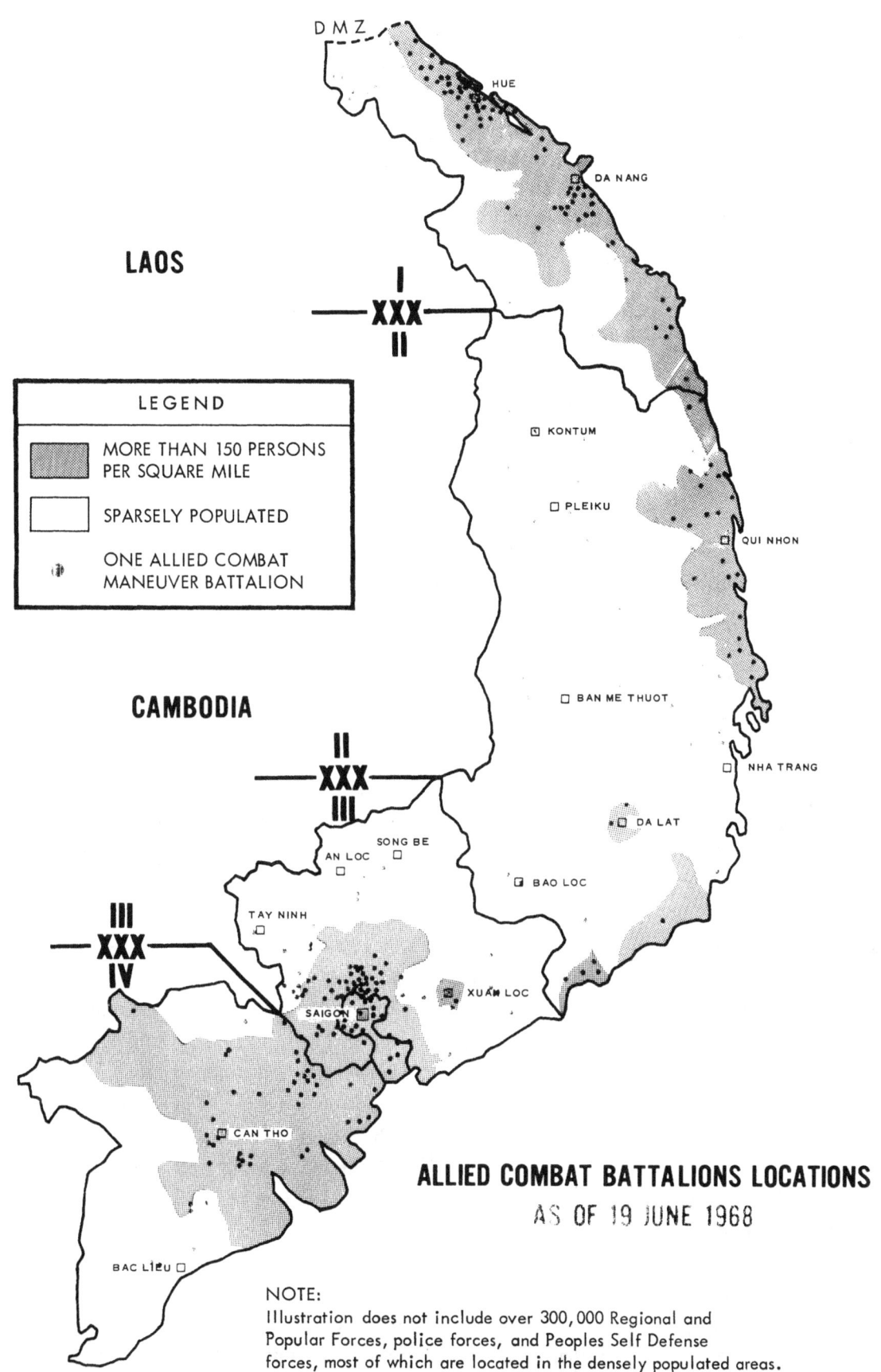

CHRONOLOGY—1968

January

A 36-hour New Year's truce ended at 0600 on 2 January. The enemy initiated 64 major and 107 minor incidents during the period. U.S. forces lost 27 men killed and 191 wounded; the South Vietnamese, 50 killed, 137 wounded. The enemy lost 598 killed.

During the period 3 through 5 January the tempo of enemy activity increased, and the Da Nang Airbase received successive attacks by 122-mm rockets.

In mid-January the North Vietnamese 304th Division infiltrated across the border from Laos and joined the 325C Division in the vicinity of Khe Sanh. Intelligence analysis by MACV indicated that these two divisions would mount a full-scale attack on Khe Sanh in the last half of January, while the North Vietnamese 320th Division along the DMZ appeared to be preparing an attack along Highway 9 toward Camp Carroll, the location of a battalion of U.S. Army 175-mm guns providing artillery support for Khe Sanh.

Amid indications of mounting North Vietnamese strength in the two northernmost provinces, I began to shift additional forces northward: the 1st Cavalry Division north of Hue; elements of the U.S. 1st Marine Division to Phu Bai, just south of Hue; and the 2d Brigade, 101st Airborne Division to the vicinity of Hue. The 2d Brigade of the Republic of Korea Marine Corps moved to the vicinity of Hoi An in Quang Nam Province to strengthen the defenses for Da Nang and to permit the northern movement of elements of the 1st Marine Division.

Enemy activity, including shelling, increased day by day around Khe Sanh. On 21 January a prolonged NVA mortar and rocket attack destroyed the largest Marine ammunition dump at Khe Sanh. The proximity and strength of the enemy and the marginal ammunition supplies remaining in Marine hands created a potentially serious situation. However, the initiative of the tactical logisticians and the magnificent support provided by the cargo aircraft of the U.S. Air Force and Marines quickly restored the situation. Despite almost continuous enemy fire, air-delivered tonnages were nearly doubled in a matter of days and no unit operation suffered from ammunition or supply shortages.

During this period, a rallier from the 325C Division reported that in addition to the 304th, 320th, and 325C Divisions, the North Vietnamese Army had committed elements of the 308th and 341st Divisions to the northern region of the I Corps. Prisoner interrogations revealed that the enemy considered Khe Sanh to be for the Americans what Dien Bien Phu had been for the French. On 22 January U.S. aircraft evacuated 1,112 civilian refugees who had fled enemy actions in and around Khe Sanh. To counter the buildup against Khe Sanh, U.S. air and artillery began an intensive SLAM operation known as NIAGARA II.

On 23 January MACV noted the likelihood of a strong enemy attack against Hue, probably to be staged just before *Tet,* with other strong attacks in the Central Highlands against Kontum City and Dak To. In the closing days of the month the enemy mounted small mortar and ground attacks on airfields at Pleiku and An Khe, killing 2 U.S. troops, wounding 29, and destroying 26 helicopters and 3 observation planes. Two C–130 aircraft were damaged.

On 24 January a South Vietnamese convoy arrived in Quang Tri City from Saigon by way of Route 1, the first convoy to travel the entire route since it was cleared. The convoy made the trip without significant incident, except as it moved over the mountainous Hai Van pass between Da Nang and Hue, where the column was harassed by fire.

North Vietnamese forces employing tanks on 25 January overran a Laotian Army post along Highway 9, west of Khe Sanh, just inside the Laotian frontier. Following the attack, observers spotted five Russian PT-76 amphibious tanks inside South Vietnam moving along Highway 9 in the direction of Khe Sanh. Attacking U.S. aircraft destroyed one.

On 27 January the Vietnamese 37th Ranger Battalion arrived at Khe Sanh from Phu Loc.

The enemy's announced cease-fire in observance of *Tet* was scheduled to begin at 0100 on 27 January and run through 0100 on 3 February. The allied *Tet* truce began at 1800 on 29 January in all corps zones except I Corps and the extended battle area north of the DMZ, where, because of the enemy buildup and threat of large scale attack, I proposed, with the concurrence of the South Vietnamese government, that no cease fire be observed.

Before daylight on 30 January the enemy launched a series of attacks against towns and installations in the zones of the I Corps and II Corps, prompting allied forces at 1100 on the 30th to cancel their announced cease fire. In the first 17 hours of the truce, the enemy had initiated 21 major and 29 minor incidents.

These marked the beginning of a nationwide offensive that erupted in full fury before daylight on 31 January. The enemy initially bombarded or attempted to invade 36 of 44 provincial capitals, 5 of 6 autonomous cities, 64 of 242 district capitals, 50 hamlets, and a number of military installations, including most airfields. Ten of the provincial capitals fell under at least partial Communist control, and heavy fighting raged in Saigon and Hue. In most places the South Vietnamese Regional and Popular Forces bore the first brunt of the offensive, and in Saigon, the National Police. The attacks included a sapper assault against the U.S. Embassy, launched at 0300 by an estimated 19 Viet Cong in civilian clothes. Although the VC succeeded in penetrating the compound, U.S. Military Police, U.S. Marine Corps guards, and a platoon from the 101st Airborne Division prevented entry to the Embassy building and by 0923 had killed all 19 of the attackers and secured the compound. U.S. forces lost 6 men killed and 5 wounded. In view of the widespread nature of the enemy attacks, President Thieu decreed martial law.

February

On 1 February the enemy attack continued near Tan Son Nhut airport, the nearby Vietnamese Joint General Staff compound, and in various areas throughout Saigon. In Hue, North Vietnamese forces occupied the Imperial Citadel, and U.S. Marine Corps forces coming to the relief of the city from the south became heavily engaged in that part of Hue lying south of the Perfume River. Enemy units held on long enough to warrant intervention by U.S. units in Saigon, Hue, Quang Tri City, Kontum City, Phu Loc, My Tho, Ben Tre, and a few smaller towns and outposts. Contingents of the U.S. 1st Marine and 1st Cavalry Divisions moved to the relief of Quang Tri City, and other elements of the 1st Marine Division entered Phu Loc. In Kontum City the ARVN headquarters and the MACV advisors were for a time isolated in the MACV advisory compound, and the airfield, under small arms fire, was closed. In the Mekong Delta the Viet Cong held most of Ben Tre, capital of Kien Hoa Province, and part of Chau Doc, capital of Chau Doc Province. Headquarters of the Vietnamese 9th Division in Sa Dec (Vinh Long Province) came under attack by six enemy companies. I decided to commit a two-battalion brigade of the U.S. 9th Infantry Division, which supported a regiment of the Vietnamese 7th Division in clearing the enemy from Ben Tre. Units of the 9th Division's Mobile Riverine Force also helped the Vietnamese 7th Division to clear My Tho, capital of Dinh Tuong Province. In the southern portion of the I Corps, the Korean 2d Marine Brigade helped clear Duy Xuyen, southwest of Hoi An.

By 2 February South Vietnamese, U.S., or Free World forces had cleared almost all towns and cities except Saigon and Hue. Tan Son Nhut airfield was in full operation on the 2d, as were 20 of 23 other airfields hit during the first 72 hours of the offensive. Only those airfields at Kontum City, Vinh Long, and Ban Me Thuot East were still closed.

By 5 February fighting was still heavy on both sides of the Perfume River in Hue, and the enemy continued to hold a large part of the Imperial Citadel. One U.S. Marine and five Vietnamese battalions were operating in the city. In Saigon 15 allied battalions were clearing the city of remnants of local force units, but a major threat still remained in the presence of the Viet Cong 9th Division deployed a few miles away to the north, northwest, and west. Two Vietnamese Marine battalions were airlifted from northern Binh Dinh Province, where they had been engaged in pacification support operations, to reinforce operations against the enemy near Saigon. The North Vietnamese 2d Division appeared to be preparing to attack Da Nang. All enemy resistance in Kontum City had ended, and in the Delta all major cities were clear, although some were still subject to harassing shellfire.

On the evening of 5 February President Thieu announced creation of a Central Recovery Committee under the direction of Vice President Ky to restore order and security, assist in reconstructing damaged population centers, and organize Peoples' Self Defense Groups. A special task force from the U.S. Mission headed by Ambassador Komer would assist and support the Vietnamese committee.

An estimated North Vietnamese battalion supported by nine amphibious tanks on 7 February overran a Special Forces camp at Lang Vei, a few miles southwest of Khe Sanh. Of 20 U.S. Special Forces troops, 14 had been recovered by nightfall, along with between 70 and 100 CIDG troops.

A MACV Forward command post under General Abrams opened on 9 February at Phu Bai to supervise the planned deployment of joint U.S. combat and logistic forces in the northern provinces.

On 23 February the U.S. 27th Marine Regimental Landing Team completed movement by air from California to Da Nang. Three days later on the 26th, the 3d Brigade, 82d Airborne Division, also completed movement by air from North Carolina, arriving at Chu Lai. The 27th Marines deployed south of Da Nang and relieved other Marine units, which proceeded to the Hai Van pass between Da Nang and Hue to open up Highway 1 and to secure it for use and subsequent repair and upgrading by our engineers. Earlier in February, the enemy had seized control of the pass and cut the highway in a number of places. Additionally, the northeast monsoon had caused erosion of the road. Operations north of the pass, including those along the DMZ and around Hue, were greatly dependent on the movement of supplies and ammunition on Highway 1, especially during bad weather when airlift was hindered and high seas made over-the-beach supply operations very difficult. The 3d Brigade of the 82d Airborne Division was attached to the 101st Airborne Division in the vicinity of Phu Bai, thereby giving that division three brigades. It had been necessary for me to retain the 3d Brigade of the 101st Airborne Division in the III Corps area to support operations in that critical area around Saigon. The arrival of the Marine regiment and the Army paratroop brigade was of great and timely assistance. These reinforcements permitted me to deploy sufficient forces to the northern area to confront the major enemy attack and to go on the offensive when favorable weather arrived in early April without assuming unacceptable risks by the deployment of forces from other areas.

On 25 February South Vietnamese units secured the grounds of the Imperial Citadel in Hue, and the next day the last enemy troops were cleared from the city. The battle had been a costly one in terms of damage to property, civilians killed (mostly a result of Viet Cong executions), and military losses. The Vietnamese Airborne Task Force flown into Hue, for instance, suffered such severe losses in its well fought engagements that it was replaced in Hue by Vietnamese Marine battalions. The airborne units returned to their base area near Saigon where, because of extraordinary measures, they were quickly reconstituted and returned to action in a matter of weeks.

Throughout the month, heavy enemy pressure continued against Khe Sanh, including ever increasing shelling, sharp reaction to U.S. patrols, and ground attacks against outposts. By the end of the month the main defensive position beside the airstrip was defended by three U.S. Marine Corps battalions (less two companies), an ARVN Ranger battalion, a U.S. Army Special Forces detachment, and a CIDG company. A battalion and two reinforced companies of U.S. Marines held outposts on nearby heights. Artillery, including 175-mm gunfire, and tactical airstrikes, including massed B–52's, pounded the lucrative targets presented by the encircling enemy divisions. The expanded B–52 airbase facilities at U Tapao in Thailand not only provided additional B–52 sorties, but because of shorter turn-around time also gave us a greater degree of responsiveness and flexibility than ever before.

Following the fall of Lang Vei and the intensification of the battle around Khe Sanh, our military efforts were briefly complicated by the influx of large numbers of Montagnard refugees into the area. We fed and provided medical care for these individuals and, in coordination with the Vietnamese government, made the necessary arrangements to transport them to established refugee camps as soon as possible. The sense of urgency demonstrated in evacuating these individuals not only insured their safety but prevented the refugee situation from becoming a major obstacle to our operations.

March

Enemy shelling on at least two occasions revealed a new tactic of firing from several sites at once, creating a quick concentrated effect and hampering counterbattery fire. On 3 March, 49 rockets fired from at least three launch sites hit Camp Enari near Pleiku, and twenty-seven 122-mm rockets were fired from two or more sites at the Kontum City airfield on the 17th.

On 5 March crater analysis and the discovery of five 70-mm shell casings—of World War II Japanese manufacture— revealed that the enemy in an attack northwest of Tam Ky (Quang Tin Province) used both 122-mm rockets and 70-mm howitzers.

On 5 and 6 March the Vietnamese 32d Regiment, supported by air and artillery, drove off an estimated enemy battalion that penetrated the city of Ca Mau in An Xuyen Province. The enemy lost 283 killed; the South Vietnamese, 11 killed and 45 wounded. Two U.S. advisors also were wounded.

On 10 March I inactivated MACV Forward headquarters, which had served its purpose, and at the same time activated the Provisional Corps, Vietnam (PROVCORPV) under command of General Rosson. The tactical headquarters was to control the large number of U.S. units in the northern part of the I Corps. In general, the PROVCORPV zone extended from the DMZ southward to the Hai Van pass, or essentially most of the area of the two northernmost provinces. The new headquarters exercised operational control over U.S. ground forces within its zone, and, in turn, was under operational control of the Commanding General, III Marine Amphibious Force.

Also on 10 March the 101st Airborne Division, controlling its own 2d Brigade and the 3d Brigade, 82d Airborne Division, began to conduct combat and security operations in the vicinity of Hue and Phu Bai.

The confrontation at Khe Sanh continued, with the enemy making every effort to halt supply of the garrison by air. There was evidence of enemy tunneling attempting to get within close assault distance of the U.S. and South Vietnamese position, and scientific teams were dispatched to the area to investigate that possibility but with inconclusive results. The rate of enemy shelling fluctuated, possibly a reflection of the effect of U.S. artillery and air strikes, the latter sometimes sharply curtailed by the monsoon weather. On the first day of March, for example, the North Vietnamese fired 195 rounds of artillery, rockets, and mortars, and on the 7th, 115 rounds; but on 23 March 1,100 rounds, including 92 rockets, hit the defensive position. On the 7th the enemy antiaircraft fire increased sharply, firing upon 13 U.S. Marine aircraft and causing the crash of a C–123 with 47 passengers several miles east of Khe Sanh. Despite continuing massive support from artillery, B–52's, and tactical aircraft averaging 300 sorties a day, toward the end of the month almost all supplies had to be air dropped or delivered by helicopter. Although the North Vietnamese from time to time probed the defensive perimeter, as on 18 March when the Vietnamese 37th Ranger Battalion repulsed a probe against the eastern arc, no full-scale ground attack developed.

An ammunition cache discovered southwest of Hue on 24 March contained 76-mm shells, the kind used by Russian PT-76 tanks, and 23-mm shells, which are used in the ZU-23 antiaircraft weapon. Enemy employment of the ZU-23 in the zone of the I Corps was later confirmed.

On 30 March the 173d Airborne Brigade moved into Binh Dinh Province and relieved the 3d Brigade of the 4th Infantry Division; the 3d Brigade, in turn, joined its parent division in the Central Highlands, the first time that the 4th Division had operated with all three of its brigades together since arriving in Vietnam in the summer of 1966.

On 31 March in an effort to induce the North Vietnamese to enter negotiations, President Johnson announced cessation of bombing against North Vietnam except for the "southern panhandle" immediately adjacent to the Demilitarized Zone.

April

On the first of April the 1st Cavalry Division, 1st Marine Regiment, and South Vietnamese airborne forces launched Operation PEGASUS/LAM SON 207 to open Route 9 and establish ground communications with the Khe Sanh plateau. At the same time, Operation NIAGARA II terminated and all B-52 and tactical air strikes in the area shifted to support of the drive along Route 9.

On the first day of the attack, the 1st Marine Regiment seized the first objective along Route 9 west of Ca Lu, and the 3d Brigade, 1st Cavalry Division, air-assaulted into a fire support base five miles east of Khe Sanh. Enemy contact was light.

The North Vietnamese on 3 April accepted President Johnson's invitation to establish direct negotiations. The two parties subsequently agreed on a meeting site in Paris.

Forces within the Khe Sanh base attacked southeastward on 4 April to link with the forces of Operation PEGASUS/LAM SON 207. The operation was supported by 36 B-52 sorties and 176 tactical air sorties.

On 6 April troops of the 1st Cavalry Division established contact with the 1st Battalion of the 9th Marines attacking from Khe Sanh, whereupon the Marines began a sweep to the northeast. Later in the day Vietnamese paratroopers and air cavalrymen reached the Khe Sanh combat base, and on the 10th, for the first time in 48 days, no enemy shells hit the base.

Several joint U.S.-South Vietnamese operations in the vicinity of Saigon and in the Mekong Delta culminated in Operation QUYET THANG (Resolve to Win), a massive 28-day search operation in the environs of Saigon, ending on 7 April. Three U.S. divisions lost 105 men killed and 922 wounded, and South Vietnamese forces lost 193 killed and 472 wounded. U.S. troops killed 1,420 of the enemy, detained 442, and captured 505 weapons. The South Vietnamese killed 1,238 of the enemy, detained 79, and captured 490 weapons. Total enemy losses were 2,658 killed, 521 detained, and 995 weapons.

On 12 April Route 9 was opened to traffic to Khe Sanh, and there were strong indications that the enemy was withdrawing from the vicinity of Khe Sanh and central Quang Nam Province while reinforcing in the vicinity of Hue. Heavy casualties from artillery, tactical air, B-52's, and ground actions had apparently convinced enemy commanders to abandon their efforts to take Khe Sanh.

On 16 April the 4th Battalion, 21st Infantry, arrived in Duc Pho from Hawaii for assignment to the 11th Light Infantry Brigade of the 23d (Americal) Division. That brought the total of U.S. maneuver battalions in Vietnam to 110, of which 24 were Marine Corps battalions.

Earlier indications that the North Vietnamese had begun to reinforce Viet Cong units in the zone of the IV Corps with other than key cadre and advisory personnel were confirmed on 18 April with the capture of a North Vietnamese soldier by the U.S. 9th Division. The prisoner revealed that he had come south in a packet of 130 men, 50 of whom had been assigned to the same company with him.

A joint operation by ARVN units and the U.S. 9th Infantry Division in the Mekong Delta, Operation TRUONG CONG DINH (named for a national hero), had by 19 April accounted for 1,716 enemy killed, 999 detained, and 858 weapons captured. U.S. forces lost 57 men killed; ARVN forces, 268.

The 1st Cavalry Division, 101st Airborne Division, and a regiment of the Vietnamese 1st Division on 19 April began Operation DELAWARE/LAM SON 216 in the A Shau Valley and along Route 547 leading into the valley, introducing the first major allied presence in the valley since loss of a Special Forces camp in 1966. A reconnaissance in force, the operation was designed to find and destroy a large logistics base the enemy had constructed in the valley, from which he had supported the *Tet* attack on Hue. After heavy initial contact, enemy resistance tapered off. The troops found a vast storehouse of material, including 2,500 individual and 93 crew-served weapons, 31 flamethrowers, eighteen 1½ ton trucks, several Soviet PT–76 tanks and 120-mm artillery pieces, and tons of munitions. The intelligence find included 90,000 pages of documents. Over 850 of the enemy were killed. Operations along Route 547 were made more effective by the excellent job performed by the combined Vietnamese-U.S. long range reconnaissance force. Its elements located numerous enemy targets, called in effective air and artillery strikes against them, and carried out a number of successful ambushes against the enemy.

On 22 April the 196th Light Infantry Brigade moved to Camp Evans in the Provisional Corps zone to provide rear area security and serve as a reserve for the DMZ area during Operation DELAWARE/LAM SON 216.

During the month, our interests in improving the tactical proficiency of the Vietnamese Air Force helicopter squadrons continued. Although U.S.-sponsored training programs were in effect, a number of the helicopter crews had little actual experience in airmobile operations. In this context, the movement of one Vietnamese H–34 squadron from Tan Son Nhut to Binh Tuy was decided upon. This deployment would place two Vietnamese Air Force helicopter squadrons near Can Tho to support ARVN operations in the IV Corps area. The move was completed by the end of April. The U.S. Army 12th Aviation Group was now capable of assuming additional helicopter support duties in the III Corps. I considered that the tactical experience to be gained by Vietnamese helicopter crews and the additional helicopter support for Vietnamese units in IV Corps far outweighed any disadvantages. Lt. Gen. Nguyen Duc Thang, the aggressive commander of the IV Corps, made excellent use of this reinforcement.

May

Beginning around midnight on 4 May, the enemy launched another wave of nationwide attacks against 109 military installations and cities, including 21 airfields. U.S. and South Vietnamese units lost 65 men killed and 320 wounded. Six aircraft were destroyed and 72 damaged.

The 4–5 May attacks lacked the intensity and coordination of the *Tet* offensive. Bien Hoa Airbase was hardest hit, with strong attacks also in Binh Duong and Hau Nghia Provinces. In the vicinity of Saigon, the enemy tried to seize the Saigon-Bien Hoa highway bridge. Heavy contact continued near Dong Ha in the northern portion of the I Corps on 6 May, while moderately heavy fighting persisted around Saigon for several days, including attacks by fire and infiltration into the southwestern part of the city. Rockets hit Da Nang on 8 and 9 May.

Heavy mortar and recoilless rifle fire struck the Kham Duc Special Forces camp in Quang Tin Province on 10 May. Two days later U.S. and CIDG troops and Vietnamese dependents were extracted from the camp by air.

On 13 May preliminary discussions designed to

lead to negotiations began in Paris between the United States and North Vietnam.

Premier Nguyen Van Loc and the South Vietnamese Cabinet resigned on 18 May at the request of President Thieu. The new Premier was Tran Van Huong.

On 19 and 22 May troops of the 3d Brigade, 82d Airborne Division, uncovered five 85-mm guns in two different locations southwest of Hue, the first time we had captured such large weapons, although we were aware from photo interpretation that they existed in the zone of the I Corps.

During the latter days of May, indiscriminate mortar and rocket fire hit residential sectors of Saigon periodically, starting a number of fires but causing relatively light civilian casualties. Despite indications of a drop in the enemy's combat effectiveness (attributable to heavy losses and insufficiently-trained replacements), his activity continued heavy in some sectors, particularly in Thua Thien Province in the vicinity of Hue and north of Dong Ha in Quang Tri Province. On the 25th and 26th the enemy shelled U.S. positions along the DMZ and at Khe Sanh.

On 30 May 13 rounds of 100-mm artillery fire struck Fire Support Base 29, located 10 miles west of Dak To in Kontum Province, the first confirmed use of that caliber weapon in the II Corps.

On the last day of May, Operation TOAN THANG (Complete Victory), the largest operation of the war, came to an end. Employing 42 U.S. and 37 Vietnamese maneuver battalions, the operation extended over 60 days. Although unspectacular, consisting primarily of small search operations during the day and ambushes at night, TOAN THANG was nevertheless highly effective, killing 7,600 members of the enemy's local forces, guerrillas, and infrastructure.

June

On 1 June the 4th Battalion, Royal Australian Regiment, replaced the regiment's 2d Battalion. All three Australian battalions were based at Nui Dat in Phuoc Tuy Province, although the 3d Battalion was conducting operations at the time in Bien Hoa Province.

After I had discussed the matter for several months with Vietnamese authorities, the South Vietnamese Government announced on 3 June that Maj. Gen. Nguyen Van Minh, commander of the ARVN 21st Division, was to be reassigned as Military Governor of Saigon and Gia Dinh Province under the Commanding General, III Corps. General Minh would have operational control of all South Vietnamese forces involved in the security of Saigon and Gia Dinh Province. To parallel the assignment, MACV named Maj. Gen. John H. Hay, Jr., Deputy Commanding General of the II Field Force, as senior advisor to the Military Governor and commander of U.S. forces assigned to the defense of Saigon and Gia Dinh Province.

After almost four and a half years of duty in South Vietnam, on 11 June I passed command of U.S. forces to General Abrams. He would serve as acting commander until I was sworn in as Chief of Staff of the U.S. Army on 3 July.

In the largest enemy capitulation of the war, a total of 141 enemy from the Viet Cong Quyet Thang Regiment surrendered on 18 and 19 June to two Vietnamese Marine battalions just north of Saigon. About half were North Vietnamese.

On 19 June President Thieu signed into law a general mobilization measure which could expand the South Vietnamese Armed Forces by nearly 20 percent. This was the culmination of many months of study and discussion.

In late June MACV announced the dismantlement of the defenses near the Khe Sanh airfield and the abandonment of the airfield. The Khe Sanh plateau would henceforth be defended by operations initiated and supplied from the Ca Lu base constructed during Operation PEGASUS/LAM SON 207. Following Operation DELAWARE, portions of the 1st Cavalry Division returned to the Khe Sanh plateau and operated there for several weeks, in the process consuming the supplies stockpiled at Khe Sanh and destroying the fortifications.

CONCLUSIONS

As I left Vietnam, I remembered the predictions and the evaluations of General Giap in January of 1966:

> He was wrong when he predicted we would not put sufficient forces in the field.
>
> He was wrong when he thought we would antagonize the people to a point where they would turn to the Viet Cong. They have done the opposite.
>
> He was correct that pressure against the war would mount in the U.S. and throughout the world. He was also correct when he said the costs of the war would be high.
>
> He was wrong about the decline in morale of South Vietnamese forces.
>
> He now knows that U.S. equipment is suited for this kind of war, geography, and climate. Surely, he also knows that:
>
> U.S. troops are not and have never been encircled so that they cannot move;
> U.S. troops are not demoralized;
> U.S. infantry is not cowardly;
> U.S. tactics are not ineffective; and
> U.S. commanders are not incompetent.

I think it is safe to say that the war in Vietnam has been more difficult to describe than earlier wars for a variety of reasons. It is not possible simply to record the progress of the battleline as it sweeps over the terrain toward a final objective and a final victory. Secondly, the war is by no means a purely military affair.

From the beginning we have struggled with various means and methods to measure and illustrate the progress of the war. As the years went by methods for the measurement of progress (or the lack of it) have multiplied and become more sophisticated. By the middle of 1968 systems had been adopted to measure the effectiveness of Vietnamese forces both regular and territorial, the pacification conditions in the hamlets, economic and social development projects, and many others. All of these measurement systems have been imperfect and without exception there have been skeptics and critics.

For the purposes of this conclusion I have selected five illustrations which, to me, most accurately reflect significant trends in the war. There are, of course, many others. The five which I have selected are:

> The ratio of enemy to allied casualties.
> The ratio of enemy to allied weapons losses.
> The proportion of North Vietnamese to Viet Cong combat maneuver battalions fighting in South Vietnam.
> The relationship of U.S. and Free World fighting strength to the contribution of the government of Vietnam.
> The overall progress in providing security to the population of South Vietnam.

CHART 1

The chart on the facing page shows the general upward trend in the ratio of friendly to enemy casualties. You will notice that in the early years this ratio was in the range of 1.5 to 2 enemy casualties for each friendly loss. Thereafter, there have been many ups and downs. The most dramatic event occurred during *Tet* when the enemy exposed very large numbers of his troops to allied firepower in Saigon, other major cities, and province and district capitals. However, the important point is the trend over the four years. The trend is clearly up, and at the present time it has reached a ratio in which six of the enemy are killed for each allied soldier lost. From a purely military standpoint this trend shows the impact of the introduction of U.S. troops, the steady improvement in performance by all allied forces, and the steady decline in battlefield performance by the enemy.

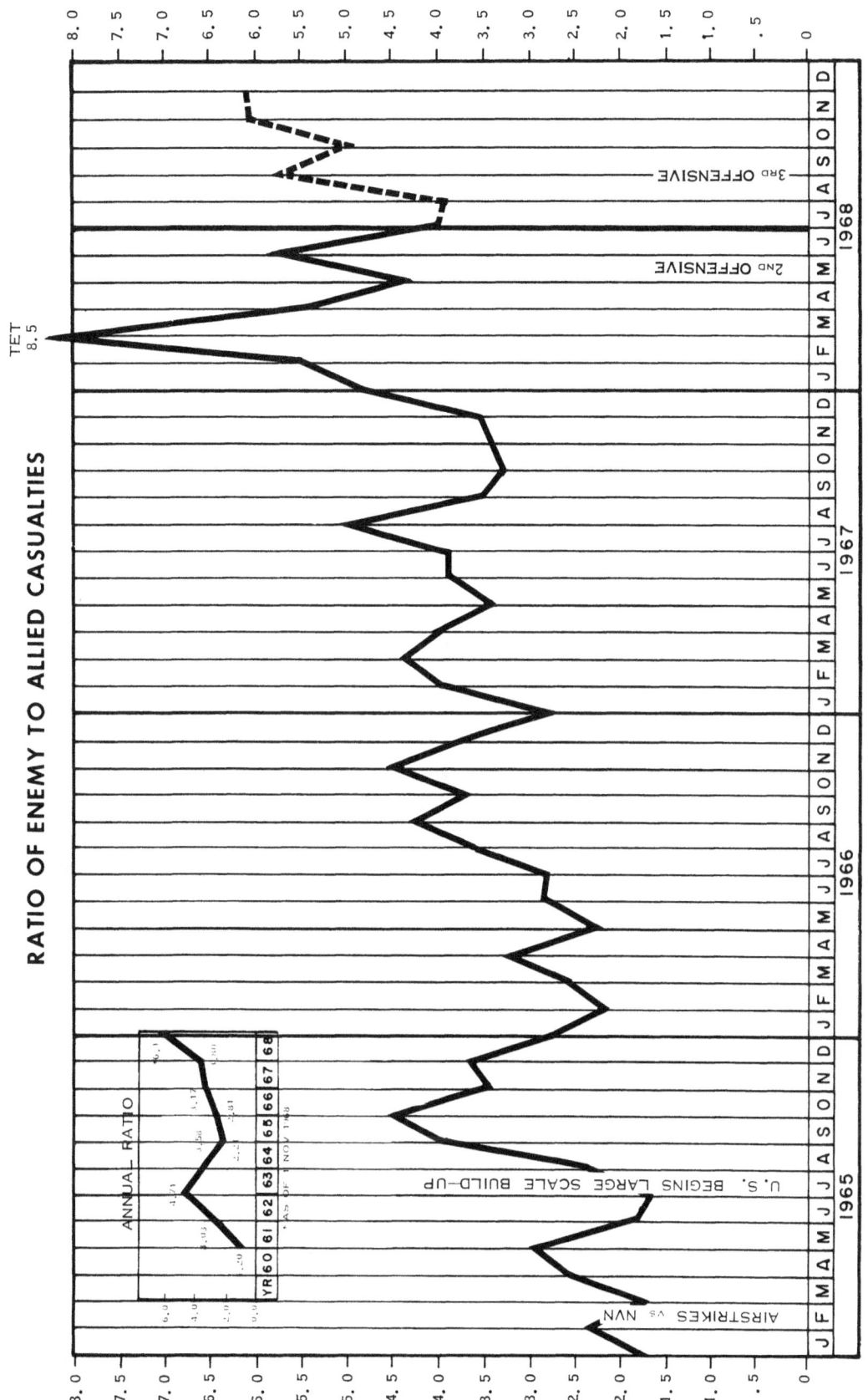

CHART 2

The chart on the facing page shows the trend of weapons losses in terms of a ratio. You will notice that in the first half of 1965 the Vietnamese Armed Forces were losing more weapons *to* the enemy than they were capturing *from* the enemy. The year 1964 showed an equally discouraging picture. Starting with the introduction of U.S. troops, the ratio steadily but unevenly improved. A word of explanation is required with respect to the very high ratios in 1968. The figures include not only weapons taken on the battlefield from enemy dead and wounded soldiers but also include the caches of weapons which have been found—and are still being found with increasing frequency as allied forces search the countryside. As in the case of the ratio of casualties, this picture of weapons losses is a clear indication of a major trend in the war. Surely the combination of these first two charts reflects a situation which must be of major concern to the enemy.

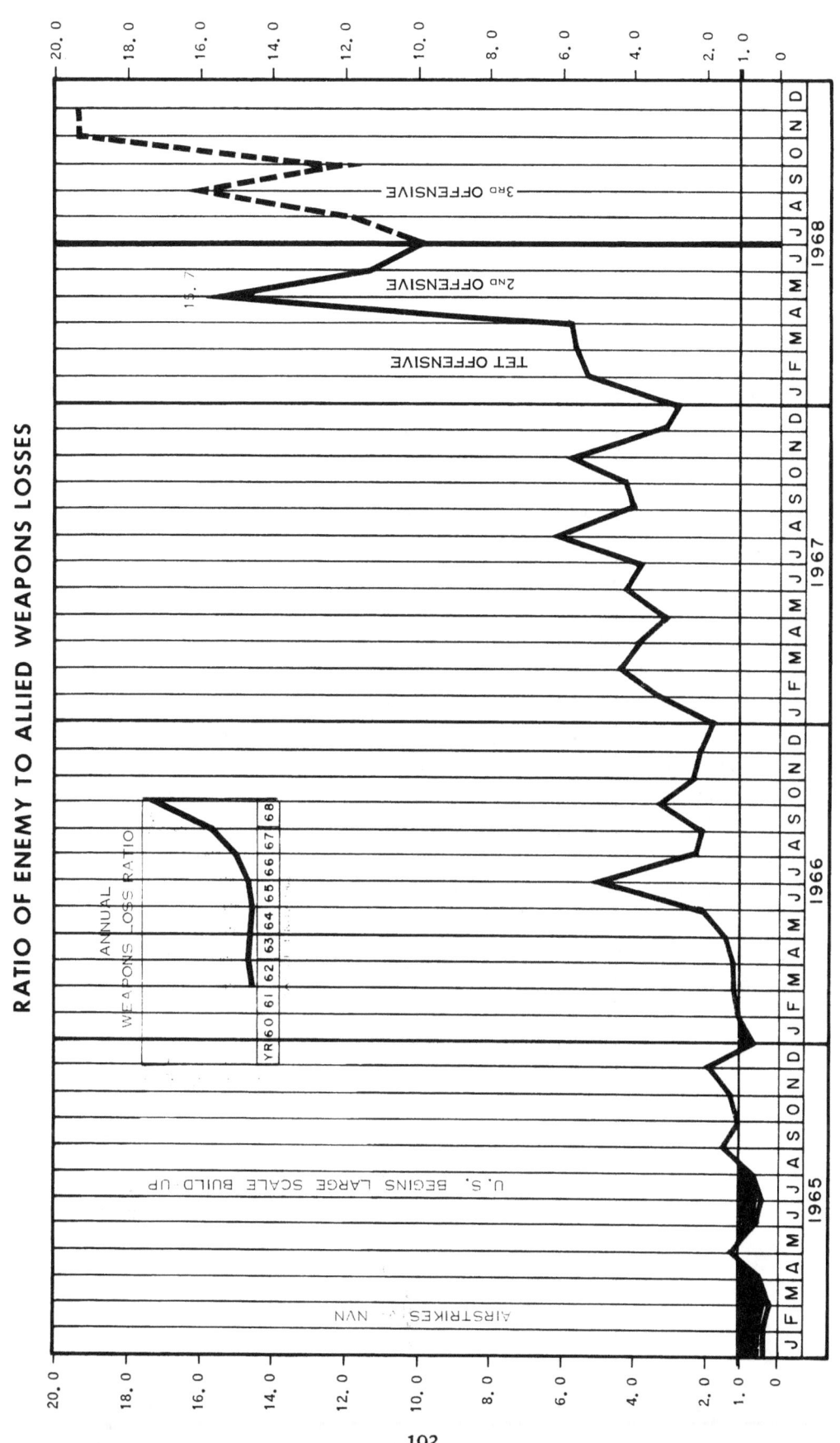

CHART 3

The chart on the facing page shows the growth of North Vietnamese Army forces in South Vietnam. It portrays battalions of ground fighting troops as opposed to total strength and therefore, it relates primarily to the so-called main force war. It does not include the guerrilla forces of the Viet Cong and therefore, is only part of the picture. However, this chart carries two highly important messages. First it shows that the North Vietnamese have assumed progressively an increasing share of the war in the south—that they have assumed the major share of the main force troop commitment, and therefore the heaviest fighting. The second major message is that over the same period of time the replacements for Viet Cong battalions have come increasingly from North Vietnam in the form of individual replacements. In 1966 approximately 10 percent of the personnel in Viet Cong battalions were North Vietnamese replacements. By mid-1968 over 30 percent of the soldiers in Viet Cong battalions were North Vietnamese. When these two developments are combined it adds up to the simple fact that the war has become to a very large extent a North Vietnamese effort. In the first half of 1968 North Vietnam had sent to the south nearly 200,000 men in units and as replacements. Enemy casualties during that same period have at least equaled that figure.

PROPORTION OF NORTH VIETNAMESE AND VIETCONG COMBAT BATTALIONS IN SOUTH VIETNAM
(IN PERCENT)

* ESTIMATE OF NVA FILLER PERSONNEL IN VC UNITS NOT AVAILABLE PRIOR TO NOV 1967.

CHART 4

The chart on the facing page shows the numerical effort in armed manpower between U.S. and Free World forces on the one hand and the forces of the government of Vietnam on the other. I would not suggest that the U.S. contribution is small, nor do I underrate the contribution of U.S. and Free World forces in terms of impact on the battlefield. Nonetheless, the graph clearly shows that the trend is one of increasing government of Vietnam participation. The numbers do not show the whole story. Not only have the numbers of South Vietnamese troops increased, but also their level of activity and effectiveness is on the upswing. As I stated in November 1967, I foresee a time when these increasingly large, increasingly effective Vietnamese forces will permit a gradual replacement of U.S. fighting elements in South Vietnam.

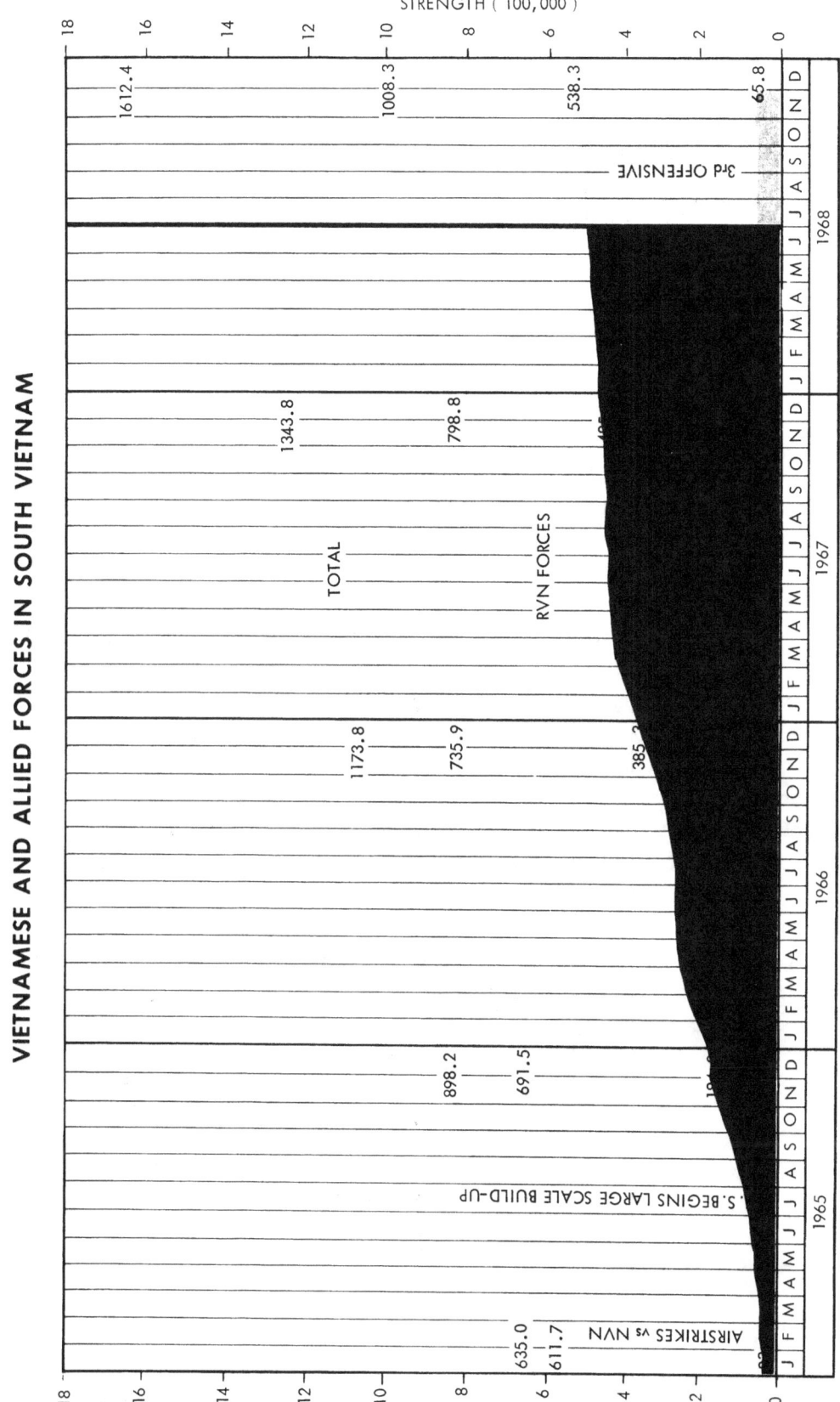

CHART 5

The last chart shows the slow, painful progress of pacification since mid-1964. The statistics reflected in this chart beginning in 1967 have been provided by the new computerized Hamlet Evaluation System. Prior to 1967 the measurements were those of the government of Vietnam. I recognize that such measurements themselves are difficult to make and may be imprecise, but the trends they reflect should be valid. The chart deserves some elaboration on one very important point. The growth in relatively secure population includes hamlets which have a sufficient level of security so that the enemy cannot operate freely in them and reasonably normal social and economic activity is possible. This is not to say that enemy efforts have ceased entirely or even that their clandestine organizations may not be active. Conversely, that area which is labeled contested does not suggest an absence of government activity. In fact, the bulk of the pacification effort, at any given time, is centered precisely in these contested hamlets. The label simply means that the process is not sufficiently advanced so that normal life can be resumed. The sharp decline in early 1968 represents the impact of the enemy's *Tet* offensive. Steady progress has been made since early March in recovering from this temporary pacification setback.

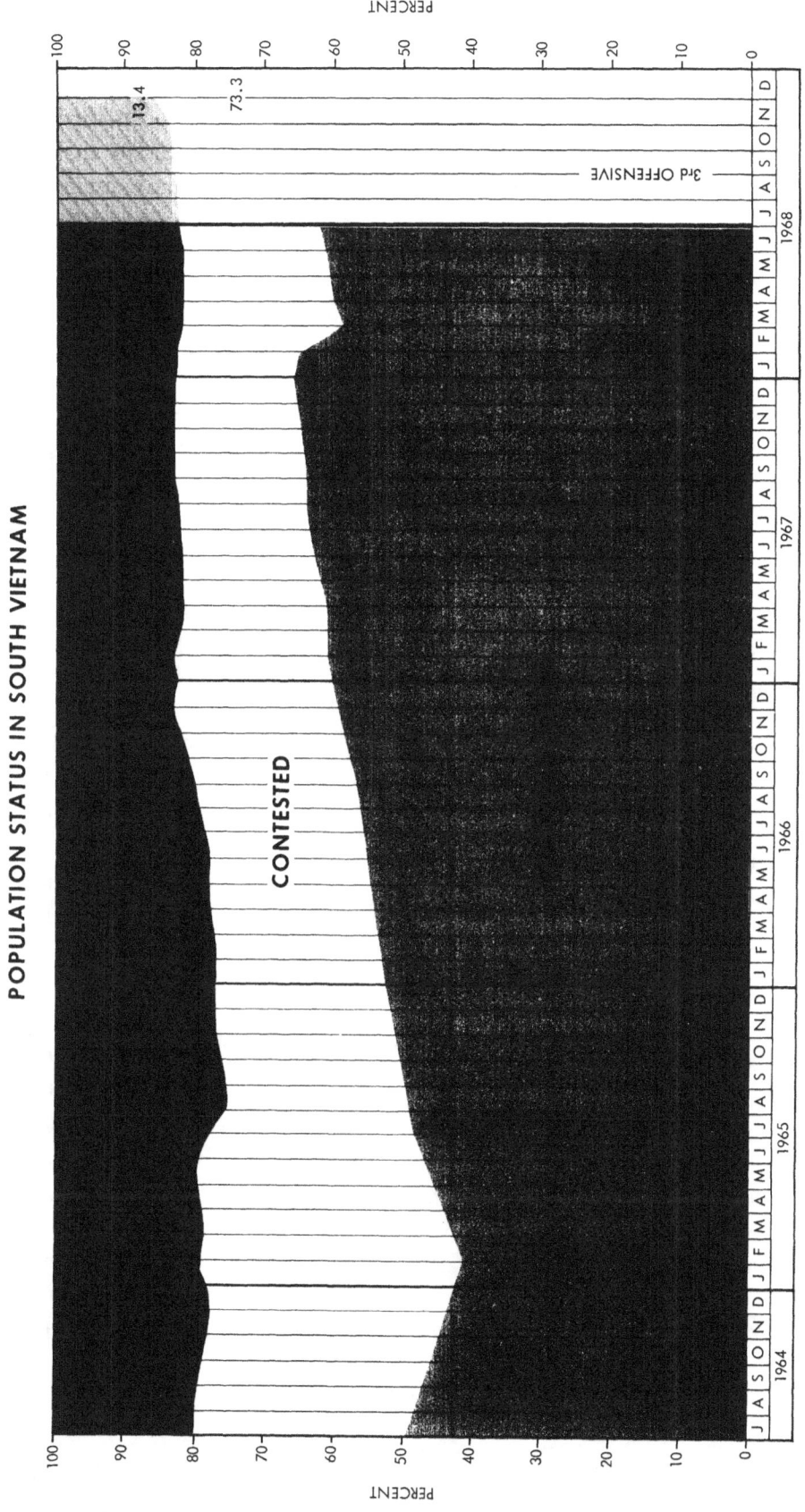

It is not possible to draw final conclusions regarding a war which is not over. I will not attempt to do so.

However, as I look back over the years both preceding and during my period of command I am increasingly impressed with the importance of major decisions which were taken by the two opposing sides—how they related to one another and how accurately they portray developments up to this time.

It seems to me that there were nine major decisions which have affected the progress and the nature of the war. Four of these decisions were taken by the enemy and four by the United States government in conjunction with the government of Vietnam and other free world nations. One decision was taken by the South Vietnamese government.

The first decision was taken by Hanoi when it decided in the late 1950's to resume the war in Indochina which had been interrupted by the Geneva Accords in 1954. This decision included a determination to build progressively a large and effective military force patterned along the lines of the Viet Minh. It also included a decision to create a broad political front organization through which the functions of government could be exercised and through which the participation and support of nationalists and non-Communist elements could be enlisted. The driving and organizing force behind this effort, as was the case during the earlier war against the French, was the Communist Party of Indochina, the Lao Dong Party, the southern branch of which is called the People's Revolutionary Party of South Vietnam. The objective was total victory, including control over South Vietnam in accordance with the long-standing objectives of the Central Committee of the Communist Party in Hanoi.

The second decision was taken by the United States when it established a national policy "to defeat aggression so that the people of South Vietnam will be free to shape their own destiny." This decision led first to materiel support of the South Vietnamese Armed Forces, then to an extensive advisory effort, and later to an increasing level of operational support and assistance.

The third decision was taken by Hanoi in 1964 when it decided to commit the regular army of North Vietnam in order to hasten a victory which, to the North Vietnamese, appeared close at hand.

The fourth decision was taken by the United States when it decided, in 1965, to initiate the bombing of North Vietnam.

The fifth decision, taken later in 1965, was to deploy U.S. ground combat forces to meet directly the rapidly increasing military threat to the existence of the government of South Vietnam.

The sixth decision was taken by the South Vietnamese government when it decided in 1966 to draft a new constitution and to hold elections for a new government.

The seventh decision was taken by Hanoi in the summer of 1967 to intensify, and thus hopefully to shorten, the war through a maximum effort in 1968.

The eighth decision was taken by the United States, together with the government of Vietnam, when the bombing of most of North Vietnam was stopped and immediate negotiations with Hanoi were simultaneously offered.

The ninth decision was made by Hanoi when it accepted negotiations and presumably decided that talking and fighting was a better method of pursuing its objectives.

How and when the war in Vietnam will end is not known. One thing, however, is clear. From the very beginning the enemy has endeavored to achieve three fundamental objectives:

1st—To destroy the Armed Forces of the government of Vietnam.

2d—To destroy the government of Vietnam at every echelon from Saigon to hamlet level.

3d—To enlist the participation and support of the people of South Vietnam on behalf of its political and military objectives.

As I left South Vietnam in June of 1968 I took with me the conviction that the enemy not only had failed to attain these objectives but that in each case they lay farther from his grasp than at any time since the dark days of 1965 when the United States intervened in strength. Additionally, I was convinced that these objectives were receding before the enemy's eyes and thus his prospects for attaining them were steadily diminishing.

Appendix A

ENEMY ORGANIZATION FOR THE CONDUCT OF THE WAR IN SOUTH VIETNAM

From the beginning, the insurgency in South Vietnam has been directed by the Vietnamese Communist Lao Dong (Worker's) Party in Hanoi. However, the North Vietnamese have gone to extraordinary lengths to attempt to conceal their dominant role. For example, in 1962 Hanoi changed the name of the South Vietnamese branch of the Communist Party to the People's Revolutionary Party in order to make the Communist movement in South Vietnam appear independent of Hanoi.

Actual direction of the insurgency in South Vietnam is exercised through a complex, interlocking political and military organization. The dominant feature of this organizational arrangement is Hanoi's control of both the military and civil aspects of the war through the various levels of the Communist Party in South Vietnam (figure on page 205).

The major link between Hanoi and Communist aggression in the South is the Lao Dong Party regional committee for South Vietnam—the Central Office for South Vietnam (COSVN). This agency is located near the Cambodian border north of Saigon in War Zone C and its personnel are the leaders of the Communist Party in the south. The various elements of the total Communist organization in South Vietnam, both military and civil, are responsive to directions issued by COSVN.

The political strategy of the Vietnamese Communists (Viet Cong) includes the classic Communist "united front" technique. This technique, as applied in South Vietnam, involves the creation of a Communist-dominated administrative organization and numerous mass associations. The National Liberation Front (NLF) provides the administrative apparatus—popularly referred to as the "VC shadow government." Mass associations are organized along functional lines such as the Farmers' Liberation Association and the Youth Liberation Association. Communist propaganda invariably proclaims mass association support of the NLF.

During the 1968 *Tet* offensive the Communists surfaced another front organization—the Alliance of National, Democratic, and Peace Forces (The Alliance). The Alliance is ostensibly urban based and seems intended to complement the largely rural base of the NLF.

A typical Communist political structure at the province level is shown in the figure on page 206. Although the diagram depicts a party cell in each section, this may not always be the case. However, to insure rigid control of crucial decision-making, a Communist cell is found in the executive committee and the military affairs committee.

At the village and hamlet level the Communists attempt to create a "Revolutionary Administration." In 1698 this effort took the form of "Liberation Committees" as seen in the figure on page 207. This "Revolutionary Administration" is responsible for a host of activities among which is the creation and often the direction of guerrilla units.

The Lao Dong Party Central Committee in Hanoi occasionally sends military policy directives directly to COSVN. Normally however, military guidance comes to COSVN from the North Vietnamese Army High Command. Based upon this guidance, COSVN issues military and political directives to the Party Committees at the region, province, and district levels. The Party Committee at each echelon is responsible to see that the orders are carried out by military units and by corresponding echelons of the "shadow government."

The South Vietnamese Communist Liberation Army includes main force, local force, and guerrilla units with a party chapter or cell in every unit (figure on page 205). The Liberation Army includes large North Vietnamese Army forces which are disguised as Viet Cong units in order to maintain the fiction of a totally indigenous South Vietnamese insurgency.

Although the Liberation Army is subordinate to the COSVN, it also communicates directly with the North Vietnamese Army High Command in Hanoi. In 1967 and 1968, as the North Vietnamese commitment to the south increased, the High Command of the North Vietnamese Armed Forces in Hanoi took direct control over a number of battle "fronts" as a matter of military necessity. These included the "Khe Sanh front," the "DMZ front," and the "B3 (Highlands) front." The deployment of the North Vietnamese Home Army and Hanoi's assumption of direct command of operations provide clear, unequivocal evidence that North Vietnam is responsible for Communist aggression in the south.

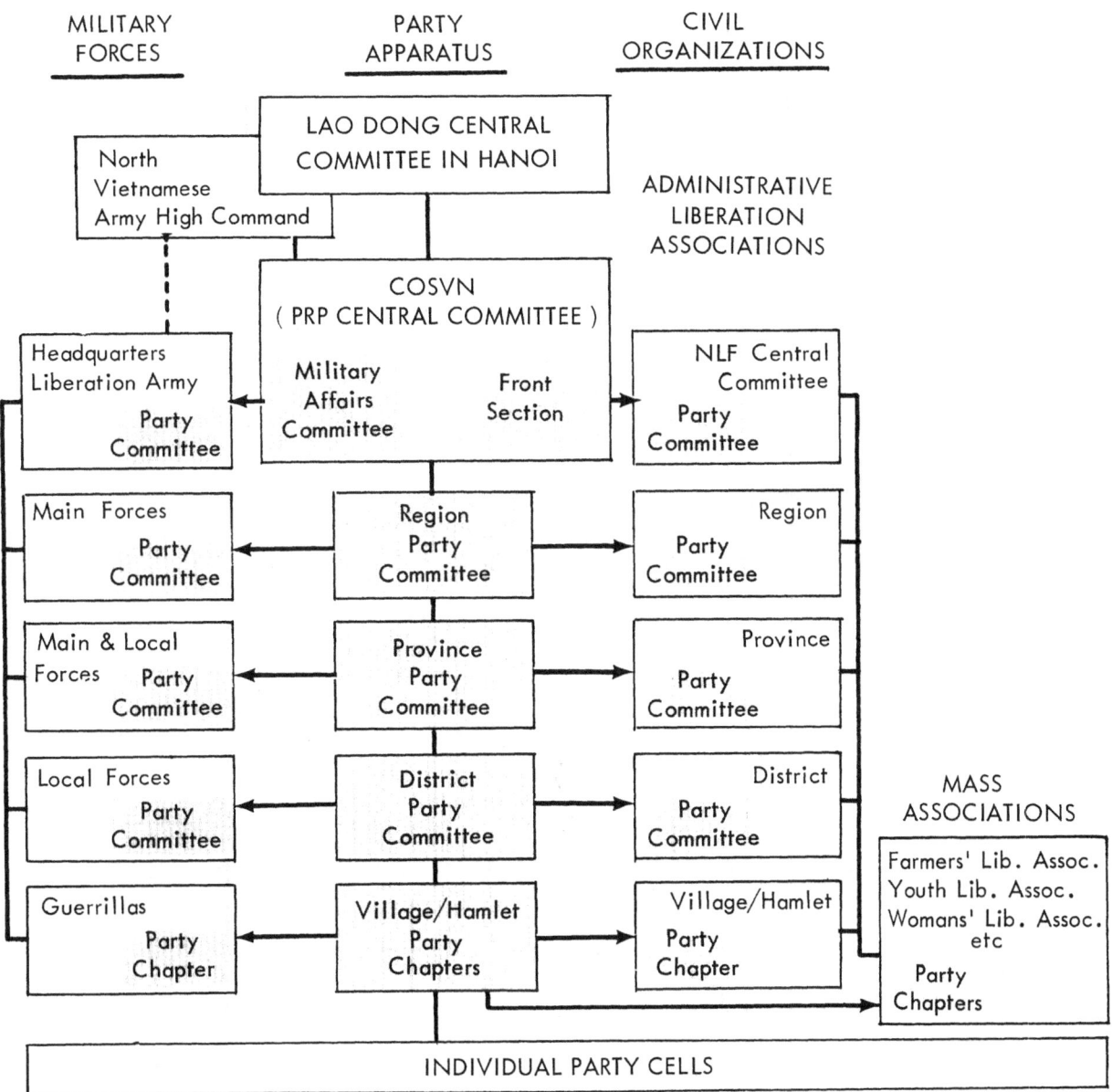

This chart shows the relationship between the major elements of the enemy organization. Although the military and civilian elements are portrayed as seperate entities — with the military and civilian headquarters controlling each echelon of their organization directly — their real organizational substance comes from, and is irrevocably tied to the party. The arrows leading left and right from each level of the party apparatus indicate the true lines of control.

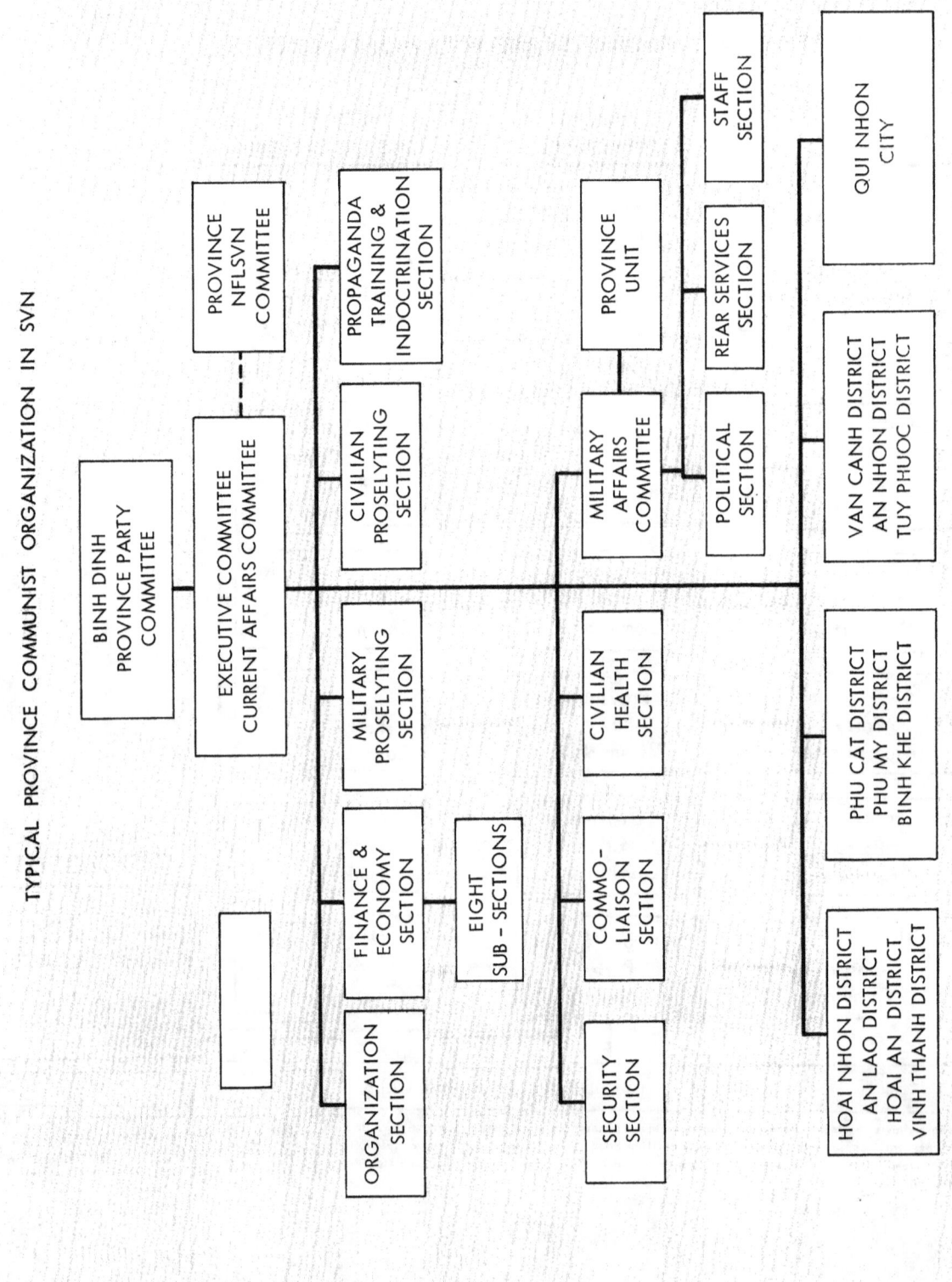

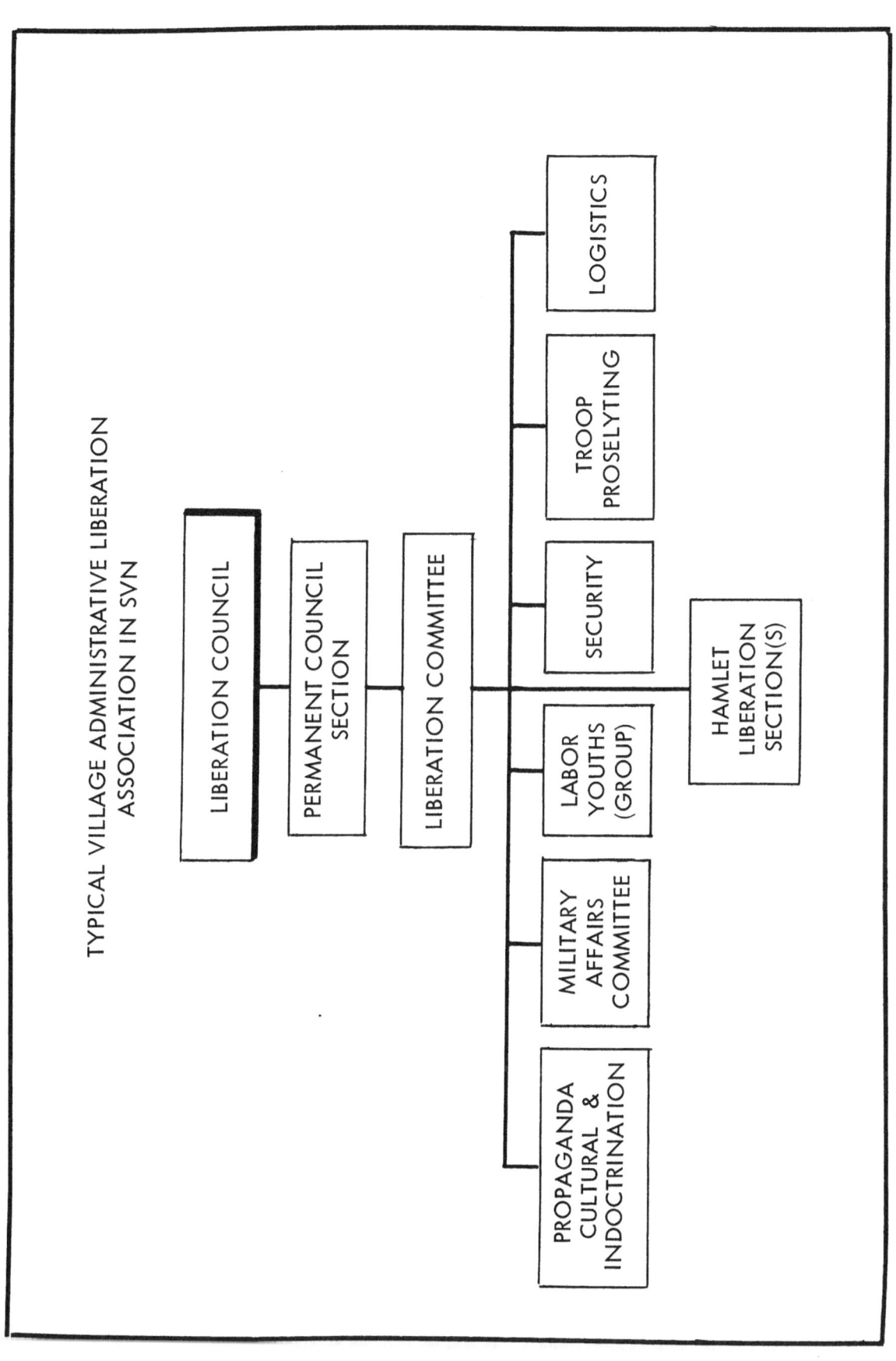

Appendix B

REPUBLIC OF VIETNAM ARMED FORCES

It has been our goal from the beginning to develop strong, confident, and effective Vietnamese military forces able to defend their own country and provide security for their own people. Without such forces little could be done even by strong allies to prevent a Communist takeover of the country. Thus to a large degree the history of the insurgency is a history of our efforts and problems in developing the Vietnamese Armed Forces. This appendix will highlight some of the key points in that history during the years from 1964 to 1968.

Composition

The Republic of Vietnam's Armed Forces include Army, Navy, Air Force, and Marine elements. By far the largest component, the Army is responsible for both mobile combat and local security in land areas of the country. To carry out the mobile combat mission, the Army includes a regular force organized into conventional divisions with supporting elements. Security of local areas is the primary responsibility of the territorial forces. These are of two types—Regional Forces, which are organized into companies under the control of the province and district chiefs, and Popular Forces, which normally operate within or close to a particular village or hamlet.

The Vietnamese Air Force is designed to support the Army and consists primarily of tactical fighters and transport aircraft, including troop-carrying helicopters. This situation contrasts with the practice in United States Armed Forces of including transport helicopters as a part of the Army.

The Vietnamese Navy, which is responsible for protection of the coasts and inland waterways of the nation, is built around a Sea Force, a Coastal Force, and a River Force. The River and Coastal Forces are designed specifically for inland and near-shore counterinsurgency operations, while the Sea Force is organized to stop the enemy's infiltration of men and supplies by sea from North Vietnam. The Vietnamese Marine Corps was organized to operate with the Navy in amphibious and river operations.

In any counterinsurgency effort, the police forces—both regular police and specialized elements—play an essential role in maintaining security and combating the enemy's control apparatus. Appendix D discusses the role of the Vietnamese National Police in carrying out the pacification program in Vietnam.

U.S. Support

U.S. military assistance to the Vietnamese Armed Forces commenced on 23 December 1950 while the French Indochina War was still in progress. With the end of that war and the departure of the French, the United States assisted the fledgling Republic of Vietnam to get on its feet and to build effective armed forces. At that time primary emphasis was directed at the development of South Vietnamese forces capable of meeting an overt thrust across the Demilitarized Zone. As a consequence, the armed forces were initially organized, equipped, and trained along conventional lines. In retrospect, this approach may have failed to pay sufficient attention to the theories of Mao Tse-tung for the achievement of Communist objectives through insurgency warfare.

As advisors to the Vietnamese forces, our objective has been to guide and assist them until they are capable of protecting the nation without our help. In Saigon, MACV Headquarters directs and coordinates all U.S. military assistance. Members of the MACV staff act as advisors to their counterparts in the Vietnamese Joint General Staff, with whom they work in planning the overall development of the Vietnamese forces. In the field advisors are provided down to battalion level in regular force units. Initially these advisors were concerned primarily with distributing American equipment and training the Vietnamese in its use; however, as the insurgency was stepped up in the early sixties, U.S. advisors became more and more concerned with tactical training of their units and with advising Vietnamese commanders in the actual conduct of operation.

1964 Situation

During 1964 the Vietnamese Armed Forces had an overall authorized strength of 435,000. Of these, approximately 200,000 were in the regular army, and another 200,000 in the Civil Guard and Self-Defense Corps—the forerunners of the Regional and Popular Forces. The regular army consisted of 9 infantry divisions, an airborne brigade and 20 separate Ranger battalions with supporting artillery, armor, and service troops. In all there were 123 maneuver battalions. Regular troops were equipped with standard U.S. World War II weapons such as the M1 rifle, the Browning automatic rifle, and the Browning light machine gun. Territorial Forces were lightly armed, principally with the semiautomatic M1 carbine; they had neither automatic weapons nor mortars.

The country was divided into four corps tactical zones. Divisions and separate regiments operated under control of the corps commanders and, like the corps, had territorial responsibility. The Ranger battalions were provided as a reserve for each corps, while the battalions of the airborne brigade together with the Marine battalions constituted a General Reserve under control of the Vietnamese Joint General Staff.

The most valid criticism of the Army at that time was that it was overly conventional in its organization, equipment, and tactics. It tended to stay too close to its bases within the populated areas and to travel habitually by roads. Consequently, it was highly vulnerable to ambush and attack by the Viet Cong and was poorly suited to contest the guerrilla on his own ground in the jungles and the swamps.

The Vietnamese Air Force at the beginning of 1964 consisted of 8,400 men, two fighter squadrons, and 190 aircraft, primarily armed T–28 training planes. During that year we began replacing the T–28 with the A–1 "Skyraider," which was faster and far more versatile, had greater endurance, and carried a much bigger load of bombs and ammunition. We also replaced the older UH–19 with the more modern CH–34.

The Navy in 1964 was authorized 7,100 men for both Sea and River Forces. Fourteen River Assault Groups located at bases throughout the Delta made up the River Force. Their main vehicles were armed and armored landing craft, used to transport South Vietnamese Army and Marine units on offensive operations as well as to patrol the major waterways of the Delta and the Rung Sat. The Sea Force consisted of patrol boats, minesweepers, and landing craft based at Saigon. At that time the Coastal Force was a paramilitary group known as the "junk force." It was organized into 28 divisions deployed along the entire coast of Vietnam working in conjunction with the Sea Force. In 1965 these junks were made a part of the regular navy.

At the beginning of 1964 the Vietnamese Marine Corps had a strength of 6,100, organized in a brigade of four infantry battalions and one amphibious support battalion. Although organized for amphibious operations along the rivers and the coast, the Marine battalions participated in ground operations throughout South Vietnam as a part of the General Reserve.

Deterioration During the "Coup Era"

During early 1963 progress in the development of the Vietnamese Armed Forces had produced an air of cautious optimism, but the turbulent political situation that followed the overthrow of President Diem created a situation of uncertainty and lack of direction which started a process of military deterioration. Frequent changes in the upper echelons of the government resulted in changes among military leaders as political favorites were assigned key jobs. Desertions in the regular and Regional and Popular Forces in 1964 were nearly double those of 1963, while among the Popular Forces they increased by 50 percent. (It was exceptional for these deserters to join the enemy; they simply returned to their homes.) The effectiveness of all forces declined sharply as morale dropped and personnel strengths shrank. Sensing the deterioration of the government forces, the enemy stepped up the tempo of his operations and began to win a series of victories.

A new draft law was promulgated during 1965, making all male citizens from age 20 through 33 subject to military service. Although the new law was adequate, so scant was the government's control and so ineffective its methods that the number of men inducted fell below requirements. To supplement conscription, the government and the Joint General Staff upon MACV advice undertook a comprehensive volunteer recruitment campaign involving extensive publicity, enlistment bonuses, special training for recruiters, and accelerated quotas for unit recruiting. Together with the callup, this campaign enabled the regular forces by the end of 1965 actually to exceed authorized strength.

The encouragement provided by this increase lasted only briefly as desertions soon eroded the gains. Many factors contributed to the high desertion rate—overly restrictive leave policies, lack of command attention to personnel management and soldier welfare, overtaxed military training facilities and a shortage of qualified instructors, tolerance of desertion by military and civil authorities, public apathy toward the war, increasingly heavy combat losses, and misuse of some types of units. The number of desertions also reflected a nationwide malaise of inertia and defeatism.

By the middle of 1965 the problem was becoming critical. At the rate manpower was pumped into the armed forces and drained off by desertion, the primary sources of manpower would be exhausted by mid-1968 and secondary sources by the end of 1969. Of more immediate concern, new units to fill out the force structure were being created at a faster rate than manpower could be provided to replace combat and desertion losses, with the result that existing units could not be brought to full strength. In particular the strength of maneuver battalions (the cutting edge) was dropping lower and lower. Low fighting strength bred caution, a defensive attitude, pressures to avoid casualties, and thus poor morale and more desertions. I was equally concerned that we were outdistancing the Vietnamese ability to produce leaders. We were on the verge of wrecking the Vietnamese forces by attempting to expand them too rapidly.

Thus, by mid-1965, as U.S. forces were being introduced to forestall an immediate Communist victory, it was obvious that vigorous efforts would have to be directed toward solving the morale crisis within the Vietnamese forces and building them into a much more effective combat force.

Improving Leadership And Morale

Coming to office in mid-1965, the Thieu-Ky government finally brought a measure of political stability within South Vietnam which provided an atmosphere conducive to progress. In June of that year I called for a temporary moratorium on activating new units until all maneuver battalions were built up to a 450-man strength for operations. In

April 1966 the government issued a series of decrees to enforce the draft laws and to provide for punishment of deserters and their accomplices. During the remainder of the year and continuing into 1967, we attacked the root causes of the desertion problem by improving leadership, personnel management, personal services, and training centers. We also made progress in reorganizing, retraining, and reequipping units. These measures, along with increased U.S. and Free World presence, helped create marked overall improvement of morale. The desertion rate for 1967 reflected these gains: desertions fell 30 percent below those of 1966.

A key factor in bringing about this improvement was a leadership development program which we began in the latter part of 1965. The aim was to improve the quality and leadership behavior of the officer corps through proper selection and training of officer personnel and through a comprehensive career management program. The Joint General Staff established personnel records and efficiency reporting procedures and centralized such personnel actions as promotions, discharges, retirements, schooling, and transfers. Both through formal training and through the example of U.S. advisors, we attempted to indoctrinate Vietnamese commanders in their responsibilities for the health, welfare, and morale of their troops. We sought to strengthen the chain of command from top to bottom.

To provide the trained leaders and specialists that the armed forces required and to insure their continued development, the Vietnamese had, with our advice and assistance, developed an extensive system of armed forces general, technical, and administrative schools. We sought at this point to improve those schools and to create new ones where voids existed. Of particular value was an upgraded Noncommissioned Officers Academy. As is the case in all armies, the Vietnamese noncommissioned officers are the backbone and provide the first line of leadership. This revitalized school began infusing the ranks with a leaven of well-trained enlisted leaders.

We assisted the Vietnamese high command in modernizing the curriculum at the Military Academy, expanding the course from two years to four, and elevating the Academy to a degree-granting institution similar to the United States Military Academy. The first class to complete the four-year curriculum will graduate in 1969. To meet more immediate requirements, officer candidate courses as well as courses at branch schools were expanded. By 1967 a steady stream of trained leaders, technicians, and specialists was beginning to flow into the ranks, greatly improving the administration and combat effectiveness of the armed forces.

An evaluation of battalion commanders in 1965 and 1966 revealed that many lacked knowledge of tactical and administrative principles. To correct the situation, a Battalion Commander's School was established in late 1966. The curriculum provided a concentrated course in battalion tactics and also a review of small unit tactics. The latter served both as a valuable refresher and as preparation for the commander's role in direct support of pacification, a mission in which the Army was becoming increasingly involved.

To improve the quality of instruction at the Command and General Staff College, we arranged for recent Vietnamese graduates of the United States Army's Command and General Staff College to be assigned as instructors. Under the tutelage of our advisors, the Vietnamese took steps to revise, revitalize, and extend the course of instruction. We also promoted a selection system for attendance at the course to insure that only qualified officers with career potential were selected.

Just as in the lower echelons of command, leadership at the national policy and planning levels long had needed improvement. In mid-1967 the Vietnamese acted to correct the deficiency. On 1 August Premier Ky signed a decree establishing a National Defense College in Saigon. The opening of this school in the spring of 1968 placed the capstone on a leader training and education system which now covers the entire spectrum from squad to national level military leadership.

Many morale problems are directly traceable to administrative mistakes and delays on matters which are of keen personal interest to the individual soldier. Faulty administration also provides opportunities for graft and corruption.

During 1966 we succeeded in streamlining significantly the Vietnamese Armed Forces' administrative procedures. On 1 January the Vietnamese started a "by name" personnel strength accounting system, employing a punch card computer process to establish rosters by unit. The Regional Forces came under this system on 1 July 1967 and the Popular Forces were scheduled to follow by the end of 1968. The new system produced many advantages, some of them unexpected, such as savings to the government on the pay of personnel who had deserted. Closer scrutiny of personnel records disclosed payroll discrepancies amounting to hundreds of thousands of piasters. In the first month that Vietnamese commanders faced the possibility that a survey would be made on all future deserters, the unprecedented sum of 33,000,000 piasters (about $280,000) was turned back to the finance office.

In November 1967 we helped form an ARVN Adjutant General Corps to improve and refine administration and management. To handle the training for the various skills that would be required, we helped set up an Adjutant General School that presented a program of instruction similar to our own. To improve the lot of the individual soldier, a number of pay adjustments, refinements, and increases were introduced to reduce financial pressures and inequities. The Vietnamese government instituted a liberal awards policy, revised and improved leave policies, regularized promotions, initiated a system of battlefield promotions, sanctioned direct appointments from enlisted to commissioned ranks, and encouraged admission of regular enlisted men to Officer Candidate School.

While working to improve administration, we also strove to raise the standard of living of the individual soldier and his dependents. The South Vietnamese soldier's living conditions had to be made as good as those of his civilian counterpart and much better than those of his adversary. If the soldier was to be able to devote his attention to fighting the war, he had to know that his family was adequately provided for, a particularly important factor in a society that stresses family relationships. Increased high-level concern for the soldier's lot and that of his family engenders greater personnel stability in the forces, which in turn insures a better armed force.

In 1967 MACV and the Vietnamese Joint General Staff took joint action to expand the commissary system in order to improve the diet of Vietnamese servicemen and their dependents while reducing the price they had to pay for subsistence items. The U.S. contributed a one-time grant of 42 million dollars worth of food items, which when sold provided self-regenerating funds from which stocks were replenished. Sales of the new items began in September. By the end of the year revenues exceeded a million dollars, covering the cost of overhead, construction, and equipment for further expansion. By the end of June 1968, 201 retail outlets were in operation, serving troops and dependents throughout Vietnam.

In July 1967 we began providing military engineering assistance to the Vietnamese to supplement two self-help dependent housing programs, one for the regular forces particularly in the III Corps and one for the Popular Forces countrywide. Our men supplied and transported materials to the construction sites and provided technical advice, but the Vietnamese remained in charge of the projects and did the actual construction work. In the first six months of 1968 over 4,000 Popular Forces housing units were improved. Overall, however, because of the lack of skilled labor and materials and the major destruction from the enemy's *Tet* offensive, progress in the dependent housing program has been no more than modest.

The Vietnamese soldier, like soldiers everywhere, is concerned about his future. Peace will someday come to the nation, and when it does there will be a vast number of veterans. Already a quarter century of war has produced a significant veteran element in the population, many of whom require assistance from the government. This need will greatly increase as the ranks of veterans swell.

In 1968 the Ambassador approved my recommendation to transfer responsibility for the veterans' program from the Agency for International Development to MACV. Working closely with the Vietnamese, my staff gave priority to appropriate hospitalization and medical treatment for veterans, classification and vocational training for the disabled, and job placement. The new program removed men who were physically incapacitated from active rolls, making room for the able-bodied. Well received by the Vietnam Veterans Administration and the military in general, the program soon showed encouraging progress.

Improving Performance

All our efforts to improve leadership and morale within the Vietnamese forces had one ultimate aim—to produce greater effectiveness on the battlefield. However, to achieve this, another element was required: we had to improve the combat skill and teamwork within the Vietnamese units. This was largely a matter of setting standards and providing practice. This, of course, was one of the major tasks of our advisors with the regular units. After 1965 we had another asset which we could use in this job: the U.S. combat units which were displaying outstanding combat skill and competence. In 1966 we developed the "Buddy System," which involved the pairing off of American and Vietnamese units. The U.S. unit in this scheme provided a team to train its companion Vietnamese unit and later to work with it on actual operations.

One of the most ambitious "Buddy System" programs was Operation FAIRFAX, a combined U.S.-Vietnamese operation in the area around Saigon, begun in November 1966 and continued into December 1967. In this operation the U.S. 1st, 4th, and 25th Divisions and later the 199th Light Infantry Brigade and the Vietnamese 5th Ranger Group integrated their forces down to squad level, and operations were planned and conducted on a completely integrated basis. The operation was highly successful.

Although FAIRFAX provided valuable training for the Vietnamese Army, we learned that only in limited and tightly controlled situations was such a thorough integration desirable. We concentrated instead on combined operations, in which U.S. and Vietnamese units operated side-by-side in close coordination, one in direct support of the other or on a coequal basis. This afforded the South Vietnamese units the advantage of training in both the planning and conduct of the operations. It also made available to the Vietnamese units extra helicopter, artillery, air, and logistical support, while providing U.S. units additional maneuver battalions. I placed great emphasis on this type of operation, and by 1968 it had become the customary way of operating throughout the Republic. As we gained experience, the effectiveness of the system steadily improved.

The problem of improving performance of the Regional and Popular Forces was significantly more difficult than with the regular forces. There were no U.S. advisors with the territorial units; and with thousands of these units deployed throughout the country, any attempt to provide a permanent U.S. presence with them would prove expensive in manpower. The demand could only be met by tapping our American combat units.

A number of factors caused us to delay before instituting a standard approach to improving the training and effectiveness of territorial forces. We had to bring the enemy main force threat under control—because the territorial forces were never designed to stand off regimental-sized enemy forces. We had also to await our own troop build-up before we could find experienced officers and men in the required numbers. We needed to train the necessary interpreters; and finally, we had to sell the Vietnamese on the usefulness and importance of the program. In the meantime, we experimented on a broad basis to find the most efficient arrangement. To this end, I delegated responsibility to my principal American subordinates to devise and carry out schemes to improve performance of territorial units within their areas.

In the I Corps, the Marines developed the Combined Action Program, in which a squad of Marines lived in a village with a Popular Forces platoon for an indefinite period. While training and assisting with the local civic action program, the Marines added to the security of the village and assured a proper climate for pacification. Under these conditions the program has been singularly successful and has been further expanded as the Marines could afford additional teams.

In other areas, commanders devised mobile training teams which rotated among Regional or Popular Force units conducting training and supervising performance. These mobile teams had the advantage of being able to conduct training for many territorial units, but the amount of time which they could spend with each was limited. Further, even under this system the demand for U.S. manpower from tactical units became excessive as the Regional Force companies increased by the hundreds and the Popular Force platoons by the thousands.

In October of 1967, under the supervision of my deputy, General Abrams, the MACV staff joined representatives from the field commands in an intensive study of ways to improve the combat effectiveness of Regional and Popular Force units. The training programs already adopted in various localities served as points of departure. In the end we adopted a massive improvement program that addressed all aspects of the administration, logistical support, and tactical operations of territorial units.

Basically, we adopted the concept of Mobile Advisory Teams which had been previously tried by General Weyand's II Field Force. Mobile Advisory Teams consisted of two American officers, three enlisted men, and a Vietnamese Army interpreter. Each team worked in a specific area with three to six Regional Forces companies and a number of Popular Forces platoons. Like the Marine Combined Action Platoons, they were required to live with the Vietnamese unit with which they worked. They supervised small unit training and developed programs of instruction geared to the specific needs of the particular companies and platoons, including instruction in small unit operations, employment of artillery and air strikes, and construction of field fortifications. We also added Mobile Administrative and Logistical Teams—seven-man advisory teams designed to provide assistance to depots and area logistical commands, as well as to smaller units.

I approved this comprehensive program and directed speedy implementation. By mid-1968 seven Mobile Administrative and Logistical Teams and 192 Mobile Advisory Teams were functioning, with another 161 teams programmed for the last half of the year.

During 1967 and 1968 the Vietnamese Joint General Staff with our assistance and encouragement also developed programs to improve the combat effectiveness of territorial units. Regional Forces companies attended the National Training Centers to undergo the same 12-week program of instruction given to the regular army soldier. Upon completion of this training, each company took training tests to determine what had been learned. Also, the Central Training Command conducted training inspections of units in the field to determine how well they were maintaining proficiency.

Even as we worked to improve the effectiveness of South Vietnamese units through training, we had constantly to seek to upgrade weapons and equipment. The matter of weapons was particularly critical, since as early as 1964 the enemy had began introducing modern Communist-bloc weapons, including the highly effective AK–47 automatic rifle. By 1967 all enemy main force and many local force units were equipped with this weapon, which has a much higher rate of fire than any of the U.S. World War II weapons with which South Vietnamese troops were armed.

The long-sought M16 automatic rifles for issue to the South Vietnamese forces began to arrive in April 1967 but in quantities that would equip only the airborne and Marine battalions of the General Reserve. After strong recommendations on my part, an accelerated schedule of M16 shipments was approved in the fall of 1967, and by mid-1968 all regular infantry maneuver battalions had received the new weapon. By enabling the Vietnamese soldier to meet the AK-47 on equal or better terms, the M16 provided a major morale and psychological boost. Although the Regional and Popular Forces were still fighting with older weapons, we made priority plans to start equipping numbers of them with M16's as they became available during 1968.

One particular difficulty in our efforts to improve the performance of Vietnamese forces was the lack of adequate data to determine where their major deficiencies lay. Advisors submitted a monthly report describing the conditions of their units, but these reports lacked sufficient data to provide a clear understanding of the situation at MACV level. To correct this lack, we instituted a comprehensive reporting system in January 1968. Known as the System for Evaluating the Effectiveness of the Republic of Vietnam Armed Forces (or SEER for short), the report had two major subdivisions, one for the regular forces and one for the territorial forces. Both reports were designed for machine processing of the data, thereby simplifying the clerical and administrative work required under the former reporting system. By pinpointing specific shortcomings for correction, these reports proved to be particularly valuable management tools in our overall effort to improve Vietnamese performance.

Force Growth

By the end of 1965 the immediate manpower crisis which had led to the moratorium on activation of new units had passed, and expansion of the force structure had been resumed. A substantial increase appeared essential to provide security for the pacification program. With MACV assistance, the Vietnamese government took steps to increase the size of its regular army by some 30,000 men and the territorial forces by 110,000. The total for all the armed forces was to be 622,000 men. The figure was limited by a piaster ceiling imposed on the Vietnamese budget by the U.S. Mission in coordination with the Vietnamese government as a hedge against inflation. The ceiling continued during the 1966–67 period to restrict the size of the Vietnamese Armed Forces. It was not until late in 1967 that the control was lifted, permitting further expansion.

Up through 1966 support for the Vietnamese forces was still being funded through the Military Assistance Program, which was proving more and more inflexible and unresponsive to the changing requirements of the combat situation. This was rectified in March 1966 by an executive order, signed by President Johnson, which transferred funding responsibility for support of the Vietnamese Armed Forces from the Military Assistance Program to the separate Services of the United States Armed Forces. This was a significant improvement since it allowed each U.S. Service to program materiel and services for its Vietnamese counterpart in a flexible, responsive manner.

By the end of 1966 Vietnamese forces had reached a strength of 623,000 with regular army troops numbering some 302,808 men. The Army contained 158 maneuver battalions, of which 153 were considered combat effective. The great challenge facing these units was to alter the image of a defeated, demoralized army.

During 1967 Vietnamese forces were assigned the role of providing security for pacification as a primary mission. Each month of the year, somewhere between 50 and 60 battalions were committed to that role. Since the emphasis in support of pacification was on small unit operations against lower elements in the spectrum of enemy forces, the Vietnamese conducted fewer large operations than in the preceding year, but the number of smaller operations more than doubled, as did the number of enemy contacts. Nearly three-quarters of all small unit operations were conducted at night. In terms of battalion-days spent on operations, combat activity increased in the last nine months of 1967 by 20 percent over the average of the first three months. Throughout the year the South Vietnamese troops displayed an increased willingness to close with and destroy the enemy.

Although the tremendous strides made by the Vietnamese Armed Forces in the twelve-month period beginning in mid-1967 were the result of many factors, one of the more important was the enactment and enforcement of mobilization during 1968. Having recognized as far back as 1966 that the Vietnamese government would probably have to resort ultimately to general mobilization, I had recommended to the Ambassador in June that planning be started. I considered it mandatory that early advance planning be done on a Mission-wide basis, since mobilization would affect every aspect of Vietnamese national life and extend far beyond the areas of MACV responsibility. As the Vietnamese government at the time had no organization to meet this eventuality, I urged that we prepare the way by establishing an American committee under the Ambassador's direction to study Vietnamese mobilization. Based on this committee's report, a joint U.S.-Vietnamese commission could then draft a mobilization program that could be instituted at a propitious time.

Since my proposal was not acted upon, I renewed it in May 1967. I stressed the immediate need for a mobilization plan in the belief that the forthcoming general elections in September would set the stage for action. Upon the Ambassador's request, a special manpower advisory mission composed of economists and labor and management specialists arrived from the United States. Working with the Embassy and MACV staff, this mission developed the basic planning necessary for mobilization. Discussions then began with the Vietnamese government.

On 24 October 1967 the Government Central Executive Committee decreed partial mobilization. The next day it was announced that on 1 January 1968 all males from 18 to 33 years of age would be eligible for conscription and that specialists and technicians in the age group 34 to 45 were liable to involuntary recall to active service. Later, as the result of the *Tet* offensive, reservists with less than five years active service were made subject to recall. On 1 April 1968 19-year-olds began to be called up, and on 1 May, 18-year-olds. These callups were far more effectively enforced than those of the past, a direct reflection of the strength and ability of the government. In June the National Assembly voted general mobilization into law and, upon approval by President Thieu, the interim period of mobilization by decree came to an end.

Under the mobilization decrees and later laws, the strength of the Vietnamese Armed Forces rapidly increased. In the first six months of 1968 total strength rose by some 122,000 men. The upsurge in volunteers was mainly attributable to the mobilization, effective enforcement of the draft, and, in the wake of the *Tet* offensive, a noticeably greater allegiance to the central government on the part of the people as a whole.

This kind of growth of the South Vietnamese Army had been our goal for years. In 1965 we had paid particular attention to expanding the General Reserve—the airborne and Marine battalions. By year's end two new airborne battalions had been organized, bringing the total to eight. The same year we supported organization of a tenth infantry division, located east of Saigon in the III Corps, in a step toward providing security in that vital area. We also began strengthening the other divisions during the year by adding a fourth battalion to each regiment; but because of manpower, leadership, and training limitations, this program had to be carried out gradually and extended into 1968.

In 1967 we converted the airborne brigade into an airborne division and started actions to make it capable of taking to the field and fighting as a mobile independent force. Prior to this time single battalions or task forces of two to three battalions had been used separately to reinforce corps and divisions. To fill out the division, a ninth airborne battalion was created and became operational at the end of March 1968.

By mid-1968 South Vietnamese regular army forces had reached a strength of 358,000 and included ten infantry divisions, three separate infantry regiments, an airborne division, a Ranger command of 20 battalions, special forces, 11 armored cavalry squadrons, and attendant supporting units. In all, there were 161 maneuver battalions in the army structure. Regional Forces, consisting of 1,053 companies, had a strength of 198,000; and Popular Forces, with 4,561 platoons, totalled 164,000.

By 1967 and 1968 capability of the South Vietnamese Army was keeping pace with its growth. In November of 1967 a Vietnamese regiment replaced U.S. Marine units manning the eastern portion of the line facing the Demilitarized Zone. In mid-December the 5th Ranger Group, after having operated for a year in close harmony with the 199th Light Infantry Brigade in the integrated Operation FAIRFAX, was specially tailored with infantry and artillery augmentation and given responsibility by the Vietnamese Joint General Staff for the defense of the area around Saigon. Similarly, the airborne units developed into truly professional outfits in 1967 and made outstanding contributions to the overall effort.

The ultimate test of the Vietnamese Army's improvement came with the 1968 *Tet* offensive. During this violent attack, units defended their positions well, even though many were undermanned because of holiday leaves. In a number of instances, the South Vietnamese launched effective counterattacks. Of the 149 ARVN infantry battalions, 42 performed exceptionally well and only eight unsatisfactorily. Although one of the enemy's goals was to promote large-scale defections, that failed to happen. Morale and esprit of the Vietnamese Army was good and in many cases higher than before the *Tet* offensive. In Saigon two provisional battalions were formed from soldiers who voluntarily returned from leave status to take up the fight. Instead of routing the South Vietnamese, the enemy came up against unexpected resolution.

Since that time it has become increasingly evident that the Republic's Army has gained confidence and resolve and is making even greater efforts to find the enemy and drive him from the field. The fighting in and around Saigon in May and June 1968 again provided South Vietnamese forces the opportunity to prove their mettle. In these battles they decimated unit after unit of Communist infiltrators.

In the spring of 1968 the South Vietnamese Army had never been in better shape. With volunteers and an effective draft swelling its ranks, the training centers were filled to capacity and turning out a record number of well-trained replacements. The present-for-duty personnel strength in the maneuver battalions, which are the cutting edge of an army and the true measure of its strength, had reached an alltime high in a third of the battalions and the others were filling up rapidly. The number of maneuver battalions also was at a peak, and the battalions had reached a quality and combat effectiveness far surpassing earlier achievements. One dark spot appeared, however. Desertions, having dropped to an alltime low in January, had risen sharply again by mid-year.

In 1964 we undertook a program to increase the number of Vietnamese Air Force fighter squadrons to six, which when completed in 1965 gave the Vietnamese a total of 150 A–1 fighters. At the same time we increased the number of liaison aircraft from 62 to 126. Concurrently, we worked to improve combat effectiveness, and by 1967 the Vietnamese were flying 25 percent of all sorties flown inside South Vietnam. By 1968 the personnel strength had risen to over 16,000, and a total of 398 aircraft included one squadron of F–5 "Freedom Fighter" jets. During the *Tet* offensive several Vietnamese fighter squadrons performed superbly, flying a record number of missions and delivering accurate and timely strikes. However, the performance of some other squadrons, even by mid-1968, still left something to be desired.

Since 1967 Vietnamese Navy personnel have manned Coastal Surveillance Centers with U.S. Navy counterparts. In the latter half of 1967 Vietnamese ships for the first time relieved American ships on coastal barrier stations, part of a continuing program to phase out our Navy in the coastal surveillance effort. In 1968 the Vietnamese Navy also assumed responsibility for minesweeping operations on the shipping channels leading from the South China Sea to Saigon. The U.S. Navy turned over several of its minesweeping boats and river patrol boats to the Vietnamese for this purpose. By the beginning of 1968 the Vietnamese Navy had more than doubled in size since 1964 and consisted of some 16,000 officers and men. It was a combat effective force and had developed a capability for sustained operations.

Vietnamese Marine strength had by 1968 reached 8,900 men organized into six infantry battalions and one artillery battalion. Marine units played a significant role in the defense of Saigon during both the *Tet* and May/June offensives. During 1968 plans were made to augment the Marine brigade and organize it as a light Marine division.

The Future

By late 1967 I was able to conclude that the trend of development of the Vietnamese Armed Forces was such that, given additional modern equipment, they could progressively take over a larger part of the war. I therefore projected a program that would give them the capability to replace some U.S. troops by 1970. The Vietnamese leadership readily accepted the concept and aggressively pursued the program. To prepare for such a takeover will require continued effort to increase the size and quality of the Vietnamese military forces and to accelerate to the extent possible the required balance between combat, combat support, and service support elements of the total force.

By mid-1968 with the national mobilization program filling the armed forces personnel needs, expansion was proceeding on a sound basis. A weapons modernization program, including the M16 rifle, was well underway. Above all, a new confidence permeated the Vietnamese Armed Forces and an air of professionalism was becoming evident within the leadership. All signs pointed toward the day when they would indeed be able to relieve American troops of an ever greater share of the war.

Annex to Appendix B

FINAL ADVICE TO VIETNAMESE COMMANDERS*

1. The most competent and honest officers should be installed as province and district chiefs. Your best fighters and disciplinarians should be placed in command of combat troops.

2. Insure that each commander takes a personal interest in the welfare of his troops and their dependents.

3. Continuously concentrate on timely intelligence and gear your organization to react immediately thereto, both with respect to enemy military elements and political infrastructure.

4. Take extraordinary steps to deny the enemy knowledge of your plans and operations.

5. Emphasize night operations to gain the initiative on the enemy and deny his freedom of movement.

6. Appreciate that the greatest gain that can be made with minimum resources is improvement in the performance and morale of the Regional and Popular Forces.

7. Give more emphasis to administrative and logistical support organizations that are essential to sustained combat operations.

8. Training must be a continuous process with more attention given to in-place classes and exercises, when the tactical situation permits. Psywar and motivational training are essential parts of this program.

9. Pacification must be supported by all elements of the Government of Vietnam, of which the RVNAF is a major part. All soldiers must realize their important role and be required to assume always a proper, friendly, and helpful attitude toward the people.

10. Maintain the offensive spirit.

---

*At a farewell luncheon given by Vietnamese senior commanders in his honor on 26 May 1968, General Westmoreland reemphasized a number of fundamentals. Although not new, these matters were of such importance that they demanded constant attention of all Vietnamese commanders. Each Vietnamese, U.S., and Free World commander was given this summary of major points made.

Appendix C

FREE WORLD ASSISTANCE

In April and December of 1964 President Johnson publicly requested that nations of the Free World unite in the effort to stop the spread of communism in the Republic of Vietnam. Such a request was not unexpected in view of the worsening military situation and the earlier expressed SEATO concern that the defeat of the Communist-supported insurgency in Vietnam was essential to the safety of all of Southeast Asia. While recognizing the seriousness of this threat and its consequences to future security, many of the Free World nations had internal and domestic problems that argued against active contribution to this effort. Despite these obstacles, however, many nations did respond and the total of 500 Free World participants in Vietnam in 1964 rapidly grew to over 22,000 by the end of 1965. This total continued to expand through the succeeding years until over 62,400 non-U.S. Free World participants were actively engaged in Vietnam by mid-1968. Apart from the actual combat forces provided by four of the Free World nations, 35 other nations contributed food, medical supplies, technical advisors, equipment, educational facilities, instructors, and over $200 million in grants, loans, credits, or gifts to support the Vietnamese war effort.

Not only have these military and nonmilitary contributions of the Free World been significant in thwarting a Communist victory, but they have also been of major importance in supporting the nation-building efforts of the Vietnamese people. The involvement of ethnically and culturally dissimilar nations in the common defense of Vietnam provided heartening evidence of the unity of nations in the cause of freedom and discredited the Communist propaganda theme that the Vietnamese conflict was the product of American "imperialism."

As in the defense of any worthy cause, the combating of Hanoi's aggression was not achieved without national sacrifice and the cost of human lives. During the period from January 1965 until late 1968, the participating military forces of the non-U.S. Free World suffered 8,500 casualties. Of this number, over 2,500 soldiers were killed.

In order to better appreciate the scope of participation of these nations, a brief résumé of some of the major contributions follows.

Australia

Australia was the first Free World nation to provide assistance to the Republic of Vietnam, beginning even before President Johnson's appeal. Early in 1962 Australia sent a 30-man group of training advisors to the nation. These individuals were jungle warfare specialists and proved a valuable addition to the U.S. advisory program. In August 1964 this initial effort was supplemented with an aviation detachment consisting of six light transport aircraft and 73 maintenance and operational personnel. The detachment was quickly integrated into the Southeast Asia airlift capability and provided valuable logistic support to dispersed Vietnamese military units.

In response to the growing intensity of the Communist offensive, Australia made its first commitment of combat troops in June 1965. The initial task force was comprised of the Headquarters, Australian Army, Far East, and the First Battalion of the Royal Australian Regiment reinforced with signal and logistic support elements. Included in this total of approximately 1,400 personnel were 100 additional jungle warfare advisors to support the original training detachments. Although the combat actions of this contingent were limited to local security operations during 1965, their professionalism and aggressiveness were praised by U.S. advisors and members of the 173d Airborne Brigade to which the infantry elements were attached. A military working agreement between the commander of the Australian Army Forces, Vietnam, and the commander of MACV placed all Australian forces in Vietnam under the operational control of the U.S. commander. With the exception of Korea, comparable command arrangements were concluded with other Free World military forces.

In April 1966 Australia expanded its original task force with an additional infantry battalion augmented with artillery, armor, and support elements. Included in this force was a squadron of the Special Air Service, a highly specialized reconnaissance unit. This commitment raised the Australian combat strength in Vietnam to slightly over 4,500 troops. Upon the arrival of these reinforcements, the First Battalion, Royal Australian Regiment, having completed almost a year of combat service in Vietnam, departed.

After a brief training period, the task force came under the operational control of the U.S. II Field Force and moved to Phuoc Tuy Province with the mission of supporting pacification operations along Highway 15 and in the eastern portion of the critical Rung Sat Special Zone. The effectiveness of the Australian contingent was clearly illustrated during a series of operations in August-December 1966. They destroyed over 300 of the enemy, captured large stores of materiel and assisted in securing Highway 15.

In early 1967 the Australian Government declared its intention again to expand its military contribution to Vietnam and the first aircraft of a Royal Australian Air Force Canberra light bomber squadron arrived in Phan Rang in April of that year. This action was closely followed by the addition of the HMAS *Hobart*, a guided missile destroyer, to the U.S. Navy's surveillance force off the eastern coast of Vietnam. In addition to its normal patrol mission, the *Hobart* participated in regular naval gunfire support operations during this period. As the year ended, another battalion combat team of nearly 1,900 troops with supporting engineer, armor, and helicopter elements began debarkation in Phuoc Tuy Province. With this increase, Australian strength in Vietnam approximated 7,500 personnel.

The tactical value of the Australian force was repeatedly demonstrated in operations which produced heavy enemy casualties and the capture of large quantities of Communist weapons. The activities of the Special Air Service Squadron were particularly noteworthy and significantly contributed to the successful operations of the task force. This highly-trained reconnaissance group provided continuous surveillance throughout the area of operations, detected the enemy, and permitted the infantry battalions to concentrate rapidly on forces moving through the zone or established base areas. As prisoner-of-war interrogations revealed, the ubiquitous and secretive operations of the squadron enervated the enemy and greatly reduced his initiative. The advisory efforts of the Australians were also commendable. They provided skilled and sensitive advisors to the sectors and subsectors of the province as well as reorganizing and training Vietnamese Regional and Popular Forces throughout the area.

Australia's support of the Vietnamese war effort was not solely confined to military operations in the field. As early as July 1964, a 12-man engineer civic action team arrived to assist in local development projects. In April 1967 two civilian surgical teams began ministering to the needs of the Phuoc Tuy population and initiated an extensive program of home nursing classes. From these modest beginnings, Australia provided an increasingly wide range of aid to Vietnam under the Colombo Plan and by direct bilateral negotiations. Economic and technical assistance has totaled more than $10.5 million since 1966, and includes the provision of water and road construction technicians, experts in dairy and crop practices, and the training of 130 Vietnamese in Australian vocational and technical schools. In the field of refugee resettlement, Australia has provided over 1¼ million textbooks, thousands of sets of handtools, and over 3,000 tons of construction materials for resettlement villages. Recognizing the necessity and importance of an adequate communications system to disseminate government policy to the people, Australian technicians constructed a 50-kilowatt broadcasting station at Ban Me Thuot and distributed over 400 radio receivers to civilian communities in the transmission area.

Republic of Korea

Next to the United States, the nation supplying the greatest amount of assistance to the Republic of Vietnam has been the Republic of Korea. This is particularly significant considering the potentially explosive security situation existing along the Republic's borders with the Communist regime of North Korea. It is also indicative of the concern the Republic of Korea has manifested for the freedom, progress, and liberty of its Asian contemporaries.

Reacting to President Johnson's call for "more flags" in the Vietnamese struggle, Korea dispatched a 130-man mobile surgical hospital and a small group of karate instructors in August of 1964. The surgical hospital was employed to meet the burgeoning medical needs of the civilian population while the karate instructors were used in training Vietnamese Army personnel in close-combat techniques. The favorable impression created by the Korean contingent resulted in a second Vietnamese government request for additional noncombatant forces to assist in projected civic action and training programs. Korea responded in March of 1965 by furnishing an army engineer battalion with associated support and self-defense troops. The "Dove Unit," aptly titled in consideration of its peaceful mission, was based in Bien Hoa Province and systematically initiated a series of comprehensive local improvement programs oriented toward public health, sanitation, rural development, and transportation improvement. The Koreans proved themselves adept in establishing a rapport with the local population by stressing the kinship of aspirations and the "brotherhood" of the Asiatic peoples.

As the military situation in Vietnam became more grave, the Korean government approved a proposal to send major combat forces to the Republic of Vietnam. As a result of this decision, elements of the two-regiment Capital Infantry (Tiger) Division and the Marine (Dragon) Brigade landed in October 1965 and were assigned the mission of providing security for the Cam Ranh Bay and Qui Nhon areas. While units of the infantry division remained in the vicinity of Qui Nhon, the Dragon Brigade assumed the role of a mobile "trouble shooter" and displaced from Cam Ranh Bay to Tuy Hoa, then to a zone south of Chu Lai, and finally to the Da Nang area in Quang Nam Province.

In response to a further request, the Republic of Korea sent the 9th (White Horse) Division and a regimental combat team to round out the Capital Division during the April–September 1966 period. With the influx of these troops, approximately 45,600 Korean soldiers had become actively engaged in combat operations against the Communist enemy. Upon its arrival, the White Horse Division assumed responsibility for security missions in the coastal area extending from Phan Rang to Tuy Hoa. Eventually the two divisions linked their sectors and the Koreans, in coordination with Vietnamese and U.S. forces, provided security for the greater part of the coastal area of the II Corps zone, which included several key logistic ports and a critical portion of Highway 1. Within the area assigned to the Korean forces, the enemy has been progressively destroyed—not only combat units but political and subversive infrastructure as well.

From the time of their entry into the country, the Korean units showed themselves to be highly professional, tactically skilled, and dangerous adversaries. Indicative of their proficiency was the MAENG HO 6 campaign of September-November 1966, in which the Koreans decimated two major Communist units and killed nearly 1,200 of the enemy. Korean forces have conducted a number of the most imaginative and skillful operations of the war. They are masters at the patient collection of intelligence and the violent and effective exploitation of that intelligence once they have it in hand.

During the summer of 1967 Korea furnished another 2,962 combat troops. A Marine battalion was provided to reinforce the Dragon Brigade and additional service personnel arrived to support the expanded Korean force. The Korean Marines celebrated the arrival of their brother battalion in Operation DRAGON FIRE (September-October 1967) by disposing of nearly 600 of the enemy who had persisted in their operations in the Quang Ngai area.

Although Korean military forces work closely and in a spirit of mutual cooperation with U.S. and Vietnamese units, they are a separate tactical entity and not under U.S. operational control. Under the provisions of a working military arrangement between U.S., Korean, and Vietnamese commanders, it was agreed that the Korean Task Force would function within the operational and policy parameters established by what later came to be known as the Free World Military Assistance Council. This Council was composed of the Commander, U.S. Military Assistance Command Vietnam (COMUSMACV), the Commander of Korean Forces in Vietnam, and the Chief of the Vietnamese Joint General Staff serving as the Council Chairman. Through the efforts of the council, operational or policy problems regarding the participants were minimized and combined operations were proven both feasible and successful.

While the financial and materiel assistance provided by Korea to Vietnam was necessarily limited, the Koreans initiated comprehensive and imaginative civic action programs among the populations within their areas of operation. Since a sizeable percentage of the Korean troops had agricultural backgrounds, a natural kinship existed with the rural inhabitants of Vietnam and improvements in farming techniques and village accommodations resulted. Korean military units tended to identify themselves with specific hamlets or areas and concentrated their talents and resources on these specific targets. As a result, a continuity of programs and progress was established. In addition to military medical assistance, seven Korean civilian medical teams, comprised of 118 doctors, nurses, and technicians, donated their services toward instituting several provincial health programs. As with the military effort, this overture was well received by the civilian population.

Thailand

Historically, Thailand had pursued a course of neutrality and nonintervention in the affairs of its neighbors. Consequently, Thailand's welcome decision to participate actively in the defense of Vietnam represented a departure from its ancient and traditional philosophy of nonalignment. The fact that this departure was taken in the face of Chinese Communist threats of reprisal and indications of an incipient insurgency in its own northeastern provinces commends the courage and resolve of the Thai nation.

Thailand's first contribution to the Vietnamese war effort was made in late 1964, when a 13-man Royal Thai Air Force training contingent was sent to Vietnam to assist in flying and maintaining some of the cargo aircraft possessed by the Vietnamese Air Force. As an adjunct to this program, the

Royal Thai Air Force also provided jet aircraft transition training to approximately 24 Vietnamese pilots.

In mid-1966 Thai concern over the course of the war resulted in the decision to provide the Republic of Vietnam with several cargo and patrol boats plus a 200-man Royal Thai Navy support and training detachment. Concurrently, the aviation detachment was expanded to a strength of 31.

Motivated by the fact that Thailand could well become the next target of the Communists if Vietnam should fall, the Thai government announced the decision to send combat units to that nation. On the date of the announcement (30 December 1966), over 5,000 civilians in Bangkok volunteered for duty with the expeditionary force. The first element of the Royal Thai Volunteer Regiment, the "Queen's Cobras," arrived in Saigon on 15 July 1967. This force soon reached a strength of 2,207 with its augmentation of engineer, cavalry, and support elements. Following an orientation period with the U.S. 9th Infantry Division, the Thai regiment was assigned a security mission on the eastern approaches to Saigon.

Upon the completion of a series of small unilateral and larger combined operations with Vietnamese units, the Thai regiment launched its first large-scale separate operation (NARASUAN) in October of 1967. The efforts of the Thai forces greatly assisted the pacification of the Nhon Trach District of Bien Hoa Province and resulted in 145 enemy killed. As combat soldiers, the Thai were found to be resourceful and determined individuals who took great pride in their professionalism.

It was announced in late 1967 that the Thai government would increase the size of its contingent in Vietnam to that of a division of two brigades with a total strength of over 11,000 men. The remainder of the volunteer "Black Panther" Division was scheduled to join these forces in January 1969.

The Thai units have been especially active in civic action projects within their areas of responsibility. Their ability to engage in an effective people-to-people program has made them close and participating members of the local Vietnamese communities. A typical example of their efforts was demonstrated during the NARASUAN operation during which time a hospital was built for the local populace, 48 kilometers of new roads were constructed, and nearly 49,000 civilian patients were treated by Thai medical units. In both military and nonmilitary operations, Thailand's support of the Vietnamese war has been of outstanding value.

New Zealand

New Zealand first contributed assistance on 20 July 1964, in the form of a military engineer platoon and surgical team for use in local civic action projects. These teams were replaced in 1965 by a 105-mm howitzer battery whose primary mission was support of the Australian Task Force in Phuoc Tuy Province. The battery was increased from four to six howitzers in mid-1966 to provide additional fire support. In December 1967 an infantry company reinforced by an engineer detachment and support personnel were added to the New Zealand contingent, bringing the total commitment to approximately 517 men. As the battery and its security element are primarily in support of the Australian Task Force, the tactical successes of the Australian Task Force are equally the successes of the New Zealand elements.

New Zealand financial aid commenced in 1966, and has averaged approximately $350,000 (U.S.) annually. This sum has financed several mobile health teams to support refugee camps, the training of village vocational experts, and the establishment of a 15-man surgical team in the Qui Nhon/Bong Son area. Other appropriated support has funded the cost of medical and instructional material for Hue University and the expansion of Saigon University. During 1967–68 nearly $500,000 (U.S.) of private civilian funds were donated for Vietnamese student scholarships in New Zealand and increased medical/refugee aid.

Republic of the Philippines

The Republic of the Philippines initially provided three medical teams and 18 civic action/psychological operations advisors to the Vietnamese effort in August 1964. By the end of 1965 this element had been expanded to a total of 72 individuals and included a public health detachment. Although small in numbers, it was estimated that this organization treated nearly 100,000 patients during its existence and that over 16,000 of these cases required some form of surgical care.

In August 1966 a 2,000-man Philippine Civic Action Group (PHILCAG) was sent to assist the Vietnamese authorities in Tay Ninh Province with small teams in several other provinces. The PHILCAG was a self-contained organization consisting of an Army engineer battalion, rural health and civic action teams, a station hospital, and a security group of infantry, armor, and artillery detachments. U.S. troops provided area security until Philippine security forces became fully operational and thereafter worked in close cooperation with them.

During the past two years (1967–1968) the civic action group has cleared a large section of the Thanh Dien forest, long an enemy stronghold, and has constructed a resettlement village for 1,000 families. It has also undertaken substantial road repair projects, renovated schools and dispensaries, constructed playgrounds, and provided extensive medical assistance and training to the population. The Philippine contribution has been appreciated and respected by all who have come in contact with it.

Other Nations

It would be impractical to cover in detail the multitude of nonmilitary contributions made to the Vietnamese conflict by other nations of the Free World. This is not to imply that these contributions were not important, but rather to indicate the necessity of limiting comments regarding support or participation to those nations most directly involved in the war.

Republic of China—Since 1966, the Republic of China has provided an 80-man agricultural team, an 18-man military psychological warfare team, and a 9-man electric power mission to supervise construction and operations of the 33,000 KW power plant located at Thu Duc. In 1967 the team of electric power advisors was expanded to 34, and a 16-man surgical group was introduced into the country to assist in expanding public health programs.

China has also arranged technical training for more than 200 Vietnamese in Taiwan. In the way of goods and materials, they have provided aluminum prefabricated warehouses, agricultural tools, seeds, fertilizers, 500,000 copies of mathematics textbooks, and over 5,000 tons of rice.

Japan—Japan has provided over $55 million worth of economic assistance to Vietnam since 1966. Principal aid in the 1967–1968 period included scholarships for students, the construction of a neurological surgery ward in Saigon, and the provision of 25 ambulances to the Vietnamese government. Of particular importance to the future economy of the nation has been the provision of technical personnel and funds for the construction of a large power dam across the Da Nhim River and the creation of an electric power distribution system to support this project.

Germany—German economic and humanitarian aid has averaged about $7.5 million annually since 1966, and more than 200 German nationals are now serving in Vietnam. In 1966 the Federal Republic of Germany also contributed the $2 million hospital ship *Helgoland* to provide medical assistance to the civilian population. The ship was initially stationed near Saigon where more than 21,000 out-patient treatments were given to approximately 6,700 patients from September 1966 until 30 June 1967. Over 850 major surgical cases were also treated. In October of 1967 the *Helgoland* shifted its operations to Da Nang. To date, it has remained in this location.

In March 1967 the German government's Maltese Aid Service team for the care of refugees was increased from its 1966 level of 25 people to 47, consisting of six doctors, two dentists, and 39 nurses and vocational teachers. Operating from subbases in An Hoa, Da Nang, and Hoi An, the teams have dispensed regular health and refugee care. The dedication of the Maltese Service personnel has won universal recognition and appreciation from the civilian populace, the Vietnamese authorities, and members of the Free World military effort.

German teachers are supporting the new Technical High School at Thu Duc as well as serving on the faculty of Hue University. Other assistance has included the construction and staffing of nine social centers in Saigon, the establishment of a training center for Vietnamese social workers, and the operation of an orphanage in Phuoc Hoa. In support of these projects, the Federal Republic has made substantial contributions of medical equipment and pharmaceuticals.

Through the provision of liberal credits, the same government has encouraged the development of a major industrial complex in the An Hoa-Nong Son vicinity.

Malaysia—Since 1964 Malaysia has trained almost 3,000 Vietnamese military and police officers. Groups of 30 to 60 men are regularly sent for training in counterinsurgency techniques with the Malaysian Police Special Constabulary. Malaysia has also provided some counterinsurgency equipment, primarily police and military transport vehicles.

The Netherlands—The Netherlands aid program, which began in 1965, has financed scholarships for Vietnamese doctors, the construction and equipping of three tuberculosis centers, and the renovation and expansion of hospital facilities in Cholon. The Dutch government has also designated $1 million in funds in trust for United Nations projects in Vietnam.

United Kingdom—The United Kingdom has supplied economic aid valued at $2.4 million since 1965. It has provided police advisors, teachers, technical experts, and a 26-member pediatric team to assist in the Saigon area.

While only a few of the larger contributions of the Free World to Vietnam have been cited, it should be recognized that significant funds, materiel, and humanitarian aid from Europe, the Middle East, India, Pakistan, Africa, Canada, and South America have been contributed to ease the war-torn conditions of Vietnam. Taken collectively or singularly, each of these contributions has exercised a helpful impact upon the conduct of the war and has, either directly or indirectly, supported the tactical operations of the Free World's military forces and the nation-building efforts of the Vietnamese government.

The assistance provided by other nations of the Free World to the Republic of Vietnam since 1964, has clearly revealed a sense of common purpose and unity among these nations. It has further served notice to the Communist powers of Asia that the Free World will forcibly and collectively resist the destruction of one of its members by a Communist-inspired or supported insurgency. It has clearly demonstrated that the desire for national identity and independence is stronger than the divisive factors of culture, custom, or ethnic dissimilarity.

Appendix D

PACIFICATION

The Concept

Pacification is the very difficult process of establishing or reestablishing effective local self-government within the political framework of the legitimate central government and its constitution. Putting it the other way around, it aims to reassert lawful governmental control by removing the enemy's underground apparatus. It includes the provision of sustained and credible territorial security and the genuine, voluntary involvement of the people as well as the initiation of self-sustaining and expanding economic and social activity. The economic element of pacification includes the opening of roads and waterways and the maintaining of lines of communication important to economic and military activity.

The objectives of pacification are not so difficult to describe but the attainment of those objectives involves cultural and social forces not so easy to understand and certainly not easy to manage. The aspects of pacification most easy to measure are often not the crucial aspects—and conversely, the less tangible aspects are not easy to perceive, let alone measure.

We concluded early that the provision of sustained territorial security was fundamental to the success of pacification—security from the Viet Cong local armed forces and guerrilla units and the main force VC and North Vietnamese regular armed forces. Territorial security also included the protection of the people within a hamlet from the Viet Cong underground government and terrorist and subversive elements.

Pacification is a two-way street. The South Vietnamese government has to demonstrate its willingness and ability to communicate with the people, assure them of an environment in which they could better their living conditions, and afford them an opportunity to have a voice in their own affairs. The people, in turn, are expected to commit themselves actively to supporting the government and rejecting the Viet Cong insurgency.

To succeed, pacification has to be a genuinely Vietnamese endeavor although supported by United States advice, military support, commodities, and funds. That pacification has succeeded to the degree that it has attests to the growing competence of the South Vietnamese government and also to the sincere devotion to duty and considerable sophistication of the various representatives of the many U.S. governmental agencies serving in Vietnam.

History

After the French departed in 1954, the Diem government approached pacification by establishing Land Development Centers and then *agrovilles*—protected farming communities. The latter were relatively unpopular because they were generally constructed by forced labor and involved relocation from traditional hamlet and village areas. Nevertheless, these efforts did include rather thoughtful economic planning in those areas selected for development.

The *agrovilles* were followed by the Strategic Hamlet program patterned very much after the British experience in Malaya. Unfortunately, the two situations were only superficially similar, and the scheme was destined for failure from the outset. This program intended to protect the populace from the Viet Cong by gathering the people into fortified hamlets. It meant, in most cases, moving farmers away from their ancestral holdings where earlier generations had built their homes, farmed their land, and buried their dead. Since these procedures tended to dislocate traditionally close Vietnamese family ties, the program was not popular among the people, to say the least. Of the 16,000 hamlets planned, 9,000 were built. Additionally, the program was overly ambitious and tried to move too fast without rooting out the VC infrastructure as it progressed. Because of a shortage of security forces, the hamlets were vulnerable to enemy attack and, even more frequently, to infiltration and subversion by the Viet Cong. The program collapsed shortly after the Diem government was overthrown in November 1963.

During the next several months, governmental instability caused security in the countryside to degenerate to the point where the Viet Cong were able to consolidate their holdings in the rural districts and extend their sphere of influence. Nevertheless, in 1964 the government tried to renew the pacification effort with a *Chien Thang* (Victory) National Pacification Plan, which relied on a "spreading oil spot" concept. The idea was to expand slowly and thoroughly from loyal areas by annexing and consolidating adjacent areas and thus spreading slowly outward from a firm base. It was a rather mechanistic concept with no real political content. Although this plan put somewhat greater emphasis on economic assistance than had earlier plans, it treated pacification as an adjunct of military planning and operations.

HOP TAC

By mid-1964 political upheavals and military defeats had thrown the country into a deep crisis. A series of coups and attempted coups caused a steady decline in government effectiveness. Institutions of government formed during the regime of President Diem progressively deteriorated. The gains of the previous eight years were steadily vanishing.

To counter the ominous and growing threat to Saigon itself, I persuaded the Vietnamese high command to participate in a combined effort to plan and execute a major operation which would use the "spreading oil spot" concept to extend government influence outward from the capital of Saigon. In those days we had little to offer but good ideas and moral support but we did all that we could. They called the program HOP TAC, which means cooperation or coordination. Its principal distinction from previous pacification attempts lay in the comprehensive nature and format of the combined planning effort on which it was based, including participation by all the responsible governmental ministries. For the first time, a concept of pacification was hammered out which not only defined more precisely the missions of the military and paramilitary forces but also sought to complement the military/paramilitary functions with the essential civil activities. A full description of HOP TAC is included in my observations in the chapter covering the year 1964. Unfortunately, the government was not strong or effective enough to carry off such a program, and it did not prosper. However, the troop disposition associated with it may well have saved Saigon. The year 1965 was one of great labor which gave forth a very modest result.

Revolutionary Development

Two developments were underway that were to influence the course of events. Certain U.S. civilian agencies took an imaginative lead in these matters. The first was the integration of the various disparate cadre elements into unified 59-man Revolutionary Development Cadre teams operating under the Ministry of Revolutionary Development. Heretofore, there had been the Mobile Administrative Cadre, the Rural Political Cadre, and People's Action Teams, to name a few. The core of the new Revolutionary Development Cadre team was a People's Action Team, which was to undergo a new program of training at the National Cadre Center at Vung Tau. The teams also included subelements to start the rudimentary aspects of political, economic, and social development at the hamlet level. The second change was the application of the HOP TAC concept to the other three corps areas, thereby establishing four National Priority areas in Quang Nam, Binh Dinh, and An Giang Provinces, and the Saigon periphery.

Since we had long realized that security against enemy attacks and acts of terrorism was the first order of business on which all other activities depended, all the members of the Revolutionary Development Cadre team were armed and trained in basic military tactics and techniques. Over half of the 59 men had the mission of providing security for the team and the hamlet to which they were assigned and of organizing and training people's self-defense groups in each hamlet. Another part of the team was charged with setting up a hamlet government, conducting a census, and acting upon the grievances and complaints of the residents as well as motivating the people to support their local non-Viet Cong government. A third part of the team was concerned with economic and social processes such as organizing farmers' associations; developing public works projects; and improving hygiene, sanitation, education, and medical facilities.

The idea was that each Revolutionary Development team would remain in its assigned hamlet for three to six months. We soon found that some could move on more quickly while others needed to stay for a year or more. We were dealing with attitudes—not solely with bridges and schools. Although the Ministry of Revolutionary Development would assist the team, most help was to be provided by the other governmental ministries. Unfortunately, in the early days those ministries were, in most areas, not up to the job.

The Revolutionary Development teams themselves required a measure of sophistication seldom available. Recruited from the local areas to which they would return, many members of the teams had limited education and a limited understanding of the process in which they were involved.

Three other kinds of teams performed duties similar to those of the Revolutionary Development teams. In the highlands, *Truong Son* (the Vietnamese name for the Annamite Mountain Chain) groups composed mainly of members of Montagnard origin conducted a program modified to meet the particular needs of the highland tribal populations. When progress in achieving security outdistanced available Revolutionary Development teams, so-called Civil-Military teams were formed. These teams were first established in Binh Dinh Province in the II Corps and were tailored to meet local needs. They consisted of an armed element from the Popular or Regional Forces, a civic action team, and a propaganda team.

In the I Corps, the U.S. Marines employed Combined Action Platoons, consisting of 15 U.S. Marines and 34 Vietnamese Popular Forces soldiers. The Marines lived with their Popular Forces compatriots in the hamlet or village which they were assigned to secure. While adding considerable fighting strength, the Marines trained their counterparts in military matters and instituted many civic action projects. Providing both combat and logistic support, the Marines did much to establish mutual respect between themselves and the Vietnamese. I encouraged the expansion of this highly successful program, and by the end of June 1968, 82 Combined Action Platoons were functioning in the zone of the I Corps.

The Revolutionary Development effort grew steadily. On 1 January 1967 588 Revolutionary Development Cadre and *Truong Son* teams were operating in the countryside. Including 4,400 trainees, a total of 38,600 Vietnamese were by then engaged in the Revolutionary Development program. By June 1968 the number of teams had increased to 777, and a total of 53,000 Vietnamese including 10,500 trainees, were involved. In addition, there were approximately 90 Civil-Military teams operating.

To further coordination and the integration of activities, the South Vietnamese government established Revolutionary Development councils at district, province, and corps level. The council chairman at each echelon was a member of the next higher level's council. The Minister of Revolutionary Development was the Secretary General of the National Central Council, and his ministry served as the council's executive agency. Other members at the national level included the ministers of the agencies responsible for the various aspects of the many-faceted pacification program. In addition to the representatives of the ministries, councils at the lower levels included the military representatives of the command responsible for providing overall security for the area.

Territorial Security

Although the presence of U.S. and Free World military forces in an area improved security, the primary responsibility of these forces was to find and defeat the enemy's main forces and thereby drive the enemy away from the populated regions. Since the South Vietnamese military forces were better able to identify the enemy guerrillas, local forces, and infrastructure, they assumed the primary responsibility for providing security in the pacification areas. By early 1967 the crucial importance of territorial security was recognized by the Vietnamese as more than 50 regular Vietnamese Army battalions and almost all of the Regional and Popular Forces were committed to this effort.

While operating against the enemy's local and guerrilla forces, the Vietnamese regular battalions were prepared to counter any move into an area by the enemy's main forces. The Regional Forces, generally of company size, also operated against the enemy's local forces and provided security around and between the hamlets of a village. They, in turn, supported and reinforced units of the Popular Forces, usually of platoon size, which were charged with augmenting the security of hamlets and villages, as well as protecting roads, bridges, canals, and other government facilities.

Security within the hamlets was the responsibility of the Revolutionary Development Cadre teams and Popular Forces or in some cases people's self-defense forces. In addition, the National Police operated against the Viet Cong infrastructure with support from all the military and civil intelligence agencies. The National Police also were responsible for normal law and order functions.

The main internal security problem in all Revolutionary Development areas was the Viet Cong infrastructure or underground organization. Only by ferreting out the members of these groups was there hope for lasting success in pacification. One purpose of the census taken by the Revolutionary Development Cadre teams was to identify the people of the hamlet so that strangers could be readily recognized. These teams also assisted in identifying the members of the underground so that the National Police Field Forces and the National Police Special Branch could apprehend or eliminate them. Provincial Reconnaissance Units, a paramilitary group normally under the control of the Province Chief, assisted in this process with unusual success.

Ultimate success of the pacification program thus hinged upon the manner in which the various Vietnamese military and paramilitary organizations performed their duties. For that reason we devoted much of our advisory effort to increasing the effectiveness of the territorial security forces.

U.S. Support

Prior to November 1966 our efforts to support the South Vietnamese pacification program were directed by the Embassy under the guidance of the Ambassador. The civilian effort included the Agency for International Development (AID), then called the United States Operations Mission, the Joint United States Public Affairs Office, and the Office of the Special Assistant. Within its particular sphere of influence, each agency was autonomous and dealt directly with its Washington headquarters. MACV formed a Revolutionary Development Division to coordinate the military support aspects of pacification.

In November 1966 the efforts of the civilian agencies were consolidated in the Office of Civil Operations with Mr. Lathram as its director. Although these changes went a long way toward consolidating all aspects of U.S. support of the pacification program, a division of responsibility still existed between the Office of Civil Operations and MACV.

Because the civilian and military efforts were closely interwoven at province and district levels where MACV personnel were predominant and because the forward momentum of pacification depended initially upon military security, the very high level conferees at Guam in March 1967 decided to integrate the two U.S. support efforts under MACV. This was a major change destined to have a sharp and lasting effect on the pacification program. On 11 May 1967, shortly after his arrival in South Vietnam, Ambassador Bunker announced that MACV would assume responsibility for the management and coordination of pacification support. Although separate U.S. civilian agencies continued to deal with their Vietnamese functional equivalents at the national level in Saigon, pacification support and direction now ran to the field agencies and commands through MACV channels. All aspects of the advisory effort below the national level came under my supervision and operational control. This decision was entirely appropriate considering the nature of the conflict. It required the integrating of some 1,200 civilian advisors throughout the already existing military advisory structure. By June 1968 approximately 1,600 U.S. civilians and 6,000 U.S. military personnel were engaged primarily in support of the pacification program.

On 28 May 1967 Mr. Komer was assigned as my deputy for Civil Operations and Revolutionary Development Support (CORDS) with the personal rank of Ambassador. To perform the complex pacification support tasks at the staff level, we formed a single agency under an Assistant Chief of Staff for Civil Operations and Revolutionary Development Support (CORDS). This staff agency absorbed the MACV Revolutionary Development Support Directorate and assumed responsibility for the field functions of the Office of Civil Operations, including Refugee, *Chieu Hoi*, Psychological Operations, Revolutionary Development Cadre, New Life Development, and Public Safety Programs.

To provide unity of effort at all levels, we established a similar organizational structure in the U.S. advisory headquarters at corps level. Although the principal advisor to the Vietnamese commander was the senior U.S. commander in the area, a civilian deputy for CORDS with a separate staff was provided to assist him. At the all-important province level, we fused a hitherto dual effort into one organization. At this level the Province Senior Advisor might be a civilian with a military deputy, or vice versa. Because one of the principal tasks at the district level was improving security, the senior advisors for the districts were for the most part military. Furthermore, the civilian agencies of government were unable to find persons of adequate talent willing to take on these jobs in Vietnam.

At each level, our advisors worked daily with their counterparts on matters concerning psychological operations, public safety (National Police), refugees, Revolutionary Development Cadre, the *Chieu Hoi* program, education, agriculture, public health, public works, the attack on the Viet Cong underground, and the Regional and Popular Forces. Technical guidance for essentially nonmilitary problems came from other U.S. governmental agencies, but since all issues had some impact on the pacification effort, extremely close political-military coordination was essential. The CORDS organization furnished the forum and the machinery.

We were particularly concerned that South Vietnamese troops establish proper rapport with the people. Therefore, we undertook special training intended to inculcate suitable standards of public conduct in units assigned to support pacification. Above all, they had to learn to respect the rights and property of civilians.

Training all units to the necessary standard was a time-consuming task. This was particularly true when the dramatic increase in military support to Revolutionary Development occurred in 1967— regular force battalions supporting pacification increased from 14 in 1966 to 55 in 1967, and about 200 Regional Force companies and 568 Popular Force platoons were added to the effort in 1967.

The most rapid solution to this training problem was the use of mobile training teams. With Vietnamese agreement I proposed the formation of highly skilled and motivated Vietnamese mobile training teams aided by U.S. advisors to give to all Vietnamese Army battalions a concentrated two-week course of instruction. Progress was slow. We later adopted a modified version of this program, a predominantly U.S. Mobile Advisory Team, in order to extend this training to the Regional and Popular Forces.

Improved training of the military met only one portion of the total problem. We also needed an effective effort to induce the Viet Cong to return to the government side. This was the purpose of the *Chieu Hoi* program which began in 1963. The program produced an encouraging number of ralliers at first, but faltered as government control waned in 1964. It revived in 1965 with the arrival of U.S. and Free World forces. During that year, 11,000 VC rallied to the side of the government. In 1966 just over 20,000 returned, and in 1967, over 27,000 although that number fell far short of the ambitious goal of 40,000.

Two of the more unusual ways in which the returnees (*Hoi Chanh*) were used against their former compatriots were as members of the Armed Propaganda Teams and as "Kit Carson scouts." In the first instance, ralliers were formed into teams which returned to their old operational areas to try to convince others to rally or in some cases to capture important members of the Viet Cong. As "Kit Carson scouts," ralliers led U.S. units to enemy caches, camps, and routes of communication.

The attack on the Viet Cong infrastructure or underground government was one of the highest priority items in pacification. Accordingly we assisted the government to develop the first coordinated effort on a nationwide basis to attack the basic source of enemy strength, his subversive organization. This effort was called the PHOENIX program. The primary responsibility to identify and eliminate the VC infrastructure rested with the Vietnamese police agencies at province and district level. To assist the police, Provincial and District Intelligence and Operations Coordinating Centers were organized. Usually composed of representatives of the National Police Special Branch, Revolutionary Development Cadre, Census Grievance Teams, Vietnamese Army, Regional and Popular Forces, as well as special reconnaissance and intelligence agencies, these centers gathered and evaluated intelligence on the enemy organization and personalities. Each center had a U.S. advisor as a PHOENIX officer. In June 1968 President Thieu lent his full support to PHOENIX by ordering a complete integration of Vietnamese police and military interests and resources in a priority effort to destroy the infrastructure.

Another priority effort was aimed at improving and maintaining roads and highways in order to facilitate the free flow of consumer products. To this end, we assumed the obligation to construct and maintain the highways in support of the Vietnamese Ministry of Public Works.

The Tet Offensive—A Temporary Setback

The enemy's *Tet* offensive in January and February 1968 had an adverse impact on pacification. Using the computerized Hamlet Evaluation System which we had developed in 1966, we found that the percent of population under Viet Cong control had risen from 16 percent to a little more than 18 percent after *Tet*. By the end of June 1968 that percentage had dropped to about 17 percent. Similarly, the percentage of population classified as relatively secure was about 67 percent before *Tet* and by the end of February had fallen to just under 60 percent. At the end of June it was up to slightly more than 63 percent and continuing to rise. Certainly by the end of the year our loss at *Tet* would be at least overcome.

The national government appeared at first to be in a state of shock from the *Tet* attacks and was slow to respond to such immediately critical needs as refugee relief and food distribution. Four days after the first attacks, the government responded enthusiastically to our offer of assistance and formed a Central Recovery Committee under the direction of Vice President Ky. With U.S. advice and assistance, this committee organized programs to alleviate civilian suffering, which was especially critical in Hue and Saigon. They provided for countrywide emergency assistance to the growing number of refugees, distributed food supplies, and supplied building material for priority reconstruction.

When the Viet Cong launched another series of attacks in Saigon in the first week of May, thousands of additional refugees were added to the still unsettled refugees from *Tet*. To meet this crisis, I consulted with General Vien and we launched Operation DONG TAM (United Hearts and Minds) to relieve the pitiable conditions of the thousands of refugees in and around Saigon. We employed engineer and medical resources of the U.S. and Vietnamese Armies and the U.S. Navy and Air Force. On 20 May the engineers began clearing rubble, restoring utilities, and erecting almost 1,500 family housing units from prefabricated materials, and providing assistance to civilians who wanted to rebuild their own homes. U.S. and ARVN psychological operations resources were used to explain this project to the people. Vietnamese government officials and the affected population were enthusiastic. One of the most heartening aspects to emerge was tangible evidence of a shift in the attitude of the South Vietnamese Army from complacency to concern about the needs of the civilian population.

As a result of the *Tet* offensive, our plans for pacification had to be restudied and revised. Our progress in 1967 caused us to expand the National Priority Areas to encompass 26 provinces in 1968. When the Vietnamese drew their military forces back to the population centers after *Tet*, we altered our plans to concentrate our pacification resources and managerial skill to address the most pressing problem—restoration of government control in the largest population centers. We crossed administrative boundaries and concentrated on the geographical areas which appeared to afford greatest expectation of success.

The *Tet* offensive pointed up the inadequacy of the basic weapons of the Vietnamese territorial security forces in comparison with the automatic weapons supplied to the enemy by his Communist allies. We instituted intensive efforts to replace the slow-firing pistols, carbines, and rifles of the territorial forces with the rapid firing American carbines and M16 rifles.

Despite the damage dealt to pacification by the *Tet* offensive, several promising developments had emerged. South Vietnamese military and paramilitary units had for the most part fought well, and in some cases exceptionally. The government showed signs of recognizing its obligation to the people, and the people responded with gratitude. Hopefully, pacification had at last come of age.

Appendix E

PSYCHOLOGICAL OPERATIONS/CIVIC ACTION

The psychological operations program is the least understood, the most difficult to explain, and surely the hardest to measure of any of our efforts in Vietnam. Progressively, over a long period of time American civilian and military advisors have worked with the Vietnamese government and Armed Forces to improve and expand their informational programs. There are a number of aspects which are interrelated but lend themselves somewhat to individual treatment.

Perhaps the most important part of the program has been the effort to explain to the Vietnamese people what the war is all about, the issues which underlie it, and what the government and its allies are trying to do about it. This part of the program has involved every conceivable method of communicating with the people from radio and television to newspapers, leaflets, posters, banners, and face-to-face discussion. For example, the government of Vietnam operates 14 radio transmitters as a part of this program and an extensive country-wide TV network. The primary responsibility for this part of the program fell to the Vietnamese Ministry of Information supported and advised by U.S. Information Agency (USIA) representatives working both in Saigon and throughout the country.

The second major element in the program had to do with the enemy. Again through leaflets and radio broadcasts and through ground and airborne loudspeakers, the armed forces endeavored to lower the effectiveness and morale of enemy troops and political cadre and induce them to rally to the government side.

The third element involved a similar effort targeted against the government, the people, and the military forces of North Vietnam. This involved primarily radio broadcasts and the dropping of leaflets.

This description of the program in terms of the objectives and the mechanics, of course, does not address its most important aspect. It is not how many broadcasts are made or how many leaflets are dropped but rather how skillfully composed and effective are the messages which are thus transmitted. For each different audience in each different location and on each different occasion the message must be persuasive, credible, and couched in terms to which the recipient is most apt to be susceptible. In order to coordinate the effort and provide consistence and purpose, the Joint U.S. Public Affairs Office was established with my strong support in 1965 under Mr. Barry Zorthian of USIA. The overall policy and general thrust of the program emanated from his office. The execution was assigned both to military forces and to civilian agencies.

I considered the psychological effort so important that I provided extensive support to Mr. Zorthian in the form of military personnel, units, and facilities. The armed Services, particularly the Army, also furnished over 120 specially trained officers to work with USIA and the Vietnamese Information Service at province and district level.

On the tactical side, psychological warfare units were organized and provided with special equipment for broadcasts of all kinds and for the printing and distribution of leaflets. The U.S. Army has a Psychological Operations Group of four battalions with one battalion operating in each corps area. The Air Force has two special operations squadrons devoted exclusively to the PSYOP mission. Most of the design and printing was done by Army units while Air Force aircraft and Navy Riverine units handled the distribution or airdrop. For example, in 1967 over 600 million leaflets were dropped over North Vietnam and almost 6 billion leaflets were dropped in South Vietnam, utilizing 35,000 sorties by all kinds of aircraft.

One of the major efforts by the government of Vietnam involved the *Chieu Hoi* program. This program endeavored to induce the enemy to defect from his unit or his post and rally to the side of the government. Surrender and *Chieu Hoi* leaflets were distributed by the millions. We found that almost every prisoner or rallier had concealed somewhere upon his person one of these leaflets. Since 1964, over 64,000 of the enemy have rallied to the government side under this program. Many of the ralliers have volunteered to serve in one of 45 Armed Propaganda Companies which conduct psychological operations in contested or VC areas by speaking directly to the people.

As I mentioned at the beginning, the psychological operations program is difficult to evaluate or measure. This is because no single effect can be attributed solely to the psychological operations program. For example, *Chieu Hoi* ralliers are inclined to increase in number as military pressures increase or as enemy fortunes ebb, thus the leaflet and broadcast program is simply one contributing cause. Secondly, it is necessary to conduct extensive and expensive attitudinal surveys both to measure effectiveness of the program and to adjust and improve the content of the messages and themes which are used. More work and further study will be required before we can be definitive in measuring effectiveness. I believe very strongly that it is an essential weapon which, when used together with all other measures, contributes greatly to the attainment of objectives in a politically sophisticated war such as that in South Vietnam. I commend those who have contributed so much time, energy, and imagination to it. They have played an important and largely unsung role in Vietnam for many years.

Unlike the psychological effort, the civic action program is not difficult to describe because it is tangible—it is easy to see. Historically, wherever the U.S. has had military forces, there has always been some form of military assistance to civilians who are without the means of helping themselves. Civic action was present in Vietnam in various degrees even before the major U.S. military commitment in 1965. For example, one of the major civic action programs in 1964 involved providing Vietnamese hamlets with a source of potable water. We introduced U.S. Navy (Seabee) teams as well as U.S. Army engineer detachments to exploit their technical skills in hydrojet well drilling.

The 1965 buildup of U.S. forces required rapid expansion of civic action to help soften the psychological impact of U.S. military presence on the Vietnamese people. I undertook several measures to initiate and maintain good relations between the Vietnamese people and all foreign troops and at the same time to help offset Viet Cong efforts to exploit isolated incidents involving U.S. forces and Vietnamese.

First, we made civic action an integral part of military unit operations. I required that all operational plans state our civic action policy clearly and earmark specific actions that would be undertaken. These plans emphasized our efforts to support and help the people caught in the path of military operations. The fulfillment of the plans clearly demonstrated to the people that we were interested in their welfare—and that we did not wish to ignore their sufferings.

Next, I required all U.S. units arriving in Vietnam to develop civic action plans for assisting the people living in the vicinity of their base areas. The special skills and equipment common to any unit, particularly those of an engineering or medical nature, were utilized to reduce hardship among and raise the living standards of the neighboring people. Our troops constructed long-needed bridges over canals and streams, built schools, established medical dispensaries, and generally improved public sanitation.

We instructed U.S. troops on arrival in Vietnam that if we were to help in reducing the influence of the Viet Cong, we had to win and maintain the friendship and active cooperation of the Vietnamese civilians. My commanders emphasized that good civilian-military relationships were dependent on two factors: (1) the military man's attitude in his dealings with the local civilians, and (2) the accomplishment of carefully planned civic actions. I soon was gratified to learn that our troops still had a missionary's heart as well as a soldier's fighting spirit.

In 1965, at my request, Ambassador Lodge asked the assistance of the government of Vietnam in organizing a Community Relations Committee in each of the major Vietnamese cities. These committees, which included not only U.S., Free World, and Vietnamese military representatives but Vietnamese civic and business leaders and government officials as well, were primarily concerned with maintaining civilian discipline, preventing incidents between soldiers and civilians, solving disputes amicably, receiving and resettling refugees, and, in general, bettering military-civilian relationships.

To alleviate some of the hardships caused by military actions, the Vietnamese Civic Action Program for 1965 included a provision for modestly assisting noncombatants in cases of death of close relatives, injuries, and loss of or damage to property as the result of operations undertaken by the Vietnamese Armed Forces. By August of the same year, a similar program covering U.S. and Free World forces was underway. In witnessing our concern for losses, the Vietnamese civilian also might realize that our forces were lawful, just, and respectful of the civilian community.

A very real part of civic action was a continuing and concerted effort by allied forces to avoid civilian casualties. Many of the rules of engagement under which our troops operated were aimed at lessening the possibility of civilian losses. MACV early issued a directive specifying ways and means for "Minimization of Casualties," which included specification for close coordination of military operations with local Vietnamese officials. We constantly updated the directive. Even though reports indicated that civilian losses ran well behind those experienced in World Wars I and II and Korea, I continued to emphasize the efforts to keep losses at a minimum.

As the presence of American forces increased in 1966, so did our civic action program. During the first five months of the year, for example, U.S. military units built or repaired 78 schools, 43 bridges, 246 miles of rural roads, and 29 dispensaries, as well as numerous dwellings and community facilities. This modest effort represented only a fraction of our total program, because our many advisory teams throughout the countryside in every province routinely arranged for assistance as an integral part of their daily duties.

Because U.S. forces were automatically involved in all aspects of the civic action program, they distributed the bulk of the International Voluntary Agency supplies brought into South Vietnam. In the first five months of 1966, for example, U.S. forces distributed 12,860 tons of food, clothing, and medical supplies of the Catholic Relief Services, and about $760,000 worth of CARE commodities.

Perhaps none of the programs had a more immediate and dramatic effect than the medical civic action program, under which both U.S. and Vietnamese military medical personnel treated local civilians as a part of their normal duties. In addition to the obvious humanitarian benefits of such a program, the Vietnamese teams especially were able to present a positive and helpful image of the government of Vietnam to the rural people. In emergencies, Vietnamese civilians were treated in U.S. military hospitals. With this in mind, MACV directed construction of three hospitals in excess of anticipated U.S. military need in order that hospitals throughout the country might treat civilian war casualties. (A more detailed discussion of this activity is contained in Appendix H.)

By 1967 every U.S. unit and base camp in Vietnam had formulated civic action plans which in turn had the blessing of a provincial-level committee. Each such committee, being aware of the implementing programs to enhance Revolutionary Development throughout the countryside, could insure that civic action was an essential ingredient in the overall Revolutionary Development program.

In early 1968 the enemy's *Tet* offensive tested the established civic action mechanism severely. The attacks throughout the country caused major damage to civilian property, cut lines of communications, and strained surviving transportation facilities. At the time when the need for civic action was the greatest, resources were seriously limited. To meet the challenge, the government of Vietnam, with U.S. advice and assistance, formed the Central Recovery Committee which resulted in a prompt government-coordinated emergency program to provide food, clothing, temporary shelter, and building supplies to tens of thousands of *Tet* refugees.

When the Communists again attacked and generated more refugees in May 1968, the civic action program was again put to test. In Saigon, recovering from the effects of the earlier *Tet* offensive, thousands of refugees were added to those occupying temporary camps in the city. In a joint endeavor (Operation DONG TAM), the Vietnamese and U.S. military engineers pooled their resources to assist the people in clearing rubble, restoring utilities, and building prefabricated family housing units. Medical teams attended the people and psychological operations teams explained the project to them. The Vietnamese officials and people alike enthusiastically responded to this demonstration of concern and willingness to help on the part of combat soldiers.

Appendix F

THE STATE OF THE COMMAND

Before the entry of United States forces into the Republic of Vietnam in strength, some observers questioned whether an American of the 1960's would be able to fight in the alien environment of Southeast Asia, whether he could adjust to the persistent heat, the monsoon rains, swamps and jungles, to an environment where military hardware of the nuclear age could not be fully employed.

The answer is, he can and he has—with distinction. Our fighting men in Vietnam are the toughest, best trained, most dedicated American servicemen in history. They use sophisticated hardware, not from any inherent weakness, but to augment their strength. While the helicopter, for example, provides mobility enabling our forces to strike the enemy, it does nothing to diminish the ability of our men to meet the foe in close combat.

In adapting to conditions in Vietnam, the American fighting man has surprised even some of his most steadfast admirers. He has demonstrated the physical and mental ability to adjust to local conditions; he has shown that he is master of his own swift mobile tactics and firepower; and he has proved that he is a match for the enemy in guerrilla warfare.

The most striking aspect of our troops in Vietnam is their high sense of dedication to our cause. Officers and enlisted men alike are imbued with a well-defined sense of direction, a sense of purpose. Their excellent morale results from knowledge of their jobs, sound military policies, professional unit leadership, and unprecedented materiel support. Their medical care is superb, their food excellent, and their mail carefully and expeditiously handled.

As an individual, the fighting man I commanded is one day a tough, determined professional in battle, and the next, a sensitive, compassionate friend helping the Vietnamese people. He is a fighter, a thinker, and a doer. He has seen at first hand Communist subversion and aggression at work, and he has acquired a deeper appreciation of the importance of freedom.

Before each man arrives in Vietnam, he receives a thorough "Command Information" orientation. Once in the country he is continually apprised of the situation and advised on the part he is playing.

Beginning in 1964 I developed a series of short guidelines or lists designed principally to focus the attention of our troops on the task at hand. Each list was the result of a detailed analysis of the subject, and in each case was printed on a small card that a man could carry in his pocket. The first, "Combat Fundamentals for Advisors," was issued in October 1964, setting forth our basic goal of assisting the Government of the Republic of Vietnam in its fight for freedom and including a checklist of key points to be considered by an advisor in combat. With the influx of major U.S. forces in 1965, I developed "Nine Rules" designed to remind our troops of their purpose in Vietnam and to set the tenor of individual conduct in relation to the Vietnamese. In 1966, the year of our tactical development and learning, I devised a 15-point troop leadership and tactical guide for our commanders. (Copies of these guidelines are included at the end of this appendix.)

A major contributing factor to the high state of morale of the command was the 12-month tour. A limited tour is particularly desirable in Vietnam because of the intensity of combat and the debilitating climate and environment of Southeast Asia. Although rotation every year introduces a degree of turbulence and affects combat effectiveness, the disadvantages are more than offset by the vigor which men conscious of the short length of their tour demonstrate. The wealth of counterinsurgency experience we are amassing as a result of rotation is a bonus.

I was nevertheless concerned about command and staff continuity, particularly because of the effect of rotation on the Revolutionary Development program. In an attempt to ease the problem, I proposed that after an individual occupying a critical position had served six months in Vietnam, we provide inducements to encourage him to extend his tour. We offered several options, the most successful of which was under Public Law 89–735, whereby a man who reenlisted, extended an enlistment, or voluntarily extended a tour in Vietnam for six months received a 30-day leave with free transportation, a leave not charged against his regular leave. As of mid-1968 over 72,000 men had taken advantage of the program. In April 1968 we introduced a reduced extension program whereby men who extended their tour by from 3 to 6 months received a week's rest and recuperation leave outside Vietnam.

Medical care of unprecedented speed and effectiveness has also been important for morale. Because of a rapid battlefield-to-hospital system of medical evacuation called MEDEVAC, lives that would have been lost in other wars are saved. The death rate of wounded is one-half that of Korea and one-quarter that of World War II. Helicopter ambulances and responsive communications are the keys.

The MEDEVAC helicopters are on continuous alert, and in response to a radio call, can reach the scene of battle in minutes. They pick up the wounded virtually at the point where they were hit and move them directly to medical evacuation stations. The hours and even days that wounded soldiers in the past waited for hospital care has been reduced to minutes. Long, rough movement by stretcher and ground ambulance has all but vanished. MEDEVAC flights have averaged less than 30 minutes from the time of call to arrival at a medical facility—a speed that for hundreds has meant the difference between life and death.

In the fledgling days of evacuation by air, helicopters merely provided expeditious means of getting patients to a rear area medical facility. Today, powerful helicopter ambulances called DUST OFF carry up to four litter patients and a crew of four and resemble small mobile dispensaries. Medical personnel aboard can administer intravenous injections of whole blood or dextrose, and officer-pilots who are members of the Medical Service Corps can perform emergency medical treatment when necessary.

Mail—the universal morale booster—is as important in Vietnam as in earlier wars. To obviate the necessity of establishing extensive postal facilities and of handling postage stamps in the humid climate, the President in November 1965 authorized a free-mail privilege for letters and voice tapes from our forces in Vietnam. Later in the year we were able to begin carrying all parcel post by air on a "space available" basis.

The major problem remaining was delay of mail within Vietnam because only irregular transportation resources were available. We solved it by establishing a mail coordinating committee at the MACV level to insure integration of the postal services with transportation units. Letters from home soon were reaching the men in four or five days. Next to essential battlefield supplies, mail received the highest priority of movement to and within Vietnam.

To cope with the deluge of Christmas mail, we made plans during the summer of 1965 to insure that adequate postal personnel and transportation would be available to meet the anticipated volume and insure coordinated movement. We had so developed the system by the Christmas season of 1967, that no backlog of mail accumulated at any facility.

Our fighting men received food of a quality seldom before served under combat conditions. Commanders at all levels continuously stressed this important aspect of the soldier's life. Despite the prevailing tropical climate, we were able to provide a variety of frozen meats, locally procured fresh vegetables, and locally reprocessed dairy products. Meals of these products were served as a matter of routine in our base areas and at field positions that could accommodate unit mess sections or field kitchens. When the tactical situation made it impossible to serve a kitchen-prepared meal, we used the traditional canned C-ration of improved quality and variety.

As in past wars, chaplains contributed immensely to morale. These dedicated men were on the move seven days a week, ministering to the troops and conducting services down to the company level. Frequently traveling by helicopter along with the ammunition and food, the chaplains concentrated on visiting troops at the lowest levels and at the farthest outposts. No unit, however small or remote, was long without a visit from a chaplain, who frequently reinforced his spiritually uplifting visits with mail delivery. By 1968 over 550 chaplains of all three services and almost all denominations were serving in Vietnam. At that time in the war, 9 had been killed and 80 wounded. One had received the Medal of Honor for valor and 18 had received the Silver Star. In base areas and wherever the situation permitted, priority was invariably given to building chapels.

A problem that had long concerned me was the difficulty encountered by the individual fighting man in expressing a grievance or seeking redress of an individual injustice, a problem that tends to be particularly acute in a rapidly changing combat situation. One of the points stressed on the "Guidance for Commanders" card was the importance of commanders at all levels making themselves available to their men. To deal with the problem further, I placed strong emphasis from the first on building a responsive Inspector General system within MACV and each of the component commands. In the case of Army units, this included assigning Inspectors General down to brigade level. My objective was to insure that every man would have ready access to a qualified Inspector General, or an officer especially trained for the role, in order to be able to lodge individual complaints. In response to complaints, the Inspectors General have conducted a multitude of investigations directed toward judicious resolution of legitimate grievances. In addition, these officers conducted numerous inspections as an aid to commanders in preventing or eliminating malpractices. In a separate but related field, our Staff Judge Advocates, who are trained military lawyers, were available throughout Vietnam to provide legal assistance.

To give the men a break from combat and at the same time reduce pressure on the Vietnamese economy, we developed a Rest and Recuperation (R&R) program, providing each man during his tour of duty a week's leave at one of several locations outside Vietnam. We began in 1964 with four rest areas: Tokyo, Manila, Hong Kong, and Bangkok. Six more locations were added later to accommodate our expanding forces: Taipei, Singapore, Penang, Kuala Lumpur, Sydney, and Hawaii. Men on leave travel by chartered jet aircraft and have five full days to rest and relax in a hospitable atmosphere far removed from the scene of battle.

Inclusion of Hawaii in the program in 1966 particularly benefited the married serviceman, since his family often was able to join him there. The major U.S. airlines cooperated by offering reduced fares to wives traveling to meet their husbands, an arrangement later extended to parents. Hotel owners, car rental agencies, and other businesses in Hawaii gave reduced rates to R&R servicemen. Hawaii as a leave center had an additional attraction from an official standpoint since it cut down on the flow of U.S. currency out of the country.

The rejuvenating effect of R&R on the morale and the spirit of our men has been inestimable. The men look forward to it with an eagerness second only to the end of their tour of duty.

To lessen the impact of the massive influx of U.S. and Free World forces with their abundant purchasing power on the economy of Vietnam, and at the same time to reduce the outflow of U.S. dollars, we took measures to reduce troop purchases on the local economy to a minimum. To this end, we greatly expanded our Post and Base Exchange System with emphasis on providing both variety and quality. Our aim was to make available to our men the items they might buy on the local economy.

In base areas we constructed austere recreational facilities, mostly supported by nonappropriated funds, to provide wholesome diversion for our troops during their limited free time. Special Services and allied organizations provided service clubs, theaters, and libraries as well as athletic facilities and equipment. The United Services Organization (USO) established 16 clubs throughout the country. The USO also provided a constant stream of performers and sports personalities to entertain and visit with the men. The entertainment provided by dedicated, patriotic artists such as Bob Hope and Martha Raye, greatly boosted morale. The American Red Cross provided dozens of clubmobiles operated by Red Cross girls. These varied and excellent facilities provided healthy diversion for our men during their limited off-duty hours; and at the same time, by attracting the men away from the towns and cities, reduced the impact of our massive presence on the economic and social structure of Vietnam.

As is always the case in war, the fighting man in direct contact with the enemy rarely has much time to call his own. In Vietnam, this was true of our support, logistical, and headquarters personnel as well. They worked a minimum of 60 hours a week and usually much longer. Since there were no front lines and no rear areas in Vietnam and since the Viet Cong had infiltrated much of the country, service troops were also constantly liable to come under enemy fire.

The Armed Forces Radio Service provided seven-day, 24-hour programming throughout Vietnam. Television was inaugurated in the Saigon area in February 1966, and by October 1967 had expanded to six other locations covering all major base areas. Radio and television provided entertainment and news, the latter designed to keep the men up to date on the latest information about Vietnam, the United States, the world, command policy, and rights and benefits. As a side benefit, our military television project was of valuable assistance to the Vietnamese government in getting this important means of communication established in Vietnam, a development that I had strongly recommended as early as 1964.

In the early days of the war, we encouraged the troops to invest their surplus money in savings bonds, which met with moderate success. In 1966 we introduced the Uniform Services Savings Deposit Program to replace the Soldiers Deposit Program, in which participation had declined because the interest rate had ceased to be competitive. The new program offered an attractive interest rate of 10 percent per annum compounded quarterly and was open to officers as well as enlisted men. By April 1968 some 84,300 men were participating in the program. American banking facilities were also established in Vietnam, where the serviceman could secure his spare money without service charge at five percent interest on deposits in his checking account.

The serviceman in Vietnam also received special pay and allowances. Beginning on 1 September 1965, men on a permanent tour of duty in Vietnam, temporarily in the combat zone for at least six days in any month, or subject to enemy fire were eligible for Special Pay for Duty Subject to Hostile Fire, which amounted to $65 per month. This was an expansion of original hostile fire provisions which were in effect as early as October 1963. Beginning in January 1964, the pay of enlisted men and warrant officers serving in the combat zone was excluded from income tax, while $200 per month of officers' pay was also excluded. On 1 January 1966 the commissioned officers' exclusion was raised to $500 per month. The special pay and allowances of men wounded and evacuated from Vietnam continued during the time they were hospitalized.

To recognize those who performed heroic or meritorious service, MACV established policies and procedures for expeditious submission and processing of recommendations for awards. A decoration often was awarded within 30 days of the act or performance. At the same time we maintained the high standards established for awards.

From the first commitment of U.S. troops in Vietnam, until my departure, 38 Medals of Honor were recommended by me and awarded by the President or his designated representative. Almost 700 of the nation's second highest awards—the Distinguished Service Cross, Navy Cross, and Air Force Cross—have been awarded. The number of Silver Stars approaches 12,000 and many more men have received lesser awards for valor and meritorious service.

Every man who served in the combat area received a Vietnam Service Medal and Ribbon and campaign stars for those campaigns in which he served. Campaigns are as follows:

Vietnam Advisory Campaign	15 Mar 62– 7 Mar 65
Vietnam Defense Campaign	8 Mar 65–24 Dec 65
Vietnam Counteroffensive	25 Dec 65–30 Jun 66
Vietnam Counteroffensive, Phase II	1 Jul 66–31 May 67
Vietnam Counteroffensive, Phase III	1 Jun 67–29 Jan 68
Tet Counteroffensive	30 Jan 68– 1 Apr 68
An as yet unnamed campaign	2 Apr 68–

In recognition of the sacrifices of all U.S. and Free World forces in the common struggle, the government of Vietnam has awarded the Vietnam Campaign Medal and Ribbon to all Allied personnel serving in the country.

As stated in the text of this Appendix, during the course of my four years as COMUSMACV, I issued guidance in card form. The contents of these cards, which were prepared in pocket size, have been reproduced on succeeding pages:

COMBAT FUNDAMENTALS FOR ADVISORS

NINE RULES (STANDARDS OF CONDUCT)

GUIDANCE FOR COMMANDERS IN VIETNAM

COMBAT FUNDAMENTALS FOR ADVISORS

The goal of the United States Government in Vietnam is to assist the Government of the Republic of Vietnam in its fight for freedom. Together we will win the struggle against the Viet Cong.

In the prosecution of the war, American advisors are called upon to appraise the situation and to give sound advice. This advice must be based on an objective analysis grounded on fundamental military knowledge. Attached are combat precepts as they apply to the war in Vietnam, which are commended for your study and use. The effectiveness of your advisory efforts will be in direct proportion to the application of combat fundamentals, knowledge, past experience, and common sense.

Ambush

A favorite tactic of the VC is the ambush. By use of the ambush, the VC seek to offset their overall inferiority in manpower and weaponry through surprise and concentration of force at one location. Recognizing this typical guerrilla maneuver, anti-ambush thinking and planning should become second nature to every U.S. Advisor in Vietnam.

The combat Fundamentals for Advisors which follow in this publication are applicable in general to all military operations—but they should be constantly applied to uncover, thwart, or destroy VC ambushes. For example, a standard VC tactic is to attack a hamlet or small post as "bait," then ambush on the route which government reinforcements must take to relieve or reinforce the hamlet or small post. Since every relief column is a potential target it must take the proper security measures en route and not rush headlong down the road. Where possible, the relief column should move by two or more routes and avoid the most obvious and direct route.

One of the main problems in anti-guerrilla war is to bring the enemy to combat. When he ambushes, he volunteers to fight. Thus, the destruction of the ambush must become a main objective of RVNAF forces—as important—in some cases more important to the overall effect than the relief column itself.

Anticipate ambushes—note potential ambush sites as a result of past experience and map reconnaissance—make detailed fire support plans—use reconnaissance by fire (artillery and small arms) against likely ambush areas—use air cover—adopt ultra-secure formations—take unorthodox approaches and routes—use multiple routes—be close-mouthed and deny VC advance information—be secure in planning troop movements—screen actual movements with ground patrols operating to front and flanks of the main body to discover ambush sites before the main body arrives. Be suspicious—be practical—be professional. Apply the fundamentals and avoid the—AMBUSH.

Mission

1. Is the mission clearly understood by all?
2. Does the plan have flexibility? Is the enemy the objective, particularly after contact has been gained, rather than terrain which was assigned for control purposes?
3. Does the plan have a decisive, attainable objective?
4. Is the selection of the objective based on the means available, the enemy, and a reasonable size area of operations?
5. Is it planned to use all available means? Crew-served weapons, artillery, air, ships and/or boats, armor, airborne?

Offensive

1. Is the commander imposing his will on the enemy rather than reacting to enemy action? Only offensive action can win and prevent the enemy from escaping, reorganizing, and resuming his attack.
2. Is the commander keeping contact and pursuing with all available means—infantry, armor, artillery, heliborne and/or airborne forces, boats and air? If contact is lost, is every effort made to re-establish it through the use of aerial surveillance, extended patrols, Eagle Flights, and aggressive offensive action?
3. Are night operations used extensively to accomplish the mission and to keep the enemy on the defensive?
4. Does the plan block all VC escape routes?
5. Has the commander instilled in his troops a will to win?

Security on the Move

1. Is every possible measure being taken to prevent surprise by the full use of intelligence and counterintelligence? Reconnaissance, searches, patrols, aerial observations, PW's, information from higher and lower units?
2. Does the formation adopted by the commander during approach to contact or on reconnaissance insure the main body against ambush?
3. Does the commander move the unit by bounds when he considers contact imminent?
4. Does the commander have knowledge of the civilians and friendly forces in the area?
5. Is the commander using deception to keep the VC off balance? For example, moving at night and the use of camouflage and concealment?
6. Is there security on moves and halts? Outposts, sentinels, scouts, searches, reconnaissance, and stealth in moving units?
7. What is the reaction of the villagers, are they friendly or have they disappeared?
8. After objectives are taken, is security continuous and is the area searched?

Civic Action

1. Has the commander required his soldiers to treat civilians properly so that the citizens of RVN have a favorable impression of their Army?

2. Have the soldiers been properly briefed on respecting civilian property? Food, crops, dwellings, and animals?

Fire and Maneuver

1. In an offensive situation, does the commander use fire and maneuver to close with and destroy the enemy? (Find, Fix, Fight, Finish.)

2. Are mobility means being used to move RVNAF forces faster than VC? M-113's, helicopters, trucks, airplanes, riverboats?

3. Does the unit establish a base of fire and maneuver at the same time, taking advantage of direct and indirect fire support elements while maneuvering?

4. Has the commander tested his communications with supporting artillery, mortars, armed riverboats, and air to guarantee continuous fire support? Is the small unit commander controlling his fires?

5. Have plans been made for the pursuit and continuation of the attack?

6. Can the scheme of maneuver be changed to suit the situation? For example, when under fire, does the unit take immediate action to flank the enemy?

Command and Control

1. How can the commander best control the operation? From where? What control measures? When will the components of fire support start? What signal or command will be used to start, shift, and stop it? How, when, and where should the attack order be issued?

2. Is there a clear-cut channel of command to promote unity of effort and the decisive application of full combat power?

3. Is there coordination of all forces toward a common goal? Coordination with Province (RF, PF, Rangers), Sector, Division, Air Force, Navy, Marines?

4. Is there a single commander of the operation?

5. Have communications with lower and higher echelons been established and checked to provide control?

6. Does the commander have continuous communications with other maneuver elements? Heliborne forces, armor elements, riverboats, airborne forces?

7. Has the commander made personal visits to follow up his orders? Has he inspected his men and equipment before the operation?

8. Are the plans simple and are the orders clear? Have leaders and troops been briefed?

9. Has the commander checked food, water, medical supplies, medical evacuation, ammunition distribution, and tested essential equipment for the operation?

NINE RULES

For personnel of U.S. Military Assistance Command, Vietnam

The Vietnamese have paid a heavy price in suffering for their long fight against the Communists. We military men are in Vietnam now because their government has asked us to help its soldiers and people in winning their struggle. The Viet Cong will attempt to turn the Vietnamese people against you. You can defeat them at every turn by the strength, understanding, and generosity you display with the people. Here are nine simple rules:

1. Remember we are guests here: We make no demands and seek no special treatment.

2. Join with the people! Understand their life, use phrases from their language, and honor their customs and laws.

3. Treat women with politeness and respect.

4. Make personal friends among the soldiers and common people.

5. Always give the Vietnamese the right of way.

6. Be alert to security and ready to react with your military skill.

7. Don't attract attention by loud, rude or unusual behavior.

8. Avoid separating yourself from the people by a display of wealth or privilege.

9. Above all else, you are members of the U.S. Military Forces on a difficult mission, responsible for all your official and personal actions. Reflect honor upon yourself and the United States of America.

GUIDANCE FOR COMMANDERS IN VIETNAM

1. Make the welfare of your men your primary concern with special attention to mess, mail, and medical care.

2. Give priority emphasis to matters of intelligence, counterintelligence, and timely and accurate reporting.

3. Gear your command for sustained operations: keep constant pressure on the enemy.

4. React rapidly with all force available to opportunities to destroy the enemy; disrupt enemy bases, capturing or destroying his supply caches.

5. Open up methodically and use roads, waterways, and the railroad; be alert and prepared to ambush the ambusher.

6. Harass enemy lines of communication by raids and ambushes.

7. Use your firepower with care and discrimination, particularly in populated areas.

8. Capitalize on psywar opportunities.

9. Assist in "revolutionary development" with emphasis on priority areas and on civic action wherever feasible.

10. Encourage and help Vietnamese military and paramilitary units; involve them in your operations at every opportunity.

11. Be smarter and more skillful than the enemy; stimulate professionalism, alertness, and tactical ingenuity; seize every opportunity to enhance training of men and units.

12. Keep your officers and men well informed, aware of the nine rules for personnel of MACV, and mindful of the techniques of Communist insurgency and the role of Free World forces in Vietnam.

13. Maintain an alert "open door" policy on complaints and a sensitivity to detection and correction of malpractices.

14. Recognize bravery and outstanding work.

15. Inspect frequently units two echelons below your level to insure compliance with the foregoing.

Appendix G

LOGISTICS AND BASE DEVELOPMENT

The 1965 decision to commit major U.S. combat forces in Vietnam required immediate action to provide for a massive logistic buildup; concurrently, it was necessary to provide continued support to the expanding Vietnamese and Free World military effort. At the time of the decision, our logistic support system consisted of an extremely austere organization designed to accommodate the needs of some 20,000 U.S. personnel. The logistician's problem was to create a system, in a largely undeveloped country, while engaged in combat, which would support coalition forces exceeding one million men.

From the beginning, it was decided that the overall policies for joint logistic planning would be determined by MACV while the Service commander would see to the execution. To the extent possible, the logistic buildup and the force buildup would be complementary. The concurrent buildups would proceed apace, neither to the detriment of the other, and available shipping and resources would be allocated to insure retention of this balance.

We decided that support should be conducted on an area basis for all common supply and service activities. This meant, for example, that the Navy would support Army units in locations for which the Navy had been assigned the support mission. However, "Service-peculiar" support would remain the responsibility of the Service concerned.

In practice, the "area" approach provided that the Army would perform common-item support within the II, III, and IV Corps zones, plus any portions of the I Corps zone where major Army forces were deployed. Since U.S. Marine forces constituted the largest tactical grouping in the I Corps zone, the Navy would provide the bulk of support there. In turn, the Air Force would provide support for its airbases as well as the air and ground elements of other services stationed on or near the bases. Support of Vietnamese and Free World units would be accomplished on a basis of convenience and proximity. Although modifications of this initial concept did occur as service troop densities fluctuated in the various zones, the operational principles remained unchanged.

By the end of 1967 our logistic system was providing support to about 1.2 million troops, 500,000 of which were U.S. personnel. A U.S. increment of over 16,000 was devoted to support of Vietnamese and Free World forces. Despite these massive demands, the ratio of support troops to combat troops steadily declined. In 1966 approximately 45 percent of U.S. forces in Vietnam were assigned to the support mission. The percentage declined to 40.3 percent in 1967 and efforts continued to reduce this percentage further in 1968. When compared with the 43 percent ratio experienced in World War II and Korea, this decline represented a remarkable achievement.

The underdeveloped nature of Vietnam greatly increased the logistic burden by requiring the construction of deep-water ports, airfields, storage facilities and the rehabilitation of an entire national roadway system. Because of the nature of the war, tactical units had to be scattered throughout the nation at widespread locations. The lack of sophisticated transportation systems necessitated major units establishing their own logistic bases rather than one central depot serving a number of units. The absence of an established frontline and the insecurity of all areas dictated that large numbers of personnel be included in the support role as security elements. The extensive use of helicopters and other complicated equipment under severe weather and terrain conditions created an unprecedented demand for highly skilled maintenance personnel.

Although the need for a centralized U.S. logistic organization and development of our support facilities in Vietnam was foreseen as early as 1962, resources were not available at the time to accomplish these tasks. In 1964 it was recommended again that a logistical command and an engineer group be introduced into Vietnam promptly. In February 1965 the deployment was approved, but the numbers were limited to 38 logistical planners and 37 operating personnel rather than the 3,800 logistic troops and 2,400 engineers requested. Two months later, coincident with the introduction of U.S. combat troops into Vietnam, the decision was made to authorize a full-strength logistical command. Thus it was that the early days of the buildup were hectic and very much a matter of improvisation and unbelievably hard work by all hands. I could not pass over this period without calling attention to the "can do" attitude and approach taken by the logistical forces and especially by Maj. Gen. John Norton, then commander of U.S. Army Support Command, Vietnam.

The fact that some of the logistic forces needed were not available in the active Army for employment in South Vietnam served further to delay the establishment of a logistic base. While the support organization was being created, it was found that certain automated supply procedures used in the U.S. were incompatible with the situation and requirements existing in Vietnam. The standardized procedures, high-speed communications, and elaborate data processing equipment required to support the U.S. oriented support system were neither present nor available to meet anticipated requirements. This added to the logistic problems and required the development of new techniques and procedures to meet the challenges of the situation.

In order better to appreciate the contributions of the logisticians, the following paragraphs summarize some of their principal problems and accomplishments.

The Environmental Problem

The Mekong Delta in the southernmost portion of Vietnam is best described as a low, flat, and very fertile plain. It is poorly drained and crisscrossed by a network of tributaries and canals. This area is extensively cultivated but contains dense jungles, mangrove swamps, and coniferous forests. All of the high ground is inhabited, and little space was available for the construction and development of logistic bases. The area is served by Route 4 from Saigon, a narrow road elevated just above the paddy lands and easily cut by demolition of culverts and bridges.

The Central Highlands area comprises about two-thirds of the country and is sparsely populated—except in Binh Dinh Province—by seminomadic, unskilled tribesmen. Within the Central Highlands is the High Plateau, an area of fine, lateritic soils characterized by rolling plains 1,000 to 3,000 feet above sea level. The lines of communication entering the Highlands are limited to the roads into Da Lat and from Qui Nhon to Pleiku. The coastal plain extending from the Mekong Delta to the 17th Parallel is very narrow, rarely exceeding 24 miles in width. Shifting sand dunes adjacent to the shore protect flat fertile areas which extend to the base of the Central Highlands. National Route 1, a narrow bituminous surfaced road, and a meter-gauge railroad traversed the region parallel to the coast. Throughout the nation, the lack of adequate roads and the presence of mountains, dense vegetation, and extensive canal networks channeled movement and made surface lines of communication highly vulnerable to enemy attack.

The long monsoon season made many roads impassable, inundated runways, and turned supply points and assembly areas into quagmires. Conversely, in the dry season, dust created serious maintenance and traffic problems. The monsoon seasons also affected over-the-beach operations by creating severe high tides and surf conditions. In turn, the climatic extremes hastened the deterioration of supplies and equipment.

South Vietnam is an agricultural nation, and the majority of the population lacks industrial skills usable for military logistic purposes. Nor does South Vietnam possess sufficient raw materials or the capability to manufacture goods to provide even partially from native resources the support requirements generated by the expansion of allied forces.

Supply Support

Prior to the start of the U.S. buildup in 1965, we anticipated that the command would experience many supply shortages. Consequently, we requested that all incoming units be self-sustaining for a period of 180 days after arrival. It was planned that this procedure would be continued until our depots could accumulate sufficient stocks to meet the demands of units arriving at a later date. This was called the PUSH system. Supplies were "pushed" from the United States to recently arrived units to sustain them until depots could respond to their requisitions without depleting their stocks. As depot stocks grew, the PUSH system was gradually eliminated.

The absence of a traditional front line and a secure rear support zone necessitated the establishment of four major support areas—Saigon, Cam Ranh Bay, Qui Nhon, and Da Nang. The four Army support areas were oriented on the four principal corps tactical zones and were capable of receiving, storing and issuing all types of supplies. In accordance with our policy of central logistic direction, all support areas were directly subordinated to the 1st Logistical Command.

Support for field operations was provided from a base known as a Forward Support Area (FSA). The FSA was a grouping of logistic personnel, equipment, and supplies which was designed to support a specific military operation and then to displace or disband upon completion of the operation. These organizations were sited as close to the supported unit as the tactical situation would permit and normally located near an airfield to expedite the receipt and delivery of supplies. Supply levels of the FSAs were based upon the anticipated tactical requirements of the supported units and usually included such items as food, construction materials, petroleum products, and ammunition. FSA stocks were replenished from supporting depots automatically to insure the maintenance of established levels.

In 1967 over 550,000 short tons of general supplies and 86,000 tons of ammunition per month were distributed to units throughout Vietnam by highway, intracoastal waterway, and air. In the case of petroleum products, bulk petroleum was received at the ports in Vietnam by tanker and distributed to over fifty inland locations by trucks, pipeline, small coastal tankers and aircraft when necessary. Petroleum storage capacity in Vietnam grew from 750 million barrels in 1965 to over 3.6 billion barrels in June 1968.

In 1964 U.S. forces had limited ammunition stocks—approximately 5,000 tons. Ammunition destined for use by Vietnamese forces was processed through Military Assistance channels. The only storage facilities capable of receiving sufficient ammunition to support the buildup were old French magazines located throughout the nation. These magazines had a capacity of about 50,000 short tons, of which 32,000 short tons were concentrated in the Tuy Hoa area. Four years later,

U.S. ammunition stocks in Vietnam had grown to over 385,000 short tons of which about 70 percent were stored in improved sites, covered magazines or open, revetted, hard-surfaced pads.

As the buildup progressed, the technology for the management of supplies improved and new and imaginative concepts and procedures were developed. In late 1965 the control of stocks in storage and on order was accomplished by a laborious manual process. Each depot was considered a separate entity and requisitioned replacement supplies directly through the 2d Logistical Command in Okinawa. Under this system, there was no practical accountability of nationwide supply levels. In less than three years, this obsolete process was replaced by a complex control system involving the large-scale use of electronic computers. Coincidentally, procedures were evolved to provide continuous and up-to-date inventory accounting of all stocks within Vietnam. In late 1967 a fully automated central inventory control center was established at Long Binh. Through these improvements in control and accountability, nationwide requirements could be tabulated, interdepot shortages and excesses balanced, and requisitions evaluated as to priorities.

As a result of the successes achieved by our logisticians, U.S. forces were never restricted in combat operations by a need for essential supplies and enjoyed the highest quality of personal services ever provided to troops in combat.

Maintenance

Due to the climatic conditions and operational requirements encountered in Vietnam, the useful life of parts and components on all types of equipment was drastically shortened. The length of supply lines, the unimproved nature of the roads, and the necessary practice of overloading vehicles further aggravated maintenance problems. As an example, the average accumulated mileage on vehicles during the early days of the buildup was about 20,000 miles annually in comparison to about 6,000 miles accumulated in other theaters.

In the early phases, direct support maintenance units, whose normal mission was the repair and return of equipment to using units, were greatly overloaded. In order to meet this situation, general support maintenance units, whose usual mission was to repair and return items to supply channels, were forced to assume expedient direct support missions. The resultant lack of general support capability created serious problems regarding the repair of severely damaged equipment. This situation slowly resolved itself as additional maintenance units arrived in Vietnam and by early 1967 virtually all units were able to devote full energy to their originally assigned missions.

As with the supply function, maintenance personnel continually evaluated their situations in an effort to develop more efficient techniques and procedures. In 1966 the "Closed Loop" program was initiated. From time to time, the inventory of certain end items or major assemblies vital to combat operational requirements was such that, unless the production and prompt shipment of new items and the retrograde, overhaul, and return of combat-damaged items were intensively managed on an item basis, no assurance could be given that combat units would have equipment needed for operational missions. The "Closed Loop" program of intensive management insured that replacement items of critical equipment were available to replace like-items damaged or destroyed in combat operations.

In late 1965 an excessive amount of essential combat equipment was nonoperational because of a delay in the receipt of needed repair parts. In December 1965 the "Red Ball Express" system was inaugurated to insure prompt delivery of required repair parts. The objective of the system was to insure that requests for parts which were causing equipment to be deadlined would be expeditiously routed to the appropriate out-of-country supplier, regardless of location, who would, if necessary, provide these parts by removing them from equipment in use by units in the United States. The time-delivery goal was established as seven days from the time the unit placed a requisition on the system until the needed part was received by the requesting unit. Control agencies in the United States, as well as in Vietnam, closely monitored the flow of these requests and insured that delays were eliminated. All parts requisitioned under this system were delivered by air.

Due to the complex problems involving aircraft and missiles, the "Stove Pipe" system was instituted in early 1966. Normally, parts were supplied by one of the seven subordinate commands of the Army Materiel Command or the Defense Supply Agency; a requisition would be directed to one of these activities. Under the "Stove Pipe" procedure, all requisitions pertaining to a particular weapons system such as a missile were sent to one supply agency, in this case Missile Command; this command filled requisitions for those parts it regularly supplied and passed requisitions for other parts to the proper command for supply action.

The number of helicopters increased from 324 in early 1965 to about 2,000 at the end of 1966 and 3,500 in mid-1968. The extensive use of these aircraft and adverse environmental conditions posed particularly difficult maintenance problems. On the average, about 7.7 maintenance hours were required for each flying hour of the helicopter. The magnitude of this workload becomes evident when it is considered that the UH–1 helicopter, which was the most numerous in Vietnam, flew almost 12 million hours during a 12-month period in 1967–68.

Several actions were taken to speed maintenance and repair procedures. Direct-support maintenance detachments were provided to all separate helicopter companies. This additional maintenance capability was immediately reflected by a corresponding rise in aircraft availability rates. A major augmentation of our helicopter maintenance capability occurred in April 1966 with the arrival of the converted Navy seaplane tender, the USNS *Corpus Christi Bay*. This ship was a mobile maintenance facility which was staffed by civilian experts and a work force consisting of U.S. Army technicians. With its machine shops, technical library, and relatively safe working area, the *Corpus Christi Bay* provided a maintenance backup capability equivalent to a major rebuild facility. The ship operated near combat areas, initially in the III Corps area and later at Cam Ranh Bay and other locations in the II Corps. Through these efforts and refined experience, we were able to maintain helicopters in numbers sufficient to meet the full range of combat operations.

Transportation

In Vietnam, transportation has been a key factor in military success as well as in a political/economic role. Strategic, tactical, and logistic mobility are essential ingredients of success; and at the core of these elements lies the ability to move units, equipment, personnel, and materiel in sufficient strength and quantity where needed and when needed, to accomplish the tasks required. The fact that the few existing land lines of communication were continuously interrupted by the enemy at the time the buildup began made it necessary to rely primarily on water and limited air transport to provide logistic support.

The large troop buildup had to be accomplished simultaneously with the development of the four support areas. Time did not permit constructing water terminals, depots, and other support facilities prior to receiving thousands of men and tons of material. Therefore, it was necessary to deploy over-the-beach, using our amphibious capability to provide support until the standard, more economical facilities could be developed. This rapid buildup on the beaches magnified the problems of the supply personnel who did not yet have adequate facilities in which to receive, identify, and store these large quantities of materiel. Transportation units included terminal units, stevedore companies, terminal transfer units, amphibious truck companies, harbor craft units with tugs, barges and floating cranes. These units provided the necessary personnel and equipment to receive, discharge, and clear the personnel and materiel entering Vietnam over-the-beach. Truck battalions having light, medium, and petroleum tank truck units were also deployed to each of the port areas to clear the ports and beaches and to move materiel forward to depots and to combat units. Initially, this work was performed by civilian contract companies because the active Army lacked transportation units in sufficient quantity to accomplish this mission. Han Jin, Alaska Barge Company, and Sea-Land Corporation cleared the ports of Qui Nhon, Cam Ranh Bay, and Saigon while U.S. transportation units were being activated, trained, and sent to Vietnam.

The plan to move by water encompassed not only the four major ports but also establishment of a series of satellite shallow-draft ports along the coast. In this way, we were able to capitalize on Vietnam's long coastline by using intracoastal shipping for lateral distribution of supplies. As the major ports developed, supplies were transhipped by water to the lesser facilities and then inland by highway or airlift to the Forward Support Areas or direct to the combat elements. The success of the sea-river transportation program was illustrated by the fact that the tonnage moved on intracoastal routes increased from a few hundred thousand short tons in 1965 to over three million short tons in the period July 1967 through June 1968.

Air terminals were developed in each of our major and many of our minor port complexes. Monthly theater airlift of cargo rose from a few tons in July of 1965 to a total of 7,500 short tons in July of 1968. The lack of airfields throughout the nation initially created a demand for a large engineer construction effort. Contractors were used to develop major jet-capable airfields while troops constructed forward strips needed to support combat operations and to permit forward supply.

Movements by highway in early 1965 were negligible, although the picture improved rapidly. For example, the monthly average tonnage hauled from April to October 1966 was only 622,700 tons. The monthly average from May 1967 through April 1968 was 1,183,400 tons. These figures do not portray adequately the magnitude of this achievement. The way in which units faced the task of supporting tactical operations over inadequate roads, which were being rebuilt and were susceptible to enemy ambush, is testimony to their skill and courage.

In 1965 the once excellent narrow gauge railroad along the east coast of Vietnam was inoperative and largely destroyed. The time, manpower, and materiel required to reestablish the rail system curtailed plans for its complete rehabilitation in favor of continued development of highway, air, and coastal water supply routes. Nonetheless, sections of the railway were restored and facilitated supply movement considerably.

The port of Saigon was a source of particular concern in 1965. As the economic center of the Republic, Saigon was the bellwether of Vietnam's economy and an important factor in our ability to stabilize the economy and, in turn, the government of Vietnam. Unable to support a vast modern military effort, along with a wartime civilian economy, the port became congested as soon as large numbers of Free World forces arrived.

A major logistic problem was the clearance of commercial cargo while moving critical military supplies. Because of the troop buildup and the accompanying demand for goods and services, inflation threatened the civilian economy. To offset this inflationary tendency, the Agency for International Development (AID) was given the job of increasing Vietnamese imports to the point where civilian demands could be satisfied, thus stabilizing the economy. The AID cargo added another two to three hundred thousand tons per month to the already overloaded port of Saigon, requiring an increase in capacity from 150,000 tons a month to over 600,000 tons.

As first priority in early 1966, we began building an entirely new port for military cargoes north of Saigon on the Saigon River. Newport, as it was called, was designed to solve the port congestion problem as well as to end the temporary disrup-

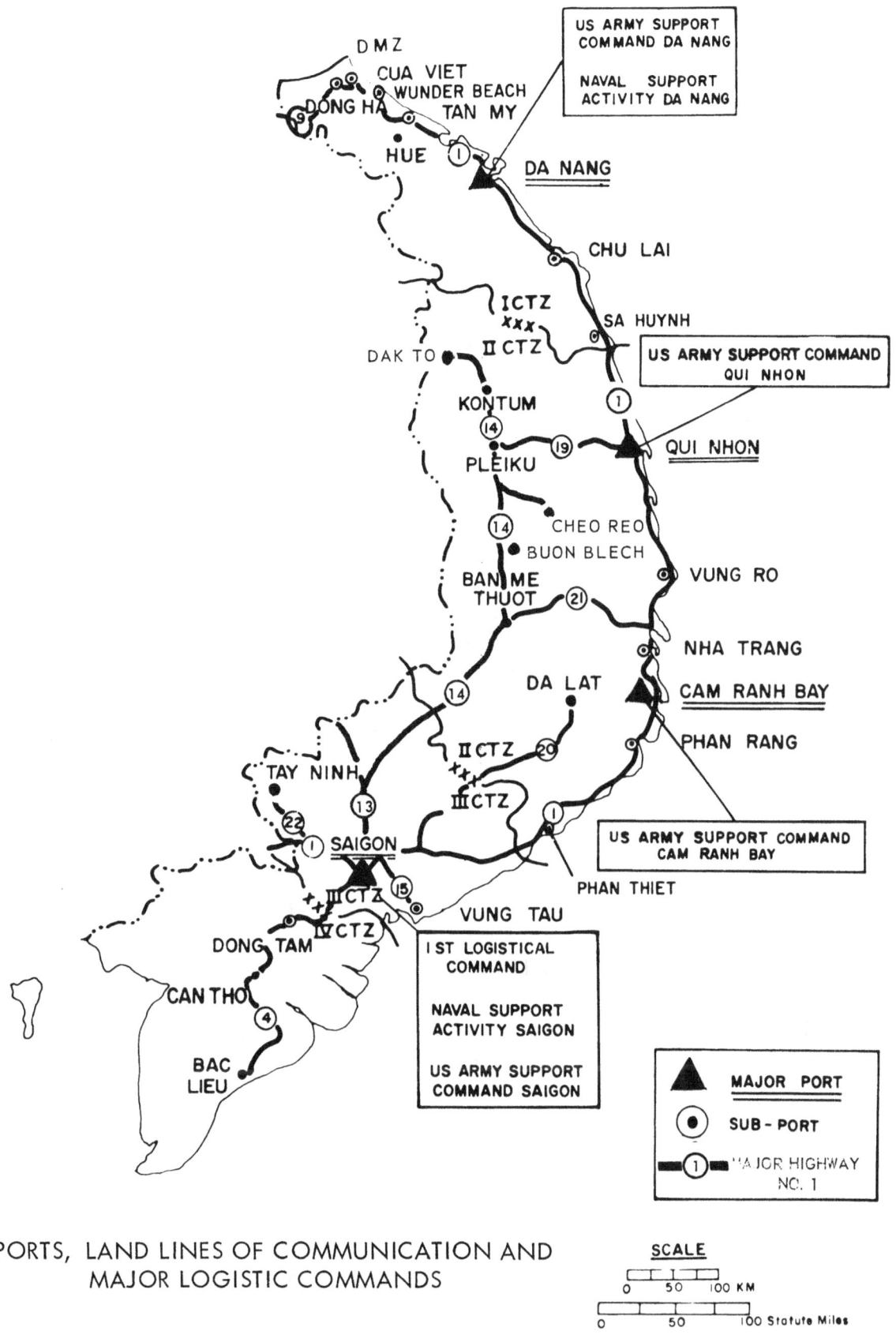

PORTS, LAND LINES OF COMMUNICATION AND MAJOR LOGISTIC COMMANDS

tion of the civilian economy caused by our large military shipments. Until the new facilities were completed, we had to continue to use the civilian port, making it necessary to modernize port operations. After consultation with U.S. agencies and with the concurrence of the government of Vietnam, the U.S. Army's 4th Terminal Command assumed the mission of receiving, discharging, and clearing U.S. military cargo entering the area and doing what was necessary to help the Vietnamese Port Authority to accomplish its mission.

Three major improvements were to be accomplished at the port complex. First, a port tariff or set of rules and regulations governing the conduct of everyone working in and around the port and specifying services available and standard charges for their use was published. Second was the requirement to help organize the Port Authority along U.S. Army major port organizational lines and collocate it with the 4th Terminal Command. Third, the badly deteriorated port was restored.

Saigon port operations steadily improved during 1966 and 1967. By May of 1967 the congestion at Saigon and elsewhere had been virtually eliminated, and ship turn-around time had been reduced to seven days. The Saigon Port Authority gradually achieved self-sufficiency, and we were able to reduce the size of our advisory effort. As of mid-1968 it was planned that the advisory function to the commercial port would be returned to the Agency for International Development. All of this activity was accomplished under the authority and in accordance with the knowledge and desires of the Port Authority and the Vietnamese government. The U.S. Army did not move in and take over as was so often recommended. Such action would have destroyed the normal commercial port-importer-customer relationship so necessary to the economy of the country.

Although the Saigon port received great attention because of its economic as well as its military importance, the other deep-draft ports were equally vital to our military effort. The story at these ports was much the same; construction went hand-in-hand with a continuous increase in capacity. Da Nang, formerly suitable only for lighterage, was expanded to include six deep-water berths and many shallow-draft slips and ramps. By 1968 Da Nang port possessed a discharge capacity of 10,560 tons per day. Formerly a fishing village, Qui Nhon was expanded to four deep-draft berths and could handle over 6,000 tons a day. Cam Ranh Bay, which originally had only a single unused pier, rivaled many of the world's finest ports, with ten deep-draft berths and a daily discharge capacity of close to 7,000 tons as well as 30,000 barrels of fuel. The more than a dozen ports and subports we built raised our discharge capability in Vietnam from 370,000 tons per month in late 1965 to 1,200,000 tons per month in 1968—almost a fourfold increase.

Construction

To provide the operational, logistic, and support facilities required for our rapidly expanding effort, facility planning and construction proceeded with urgency as the order of the day. The base development task was comparable to constructing the basic facilities for the population of a city the size of Toledo, Ohio, including such things as water supply, refrigeration, hospitals, roads, and living accommodations. In concept, the plan for base development was: to construct several deep-draft ports with satellite shallow-draft ports; to build major airfields, depots, and logistical facilities at the port complexes; to extend the land lines of communications inland from the ports; to build the necessary troop base locations throughout the country; and, finally, to expand the road and rail net to interconnect the major troop bases. Construction of this countrywide base complex proceeded concurrently with the arrival and operation of our forces and their supplies so that the base was used as it was being built. As operational plans changed to meet the changing military situations, construction effort was shifted to meet new needs. As an example, the deployment of major Army units into the northern part of the I Corps zone in 1967 required the establishment of a support facility at Da Nang to furnish Army-peculiar supplies. Eventually, this organization assumed responsibilities for Army support activities in Chu Lai and was required to establish a subordinate support complex in the Hue-Phu Bai area with a Forward Support Area at Dong Ha. In each of these developments, construction of troop billets, storage areas, roads, water supply systems, and an array of other facilities were required to provide adequate support to combat operations.

Up to mid-1965 there were no U.S. engineer troops in Vietnam, and only a small contract construction capability existed. As buildup proceeded, engineer and construction forces were given a high priority for expansion. Our U.S. construction capability increased with additions of Army engineer troops, Naval construction units, Air Force civil engineers, Marine Corps engineer troops, and civilian construction under Navy supervision. Vietnamese Army engineers and engineer troops of our other allies performed construction for their forces, thereby contributing to the overall effort.

In early 1966 I established the Directorate of Construction in MACV to provide centralized management of the U.S. construction program. As the principal staff officer for engineering and base development matters, the Director of Construction insured that construction effort was responsive to tactical needs and priorities.

As an additional mission, the Director of Construction was charged with insuring that only the minimum essential construction was undertaken and that this construction was of the most austere standard, consistent with operational needs and the accomplishment of the tactical mission. In the effort to economize, we gave major attention to the use of materials which could be salvaged upon our withdrawal from the area. Prefabricated DeLong Piers were used extensively in the development of port quays and ship's berths. Not only could these piers be installed much more rapidly than conventionally constructed docking facilities but, of great importance, they could be reclaimed when no longer required. During the initial buildup phase, great reliance was placed on tentage to support administrative and storage needs. It soon became apparent that this was not an economical substitute due to the rapid deterioration of the fabric in the tropical environment. Therefore, a simple structure was designed which combined standard and prefabricated features for use in accommodating housing and administrative requirements. This same concept of austerity applied to the construction of all buildings within the command, to include my own headquarters, which was prefabricated and could be relocated and/or salvaged when it had outlived its usefulness.

Five major jet airbases were built as well as 100 widely dispersed fields for transport aircraft. The major bases afforded the necessary runways for our tactical aircraft and for handling of airlift arriving from outside Vietnam. The smaller fields throughout Vietnam allowed the forward airlift of logistical support to dispersed forces. Newly developed aluminum and steel airfield matting enabled the construction of substantial airfields at remote sites.

Construction and improvement of the road net was of major importance because this work aided our military operations and the supply of our troops while supporting civilian traffic; this, in turn, encouraged economic development and the extension of government control in the countryside. The work primarily involved widening and paving roads and constructing bridges. Prefabricated combat bridging was used to provide tactical crossing sites and these temporary facilities were later replaced by permanent-type bridges. First priority was given to Route 1 and the routes extending inland from our coastal bases. By 1968 the priority highways had been restored in each area and increased effort could be devoted to expanding other road networks and improving secondary roads.

Upon my request, the Ambassador, in late 1967, transferred the advisory function for roads and highways from the Agency for International Development to MACV. The MACV Director of Construction was assigned supervision of this func-

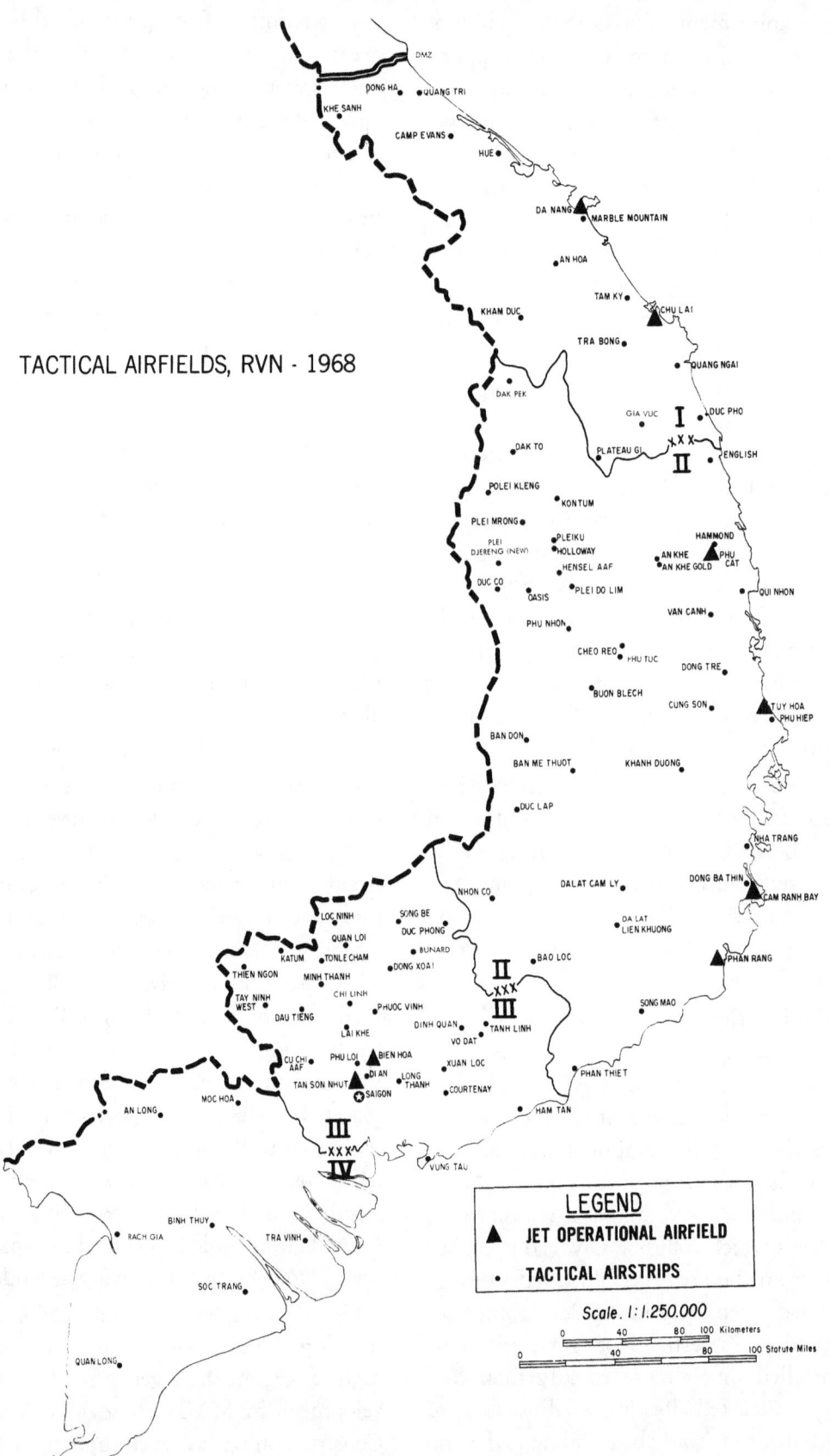

tion on 1 February 1968. This decision facilitated the coordination of all military and civilian efforts in accomplishing the countrywide highway improvement program. The function involved advising the Minister of Public Works, the Director General of Highways, the five Vietnamese district engineers, and each of the province engineers on all matters pertaining to the national and interprovincial highway programs. Shortly thereafter, control of railroad and waterway programs was also centralized.

Other construction accomplishments included: depots with over 11 million square feet of covered storage, over 5 million square yards of open storage, 2.5 million cubic feet of cold storage, and hospitals providing 8,250 beds.

The construction program in Vietnam had many unique features. It was probably the largest concentrated effort of this kind in history. This was the first time that civilian contractors were used on a major scale in an active theater of operations. The largest construction contractor was a consortium made up of Raymond International, Morrison-Knudsen, Brown and Root, and J. A. Jones construction firms. At the peak, in July 1967, their work force numbered 51,000 employees. Other construction contractors included DeLong Corporation for the prefabricated piers, Vinnell Corporation for electrical power plants and the power distribution systems, and Walter Kidde, who built Tuy Hoa Airbase.

Civilians, including U.S., Vietnamese, and third country nationals (mainly Koreans and Filipinos) were used both by contractors and under the supervision of military units. Without their contributions, more military personnel would have been required to do the job. As an ancillary benefit, Vietnamese civilians working on construction projects received training in equipment operation and in technical and supervisory skills. The advantages of this type of training to the future growth of the Vietnamese economy were substantial.

The development of the port of Cam Ranh Bay provided an excellent example of how U.S. presence in Vietnam generated favorable economic benefits. A major problem associated with the construction and operation of the Cam Ranh Bay installation dealt with the absence of an adequate local labor pool. In April 1965 we recommended that the Vietnamese government give consideration to the prospects of resettling refugees and displaced persons in the Cam Ranh Bay area. The recommendation was well received and planning was initiated with a view toward relocating about 5,000 Vietnamese to a planned model village in the vicinity of the Cam Ranh Bay site. In a relatively short period of time, plans for the village had been completed and Vietnamese government funds allocated for the project.

Settlers began arriving in the area as early as July 1965, and by mid-1968, it was estimated that over 15,000 personnel resided in the new village. The labor provided by these personnel greatly aided in the construction of the base and served as a major source of employment and security for the population. In early 1968 over 4,000 Vietnamese were employed by the Cam Ranh Bay installation. The success of this project served as an incentive for a second resettlement program initiated in 1968. It is expected to draw an additional 20,000 Vietnamese citizens into the area.

The contractor effort was concentrated primarily on the base complexes. However, military engineer troops accomplished much heavy construction while also performing combat support tasks for operational forces. By 1968 engineer troops comprised approximately 11 percent of our total forces in Vietnam; and in the USARV, engineer troop strength exceeded all other branches except infantry.

As the construction program proceeded, the job of maintenance, repair, and operation of facilities grew proportionately. The work was accomplished by a combination of military personnel, Vietnamese civilian employees, and contracts. The two major contractors were Pacific Architects and Engineers for the Army and Philco-Ford for the Navy. The total program cost about $100 million per year and employed more than 20,000 local and third country nationals.

In accomplishing the construction task, the engineers overcame numerous obstacles. The work was accomplished under severe environmental conditions. There were very few construction materials either natural or manufactured that could be obtained in Vietnam. Lumber was not available. Rock suitable for construction purposes was limited in quantity and often obtainable only at a great distance from the construction sites. Construction equipment and supplies had to be shipped 12,000 miles from the United States or purchased offshore from distant locations. Despite these obstacles, the construction mission was successfully and efficiently performed and the face of Vietnam was changed. The ports, airfields, roads, buildings, and utilities which were provided for our forces will serve the Vietnamese economy and will provide the framework for development of the nation in the years ahead.

The impact of these contributions appears even greater when measured in economic terms. The total appropriations allocated for construction in Vietnam totaled about $1.6 billion, of which 75 percent has been expended at the rate of about two percent of the yearly costs of the war. It is anticipated that at least $100 million of this sum is recoverable at the termination of hostilities. In consideration of the contributions our construction effort has provided in both the support of combat operations and the civilian economy, the investment has been prudent and productive.

Communications

As vital to the success of our forces in Vietnam as the building of bases and improving lines of communications, was the establishment of a modern communications system for command and control.

In the early stages of involvement in Vietnam, it was necessary to establish out-of-country circuits and to tie together the military advisory effort inside Vietnam. The first out-of-country systems had been established by radio and submarine cable. In 1962 action to supplement the steadily increasing level of activity required the deployment of an organization to satisfy growing communication needs. This organization, the 39th Signal Battalion, had the capability of establishing five communication centers. This was the first regular U.S. Army unit of any type to enter Vietnam and was the start of the communication buildup in Southeast Asia.

Planning for the Integrated Wideband Communications System (IWCS) was initiated to increase the overall capacity and quality of communications by extending, upgrading, and expanding existing facilities. Within Vietnam and across the Pacific, military and civilian communications specialists cooperated to develop this system, which now employs advanced techniques and equipment to serve the tens of thousands of users in combat and supporting activities.

To coordinate and control the developing communications system, the Army activated the 1st Signal Brigade in 1966. The brigade included all U.S. Army signal units not associated with tactical units and tied together strategic and tactical communications systems. The brigade's strength is now about 20,000.

Dial telephone equipment began arriving in Vietnam in 1966. Installation of automatic telephone exchanges resulted in a major improvement in service. Additional improvements also were made in the communications equipment assigned to combat units. In 1967 voice security equipment was provided for small unit radios as well as new tactical transmitters of greater power, simplicity, and range.

Personnel and Management

Probably unique in U.S. military history is the extent to which local purchasing of supplies and services has been exploited to conserve manpower and to foster economic development. The value of local contracts in force in July 1968 exceeded one-half billion dollars. The largest service contracts were for repairs and utilities on bases. In addition, contracts were awarded for transportation, equipment maintenance, laundry, and certain base operations. Supply contracts were concluded for fresh fruit and vegetables, ceramic products, and reprocessing of U.S.-produced dairy products.

While a main objective of the local contracting program was to conserve U.S. manpower, it was also possible to foster MACV-AID supported civil assistance programs. Through use of local resources and capabilities, business techniques were improved, and mechanical and clerical skills were developed.

Almost 16,000 Vietnamese employees, both blue and white collar, filled technical and professional positions. They operated in such fields as supervision, computer operation, accounting and budgeting, engineering and architecture, clerical, supply and transport, food preparation and serving, carpentry, pipefitting, welding, vehicle maintenance, and others.

To develop needed skills, the 1st Logistical Command conducted an extensive training program, preparing its Vietnamese employees to fill working level positions and in some cases eventually to assume managerial and highly skilled positions. By mid-1968, for example, some 1,800 employees had graduated from driver training school, the equivalent of over 14 Army truck companies. To mention the output of only a few of the other courses, 278 Vietnamese were trained in managerial skills; 4,000 in clerical skills; 3,600 in general industry, and over 1,000 in the English language.

Further, as the use of local nationals increased, it was possible to reduce costs. For example, at Qui Nhon, as the tonnage handled in the port increased from 100,000 to 200,000 tons, the cost per ton decreased from $12 to $5.

Throughout the course of our buildup, improvement of our managerial techniques and conservation of U.S. manpower were motivating factors. In 1966 MACV requested the first manpower survey ever conducted in a combat environment. As a result of this survey, nearly 1,000 personnel spaces were eliminated. Requests for additional personnel required the fullest justification and were monitored closely.

In 1967 a management improvement program (Project MACONOMY) was initiated under the supervision of the MACV comptroller with the objectives of enhancing efficiency and insuring the most economical use of available resources. Under this program, it was the responsibility of all managers to continually review their plans and programs, to analyze and evaluate resources with a view toward consolidation, and to increase operational capabilities at the most economical cost in men, money, and materials. Project MACONOMY's objectives received the wholehearted support of the command and the results were gratifying. By December 1967 the realized savings of MACONOMY were in excess of $100 million. In addition to these tangible savings, the program provided a valuable tool for analyzing the efficiency of our administrative and logistic operations.

During 1967 we also began to participate in another program to reduce imbalances and excesses in supplies that had developed in Vietnam as a result of our rapid buildup in preceding years and of inadequacies in depots, storage, and supply management facilities during those years. This included an extensive campaign to locate and redistribute excess supplies from one Service to another and to locate and cancel requests from other components of the Pacific Command for supplies that might be excess in Vietnam.

Summary

Although the logistical aspects of the Vietnam war offer neither the color nor drama of the combat operations, their importance cannot be overemphasized nor can it be denied that they have presented an astonishing spectacle. Despite seemingly insurmountable problems, the logisticians created an organization responsive to every tactical need. Through initiative and imagination, new solutions, techniques, and procedures were devised to cope with the problems of weather, terrain, and the ever-present enemy. Among the thousands of Americans who wrought this logistic miracle, I must call attention to the absolutely invaluable contribution of Lt. Gen. Jean Engler who as Deputy Commander of USARV brought to the job the skill and energy of a professional logistician.

The forces of the U.S. and the Free World as well as the economy of Vietnam have profited greatly from the tireless efforts of these officers and men.

Appendix H

MEDICAL

The provision of medical service for the U.S. forces in Vietnam has been a responsibility of the MACV component commands. Cross-servicing whereby one Service cares for the sick and injured of another has been carried out extensively.

Medical service in Vietnam is as complete as that found anywhere in the world. It includes not only medical evacuation and hospitalization but also medical supply and maintenance, preventive medicine, dental, veterinary and medical laboratory services, medical intelligence, and medical research and development activities.

As our troop buildup began, medical units of all types were phased in along with the tactical and logistical units they supported. Completely equipped hospitals staffed with well-trained specialists were soon located throughout Vietnam.

In January 1964 the medical support for the limited U.S. forces in Vietnam consisted of a Navy dispensary and a 60-bed infirmary in Saigon, an Air Force dispensary at nearby Tan Son Nhut Airbase, an Army hospital of 100 beds at Nha Trang, and a small Navy dispensary at Da Nang.

The Seventh Air Force since that time has established dispensaries at its other major airfields in Vietnam and in 1967 established a 475-bed Air Force hospital at Cam Ranh Bay. The Seventh Air Force has also built casualty staging facilities at the airfields at Da Nang, Qui Nhon, Cam Ranh Bay, and Tan Son Nhut. These facilities receive patients who have been treated in nearby hospitals and care for them until they are placed on aircraft that will evacuate them to hospitals in the Pacific Command or in the Continental United States. The Air Force also has placed mobile casualty staging facilities at more remote airfields when required by the level of the fighting. Personnel of the 903d Aeromedical Evacuation Squadron performed in an outstanding manner and displayed great courage many times, such as at Dak To, during the battle there in November 1967, and at Khe Sanh, during the early months of 1968.

Since 1964 the Navy has established dispensaries at its bases outside Saigon and has built a hospital of 700 beds at Da Nang. Hospital ships have been stationed off the northern coast of Vietnam since the arrival of USS *Sanctuary* in February 1966 and USS *Repose* in April 1967.

The Naval medical service also supports U.S. Marine units in Vietnam. Each Marine platoon has a Navy hospital corpsman and each battalion a medical officer and several corpsmen. A medical battalion and a hospital company are located at division level. This arrangement provides a phased system of increasingly more sophisticated treatment at successively higher levels. At each level the patient is treated and either returned to duty or evacuated to a hospital or a hospital ship.

The Army uses this same system of phased evacuation and treatment, beginning with the medical aidman who accompanies each infantry platoon and ending with the hospitals of the 44th Medical

Brigade. These and other Service hospitals have been so located that by 1968 any casualty evacuated by helicopter was within 30 minutes flying time of a hospital capable of providing definitive surgical care. The Army has 5 field hospitals, 7 surgical hospitals, and 11 evacuation hospitals in Vietnam today.

The stability of these hospitals has permitted semipermanent construction to promote efficiency and to protect from the tropical environment. All preoperative, operative, postoperative and other intensive care areas are air-conditioned, a significant contribution to better patient care. It has been possible to substitute more sophisticated medical equipment than normally found in mobile medical units. As a result, the level of medical and surgical care given is much above that normally expected within the combat zone. In addition to the constructed facilities we have equipped four of the surgical hospitals with the Medical Unit, Self-Contained, Transportable (MUST). While the MUST hospital system is still in the development stage, it represents a vast improvement over the tent hospitals of the past. The MUST is a system of shelters and equipment designed to provide the required medical-surgical capability for patient care in the field under a wide range of environmental conditions. Modules can be combined to form any desired field treatment facility and can be transported by CH-54 helicopters, although normally transported by fixed wing aircraft. The MUST system gives us the capability of applying in the field many of the advances which have been made since World War II.

Under the fluid conditions of warfare in Vietnam, hospitals have no immunity, and many have come under attack varying from sniper fire and hand grenades to mortars and rockets. The U.S. Naval Hospital, Naval Support Activity, at Da Nang has been hit by some form of attack, mainly mortar fire, an average of at least three times a year since its establishment in 1965. Although no fatalities resulted through the years, approximately 20 staff members and a few patients have incurred light wounds. From mid-1967 through mid-1968, U.S. Air Force medical installations were shelled on five occasions, but damage was minimal. The commanding officer of the U.S. Army's 45th Surgical Hospital was killed by mortar fire while visiting the hospital's future location at Tay Ninh. In November of 1967 one mortar round struck the 12th Evacuation Hospital and killed a patient. In February 1968 several rockets hit the 45th Surgical Hospital at Tay Ninh, killing a medical officer, and in a shelling of the 71st Evacuation Hospital at Pleiku the same month, a Vietnamese patient was killed. All inflatable patient shelters of the 3d Surgical Hospital at Dong Tam were deflated in a shelling in July 1967, but hospital personnel incurred only minor wounds. In June of 1967 mortar rounds striking the 8th Field Hospital at Nha Trang caused minor damage but no casualties.

The Army medical service gives medical support, including evacuation and hospitalization, to the other Free World forces in Vietnam. The Army also provides convalescent facilities for all U.S. and Free World forces in its 6th Convalescent Center at Cam Ranh Bay, which opened in April 1966, to treat men who did not require hospitalization during convalescence from wounds or illness. Since that date, the 6th Convalescent Center has returned to duty 23,000 lightly wounded or sick members of the U.S. and Free World forces who otherwise would have had to be evacuated to hospitals in the Pacific Command.

The evacuation of casualties to hospitals and the transfer of patients between hospitals within Vietnam is accomplished almost entirely by helicopters and fixed wing aircraft. Since beginning a service called DUST OFF in 1963, Army helicopter ambulances have evacuated steadily increasing numbers of military and civilian patients. In 1966, 59,722 were evacuated; 88,696 in 1967, and 99,765 during the first six months of 1968.

The courage and dedication of the crews and medical teams aboard the Air Force fixed wing evacuation aircraft has been most laudable. At the same time, the Navy corpsmen attached to ground units and the Army aidmen have given extraordinarily brave performances, as the high casualty rate among these medics clearly demonstrates.

In the past, patients have been evacuated from Vietnam to hospitals in the Pacific Command and the Continental United States by C–118 piston engine aircraft of the Military Airlift Command. Starting in June 1968 all evacuation flights were by C–141 "Starlifter" jet aircraft.

The air evacuation patients have all been regulated or programmed for particular beds in designated hospitals in the Pacific Command or the Continental United States by the Area Joint Medical Regulating Office at MACV. Activated in July 1965 this office handled the evacuation of 26,939 U.S. and Free World patients in 1966, 40,083 in 1967, and 33,932 in the first six months of 1968. The greatest numbers were evacuated in February (7,510) and May (7,051) of 1968. In one 24-hour period during the *Tet* offensive, 9–10 February 1968, over 650 patients were evacuated. Hospitals outside Vietnam supporting MACV have been those of the Navy at Guam and at Yokosuka, Japan; of the Air Force at Clark Airbase in the Philippines and at Tachikawa Airbase in Japan; and of the Army in Okinawa, Hawaii, and the U.S. Army Medical Command, Japan, with hospitals at Camp Zama, Camp Oji, Camp Drake, and Kishine Barracks.

MACV early established a 30-day evacuation policy, which meant that any patient whose hospitalization and treatment would require more than 30 days (with some exceptions, such as those with malaria and hepatitis) would be evacuated to a hospital in the Pacific Command as soon as his condition allowed transfer. This policy freed beds for patients who could be treated and returned to duty within 30 days or less.

The MACV components have striven to keep 40 percent of their hospital beds empty at all times and thus available for the treatment of the sudden surges of casualties that occur from time to time.

The overall hospital bed occupancy rates have only exceeded the desirable maximum of 60 percent on two occasions: during May 1967 when it briefly approached 67 percent and for a 24-hour period during February 1968 when it rose slightly above 65 percent.

The majority of U.S. patients admitted to MACV hospitals and other medical installations have been ill rather than wounded. During 1966, 1967, and the first half of 1968 slightly more than 69 percent of all U.S. military admissions were due to illness. During these same periods, battle casualties constituted approximately 17 percent of all admissions and nonbattle injuries approximately 14 percent.

The medical problems faced by the U.S. forces in Vietnam were not the devastating ones that predictions had indicated they might be. But they were still the most formidable that had been faced by a large military force in United States history. The fact that there has not been an undue incidence of disease and injury has been due to the high degree of professionalism displayed by the majority of commanders and staff officers and to the fact that the U.S. forces fielded the finest military medical service in history.

Five groups of diseases accounted for the majority (61 percent) of the disease admissions. These were malaria, fevers of unknown origin, and the respiratory, skin, and diarrheal diseases. Malaria, which has ranged seventh as a cause of admission to hospitals in the U.S. forces in Vietnam, has ranked third as a cause of man-days lost from duty, exceeded only by wounds and by nonbattle injuries.

With the deployment of U.S. forces into the Central Highlands in the fall of 1965, there was a significant increase in the incidence of malaria, particularly in assault elements in close contact with the enemy. By November 1965 the malaria rate was such as to constitute a serious impediment to military operations and to cause an unacceptable drain on combat manpower. It was apparent that the enemy was the reservoir of infection. Malaria control measures that had been so effective in base camps in the Delta and Lowlands were much less effective on tactical units in the jungles, and the standard chloroquine-primaquine preventive was not completely effective in preventing infection with the vicious falciparum strain of malaria encountered in the Highlands.

Upon request, The Surgeon General of the Army provided immediate technical assistance. Experienced malariologists were sent to Vietnam, bringing with them a new anti-malarial drug—dapsone. The emergence of chloroquine-resistant falciparum malaria in Vietnam did not come as a surprise to the Army Medical Department as a similar strain had been reported elsewhere in Southeast Asia in the late 1950s. An aggressive malaria research program to develop improved malaria drugs had been revitalized in 1960. Dapsone, long used in the treatment of leprosy, needed only operational field testing to prove its efficiency against the Vietnam strain of falciparum malaria.

Extensive field tests were completed on a trial basis and the drug was put into operational use at the end of 1965. This addition of daily doses of dapsone to the standard weekly chloroquine-primaquine tablet, coupled with command emphasis on stringent personal protective measures, succeeded in reducing the malaria rate to a militarily acceptable level. The incidence of malaria has since varied from month to month, depending on such factors as the type of terrain, degree of contact with the enemy, degree of infection of enemy units in contact, malaria discipline of the friendly unit concerned, and the season of the year. The problem continues to receive command emphasis.

The incidence of diarrheal diseases was greater in new arrivals in Vietnam but continued thereafter at a significant rate. The skin disorders resulted from a combination of factors such as the hot, humid climate, skin injuries from scratches, insect and leech bites that became infected, etc. Fungus infections of the feet, legs, and trunk were common after immersion in water during operations in rice paddies and other flooded areas, such as during riverine operations in the Delta.

The neuropsychiatric casualty admission rate has been the lowest of any war to date, having been 14.5 per 1,000 per year during 1966, 10.4 during 1967, and 13.1 during the first five months of 1968. This reflected the high morale of our forces and the early treatment in forward areas of such casualties as occurred.

The noneffective rate among U.S. forces in Vietnam has compared very favorably with that among U.S. forces elsewhere, having been 9.7 per thousand per day during 1966, falling to 9.0 in 1967, and to 8.7 during the first five months of 1968.

The meaning of the term "casualty" has not always been understood. As the term is used by the military, it refers to those who are missing or who have been wounded as well as to those who have been killed. For example, of every 100 U.S. combat "casualties" that occurred in Vietnam during 1967:

1. 11 were killed outright (one more died later of wounds after reaching a medical treatment facility).

2. 1 was missing.

3. 88 were wounded, and 87 of these survived. Of these 88 wounded:

a. 35 were treated and immediately returned to duty after treatment by an aidman or in a battalion aid station, division level medical facility, or hospital.

b. 7 were treated and held for a few hours or days in a division level medical facility and then returned to duty. (42 thus were treated and returned to duty without having been hospitalized.)

c. 1 of these 88 wounded died after admission to a medical facility of some kind: aid station, division clearing station, or hospital.

d. 45 were hospitalized. Of these:

(1) 20 were treated and returned to duty from hospitals in Vietnam.

(2) 25 were evacuated further for treatment in hospitals in the Pacific Command or the Continental United States.

Several varied medical programs were instituted that helped the Vietnamese military and civilian populations.

The Military Provincial Health Assistance Program (MILPHAP) was begun in November 1965 to augment the medical care available to Vietnamese civilians and to assist and develop the public health programs in the country.

The program has been carried out by 22 MILPHAP teams, each made up of 3 medical officers, 1 administrative officer and 12 enlisted technicians. These 8 Army, 7 Air Force and 7 Navy MILPHAP teams have augmented and assisted the clinical, medical, and surgical care and public health services in 25 of the 44 provinces of the Republic of Vietnam.

Civilian teams of the Provincial Health Assistance Program (PHAP), made up of medical personnel from other Free World nations and a Public Health Team from the Republic of Korea, have carried out similar programs in the other provinces of the Republic of Vietnam. The Volunteer Physicians for Vietnam Program of the American Medical Association and the programs of other religious and charitable associations have augmented and assisted these programs in the provincial hospitals.

The Medical Civic Action Program (MEDCAP) was begun in January 1963 to establish and maintain mutual respect and cooperation between the Vietnamese Armed Forces and the civilian populations by means of medical treatments given the civilians by Vietnamese military medical personnel, assisted with advice and encouragement by Special Forces medics. All U.S. and Free World medical units and all nonmedical units of battalion or larger size have also carried out MEDCAP programs and have given many millions of treatments during military operations and during their off-duty time. They have often provided complete health service for a village or hamlet or for an orphanage, leprosarium, or dispensary; and they have often been successful in gaining the cooperation of the local civilian population in the process.

The Civilian War Casualty Hospitalization Program has supplemented the hospital capabilities of the government of Vietnam's Ministry of Health. Under its provisions civilians who have received war related injuries and who have been referred for treatment from province hospitals by Vietnamese medical authorities are evacuated in U.S. military aircraft to U.S. military hospitals for treatment.

U.S. military hospitals have admitted and treated sick, wounded, and injured Vietnamese civilians on an emergency basis since they first became operational. Other Vietnamese civilians have been admitted to U.S. and Free World hospitals for elective surgical procedures such as the repair of cleft palates and harelips.

The Civilian War Casualty Hospitalization Program was designed to augment the government's provincial hospitals and to provide additional beds and treatment where these were most needed. Military hospitals were constructed for this purpose at Da Nang, Chu Lai, and Can Tho and became operational in the first part of the summer of 1968.

The Civilian War Casualty Hospital Program was begun in October 1967 in the U.S. Army's 36th Evacuation Hospital at Vung Tau and its 91st Evacuation Hospital at Tuy Hoa. Experience soon showed that the Vietnamese disliked leaving their own communities for hospitalization in another province or region of the country. In addition, experiences during the *Tet* offensive in February and March 1968, when all U.S. military hospitals admitted and treated numerous Vietnamese civilian casualties, showed that none experienced any undue difficulties due to the resulting joint occupancy by U.S. and Vietnamese casualties.

The program was therefore modified in May 1968 to allow this continued joint occupancy in all U.S. military hospitals, including the three new ones being constructed for the program. U.S. casualties have had and continue to have first priority on available beds but Vietnamese civilians now can be hospitalized and treated in hospitals much closer to their homes.

In 1967 it became apparent that there was duplication of medical effort in the U.S. medical advisory programs in Vietnam and in the Vietnamese medical programs themselves. The U.S. Agency for International Development was assisting the Ministry of Health in its civilian medical programs; MACV was assisting the Vietnamese Armed Forces in their military medical programs. On both sides there was duplication of advisory effort and duplication of medical functions.

Joint MACV–AID working committees were established early in 1968, which thereafter eliminated duplication of effort. They formulated joint plans in the areas of hospital construction, medical supply, medical education and training, and preventive medicine and public health. Soon afterwards representatives from the Ministry of Health and Vietnamese Armed Forces' Surgeon General's Office became participating members of these committees so that these programs could be carried out without duplication between the Vietnamese military and civilian agencies.

Appendix I

PRESS

No war in history has been so freely and broadly covered by the press both in detail and scope as has the conflict in Vietnam, and never before have Americans been able to sit before their television sets and watch actual battle scenes only hours after the action occurred.

My policy regarding relations with the press has been to provide as much detailed information as possible consistent with the security of our forces and operations.

Recognizing that objective and responsible press coverage of the war in Vietnam was important in forming American and international public opinion, my command and I exercised maximum candor in our relationship with the press corps and within the limits of security, imposed no censorship. A set of ground rules governed coverage of the war and required each newsman to act as his own censor to insure that information of possible value to the enemy was not revealed. Intentional noncompliance subjected the correspondent to possible loss of his MACV accreditation and thus loss of many official services. Since correspondents and U.S. field commanders often were unsure just what constituted genuine security considerations, MACV ultimately provided a duty officer on a 24-hour basis to advise and guide reporters. On only four occasions in four years was it necessary to suspend or withdraw correspondents' accreditation for violation of security.

The one major exception to our policy of full disclosure to the press was Operation DELAWARE in April and May 1968, an airmobile reconnaissance in force operation deep into a well-defended enemy base area in the A Shau valley near the Laotian border. Since surprise was essential both to the success of the operation and the safety of our forces, we employed unusual security measures. The press understood and cooperated.

An area war marked by no well-defined battle lines, the war in Vietnam is unlike any other war on foreign soil in which our country has participated. With action likely to develop anytime and anywhere, we made special efforts to provide the press with transportation and other accommodations. We granted newsmen priority seating on a number of regular C–130 flights which daily covered nearly all of South Vietnam north of Saigon. For the area south of the capital, to the extent practical, a helicopter was on standby. Members of the press also had the privilege of "hitching" rides on almost all other U.S. aircraft. Without these arrangements, the newsman's job would have been next to impossible, since his only other choice was to purchase space on Vietnam's commercial airline, servicing only a few major population centers. In addition to flight benefits, an accredited correspondent was usually entitled to enter U.S. and Free World installations, eat at cost in U.S. mess halls, have limited privileges in post exchanges, and when necessary, sleep in government billets.

Early in 1964 only about 20 resident correspondents were in Vietnam. By the start of the next year the number had multiplied to 334, and in February 1968 reached 649. Eight U.S. correspondents and ten non-U.S. correspondents have been killed.

The great interest of the press in the war in Vietnam and the massive volume of reporting have played a major role bearing upon American public opinion on the war and the situation in Vietnam. In view of the impact of public opinion on the prosecution of the war, the accuracy and balance of the news coverage has attained an importance almost equal to the actual combat operations. These factors, together with the rules and regulations under which we operated, have served to add a new dimension to battlefield command. Despite occasional divergencies between the news media and MACV in regard to emphasis placed on some actions and projects, the conduct of the press and MACV's liberal policies have brought the American people an abundance of information and many points of view.

Appendix J

MAJOR UNITED STATES AND FREE WORLD MILITARY UNITS IN VIETNAM

Unit	Date of arrival	Location in June 1968
Joint		
United States Military Assistance Command, Vietnam.	February 1962*	Saigon.
Army		
U.S. Army Support Command, Vietnam.	March 1964*	(Disestablished July 1965 on activation of U.S. Army, Vietnam.)
U.S. Army, Vietnam	July 1965*	Long Binh, Bien Hoa.
Field Force, Vietnam**	September 1965*	Nha Trang, Khanh Hoa.
II Field Force, Vietnam	March 1966*	Long Binh, Bien Hoa.
Provisional Corps, Vietnam	March 1968*	Phu Bai, Thua Thien.
1st Logistical Command	April 1965*	Long Binh, Bien Hoa.
1st Infantry Division	October 1965	Lai Khe, Binh Duong.
1st Brigade	October 1965	Quan Loi, Binh Long.
2d Brigade	July 1965	Di An, Bien Hoa.
3d Brigade	October 1965	Lai Khe, Binh Duong.
1st Cavalry Division (Airmobile)	September 1965	Phong Dien, Thua Thien.
1st Brigade	September 1965	Phong Dien, Thua Thien.
2d Brigade	September 1965	Phong Dien, Thua Thien.
3d Brigade	September 1965	Phong Dien, Thua Thien.
4th Infantry Division	August 1966	Pleiku, Pleiku.
1st Brigade	October 1966	Dak To, Kontum.
2d Brigade	August 1966	Phu My, Binh Dinh.
3d Brigade***	December 1965	Kontum, Kontum.

*Formed in Vietnam.
**Became I Field Force, Vietnam August 1966.
***Originally 3d Brigade, 25th Infantry Division.

Unit	Date of arrival	Location in June 1968
9th Infantry Division	December 1966	Bear Cat, Bien Hoa.
1st Brigade	December 1966	Dong Tam, Dinh Tuong.
2d Brigade	January 1967	My Tho, Dinh Tuong.
3d Brigade	December 1966	Saigon.
23d Infantry Division (Americal)	September 1967*	Chu Lai, Quang Tin.
11th Light Infantry Brigade (attached).	December 1967	Duc Pho, Quang Ngai.
196th Light Infantry Brigade (attached).	August 1966	Hoi An, Quang Nam.
198th Light Infantry Brigade (attached).	October 1967	Hoi An, Quang Nam.
25th Infantry Division	April 1966	Cu Chi, Hau Nghia.
1st Brigade	April 1966	Tay Ninh, Tay Ninh.
2d Brigade	January 1966	Hoc Mon, Gia Dinh.
3d Brigade****	October 1966	Hoc Mon, Gia Dinh.
101st Airborne Division	December 1967	Phu Bai, Thua Thien.
1st Brigade	July 1965	Phu Bai, Thua Thien.
2d Brigade	December 1967	Phu Bai, Thua Thien.
3d Brigade	December 1967	Phuoc Vinh, Phuoc Long.
173d Airborne Brigade	May 1965	Bong Son, Binh Dinh.
199th Light Infantry Brigade	November 1966	Long Binh, Bien Hoa.
3d Infantry Brigade Task Force, 82d Airborne Division.	February 1968	Phu Bai, Thua Thien.
11th Armored Cavalry Regiment	September 1966	Xuan Loc, Long Khanh.
1st Aviation Brigade	May 1966	Long Binh, Bien Hoa.
18th Engineer Brigade	September 1965	Dong Ba Thin, Khanh Hoa.
20th Engineer Brigade	August 1967	Bien Hoa, Bien Hoa.
1st Signal Brigade	April 1966	Long Binh, Bien Hoa.
18th Military Police Brigade	September 1966	Long Binh, Bien Hoa.
44th Medical Brigade	April 1966	Long Binh, Bien Hoa.
5th Special Forces Group	October 1964	Nha Trang, Khanh Hoa.
3/17 Cavalry Squadron (Airmobile)	October 1967	Di An, Bien Hoa.
7/17 Cavalry Squadron (Airmobile)	October 1967	Pleiku, Pleiku.
7/1 Cavalry Squadron (Airmobile)	February 1968	Vinh Long, Vinh Long.

Navy

Unit	Date of arrival	Location in June 1968
Commander, Naval Forces, Vietnam—Chief, Navy Advisory Group.	April 1966*	Saigon.

*Formed in Vietnam.
****Originally 3d Brigade, 4th Infantry Division

Unit	Date of arrival	Location in June 1968
Naval Support Activity, Saigon	May 1966*	Saigon.
Naval Support Activity, Da Nang	October 1965*	Da Nang, Quang Nam.
Coastal Surveillance Force, Task Force 115.	July 1965*	Cam Ranh Bay, Khanh Hoa.
River Patrol Force, Task Force 116	December 1965*	Binh Tuy, Phong Dinh.
Mekong Delta Mobile Riverine Force, Task Force 117.	January 1967	Dong Tam, Dinh Tuong.
3d Naval Mobile Construction Brigade.	June 1966*	Da Nang, Quang Nam.

Air Force

Unit	Date of arrival	Location in June 1968
2d Air Division	October 1962	(Disestablished on formation of 7th Air Force in April 1966.)
7th Air Force	April 1966*	Tan Son Nhut, Gia Dinh.
834th Air Division	October 1966	Tan Son Nhut, Gia Dinh.
3d Tactical Fighter Wing	November 1965	Bien Hoa, Bien Hoa.
12th Tactical Fighter Wing	November 1965	Cam Ranh Bay, Khanh Hoa.
31st Tactical Fighter Wing	December 1966	Tuy Hoa, Phu Yen.
35th Tactical Fighter Wing	April 1966	Phan Rang, Ninh Thuan.
37th Tactical Fighter Wing	March 1967	Phu Cat, Binh Dinh.
366th Tactical Fighter Wing	March 1966	Da Nang, Quang Nam.
14th Air Commando Wing	March 1966	Nha Trang, Khanh Hoa.
315th Air Commando Wing	March 1966	Phan Rang, Ninh Thuan.
460th Tactical Reconnaissance Wing.	February 1966	Tan Son Nhut, Gia Dinh.
483d Tactical Airlift Wing	October 1966	Cam Ranh Bay, Khanh Hoa.
120th Tactical Fighter Squadron	April 1968	Phan Rang, Ninh Thuan.
136th Tactical Fighter Squadron	June 1968	Tuy Hoa, Phu Yen.
174th Tactical Fighter Squadron	May 1968	Phu Cat, Binh Dinh.
188th Tactical Fighter Squadron	May 1968	Tuy Hoa, Phu Yen.

Marine Corps

Unit	Date of arrival	Location in June 1968
9th Marine Expeditionary Brigade	March 1965	(Disestablished May 1965 on formation of III Marine Amphibious Force.)
Headquarters, III Marine Amphibious Force.	May 1965*	Da Nang, Quang Nam.
Headquarters, 1st Marine Division	January 1966	Da Nang, Quang Nam.
1st Marine Regiment	February 1966	Khe Sanh, Quang Tri.
5th Marine Regiment	April 1966	Phu Loc, Thua Thien.
7th Marine Regiment	August 1965	Da Nang, Quang Nam.

*Formed in Vietnam.

Unit	Date of arrival	Location in June 1968
26th Marine Regiment, 5th Marine Division (attached).	April 1967	Da Nang, Quang Nam.
27th Marine Regiment, 5th Marine Division (attached).	February 1968	Da Nang, Quang Nam.
Headquarters, 3d Marine Division	May 1965	Dong Ha, Quang Tri.
3d Marine Regiment	March 1965	Dong Ha, Quang Tri.
4th Marine Regiment	May 1965	Khe Sanh, Quang Tri.
9th Marine Regiment	July 1965	Cam Lo, Quang Tri.
1st Marine Air Wing	May 1965	Da Nang, Quang Nam.

Free World Military Assistance Forces

Unit	Date of arrival	Location in June 1968
1st Battalion Royal Australian Regiment.	June 1965	(Returned to Australia June 1966.)
1st Australian Task Force (Includes 2d Battalion, Royal Australian Regiment).	April 1966	Nui Dat, Phuoc Tuy.
3d Battalion, Royal Australian Regiment.	December 1967	Nui Dat, Phuoc Tuy.
4th Battalion, Royal Australian Regiment (Replaced 2d Bn RAR).	June 1968	Nui Dat, Phuoc Tuy.
7th Battalion, Royal Australian Regiment.	April 1967	Nui Dat, Phuoc Tuy.
Republic of Korea Capital Division	October 1965	Qui Nhon, Binh Dinh.
Republic of Korea 9th Infantry Division.	September 1966	Ninh Hoa, Khanh Hoa.
Republic of Korea Marine Brigade	October 1965	Da Nang, Quang Nam.
New Zealand Field Artillery Battery	July 1965	Nui Dat, Phuoc Tuy.
Philippines Civic Action Group	August 1966	Tay Ninh, Tay Ninh.
Thai "Queen's Cobras" Regiment	September 1967	Long Thanh, Bien Hoa.
New Zealand Infantry Company	December 1967	Nui Dat, Phuoc Tuy.

The above listing has been restricted to major United States and Free World Military Assistance Units. Of no less importance is the contribution of hundreds of smaller units and the many off-shore organizations that provide combat support and combat service support.

Appendix K

COMMANDERS OF MAJOR UNITED STATES AND FREE WORLD MILITARY ASSISTANCE FORCES IN VIETNAM

COMMANDERS OF MAJOR USMACV COMMANDS

Command	Commander	Date of assumption of command
U.S. Military Assistance Command, Vietnam.	GEN Paul D. Harkins, USA	8 Feb 62
	GEN William C. Westmoreland, USA	20 Jun 64
Deputy Commander, U.S. Military Assistance Command, Vietnam.	LTG William C. Westmoreland, USA	27 Jan 64
	LTG John L. Throckmorton, USA	2 Aug 64
	LTG John A. Heintges, USA	5 Nov 65
	GEN Creighton W. Abrams, USA	1 Jun 67
U.S. Army, Vietnam	GEN William C. Westmoreland, USA	20 Jul 65
Deputy Commanding General, U.S. Army, Vietnam.	BG John Norton, USA	20 Jul 65
	LTG Jean E. Engler, USA	24 Jan 66
	LTG Bruce Palmer, Jr., USA	1 Jul 67
2d Air Division	LTG Joseph H. Moore, USAF	31 Jan 64
7th Air Force	LTG Joseph H. Moore, USAF	2 Apr 66
	GEN William W. Momyer, USAF	1 Jul 66
Naval Advisory Group	RADM Norvell G. Ward, USN	10 May 65
Naval Force, Vietnam	RADM Norvell G. Ward, USN	1 Apr 66
	RADM Kenneth L. Veth, USN	27 Apr 67
III Marine Amphibious Force	MG William R. Collins, USMC	6 May 65
	LTG Lewis W. Walt, USMC	4 Jun 65
	LTG Robert E. Cushman, Jr., USMC	1 Jun 67
Field Force, Vietnam	MG Stanley R. Larsen, USA	25 Sep 65

Command	Commander	Date of assumption of command	
I Field Force, Vietnam	LTG Stanley R. Larsen, USA	15 Mar	66
	LTG William B. Rosson, USA	1 Aug	67
	MG William R. Peers, USA	1 Mar	68
II Field Force, Vietnam	LTG Jonathan O. Seaman, USA	15 Mar	66
	LTG Bruce Palmer, Jr., USA	24 Mar	67
	LTG Frederick C. Weyand, USA	1 Jul	67
Senior Advisor, IV Corps Tactical Zone.	COL George Barton, USA	17 Sep	64
	BG William R. Desobry, USA	3 Jun	66
	MG George S. Eckhardt, USA	14 Jan	68
Provisional Corps, Vietnam	LTG William B. Rosson, USA	10 Mar	68
U.S. Army Support Command, Vietnam.	BG Joseph W. Stilwell, USA	1 Mar	64
	BG Delk M. Oden, USA	1 Jul	64
	BG John Norton, USA	1 Apr	65

COMMANDERS FREE WORLD MILITARY ASSISTANCE FORCES IN VIETNAM

Australian Army Force, Vietnam.	Brigadier O. D. Jackson, OBE	Jun	65
Australian Force, Vietnam	MG K. MacKay, MBE	May	66
	MG D. Vincent, OBE	Feb	67
	MG A. L. MacDonald, OBE	Feb	68
Republic of Korea Military Assistance Group, Vietnam.	BG Moon Hwan Cho	Oct	65
Republic of Korea Forces, Vietnam.	LTG Chae Myung Shin	Dec	65
New Zealand Army Force, Vietnam.	LTC W. C. T. Foley	Oct	65
	LTC R. H. Smith	Aug	66
Republic of the Philippines Contingent, Vietnam.	COL J. V. H. Banzon	Oct	65
1st Philippines Civic Action Group, RVN.	BG Gaudencio V. Tobias	Nov	66
Royal Thai Military Assistance Group, Vietnam.	LTC U. Boonsom	Mar	66
	CDR P. Montri	Mar	67
	COL Y. Samran	Apr	67
	MG D. Yose	Sep	67

Appendix L

LIST OF MAJOR OPERATIONS

Since the introduction of U.S. forces into Vietnam in March 1965, more than 300 major and many thousands of smaller operations have been conducted against the enemy. The sheer magnitude of this number precludes coverage here. The chronological listing that follows includes only those operations conducted prior to 30 June 1968 in which more than 500 known casualties* were inflicted on the enemy.

Date and duration	*Operation*	Corps Tactical Zone
18–21 Aug 65 4 days	STARLIGHT. U.S. Marine Corps operation against VC 1st Regiment south of Chu Lai in Quang Ngai Province. 700 known enemy casualties.	I
23 Oct–20 Nov 65 29 days	SILVER BAYONET. 1st Cavalry Division (Airmobile) and ARVN units operation in Pleiku Province. Operation included 3d Brigade battle of Ia Drang Valley. 1,771 known enemy casualties.	II
19 Jan–21 Feb 66 34 days	VAN BUREN. 1st Brigade, 101st Airborne Division, Republic of Korea 2d Marine Brigade, and the ARVN 47th Regt rice-security operation in Phu Yen Province. 679 known enemy casualties.	II
24 Jan–6 Mar 66 42 days	MASHER/WHITE WING/THANG PHONG II. Conducted by 1st Cavalry Division (Airmobile), ARVN, and ROK forces in Binh Dinh Province. First large unit operation across corps boundaries when Marines on DOUBLE EAGLE crossed into Binh Dinh and linked up with soldiers of the 1st Cavalry Division. 2,389 known enemy casualties.	II

---

*Known casualties include only enemy dead determined by body count.

Date and duration	Operation	Corps Tactical Zone
4–8 Mar 66 5 days	UTAH/LIEN KET 26. U.S. Marine Corps/ARVN operation in vicinity of Quang Ngai City against NVA and VC main force units. 632 known enemy casualties.	I
20–24 Mar 66 5 days	TEXAS/LIEN KET 28. U.S. Marine Corps/ARVN/Vietnamese Marine Corps reaction force operation to retake An Hoa outpost in Quang Ngai Province. 623 known enemy casualties.	I
10 May–30 Jul 66 82 days	PAUL REVERE/THAN PHONG 14. 3d Brigade, U.S. 25th Inf Div and ARVN forces border screening, area control operation in Pleiku Province. 546 known enemy casualties.	II
2–21 Jun 66 20 days	HAWTHORNE/DAN TANG 61. 1st Brigade, 101st Airborne Division and ARVN units operation in Kontum Province. 531 known enemy casualties.	II
2 Jun–13 Jul 66 42 days	EL PASO II. U.S. 1st and ARVN 5th Divisions against VC 9th Div in Binh Long Province. 855 known enemy casualties.	III
4 Jul–27 Oct 66 116 days	MACON. U.S. Marine Corps security operation for An Hoa industrial complex in Quang Nam Province. 507 known enemy casualties.	I
7 Jul–3 Aug 66 28 days	HASTINGS/DECKHOUSE II. U.S. Marine Corps/ARVN/Vietnamese Marine Corps operation in Quang Tri Province against NVA 324B Division in area of Demilitarized Zone. 882 known enemy casualties.	I
1–25 Aug 66 25 days	PAUL REVERE II. 1st Cavalry Division (Airmobile) and ARVN operation in Pleiku Province. 809 known enemy casualties.	II
3 Aug 66–31 Jan 67 182 days	PRAIRIE. A continuing 3d Marine Division operation in Con Thien/Gio Linh areas of the Demilitarized Zone. Followed HASTINGS and was initiated by one battalion left behind from that operation to keep track of the NVA 324B Division. 1,397 known enemy casualties.	I
6–21 Aug 66 16 days	COLORADO/LIEN KET 52. U.S. Marine Corps/ARVN operation in Quang Nam/Quang Tin Provinces. 674 known enemy casualties.	I

Date and duration	Operation	Corps Tactical Zone
26 Aug 66–20 Jan 68 513 days	BYRD. 1st Cavalry Division economy-of-force operation in Binh Thuan Province. Usually one or two battalions involved. 849 known enemy casualties.	II
14 Sep–24 Nov 66 72 days	ATTLEBORO. In War Zone C (Tay Ninh Province). Initiated by 196th Light Infantry Brigade. No significant contact until 19 October when a sizeable base area was uncovered. By early November the 1st Infantry Division; 3d Brigade, 4th Infantry Division; 173d Airborne Brigade, and several ARVN Battalions were involved. 1,106 known enemy casualties in largest U.S. operation to date.	III
23 Sep–9 Nov 66 48 days	MAENG HO 6. Republic of Korea Capital Division operation in Binh Dinh Province. 1,161 known enemy casualties.	II
2–24 Oct 66 23 days	IRVING. 1st Cavalry Division (Airmobile), ARVN, and Republic of Korea units against NVA 610th Division in Binh Dinh Province. 681 known enemy casualties.	II
18 Oct–30 Dec 66 74 days	PAUL REVERE IV. Continuing operation near the Cambodian border of Pleiku Province. Conducted primarily by the newly arrived 4th Infantry Division along with elements of the 25th Infantry Division and 1st Cavalry Division. 977 known enemy casualties.	II
25 Oct 66–12 Feb 67 111 days	THAYER II. 1st Cavalry Division (Airmobile) operation in Binh Dinh Province. Followed THAYER I and was in turn followed by PERSHING in the rich northern coastal plain and Kim Son and Loui Ci Valleys to the west. 1,757 known enemy casualties.	II
30 Nov 66–14 Dec 67 380 days	FAIRFAX. Started by 3 battalions, one each from 1st, 4th, and 25th Infantry Divisions, in and around Saigon and taken over by the 199th Light Infantry Brigade in January 1967. Emphasis was on joint U.S./ARVN operations. Upon withdrawal of the 199th, the area of operations was taken over by the ARVN 5th Ranger Group. 1,043 known enemy casualties.	III

Date and duration	Operation	Corps Tactical Zone
1 Jan–5 Apr 67 95 days	SAM HOUSTON. A continuation of the 4th and 25th Infantry Divisions border surveillance operations in Pleiku and Kontum Province. Followed by FRANCIS MARION. 733 known enemy casualties.	II
6 Jan–31 May 67 146 days	PALM BEACH. 9th Infantry Division operation in Dinh Tuong Province. 570 known enemy casualties.	IV
8–26 Jan 67 19 days	CEDAR FALLS. 1st and 25th Infantry Divisions, 173d Airborne Brigade, 11th Armored Cavalry Regiment, and ARVN units joint operation against VC Military Region 4 Headquarters in the Iron Triangle. 720 known enemy casualties.	III
1 Feb–18 Mar 67 46 days	PRAIRIE II. Continuation of the 3d Marine Division operations in the area of the Demilitarized Zone. 693 known enemy casualties.	I
11 Feb 67–19 Jan 68 343 days	PERSHING. 1st Cavalry Division (Airmobile) operation in Binh Dinh Province against elements of the NVA 610th Division and VC units. Followed by PERSHING II in the same area when major elements of the 1st Cavalry Division moved to I Corps. 5,401 known enemy casualties.	II
13 Feb 67–11 Mar 68 393 days	ENTERPRISE. 9th Infantry Division operation combined with ARVN and Regional and Popular Forces in Long An Province. 2,107 known enemy casualties.	III
17–22 Feb 67 6 days	LIEN KET 81. ARVN 2d Division operation in Quang Ngai Province. 813 known enemy casualties.	I
22 Feb–14 May 67 83 days	JUNCTION CITY. Largest operation in Vietnam to date. 22 U.S. battalions and 4 ARVN battalions. Elements of the U.S. 1st, 4th, and 25th Infantry Divisions, 196th Light Infantry Brigade, 11th Armored Cavalry Regiment, and 173d Airborne Brigade. Conducted in War Zone C (Tay Ninh Province) and bordering provinces. 2,728 known enemy casualties.	III
7 Mar–18 Apr 67 43 days	OH JAC KYO I. Largest Republic of Korea operation to date. Accomplished the linkup of the two Republic of Korea Division areas of operations along the central coastal area. 831 known enemy casualties.	II

Date and duration	Operation	Corps Tactical Zone
5 Apr–12 Oct 67 191 days	FRANCIS MARION. 4th Infantry Division operation in western highlands of Pleiku Province. Followed SAM HOUSTON and upon termination combined forces with GREELEY to commence MAC ARTHUR. 1,203 known enemy casualties.	II
21 Apr–17 May 67 27 days	UNION. 1st Marine Division operation against NVA forces in Quang Nam and Quang Tin Provinces. 865 known enemy casualties.	I
14 May–7 Dec 67 208 days	KOLE KOLE. 25th Infantry Division operation in Hau Nghia Province. 645 known enemy casualties.	III
25 May–5 Jun 67 12 days	UNION II. 1st Marine Division operation against NVA forces in Quang Nam and Quang Tin Provinces. 701 known enemy casualties.	I
2–14 Jul 67 13 days	BUFFALO. Continuing 3d Marine Division operation in the Demilitarized Zone. Followed CIMARRON and was followed by HICKORY II. 1,281 known enemy casualties.	I
16 Jul–31 Oct 67 108 days	KINGFISHER. Continuing 3d Marine Division operation in the Demilitarized Zone. Followed HICKORY II and was followed by KENTUCKY and LANCASTER. 1,117 known enemy casualties.	I
4–15 Sep 67 12 days	SWIFT. 1st Marine Division operation in Quang Nam and Quang Tin Provinces. 517 known enemy casualties.	I
5 Sep–30 Oct 67 57 days	DRAGON FIRE. Elements of the Republic of Korea 2d Marine Brigade operations in Quang Ngai Province. 541 known enemy casualties.	I
27 Sep–19 Nov 67 54 days	SHENANDOAH II. 1st Infantry Division operation in Binh Duong Province and extended to include the Loc Ninh area of Binh Long Province after the enemy attacks on the district town. 956 known enemy casualties.	III
12 Oct 67—(Cont.)	MAC ARTHUR. 4th Infantry Division continuing operations in the western highlands. 4,944 known enemy casualties as of 30 June.	II
1 Nov 67–31 Mar 68 152 days	SCOTLAND. 3d Marine Division operation in the westernmost part of Quang Tri Province. Action centered on the Khe Sanh area. Terminated with the commencement of PEGASUS. 1,561 known enemy casualties.	I

Date and duration	Operation	Corps Tactical Zone
1 Nov 67—(Cont.)	KENTUCKY. 3d Marine Division continuing operations in the Con Thien area of the Demilitarized Zone. 2,658 known enemy casualties as of 30 June.	I
11 Nov 67—(Cont.)	WHEELER/WALLOWA. Americal Division (2 brigades) operations in Quang Nam and Quang Tin Provinces. 8,689 known enemy casualties as of 30 June.	I
8 Dec 67–24 Feb 68 79 days	YELLOWSTONE. 25th Infantry Division operation in War Zone C (Tay Ninh Province). 1,254 known enemy casualties.	III
8 Dec 67–11 Mar 68 95 days	SARATOGA. A continuation of the 25th Infantry Division operations in the southern half of their area of operations west of Saigon and along the Cambodian border. Commenced at the same time as YELLOWSTONE in the northern half of the Division area of operations. 3,862 known enemy casualties.	III
17 Dec 67–8 Mar 68 83 days	UNIONTOWN. 199th Light Infantry Brigade operation in Bien Hoa Province. Includes *Tet* offensive operations. 922 known enemy casualties.	III
17 Dec 67–30 Jan 68 45 days	MAENG HO 9. Republic of Korea Capital Division operation in Binh Dinh Province. 749 known enemy casualties.	II
19 Dec 67–10 Jun 68 175 days	MUSCATINE. Americal Division (1 Brigade) operations in Quang Ngai Province. 1,129 known enemy casualties.	I
19 Jan 68—(Cont.)	McLAIN. 173d Airborne Brigade reconnaissance-in-force operation in support of pacification in Binh Thuan Province. Over 637 known enemy casualties as of 30 June.	II
22 Jan–29 Feb 68 39 days	PERSHING II. A continuation of the 1st Cavalry Division (Airmobile) operations in Binh Dinh Province after major division forces had deployed to I Corps. 614 known enemy casualties.	II
22 Jan–31 Mar 68 70 days	JEB STUART. 1st Cavalry Division (Airmobile) initial operation in northern I Corps following PERSHING operations in II Corps. 3,268 known enemy casualties.	I

Date and duration	Operation	Corps Tactical Zone
31 Jan–25 Feb 68 26 days	BATTLE OF HUE. ARVN and U.S. Marine Corps elements defended and drove the enemy out of Hue City during the *Tet* offensive. 5,113 known enemy casualties.	I
5–17 Feb 68 13 days	TRAN HUNG DAO. Joint General Staff conducted operation in the Saigon area with 6 Vietnamese Marine Corps, 4 ranger and 5 airborne battalions during the *Tet* offensive. 953 known enemy casualties.	III
16 Feb–1 Mar 68 15 days	MAENG HO 10. Republic of Korea Capital Division operation in Binh Dinh Province. 664 known enemy casualties.	II
17 Feb–8 Mar 68 21 days	TRAN HUNG DAO II. A continuation of the Joint General Staff (Vietnamese) conducted operation TRAN HUNG DAO in the Saigon area with slightly reduced forces. 713 known enemy casualties.	III
29 Feb 68—(Cont.)	NAPOLEON/SALINE. U.S. Marine Corps operations along the Cua Viet River to keep this supply line of communications open to the port facility in the Dong Ha area of Quang Tri Province. 3,127 known enemy casualties as of 30 June.	I
1 Mar 68—(Cont.)	TRUONG CONG DINH. Operation by ARVN units and elements of the U.S. 9th Infantry Division in Dinh Tuong and Kien Tuong Provinces of the IV Corps. On 21 May combined with Operation PEOPLE'S ROAD.	IV
11 Mar–7 Apr 68 28 days	QUYET THANG (Resolve to Win). Largest operation to date. Conducted in the Saigon area and the five surrounding provinces. Elements of the U.S. 1st, 9th, and 25th Divisions and ARVN 5th and 25th Divisions and ARVN airborne battalions and Vietnamese Marine Corps Task Forces, a total of 22 U.S. and 11 ARVN battalions. 2,658 known enemy casualties.	III
17 Mar 68—(Cont.)	DUONG CUA DAN (People's Road). Operations by 9th Infantry Division to provide security for engineers working on Route 4. Combined with Operation TRUONG CONG DINH on 21 May. In the two operations, over 1,251 known enemy casualties as of 30 June.	IV

Date and duration	Operation	Corps Tactical Zone
1–15 Apr 68 15 days	PEGASUS/LAM SON 207. 1st Cavalry Division (AIRMOBILE) with U.S. Marine and ARVN airborne battalions operation to relieve the siege of Khe Sanh. 17 U.S. and 4 ARVN battalions involved. 1,044 known enemy casualties.	I
1 Apr–17 May 68 47 days	CARENTAN II. 101st Airborne Div, and 3d Bde, 82d Airborne Div in conjunction with the ARVN 1st Division operations along the lowlands of Quang Tri and Thua Thien Provinces. 2,100 known enemy casualties.	I
8 Apr–31 May 68 54 days	TOAN THANG (Complete Victory). Largest operation to date. A combined III ARVN Corps and II Field Force offensive to destroy VC and NVA forces within the Capital Military District. 42 U.S. and 37 Vietnamese battalions were involved for total of 79 battalions. 7,645 known enemy casualties.	III
8 Apr 68–(Cont.)	BURLINGTON TRAIL. Combat sweep operation by the 198th Brigade of the Americal Division in Quang Tin Province along the Quang Nam Province border. Over 577 known enemy casualties as of 30 June.	I
15 Apr 68–(Cont.)	SCOTLAND II. Continuation of U.S. Marine Corps operations around Khe Sanh upon termination of PEGASUS. Over 2,053 known enemy casualties as of 30 June.	I
19 Apr–17 May 68 29 days	DELAWARE/LAM SON 216. 1st Cavalry Division (AIRMOBILE), 101st Airborne Division, and elements of 196th Light Infantry Brigade, plus ARVN 1st Division and ARVN Airborne Task Force Bravo, operations into A Shau Valley to pre-empt enemy preparations for an attack on the Hue area. 869 known enemy casualties.	I
4 May 68–(Cont.)	ALLEN BROOK. U.S. Marine Corps operation west of Hoi An City in southern Quang Nam Province. Over 871 known enemy casualties as of 30 June.	I
17 May 68–(Cont.)	JEB STUART III. Continuation of the 1st Cavalry Division (AIRMOBILE) operations along the border of Quang Tri and Thua Thien Provinces. Over 843 known enemy casualties as of 30 June.	I

Date and duration	Operation	Corps Tactical Zone
17 May 68–(Cont.)	NEVADA EAGLE. Continuation of 101st Airborne Division operations in central Thua Thien Province. Over 1,024 known enemy casualties as of 30 June.	I
18 May 68–(Cont.)	MAMELUKE THRUST. U.S. 1st Marine Division operation in central Quang Nam Province. Over 576 known enemy casualties as of 30 June.	I
1 Jun 68–(Cont.)	TOAN THANG II. Continuation of the II ARVN and II Field Force operations in the Capital Military District. Over 697 known enemy casualties as of 30 June.	III

Appendix M

ORIGINAL LETTER OF TRANSMITTAL

HEADQUARTERS
UNITED STATES MILITARY ASSISTANCE COMMAND, VIETNAM
OFFICE OF THE COMMANDER
APO SAN FRANCISCO 96222

MACJOO 30 June 1968

SUBJECT: COMUSMACV Report on the War in Vietnam

Commander in Chief, Pacific

FPO San Francisco 96610

1. As requested by higher authority, I submit herewith a report on my four years as Commander, United States Military Assistance Command, Vietnam.

2. The situation in Vietnam is unique. COMUSMACV is subordinate to the American Ambassador. COMUSMACV advises and assists but does not command the Republic of Vietnam Armed Forces. Furthermore, the actions of COMUSMACV are influenced at all times by the close interrelationship among military, political, economic, and psychological factors. Therefore, I feel it is appropriate to note events and express views over and above those normally expected of a military commander. In view of the vast responsibilities of the Ambassador, U.S. civilian agencies, and the South Vietnamese Government and Armed Forces, my report nevertheless can provide only an incomplete account of the complex and multitudinous happenings in Vietnam during my stewardship. I have attempted to provide some additional perspective by treating a number of special topics in detail and by including several appendices, including a brief chronology.

3. It was my privilege before assuming command to serve five months as deputy to an able and conscientious soldier, General Paul D. Harkins, and during that time to become acquainted with the country, the officials, the people, and the nature of my subsequent assignment.

4. When I assumed command on 20 June 1964, the Communist insurgents, after years of having been held in check, had seized the initiative. As always throughout my years in Vietnam, the military situation and the ability of COMUSMACV to accomplish the goal of improving the South Vietnamese Armed Forces bore a direct relationship to the stability and general health of the South Vietnamese Government. In 1964 the political situation was unstable and uncertain, government control disintegrating. Despite a gradual buildup of U.S. advisors and operational support units to a strength of 23,000 men, the Viet Cong retained the initiative.

5. My report describes the problems, decisions, innovations, operations, and other activities of the COMUSMACV and U.S., South Vietnamese, and Free World forces over the four years of my command. The conflict passed from the crises of 1964 and 1965, through the graduated commitment of major U.S. forces and the development of logistic bases, to a period of accelerated operations, and finally a position of strength in 1968. A theme of constant change runs through the entire period of this complex war, involving a fluid battle situation with no front lines. Continuous innovations were required as we fought, built, and strove to protect the Vietnamese people from terror and attack. As the enemy reacted to successive defeats with altered tactics and strategy, a premium was placed on ingenuity and new initiatives.

6. The restraints under which we conducted the war confined our general strategy throughout to defense of the sovereign territory of the Republic of Vietnam. The air campaign to the north, which except in the area immediately beyond the Demilitarized Zone did not come under my command, constituted the offensive element of our overall strategy. On the other hand, our tactics in Vietnam have been consistently offensive in character. As we gained experience and our troop strength, logistics, and helicopter and fixed wing aircraft inventories built up, our operations became increasingly effective. Our national policy of confining the ground war precluded operations across the Cambodian border where the enemy frequently sought sanctuary, north of the Demilitarized Zone where the enemy ultimately massed troops, and into southeastern Laos through which ran the enemy's main route of logistic support. These restrictions made it impossible to destroy the enemy's forces in a traditional or classic sense. Thus our main objectives were to prevent the enemy from imposing by force a Communist government on South Vietnam, to protect the people and resources of South Vietnam from Communist control or domination, to defeat attempts by the enemy to seize territory of strategic importance or terrain of tactical value in South Vietnam, and to weaken the enemy by applying maximum pressure on his ranks and means of support. We pursued these objectives by supporting the pacification and nation-building programs of the Republic of Vietnam, by defending important territory and terrain, and by offensive operations designed to inflict maximum casualties on the enemy and damage to his logistic structure.

7. Of importance equal to the accomplishment of our battlefield mission has been the development of South Vietnamese armed forces and a police force. Our goal has been to assist the Vietnamese in creating, training, and motivating well-balanced military forces and an effective police force, tailored for the tasks of providing security for the people and defending against invasion. This has been a difficult and complex undertaking and has been influenced by the political strength of the Government of Vietnam, the state of the Vietnamese economy, manpower availability, our ability to equip organized units, and other practical considerations. At all times, a dearth of Vietnamese leadership has been a major problem.

8. The situation in Vietnam today stands in sharp contrast to the dark days of 1964 and early 1965. We

have curtailed the tide of Communist aggression and prevented the overrunning of the Republic of Vietnam. In over three years, the enemy has not won a single major military victory, and declining morale reflects his repeated defeats. Our intelligence on the enemy has improved continuously, thereby making our operations more productive. In the first six months of 1968, the Communists lost an estimated 170,000 men. Large portions of the countryside have been secured and a major segment of the population brought under government control and protection. Many miles of roads and waterways have been opened. We have made great strides in developing self-sufficient Vietnamese armed forces and a police force. Vietnamese military and civilian leadership have improved. A government duly chosen by the people in a constitutional election has found broader support. Despite our large military presence, adverse effects on the economy of South Vietnam have been kept within acceptable bounds. By virtue of their understanding, discipline, combat proficiency, and humanitarian actions, our troops have earned the respect of the Vietnamese people and many have established a rapport with them. Although a serious Communist challenge remains and all goals have not been realized, the Republic of Vietnam is growing steadily stronger. The military posture of our forces, measured in terms of troops, mobility, and firepower, has developed steadily and this trend continues. Our well-balanced, flexible, and hard-hitting U.S. forces, in concert with the forces of the Vietnamese and our Free World allies, are now capable of frustrating or defeating any military offensive by the Hanoi-led enemy. The foundations we have laid are soundly constructed and, with firm resolve, an independent and viable nation should emerge.

9. To name all those individuals to whom I would like to express gratitude for their assistance and cooperation would take far too much space, yet I cannot depart this command without making certain acknowledgements:

   a. I commend and thank with deep humility the valiant men and women of all the armed services of the United States, the Republic of Vietnam, and the Free World allies, who have responded so nobly in the struggle for freedom in Vietnam. I thank also those dedicated officers, uniformed men and women, and civilians who through the years have served my command, the highly competent service component and field commanders who have worked with me, and the dedicated employees of U.S. civilian agencies.

   b. It has been a privilege to serve under and with a succession of knowledgeable and distinguished Ambassadors—Henry Cabot Lodge, Maxwell D. Taylor, and Ellsworth Bunker, whose responses to my requests for guidance in all nonmilitary matters were always freely and constructively given. A friend and colleague during my entire tour, Barry Zorthian, Director of the Joint U.S. Public Affairs Office, was of abiding assistance. During most of my last year of duty, Ambassador Robert W. Komer was of great value in guiding our efforts to assist the Vietnamese in developing and putting into effect a practical pacification program. I am grateful also for the cooperation and support of the Commander in Chief, Pacific, Admiral U. S. Grant Sharp; of the U.S. Seventh Fleet; and of the 3d Air Division of the Strategic Air Command.

   c. To my dedicated Vietnamese counterpart, the Chief of the Joint General Staff, General Cao Van Vien, I pay tribute. I thank and commend the commanders of the Free World forces who joined us in the struggle—Australia, New Zealand, the Republic of Korea, Thailand, and the Philippines. I had the professionally and personally rewarding experience of working closely with Lieutenant General Chae Myung Shin of the Republic of Korea.

d. I am appreciative also of the representatives of the press and television who dutifully and sometimes at great personal sacrifice fulfilled their responsibility to keep the world informed of the terrible and yet inspiring events in Vietnam.

e. Finally, I express my appreciation to Colonel Reamer W. Argo, Jr., USA, and Lieutenant Commander Paul S. Frommer, USN, for their research and editorial assistance and to Colonel R. H. Johnson, USA; Lieutenant Colonel Wayne E. Whitlash, USAF; Captain Charles W. Sampson, USMC; Chief Warrant Officer Charlie M. Montgomery, USA; Warrant Officer Richard A. Sauer, USA; and Petty Officer I Ronald R. Rhodes, USN, for their diligent assistance in the preparation of this report.

10. I depart my post with a sense of both pride and humility in having played some part in the emerging growth and freedom of a tortured nation and pass my command to a distinguished professional soldier—General Creighton W. Abrams—in whom the nation may repose the utmost confidence as the leader of our valiant troops.

W. C. WESTMORELAND
General, United States Army
Commander

I Incl
as

PHOTOGRAPHS

The following photographs have been selected to provide the reader a glimpse of the terrain encountered in South Vietnam and some of the more significant equipment and techniques discussed in the report.

A view of Nha Trang against the backdrop of the Central Highlands.

Aerial view of the rugged coastline near Qui Nhon.

Aerial view of coastline in Binh Dinh Province.

A view of the rugged terrain and dense vegetation of the Central Highlands.

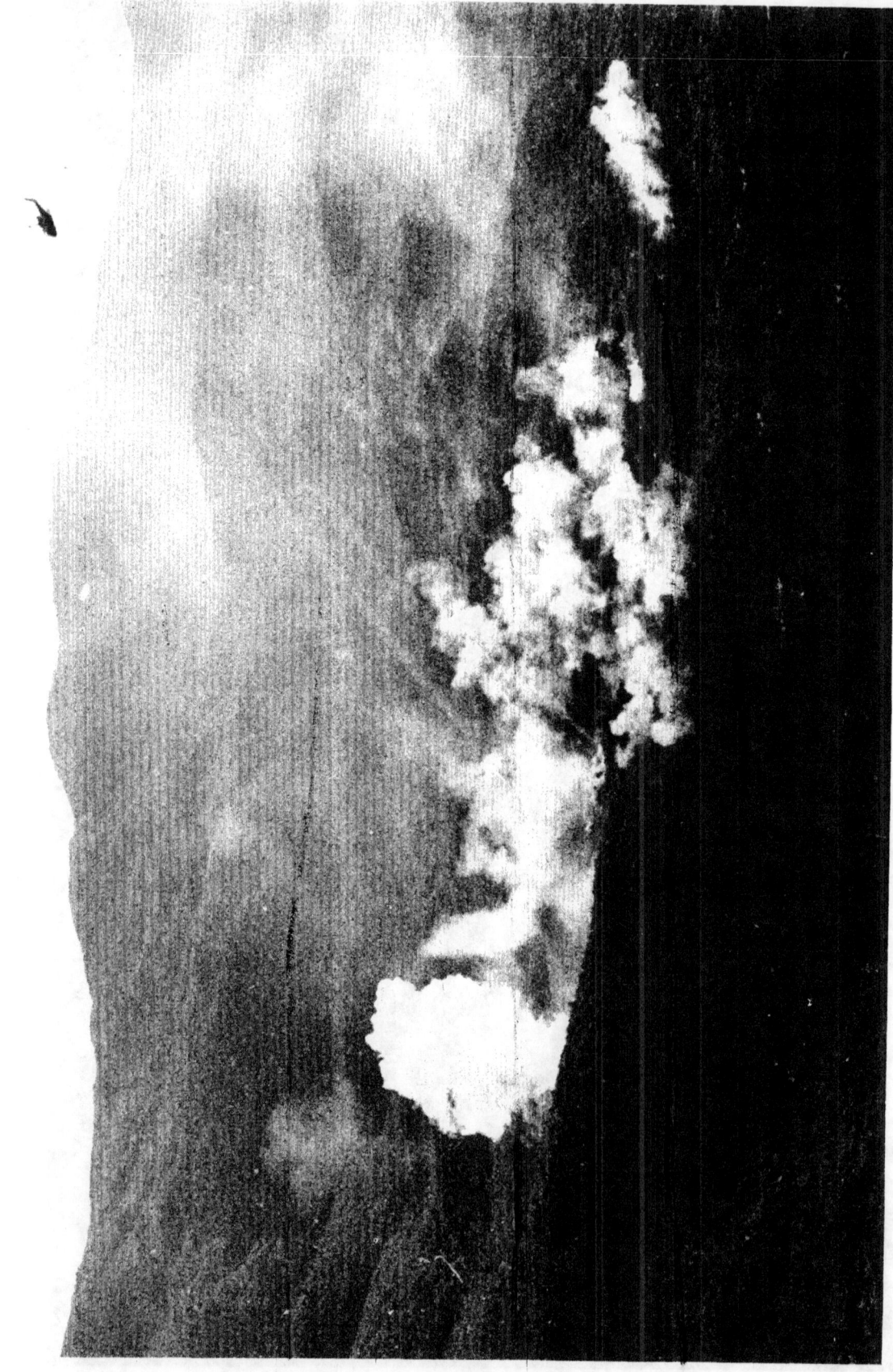

A UH-1 helicopter gunship of the 1st Cavalry Division operating over typical jungle-covered terrain in the Central Highlands near An Khe.

U.S. Air Force A-1E Skyraiders above rugged terrain of Central Highlands.

A U.S. patrol approaching dense jungle.

Men of the 25th Infantry Division conduct a sweep for guerrillas through a rice paddy bounded by tropical growth northwest of Saigon. This is typical of much of the countryside around the capital.

U.S. Army trucks move along the main highway in the Mekong Delta during the southwest monsoon.

Rice paddy area in the Delta near the Cambodian border.

Vietnamese Marines moving through a mangrove swamp in the Mekong Delta.

South Vietnamese troops landed by U.S. Army UH–1 helicopters begin an operation in the Mekong Delta.

Members of a long range reconnaissance patrol moving into ambush positions.

Australian troops rehearsing ambush prior to departing on ambush patrol in Phuoc Tuy Province.

Helicopters assembling preparatory to transporting troops on an operation into the A Shau Valley.

Homes of fishermen in the estuary of the Mekong River.

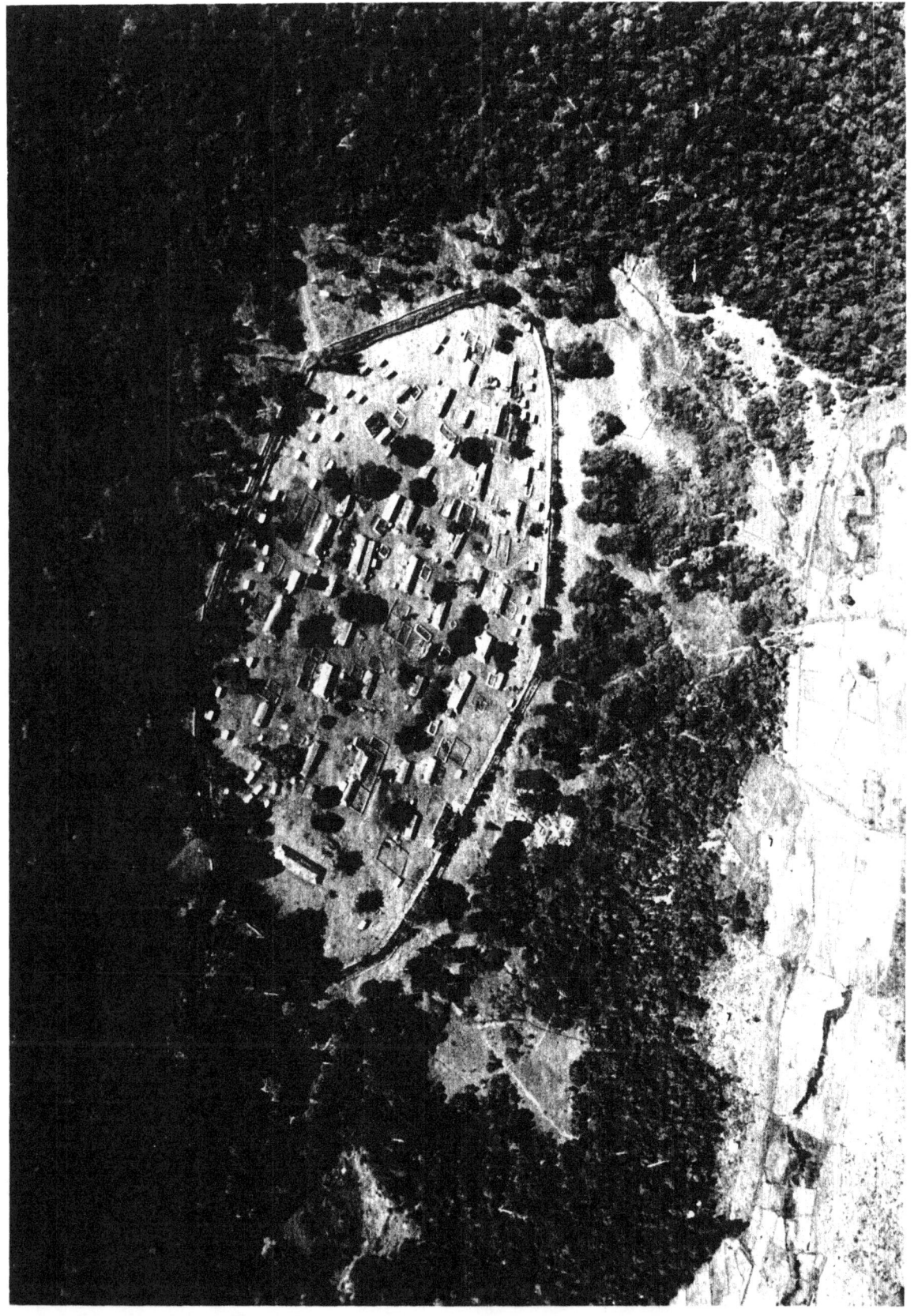
A Montagnard village in the Central Highlands surrounded by a bamboo fence.

A U.S. Army artillery fire support base in the rugged Central Highlands.

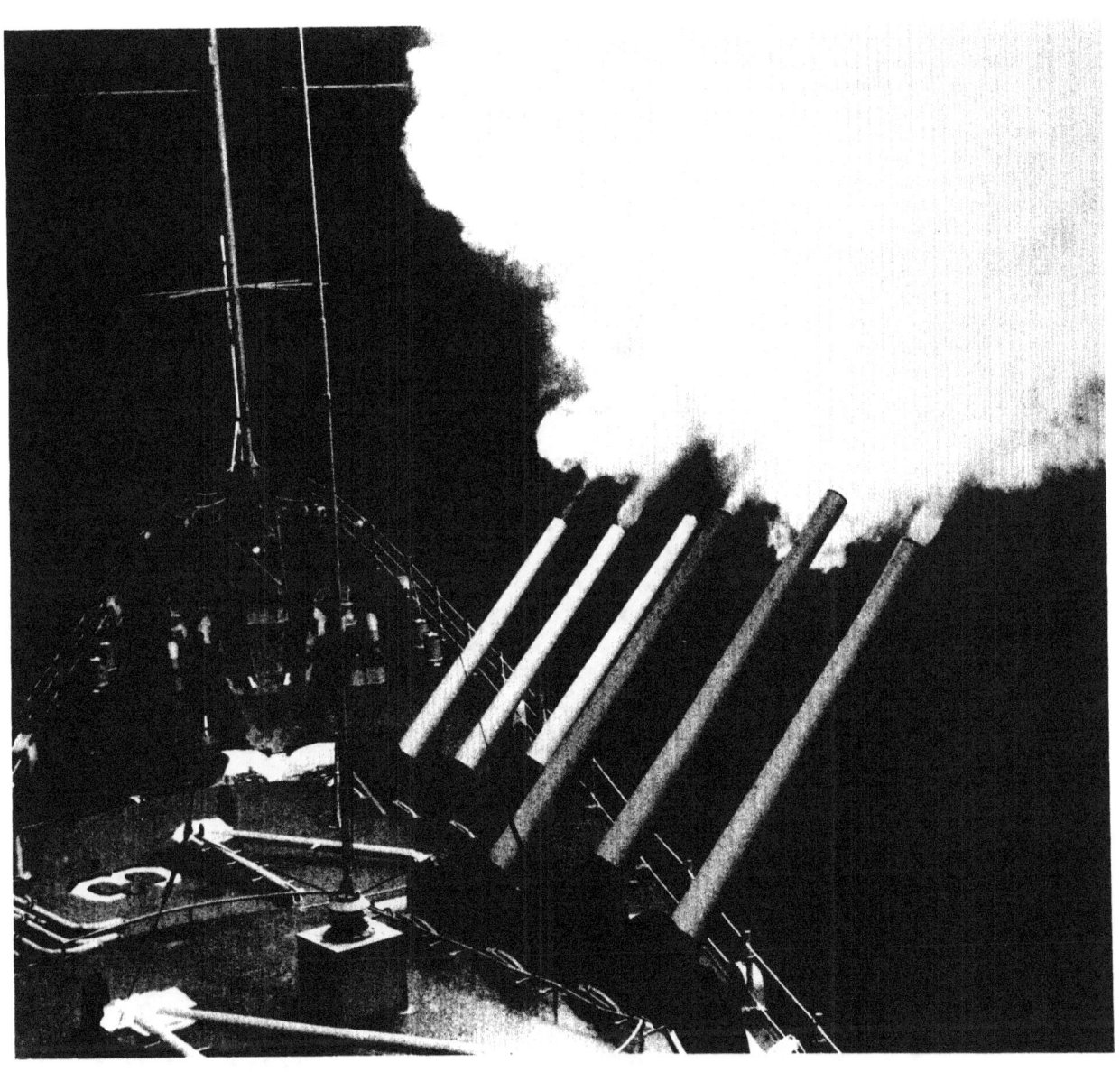
Six-inch guns of the USS *Galveston* firing at maximum range off the coast of Vietnam.

Landing craft prepare to depart Dock Landing Ships for an operation 1½ miles south of the Demilitarized Zone.

Carrying chain saws and demolitions, U.S. soldiers descend by rope ladder from a CH-47 Chinook helicopter.

Soldiers begin clearing a landing zone from the jungle.

A helicopter arrives on the completed landing zone.

Rome Plows (Bulldozer-like vehicles equipped with a special blade for leveling large trees) of the 168th Engineer Battalion clearing Viet Cong-infested jungle in Operation PAUL BUNYAN.

A "Tunnel Rat" prepares to enter an enemy tunnel.

A "Tunnel Rat" makes his way along the restricted passageway.

Scout dogs assist a patrol in tracking the enemy.

Scout dogs help South Vietnamese troops to search for hidden enemy.

Aerial view of Cam Ranh Bay showing a tanker discharging its cargo of fuel.

Cam Ranh Bay port complex as viewed toward the south.

An air cushion vehicle used for patrolling on the waterways of the Mekong Delta.

A barrack ship of the Mobile Riverine Force with helicopter landing pad and with smaller craft drawn alongside.

An early morning sky silhouettes armored troop carriers of the U.S. Navy, part of the Mobile Riverine Force operating in the Mekong Delta.

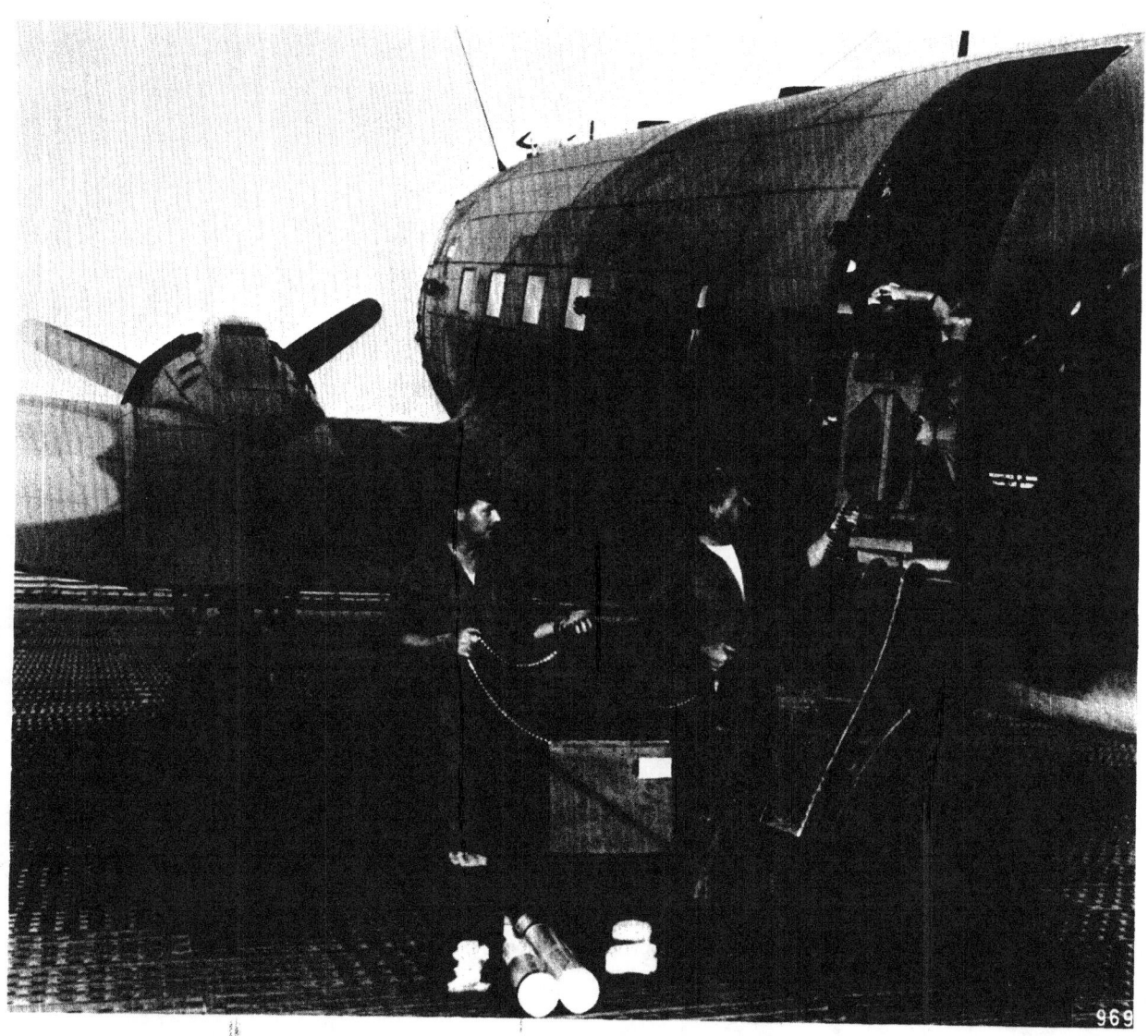
Airmen load ammunition into a 7.62-mm "mini-gun" cannon mounted in a U.S. Air Force AC–47 Dragon ship. The three guns can fire up to 18,000 rounds per minute.

A U.S. Air Force C-130 transport takes off from the dirt runway at Tay Ninh, South Vietnam after delivering Army troops and supplies in support of a ground operation. A recently delivered 105-mm howitzer is in the foreground.

Aerial view of Da Nang showing F–4C Phantom jet aircraft parked in protective revetments.

Top view of two B-52's delivering their bombs with precision accuracy upon an enemy sanctuary.

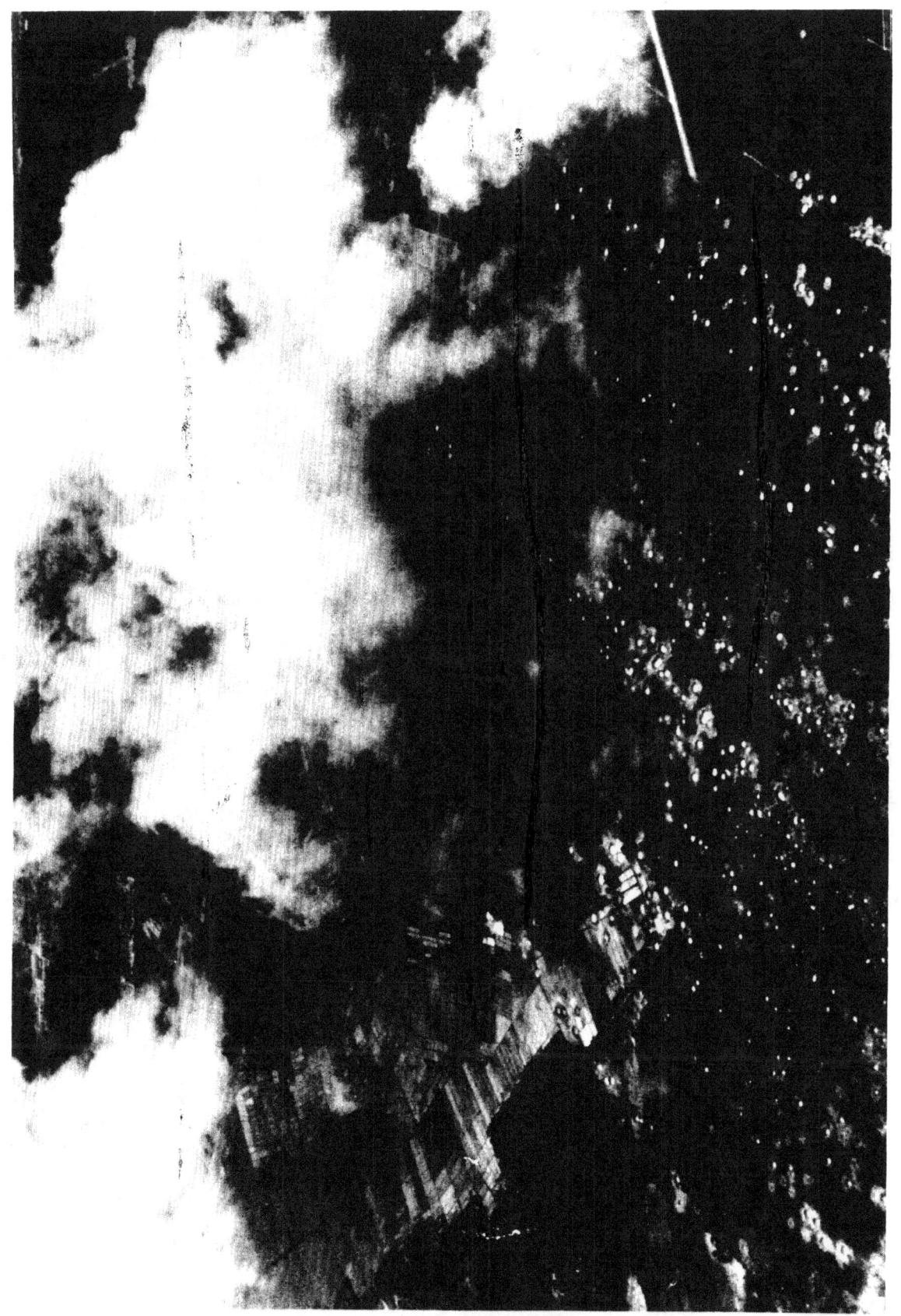

The water-filled craters appearing in the lower half of this photograph were made by 750-pound bombs dropped during a U.S. Air Force B–52 operation against Viet Cong jungle targets 20 miles northwest of Bien Hoa, Vietnam.

Closeup view of a U.S. Air Force C-123 spraying defoliant.

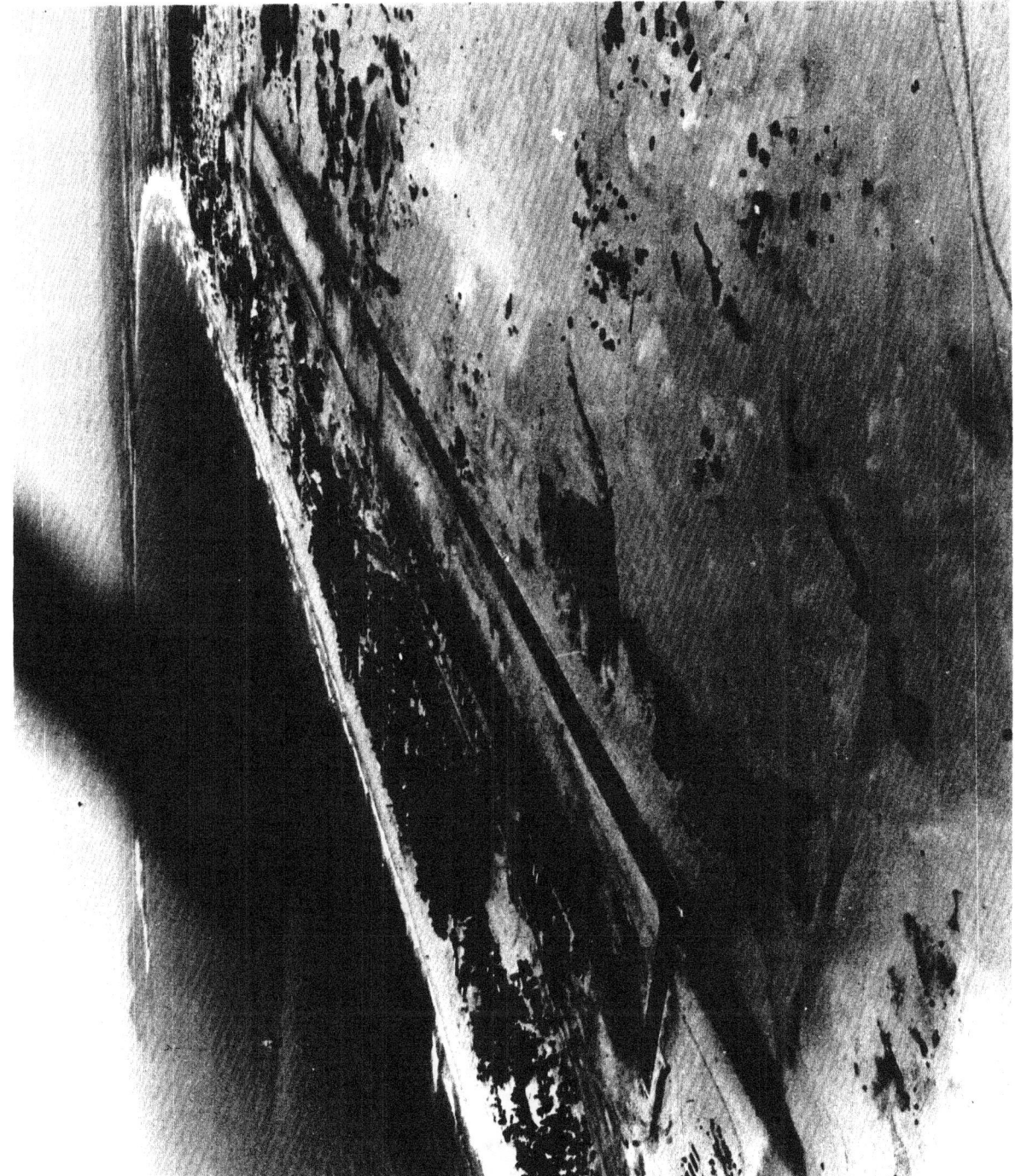

Aerial view of U.S. Marine Corps Air Base at Chu Lai after initial expeditionary construction.

U.S. Marines on the ground await helicopter resupply 2,000 meters south of the Demilitarized Zone.

Members of the 9th Marine Regiment move through a clearing past a Marine tank as a CH-46 helicopter lands to evacuate wounded near Cam Lo, Vietnam.

A soldier of the 173d Airborne Brigade helps Vietnamese civilians build a school.

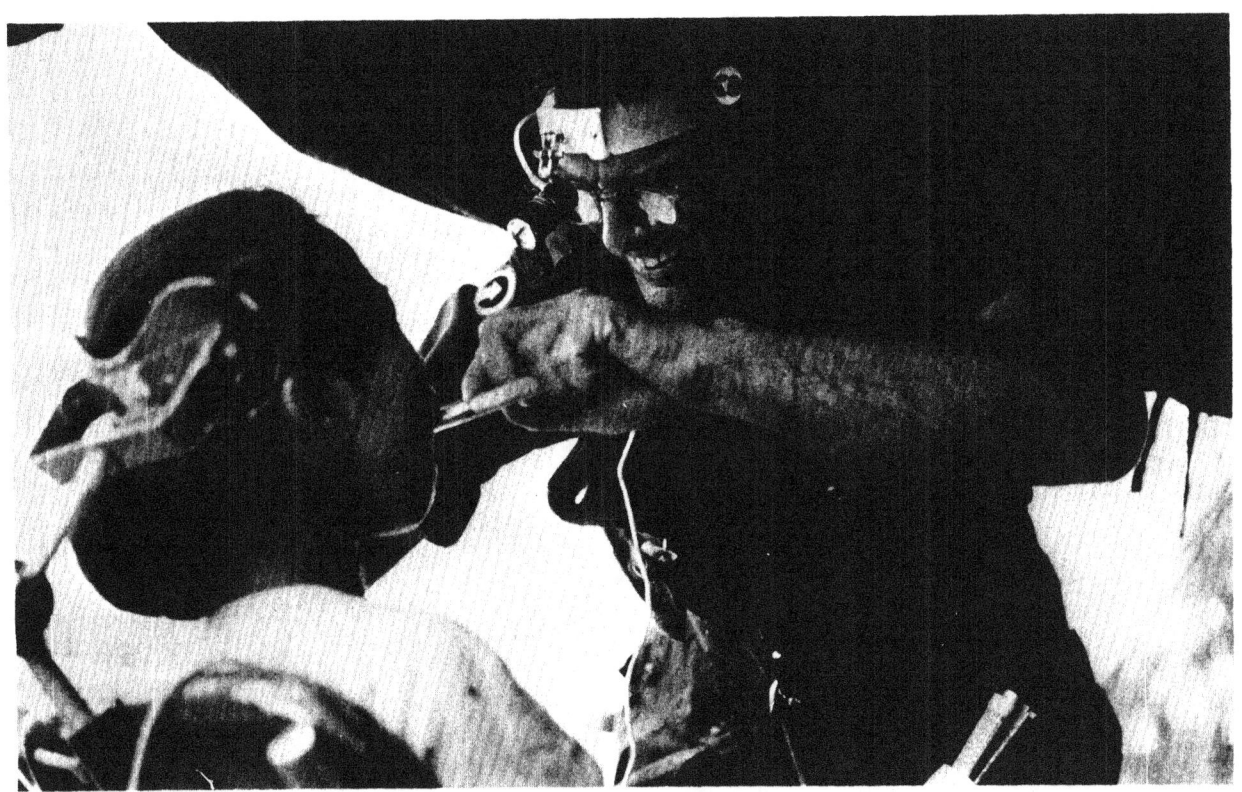
A U.S. Army dentist treats a Vietnamese woman.

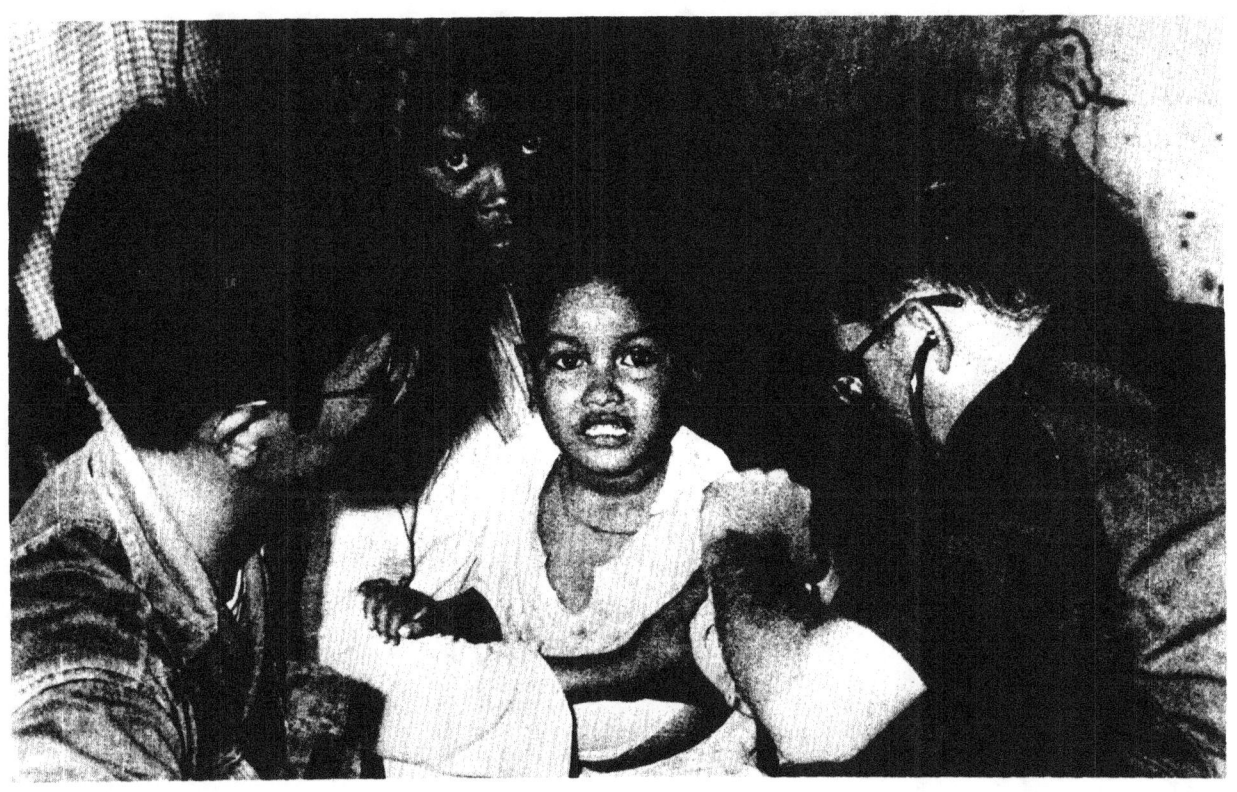
A U.S. Army medical officer examines the son of a South Vietnamese soldier.

Chinese Communist copy of the Soviet AK–47 assault rifle, a very effective automatic weapon which is the mainstay of North Vietnamese and Viet Cong units.

Soviet-made RPG–7, a lightweight rocket launcher effective against armored vehicles and fortifications.

Captured Soviet-made 122-mm rocket launcher and rocket (range: 11,000 meters).

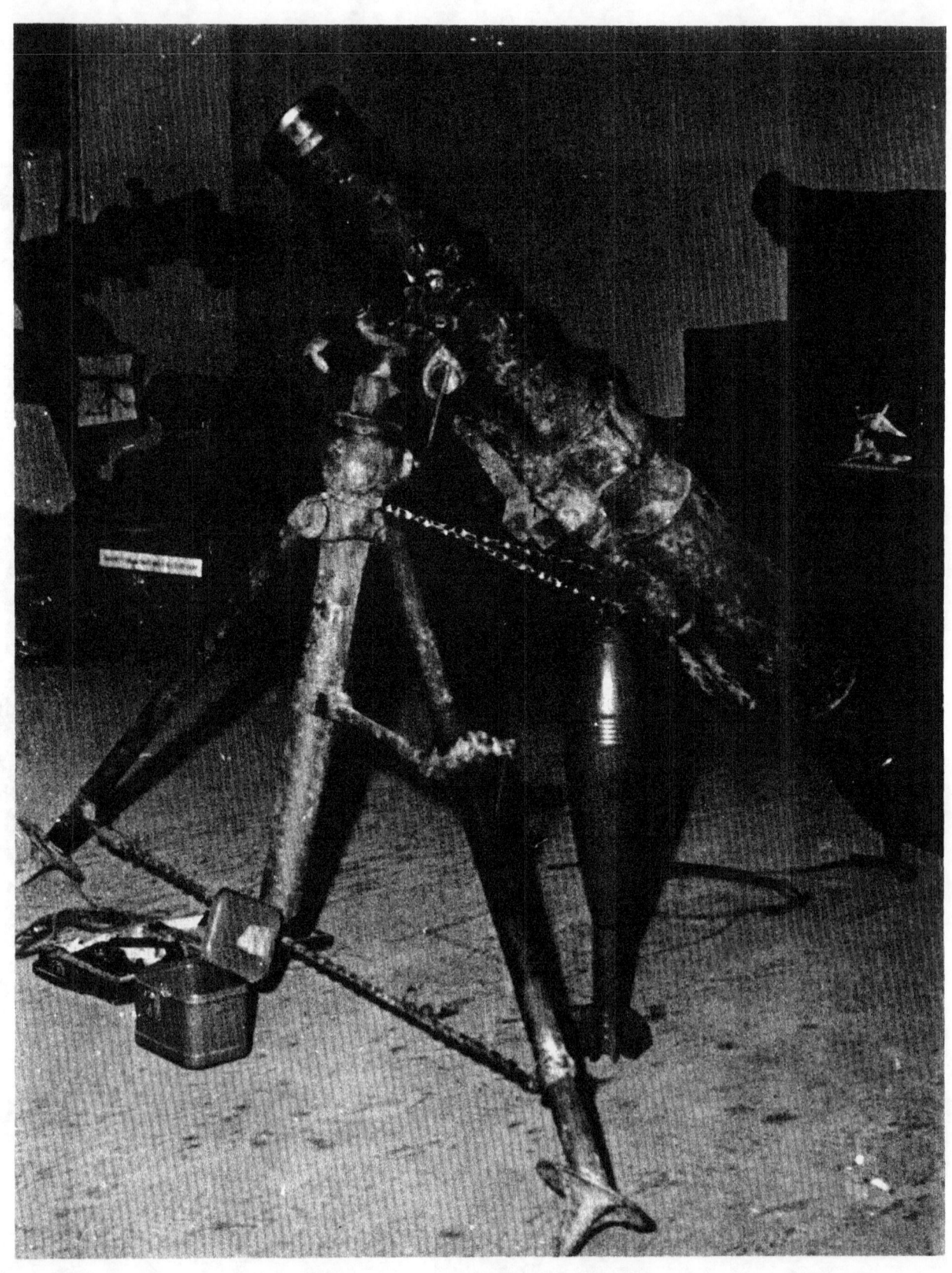

Captured enemy 120-mm mortar and round.

A captured Soviet-made 37-mm antiaircraft gun.

A large collection of enemy weapons captured by Australian forces during February 1968.

U.S. Troops examining large quantities of enemy rifles and ammunition captured approximately 25 miles northwest of Saigon in May 1967.

One of the many enemy rice caches captured by our forces.

U.S. troops move captured rice on armored personnel carriers to a nearby helicopter landing zone for evacuation.

Sampans in the Delta are typical of those used by the enemy.

Cargo bicycles of the type used by the enemy for resupply.

An oxcart loaded with wood exemplifies another means the enemy uses to conceal and transport supplies.

A Soviet-manufactured truck captured in the A Shau Valley by the 1st Cavalry Division (AM) in April 1968.

An example of an enemy elevated trellis system used to support foliage, thereby camouflaging a road from aerial observation.

Glossary

AID	Agency for International Development (U.S.)
ARVN	Army of the Republic of Vietnam
CIDG	Civilian Irregular Defense Group
CINCPAC	Commander in Chief, Pacific
COMUSMACV	Commander, United States Military Assistance Command, Vietnam
CORDS	Civil Operations and Revolutionary Development Support
COSVN	Central Office for South Vietnam
DMZ	Demilitarized Zone
FSA	Forward Support Area
FULRO	For the French term meaning United Front for the Struggle of Oppressed Races
IWCS	Integrated Wideband Communications System
MAAG	Military Assistance Advisory Group
MACV	Military Assistance Command, Vietnam
MEDCAP	Medical Civic Action Program
MEDEVAC	Medical Evacuation
MILPHAP	Military Provincial Health Assistance Program
MUST	Medical Unit, Self-contained Transportable
NLF	National Liberation Front
NVA	North Vietnamese Army
OCO	Office of Civil Operations
PF	Popular Force(s)
PHAP	Provincial Health Assistance Program
PHILCAG	Philippine Civic Action Group
PROVCORPV	Provisional Corps, Vietnam
PSYOPS	Psychological Operations
R&R	Rest and Recuperation
RF	Regional Force(s)
ROK	Republic of Korea
RVNAF	Republic of Vietnam Armed Forces
SEAL	Sea, Air, Land (Team)
SEATO	Southeast Asia Treaty Organization
SLAM	Seeking, Locating, Annihilating, Monitoring
USARV	United States Army, Vietnam
USIA	United States Information Agency
USMACV	United States Military Assistance Command, Vietnam
USO	United Services Organization
VC	Viet Cong

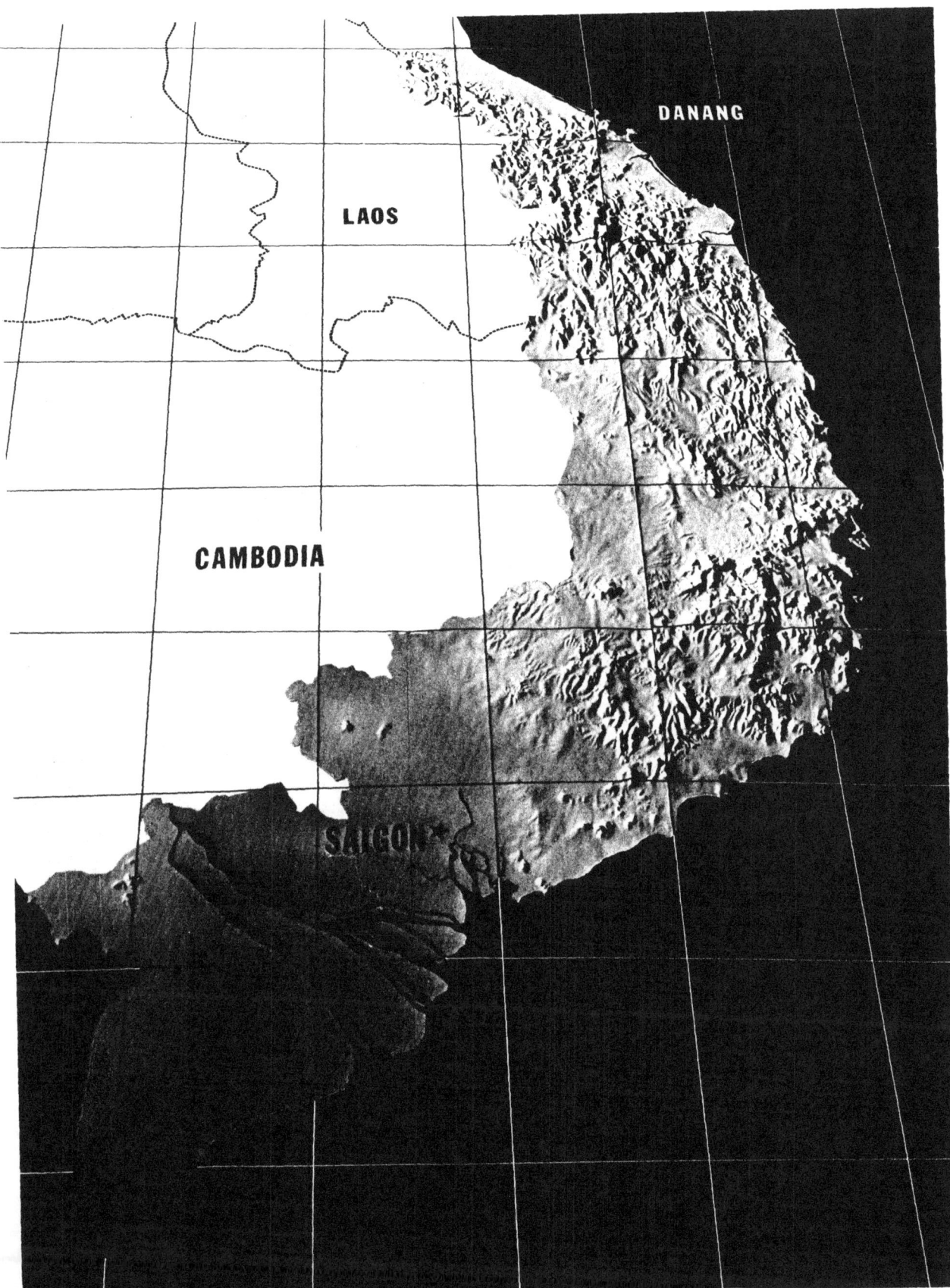

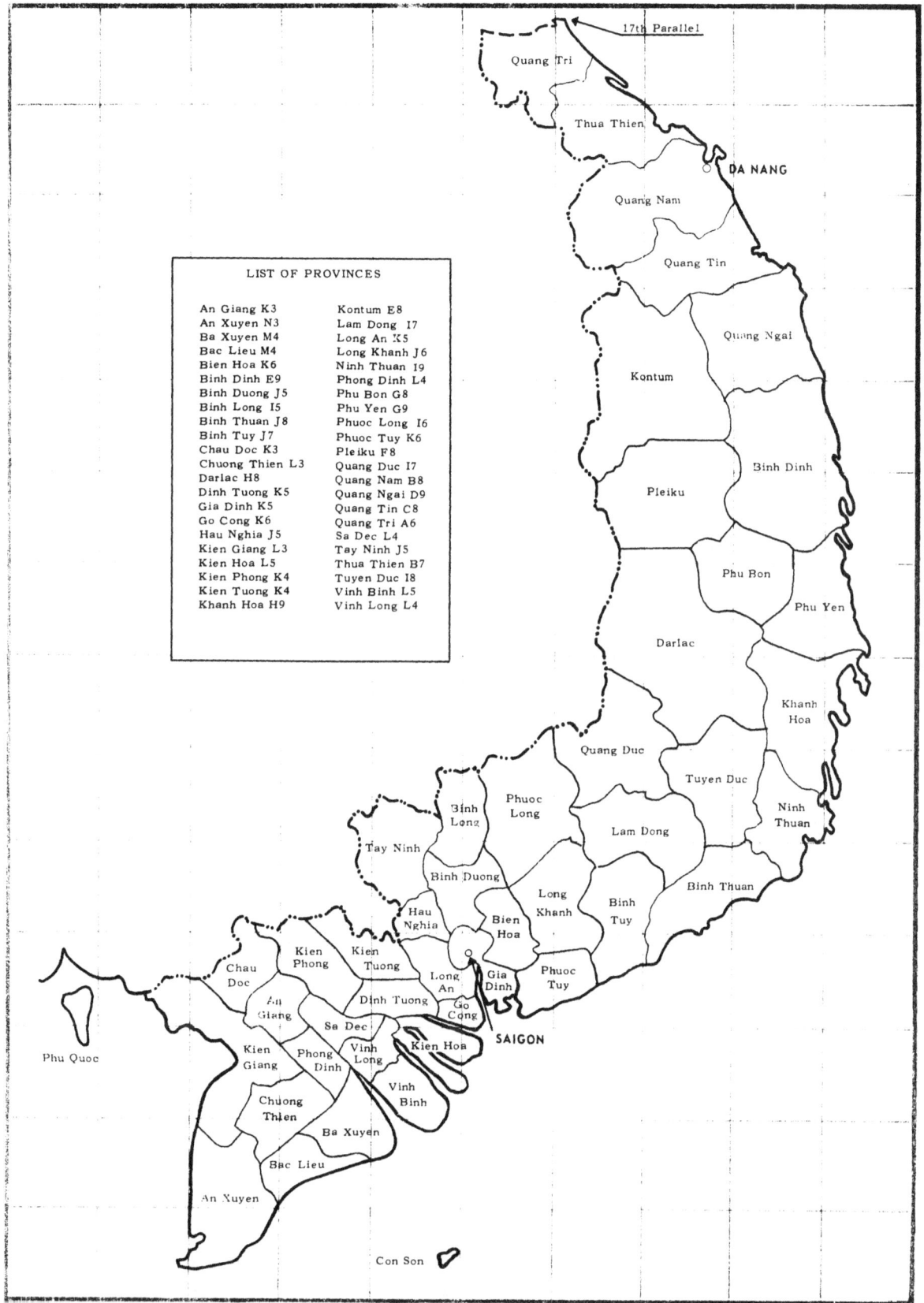